TIN CAN
SAILOR

TIN CAN
SAILOR

*One Man's Account of Navy Life
During World War II*

Capt. Harold Jervey, Jr. MC USNR

Harold Jervey

For information address:
Press-TIGE Publishing
291 Main Street
Catskill, New York 12414

First Press-TIGE Edition 1999

Printed in the United States of America

ISBN #1-57532-1718

The events described are factual. They occurred just as they are described. The names of the people are real except for a few whose names are fictitious. This was done so that family members might not be embarrassed.

This book is dedicated to the millions of young men and women who, over the centuries, have answered their countries' call to arms. When they left their homes to join in the conflict, only a few family members were present to wave them good-bye and Godspeed, AND NO BANDS PLAYED!

After months and years of war, seeing death and destruction for the first time, they returned by foot, car, bus and plane. To greet them were a few family members, AND NO BANDS PLAYED! BUT THE ANGELS DID SING.

CONTENTS

PREFACE

This book was written in the hope the readers would gain a better understanding of what life was like during WW II in the Tin Can Navy. Few realize that on a destroyer no matter how one likes or dislikes a ship mate you can run, but you can't hide. Your entire world is confined to an area 300 feet long and 15 feet wide. Early on you learn to tolerate. That trait continues through out your life.

I would like the reader to be able to relate to the vastness of the world in which we operated. The Atlantic, especially in the North during midwinter was brutal with giant waves, howling winds and unbearable freezing weather. The brief glimpse of the indigo blue of the gulf stream shading to emerald green in the shallows gave us only an idea of what to expect after passing through the Panama Canal. The Pacific was spacious with placid seas, calm winds and beautiful islands. When it became angry Typhoons of indescribable fury tortured men and ships. Many were unable to cope, gave up the fight and cruised into the next world.

Only tin can sailors can appreciate the weeks of boredom. Their major excitement were the rare letters from home. There were brief liberties on nameless islands with only coconut trees, beer and the warm water of the lagoon in which to swim. They would reminisce of their visits with their heart throb of the moment. Later would come the Dear John letter and then the talk was about who else might be available. After many months at sea their ship might report to Pearl Harbor or to a state side Navy Yard for repairs and recreation. They would get a few days leave to visit family and friends. During their stay they would visit all of the nearby bars which would provide tall tales to share during the boring hours at sea.

Their raison d'etre, the destruction of the Japanese Navy, provided excitement and terror for only a few hours, or days, in between the weeks of boredom. During the battles they experienced Dante's hell with hideous noises from the destroyer's guns and the enemy's hits shaking the ship like an earth quake. The reports from the phone talkers gave varying accounts of the battle for majority of men which were below decks. When the battle was over the decks were covered with blood and the gruesome body parts of former friends and shipmates. These were placed in sacks for the burial at sea the next day.

During the four years I spent writing this I received help from countless sources. To insure the accuracy of the events I relied on the deck logs and action reports of the destroyers. The names of everyone used are accurate with the exception of a few. They are fictitious to prevent embarrassing members of their families.

My former shipmates shared vignettes by phone and mail. I am indebted to A. Crawford Clarkson, a classmate and friend, for his critiquing and keeping me from straying too far off course. My daughters Harriet Jervey Morris and Peggy Jervey Stands provided suggestions which were of great help. With out Alice Crook contributing her editing expertise the book would still remain Incomplete. Last but not least Is my wife. Words cannot express my gratitude for her countless hours of widowhood she spent when I was at the computer. For her it was a little easier than for most writers. During my practise days she had learned to tolerate my lengthy and unpredictable hours. She did what she does best, help other people, be it our seven children, friends, or Strangers.

If the reader has gotten even a glimmer of what wartime Tin Can Sailors experienced, my years of work have been worthwhile. This is especially true for those eighty men who chased Japanese for four years seeing only a few. When the bell rang closing the war, they were baby sitting 1500. The largest number captured by Navy personnel during the war. This event provided memories and tales for their families to pass on to generations which followed.

CHAPTER 1

"It's an ill wind that blows no good"
Preparations for War

November 12, 1942: "Sorry X Unable to make rendezvous tonight X Good luck and Good hunting X Lee."

I stared at the decoded message in disbelief. The hairs on the back of my neck bristled and my hands were sweating. How the hell did Admiral Lee think Task Group 67.4 could stop the Japs? Admiral I. Yamamoto was determined to recapture Guadalcanal, a mountainous island 90 miles long and 25 miles wide, located 500 miles south of the equator and 600 miles northeast of Australia. Coast watchers and scout planes had reported at least 2 battleships, several cruisers and 12 to 14 destroyers, followed by troop transports. They were under the command of Admiral Hiroski Abe and they headed down the slot to pulverize the American Marines and destroy Henderson Field. Rear Admiral Willis Augustus Lee had the only 2 modern battleships in the South Pacific, the USS South Dakota and the USS Washington. Without them, we had no chance to carry out orders to destroy the Japanese force. Our Task Group, commanded by Admiral Daniel Callahan in the USS San Francisco, consisted of 3 heavy cruisers, 2 light cruisers and 8 destroyers. It was one-sided in favor of Admiral Hiroski Abe.

I took the message to the bridge for Commander Jessie Coward, Captain of the USS Sterett DD 407. As I handed the message board to Lt. C.R. Calhoun, the Officer of the Deck, I said, "Have the skipper read and initial this. He's going to blow his stack when he sees it."

As I stood on the wing of the bridge with the sun sinking, I could see the 8,000-foot mountain on Guadalcanal. We had been at this God-forsaken island since D-Day, 7 August. None of us had heard of the Solomon Islands until we reached Tongatabu in July and saw operation "Watchtower", nicknamed "Shoestring."

The 1st Marine Division and other elements of the Expeditionary Force had never been together until the rendezvous on 26 July, 400 miles south of Fiji. Our objective was an airfield the Japanese were building on Guadalcanal. The island's interior had a dense rain forest filled with beautiful multicolored birds and mosquitoes which would cause far more casualties than the Japanese.

The bark of the Captain interrupted my reveries: "Is this all there is? Didn't Lee explain why he can't join us?"

"No, sir. I wonder if he knows what happened this afternoon?"

"Of course he does. Both Turner and Callahan sent dispatches to Admiral Ghomerly in Noumea, and Lee was an information addressee. Check with the radio shack and see if they've got anything else. If Lee and his battleships can't make the rendezvous, we're in big trouble."

While we were unloading supplies on the afternoon of 12 November, Jap torpedo planes attacked. Admiral Turner maneuvered the transports out of the way. Only one Betty survived our combat air patrol and ship anti-aircraft fire. The Sterett shot down 4. One crashed into the San Francisco's fantail. It knocked out the after-gun director, the after-fire control radar, and inflicted 50 casualties, including the executive officer, Commander Mark Crouter. The wounded were transferred to the President Jackson. Commander Crouter insisted on staying aboard, a decision which cost him his life.

When the sun rose on 13 November, I discovered that shells have no respect for rank, race or creed. I would realize the folly of establishing a permanent relationship with any female. More importantly, I would know the work I hoped to devote my life to after the last shot was fired.

For the world, the Third Battle of Savo Island was a turning point of the war in the Pacific. Henceforth the United States would be on the offensive. Historians would describe it as the wildest, most desperate naval engagement since Jutland.

As I decoded dispatches, I asked myself: "How did I end up 10,000 miles from Columbia, SC, in this hell hole?" The memories flooded over me.....

It was the summer of 1939. I was 18, beginning my junior year at the University of South Carolina. I was happy and ready for school. The only blight had been the hurricane which had destroyed the tents and campground of the medical detachment of the 263rd Coast Artillery of the SC National Guard.

Adolph Hitler, a former carpenter and dictator of Germany since 1933, was brutally over-running Europe. He was aided by Mussolini, dictator of Italy, who, in 1936, had signed a mutual support pact. On 12 September, 1938, he assured Neville Chamberlain, Prime Minister of Britain, that if he were given Sudentenland, he would seek no additional territory. Chamberlain declared there would be "peace in our time". Peace was short lived. On 28 October, he demanded that Poland cede over the Port of Danzig and the adjacent corridor so Germany would have access to the sea. Poland refused. Over the next several months, Germany invaded Czechoslovakia. Hitler continued to pressure Poland from May through July. Britain, recognizing his intent to invade Poland, signed an Alliance on 25 August.

Author, 2nd on left, summer 1939—Private S.C. National Guard.

Shown in two pictures above, the Camp grounds after hurricane hit Sullevin Island, summer 1939.

In the far east, Japan rampaged. She rolled over northern China and Manchuria and captured Shanghai and Nanking. She disavowed the Naval Treaty restrictions placed on her after World War I and declared that she alone was responsible for all political relations and military security of the Far East. In the western Pacific, Japan controlled the Mariana, Marshall and Caroline Islands. The newspapers reminded me daily that the world was at war. I joined the National Guard to earn a few dollars in the post-depression years. In addition to weekly drills, I was required to go on a two week encampment at Fort Moultrie on Sullivan's Island, SC. The first week had not been completed when a hurricane roared in with winds gusting up to 90 miles per hour. Summer camp was over and would be made up in January during my Christmas holidays.

Europe exploded on 1 September while I registered for the fall semester at the University of South Carolina. The headlines screamed: "Poland Invaded". World War II officially started at 0445 when German troops attacked Poland. Britain and France declared war on 3 September followed by South Africa and Canada. The US and Japan proclaimed their neutrality.

The radios and newspapers reported on the clashes between the navies. Submarines sank the British aircraft carrier Courageous and the battleship Royal Oak. Poland surrendered to the Soviet Union and Finland was invaded on 30 November.

A classmate said to me, "This war is getting closer, but it still seems like it's on another planet. Girls, parties and studies are more important."

When President Roosevelt lent 25 million dollars to General Chiang Kai-shek in December, the US began getting involved. The Pope pleaded for peace on 24 December. The joy of Christmas was brief, as my encampment with the National Guard began at Sesquicentennial State Park northwest of Columbia. I put up my tent and prepared my pallet for sleeping. The temperature was just below freezing. As I snuggled under the blanket, my tent mate remarked, "I sure hope it doesn't get any colder. We haven't got a helluva lot of cover. Let's just hope for the best."

When I opened the tent flaps at dawn, it looked like Antarctica. The wind was howling and ice was everywhere. I exclaimed, "Fighting a war is one thing, but I'll be damned if I'm going to fight it on the ground freezing my butt off. I'm going to join the Navy. I may get sea sick, but at least I'll be warm." Visions of a comfortable cabin and hot food flashed through my head.

Two weeks later, I was in the Navy Recruiting Office signing up for the V-7 program. It was designed for college graduates and required four months training after which a commission would be earned.

During the next few weeks while I was resigning from the Guard[1], signing a mountain of papers, and passing the physical examination, Winston Churchill became Prime Minister of Britain.

In the spring of my junior year at USC, the war abroad spread. Norway was invaded in January, followed by Denmark and Sweden. Fighting began in North Africa. On 1 March, US Secretary of State Sumner Wells was in Berlin searching for peace. On 18 March, Mussolini met with Hitler at Brenner Pass and promised to enter the war against Britain and France. The signing of the Japanese-Soviet Non-Aggression Pact followed on 13 April.

Realizing I had enough credits to graduate in 3½ years, I requested and received orders to report to the USS Quincy, Norfolk, Va., on 1 November, 1940.

While I was studying for exams, Germany invaded Belgium and Holland. On 15 May, Holland surrendered and King Leopold of Belgium followed behind. Hitler turned to France. His advance was so rapid that 320,000 British, French and Belgium troops were evacuated from Dunkirk between 30 May and 3 June.

2nd row-third from the right, completing Apprentice Seaman Cruise on USS Quincy, November 1940.

Following the June Ball, all fraternity and sorority members went house-partying to Pawley's Island, just north of Georgetown, SC. My date for the Kappa Sigma affair was Lil Hair. She was an attractive, popular, bubbly brunette. The fun lasted one week. She became convinced I was playing around with other girls and exploded, "I've had it with you! I'm leaving. I've got a ride back to Columbia this afternoon. I never want to see you again."

It was mutual. Little did I suspect.....

Lil Hair.

That night I went dancing at the pavilion with Betty McDonald. All went well until we were returning home. She was barefooted and her back yard was filled with stickers. "Do you mind carrying me to the house?" she asked.

"Sure. No problem."

Getting almost to the back porch, I felt the ground slowly sinking under my feet and the sound of wood breaking. Holding Betty tightly, I found myself waist deep in a gooey, stinking liquid. Betty slipped out of my arms and suddenly we were sloshing around with our arms entwined.

I yelled, "This is a septic tank!"

"Smart kid," she responded.

With difficulty, I extricated the two of us. We were smelling as if we had been sprayed by a skunk. At the door, I grimaced as I said, "I'm sorry. For whatever it's worth, it has been a memorable evening. Your sorority sisters are not going to believe anything you say, so don't even try to explain."

On 10 June, when I returned to Columbia, the Germans entered Paris. The next day, Italy announced it would be at war with Britain and France. General Charles de Gaulle broadcast from London on 18 June that the Free French would continue to fight even after France surrendered. France signed an armistice on 22 June and on 11 July, Marshall Philippe Petain was declared leader of the Vichy French.

I dug ditches for the Highway Department and dated different girls.

I was happy to learn that Johnny Carroll, Buck Dupre, Lee Baker, Dave Baker, Dan McLeod, Bobby Collier and A.C. Lyles would be with me on the Quincy. I was oblivious to the war until 2 September when the US handed over 50 obsolete destroyers to Britain and received 99-year leases to bases in Antigua, St. Lucia, Trinidad, British Guyana, Jamaica and Argentia, Newfoundland. The US was one step closer to war.

USS Quincy 1940

On 1 November, Johnny Carroll, Buck Dupre and I caught the train for Norfolk, Va. After we reported aboard, our bunks were assigned and we were divided into sections. Because of my military experience, Lt.(jg) R.B. Kelly selected me to be section leader.[2] I led my men[3] to their muster station, mess hall, abandon ship station, bridge or wherever else they needed to be. I quickly learned the bow from the stern and all areas in between.

The Quincy got underway for Bermuda at 0930 on 13 November. The voyage through the Chesapeake Bay was smooth. I was now a sailor. I had not been sea sick and was sleeping fairly well in my hammock. My attitude changed upon encountering the open sea. The Quincy began to roll and pitch as the waves became higher. My stomach felt queasy. Neither I nor the others ate lunch. The hammock looked inviting. Perhaps the Navy was not for me. The Quincy was ordered to skirt the bad weather and stay at sea, which meant no Bermuda. As the waves continued crashing over the bow, the ship rolled and plunged. The bitter cold, ice and sleet on solid ground seemed better than being pounded to death by the sea. After what felt like eternity, the sun came out. The wind and sea calmed down. The indigo blue of the gulf stream extended as far as the eye could see. It was beautiful. And the night! A sliver of a moon with stars brighter than I had ever seen. This was God's handiwork as I had imagined it to be. What a way to fight a war.

Prior to the end of the cruise, I selected the Naval Academy as my choice of midshipman's schools. Entering New York Harbor and seeing the Statute of Liberty with the sky scrapers in the background was an unforgettable spectacle. We disembarked at a pier in the heart of New York City.

Johnny Carroll exclaimed to Buck Dupre and me, "We've completed 30 days sea duty, have money in our pockets and may never get back. Let's stay at the YMCA on 34th St."

The main event of that visit was my introduction to rum and coke, resulting in a deadly hangover. In the middle of the night, I vomited out of the 12th story window until only my stomach remained. I seriously considered jumping out. The following morning at the cafe next door, Buck assured me that his concoction of Tabasco sauce, vinegar, Worcestershire sauce and other ingredients would cure my problem. It didn't. Only time settled my stomach. "No more alcohol for me!" I swore.

Upon returning to Columbia, I worked at the Highway Department. I had money. I was in love with a beautiful blonde, who later would be a Miss Columbia. We danced to Buster Spann's and Henry Westbrook's Orchestras in the ballroom of the Jefferson Hotel. We embraced as we listened to Tommy Dorsey playing "I'll Never Smile Again", "Stardust" and others songs.

Life was wonderful, until the bomb fell! Opening an official letter from the Navy Department, I read with alarm: "You will report on January 5, 1941, to Midshipman School, Northwestern University, Chicago, Ill." There must be a mistake. I had been assured I would be able to finish college in the spring. I was panic-stricken, angry and depressed. My despair was short lived. My father was a long-time friend of Jimmy Byrnes, President Roosevelt's right-hand man. Mr. Byrnes assured my father that I would be deferred until June so I could graduate from college. Within a few days, my new set of orders stated that I would report on 16 June to the Prairie State, New York City. I was in heaven, even though the world was blowing up.

The fighting in Africa was furious. Hitler sent in General Rommel with reinforcements. The Allies were having a difficult time in the Middle East with Syria, Iran and Lebanon. Britain had to send troops to Greece.

On 1 January, Congress passed the Lend-Lease Bill, aligning the US closely with the allies. To coordinate efforts and plan strategy, US staff officers began meeting with British officers.

Throughout the winter and spring, the Battle of the Atlantic raged. U-boats successfully attacked convoys. In March the losses amounted to a staggering 517,000 tons. The battleship Bismarck devastated several ships, including the HMS Hood. On 27 May, the Bismarck was sunk by the King George and the Rodney.

Germany invaded Yugoslavia and Greece on 6 April. Hitler was too strong and the Allies evacuated Greece on 26 April. There were ongoing clashes in the Mediterranean between the British and Italian navies. By March, Britain had control and the Italians were bottled up in their ports. In the Far East, Japan was advancing and acquiring new territories.

To protect our sea lanes, the US established a base on Greenland on 12 April. War was inevitable. It was only a question of when. For me, the spring semester passed uneventfully until I clashed with my biology professor over the final exam.

"Professor, I understand you're not exempting anyone from the final exam."

"That is correct."

"You won't make any exceptions?"

"No, I don't think it's fair to the other students."

"The other professors don't agree with you. Everyone is exempting seniors with an A average. By staying for your exam, I'll miss half of my fraternity's house party. It's probably my last, since I report for duty with the Navy on June 16. If I didn't need this course to graduate, I'd just skip the exam and take my chances. Can't you make an exception?"

Seeing my anguish, he said, "I tell you what I'll do. If you don't take the exam, you'll get a B on the course."

"I'll take it!" I replied.

The following day I went by the registrar's office to make certain everything was in order for my graduation. After he reviewed my courses, credits and grades, Flynn Gilland said, "Everything is in order. It looks like you're eligible for Phi Beta Kappa. You've got a 3.5 grade average."

"I just blew it. I was borderline. Yesterday I agreed to take a B in Biology. The little jerk wouldn't exempt me from the exam. I don't really care. There's a war coming on and all I want is my diploma."

My date for the house party was Carole Bruton, an intellectual blonde. I had a wonderful time and my eyes moistened as I said my good-byes. Some one remarked, "Remember what Satchel Page said: 'Don't look back. Something might be catching up with you.' "

"Yeah, and I also recall Admiral Dewey's famous remark: 'Damn the torpedoes! Full speed ahead!' That's me."

The days passed quickly, and on 15 June at 10pm, George Hartness, Johnny Carroll and I boarded the Silver Meteor. Catching a cab from Pennsylvania Station, we quickly arrived at the foot of 138th St. Seeing the Prairie State, I yelled, "That's a ship? It looks more like a barn placed on top of a barge." The former USS Illinois was commissioned 16 February, 1901, and decommissioned on 15 May, 1920. Now she was the Prairie State, and on 12 August, 1940, the first class of midshipmen reported on board.

Prairie State—where I attended midshipman school summer 1941.

Summer 1941, on right midshipman on USS Prairie
State (in background) New York City—Foot on
138th Street.

My first day was spent waiting on the dock, meeting classmates and getting fitted for used uniforms, either too small, too large, or needing repair. The shoes, ties, shirts and pajamas were new and they fit.

Johnny exclaimed, "This class consists of 500 men and is over-loaded with Ivy League graduates: Harvard, Yale, Princeton and MIT. Even a couple of Phd's. There are a few from the Naval Academy who bilged out. I'm impressed and intimidated."

"Don't sweat it, Johnny. Our friends who've already graduated said we'd have no problem."

Later in the day, Captain John J. London, the Commanding Officer, announced on the drill deck: "My staff and I have reviewed the backgrounds of each of you. Based on your previous military experience, we have selected the Regimental Commander and Battalion Commanders. The four company commanders and platoon leaders are up for grabs. I want volunteers to come forward."

The classmate standing by me pushed me forward, saying under his breath, "You qualify." I couldn't back up. A voice asked: "Do you want to be considered for company commander?"

"No, sir, not really."

"How about platoon leader?"

There being nothing lower, I replied, "Yes, sir."

I was selected.

The editor of the Side Boy, our annual, was to be Robert M. Morganthau. His father was Secretary of the Treasury, a close friend of Roosevelt's.[4]

Each of us was assigned to the deck or the engineering department. The selection process seemed stupid, with history, English and economic majors becoming engineers. I automatically qualified, having majored in Chemistry and Biology. I complained to my bunk mates, "I've got claustrophobia and I ain't going to function well below decks. I expected to be on the bridge, maybe even have a command some day."

A voice responded, "If you don't shut up, you're going to end up in the brig. What'll that do for your claustrophobia?"

I settled into the daily routine. Reveille was 0600, taps at 2300. In between were classes, meals, close order drill on the pier, and calisthenics. From 1800 to 1930, I wrote letters and socialized. Study hall followed.

We were told that the three essentials to being a good Naval officer were getting a ship from one place to another with efficiency and speed, finding out where you are when you think you've gotten some place, and firing the guns accurately when you get there.

Weekly instruction was held on the USS Sylph, a yacht given to the Navy and now used as a training ship for the midshipmen. She usually cruised to the Ambrose Light Ship in New York Harbor and back and, on occasion, up the Hudson River. Her long-suffering crew repeated the same instructions and answered the same questions to new faces every day. It was said that the deck midshipmen staggered aboard with a load of books which were stowed and forgotten. The engineers marched aboard with clear heads and empty hands and went below decks into the hot, noisy engineering spaces.

There were drills and lectures. Occasionally, we rowed the life boats when abandon ship was ordered. The complaint was voiced: "What a screwed up world! I thought the crew was supposed to row and I'd give orders."

We heard the news and knew at 0330, 22 June, that Hitler was invading Russia and demanding that Japan attack also. Instead of complying, Japan advanced to the south into Indochina. Roosevelt froze all German and Italian assets and on 4 July, warned the American people that the US couldn't survive in the middle of a desert surrounded by dictatorships.

On 16 July, the Japanese Army overthrew Admiral Yonai's moderate government and replaced him with Prince Konoye. This was followed on 27 July by the creation of the Greater Asia Co-Prosperity Sphere. Needing raw materials, she declared that all islands and countries up to the northern border of Australia were under her control. The US froze all Japanese assets.

Roosevelt knew of Japan's aggressive moves to the south, because our cryptographers had broken the Japanese code. This accomplishment was named "Magic". Roosevelt had our Marines relieve the British garrison in Iceland. This was followed by the establishment of a base in Argentia, Newfoundland.

My world was not affected. The Tuesday afternoon Tea Dance from 6:30 until 8 o'clock was the social highlight of the week. The girls were New York's most beautiful and wealthiest. Every mother's daughter wanted to do her part for the war effort. In the beginning, they came alone but with the passage of time, favorites were invited back as dates. At the first dance, griping began when lemonade and cookies were served: "What kind of Navy is this? Where is the beer and pretzels?"

Determined not to look like an ignorant southern boy, I studied diligently. I remained apprehensive until the grades were posted on the bulletin board. I was happy with my B-plus average. The Ivy League graduates and I would play on a level field.

George Hartness bilged out. When I extended my sympathy, he laughingly said, "Don't worry about it, Harold. I promised my trigonometry professor at Carolina that if he'd pass me, I'd never take another math course for the rest of my life. I'm going to join the Marines. While you guys are bouncing all over the ocean trying to keep your food down, I'm going to be sitting under a palm tree drinking a beer. We'll probably meet on some South Pacific Island."

Shore leave from noon Saturday until Sunday evening was eagerly anticipated. We were given privileges at several of New York's prestigious social, athletic and golf clubs. Families with eligible daughters would call Chaplain Richards and ask him to provide up to 25 escorts for a variety of events.

Johnny Carroll and I spent our first such weekend at Ridgewood, New Jersey. Our host had a palatial house and an attractive daughter. I was impressed by the call bell in the bedroom and being told, "Just ring for the butler if you need anything." We went to the country club that night where a group of friends joined us for dinner and dancing. I was bewildered by the cocktail menu which listed exotic drinks of which I knew little.

"Try a stinger or a scorpion!" my date suggested.

"I have tried every drink ever mixed, but on Saturday night, Tom Collins is the drink for me. The others do crazy things to me on the weekend."

The dinner menu was intimidating. My date said, "You've got to try the lobsters. We're not going to take you home tonight if you don't."

I had never seen a lobster, alive or dead, only pictures. Johnny exclaimed, "Come on! Let's give it a try. The girls say order lobster, I say, order lobster."

"OK. I'll give them a try. We don't get good ones down south and our chefs aren't skilled at cooking them." (More importantly, the chefs I knew had never even seen one.)

Too quickly, the waiter arrived and, with a flourish, placed the thing on the table. Except for the bulging eyes which stared at me in scorn, it didn't look too fearsome. The utensils were strange: a nutcracker, a small fork and a steel tooth pick. I thought, "With this equipment, we ought to be eating nuts."

I watched my date's every move. I did exactly as I saw her do and looked around to see if I was being observed. Smacking my lips in appreciation, I said,

"This has to be the finest lobster I've ever eaten. Congratulate the Chef for me."

I got through the meal without a major goof and even imagined a wink of congratulations from the lobster's eyes.

The next morning, I ordered breakfast using the intercom. The butler brought in coffee, scrambled eggs, toast, jelly and orange juice. Johnny exclaimed, "Wow! This is living! I could get used to it." The day was spent at the country club around the swimming pool with several other couples.

Occasionally I went to the Hotel Astor on 45th St. and Broadway. The bar was always filled with shipmates and unattached girls. A room cost $3 a night and New York was overflowing with entertainment. The blue uniform was welcomed everywhere. There were discount tickets to the theater, free drinks at the bar and, on occasion, some kind soul would pick up my meal ticket.

Big bands were in the hotels: Johnny Long at the New Yorker, Xavier Cugat at the Starlight Roof of the Waldorf Astoria and Guy Lombardo at the Grill Room of the Roosevelt Hotel. In the Green Room of the Edison Hotel was Les Brown with Doris Day. The bar was always next to the dining room where the band was playing. For 50 cents, I could order one drink and listen for as long as I liked. One Saturday night, I heard 5 bands.

The movie theaters featured Benny Goodman, Harry James, and Woody Herman. Tommy Dorsey had Frank Sinatra, and Jimmy Dorsey had Helen O'Connell singing "Green Eyes" and "Tangerine." The hit tunes of the day included "Deep in the Heart of Texas," "I'll Remember April", "Waltzing Matilda" and "The Anniversary Waltz". A theater ticket was $2.20. I saw Ethel Merman in "Panama Hattie" and Boris Karloff in "Arsenic and Old Lace". To cap off the evening, I'd go to Sherman Billingsley's Stork Club, the 21 Club or El Morocco.

To sit under the stars at Lewishon Stadium with Toscani conducting his symphony orchestra was as close to heaven as I had ever been. I began a love affair with New York and the theater which has never ended.

The highlight of my weekends was one spent with J.P. Morgan at his estate at Glen Cove, Long Island. 25 midshipmen were invited. As the designated leader, I knocked on the door. It was opened by an elderly man dressed in a rumpled, checkered linen coat and baggy pants. I said, "We are midshipmen from the Prairie State and we've been invited by Mr. Morgan to be his guests for the weekend."

He smiled and replied, "Welcome! I'm Mr. Morgan. I'm glad to see you. Come right in."

After we exchanged pleasantries, he said, "You fellows must be hungry! Let me show you to the washroom. Lunch will be ready after you have freshened up."

When I finished freshening up and went to put on my coat, only one coat was left—two sizes too large for me. I wondered how the other fellow got into mine. I felt conspicuous as I entered the dining room. Everyone was seated six to a table. There was one vacant chair next to Mr. Morgan. I sat down and explained what had happened. Mr. Morgan laughed and said, "Don't worry about it. I learned long ago that looks don't make the man."

He asked about our families and our opinions on world affairs. I was impressed that one of the wealthiest and most powerful men in the world would be interested in our thoughts. He asked me, "What do you think of the prospects for war?"

"Mr. Morgan, you know the answer much better than I do. Your connections are far more extensive than mine."

"In a way, maybe, but I'm interested in your views. You are the ones that will do the fighting. Your ideas are important."

With some reluctance, I responded, "You're right! War is inevitable. It's just a question of when. None of us objects to dying in the service of our country. The unfairness is that those who cause wars stay home, comfortable, safe and making money. They will be winners no matter the outcome. They provide the means to fight: guns, machines and ammunition. Aristotle advocated having wars fought by the elderly. He thought there would be fewer wars if the young stayed home." That missile was aimed at him. I wanted to disappear. I was relieved when he quietly said, "You are right, young man."

The conversation shifted. He told us something about the Rembrandt, Van Gogh and Gainsborough paintings on the wall. The portrait of the strikingly beautiful lady at the front of the room was his wife, and he told us in a childish way that the artist had let him watch as it was being painted.

Some one asked, "Why do you like a picture?"

He replied, "I just do. I can't put it into words. I'm just drawn to them for some inexplicable reason."

With lunch finished, Mr. Morgan said, "Just make yourselves at home. I've got bathing suits of all sizes, enough for everyone. There's a beach behind the house. You can fish, boat, walk and explore. Let one of the servants know if you need anything."

Turning to me, he asked, "Would you like to see the rest of the house?"

Stammering, I replied, "I certainly would. Thank you."

Taking me upstairs, he pointed out objects of note and told interesting stories about each one, including his priceless collection of snuff boxes and how he had acquired them. The most memorable moment was stopping before a picture of him and his wife with the King and Queen of England. Putting his hand on my shoulder, he said sadly, "I have been privileged to be friends with world leaders, to have made more money than I can ever spend, and yet I can't buy what you have—youth and happiness. You've got your whole life before you. Live it to the hilt, enjoy every day, but never let money be your goal. It can buy things, but it can't buy what really counts—friends and happiness." I was stunned. A confession by J.P. Morgan to a 20 year old southern boy who didn't even know how to eat a lobster![5] I could only mumble, "I'll never forget."

Later in the afternoon, we went to his son Junius's estate. He had an attractive daughter who provided dates for everyone, and we went to the country club for dinner and dancing. Johnny spoke for all, "A few more weekends like this and I may leave the Navy and stay in New York."

Although I went to Frank Dailey's Meadowbrook night club on the New Jersey Turn turnpike, the Larchmont Yacht Club, Coney Island and the Glen Island Casino, nothing ever compared to the visit with J.P. Morgan.

In August, the US began sending lend-lease aid to Russia. Roosevelt and Churchill met in Placentia Bay, Newfoundland, to plan strategy. Reports of the war in Africa were encouraging. General Auchinlick, with Australian and Soviet troops, had gone on the offensive. The Allies were making progress in Iran, Iraq and Syria.

I asked advice from the officers as to my active duty request. I was told, "Destroyer duty. The tin can Navy is where the action is. You'll get more responsibility faster, but on the down side, you won't sleep or eat like those on battle ships and carriers. Ice cream and porgy bait will have to be begged or stolen. There's a saying, 'One year on a destroyer equals two on shore.'" I decided I could forfeit a couple of years and requested destroyer duty.

In late August, the Regiment was invited to attend a pre-season game of the New York Giants. We marched the several miles to the Polo

Grounds. The streets were lined with hundreds of spectators clapping and whistling as we passed. The biggest thrill was entering the packed stadium. Everyone was standing and cheering as the band struck up "Anchors Aweigh". The singing of the National Anthem followed. As the flag was slowly raised and waved in the breeze, with the new moon in the background and the crowd singing "by the dawn's early light," chills ran up and down my spine. I was proud to be an American. I was ready to defend my country. I don't remember who won the game or how I got back to the Prairie State.

In September, the drill deck became a clothing store. I felt like a millionaire. The tailor at Sack's Fifth Avenue measured me for dress blues, whites, khakis and everything that went with them.

During the last week, Fred Waring with his Glee Club performed and a Broadway show came aboard. Final exams were given. Our uniforms arrived. I was apprehensive when I heard the Public Address System boom, "Now hear this! Midshipman Jervey, lay up to the Captain's Quarters."

I joined the line of midshipmen waiting. When I was called in, Captain London smiled and said, "At ease. Don't be afraid. I think you'll be pleased with these." My hands were shaking as I opened the envelope he gave me. I relaxed when I read that the Chief of Bureau of Navigation was ordering me to report to the Commandant of the Sixth Naval District in Charleston, SC, for duty on the USS Sterett DD 407. I was authorized 10 days leave. I thanked Captain London and shared the news with my shipmates. Many were happy with their assignments, a few disappointed.

In Europe, Leningrad was under siege. The Allies were holding their own in Africa and the Middle East. Japan was preparing for a major offensive, and the war was getting closer. Our instructors assured us it would be over in 6 months; Japan didn't stand a chance. We were smarter, tougher and had much better equipment. Some of us considered this propaganda, but kept our thoughts to ourselves.

On Graduation Day, I marched across the stage, received my commission and was sworn into the United States Navy. It was anticlimactic! It was the voyage that had provided the excitement. I was going to miss my friends. We knew our paths would cross again in another part of the world. No one said good-bye in the Navy; rather "till we meet again."

For the Graduation Ball at the Commodore Hotel, I had a date with the sister of a classmate from Scarsdale, NY. I was unhappy when the band stopped playing at midnight. Johnny said, "It's too early to go home. Let's go to the Rainbow Room at Rockerfeller Center." Arriving on the 65th floor of Rockerfeller Center, the Maitre d' escorted us to our seats by the window. The entire city of New York was at our feet.

When the orchestra leader acknowledged our presence with "Anchors Aweigh", all eyes focused on us. My date whispered, "Get up. This is your big chance." My shipmates and I stood at attention. My eyes moistened as I sang:
"Tho our last night ashore, drink to the foam.

Until we meet again, here's wishing you a happy voyage home."
The cheering and applauding of the crowd continued after we sat down. Johnny exclaimed: "What an ending to our college days! There can never again be a summer like this one of '41."

The 10 days leave passed quickly. With my new love, Helen Orr, I saw "Citizen Kane" with Orson Wells and Joseph Cotten and "Dr. Jekyll and Mr. Hyde" with Spencer Tracy and Ingrid Bergman. Occasionally we'd join friends at the Carrolton Club and dance to the juke-box music, with Glenn Miller playing "Chattanooga Choo Choo" or Harry James playing "You Made Me Love You".

Always the talk turned to sports. Leon declared, "Frank Sinkwich, Georgia's fullback, is a consensus All American. Duke, Georgia and Alabama are going to have outstanding seasons."

"Whose going to win the World Series?"

"It'll be between New York and Brooklyn. Boston's Ted Williams has a batting average of over .400 and will lead the league."

The girls complained about shortages which were developing and the rationing of silk stockings. Helen exclaimed, "The government regulations limiting dress length, restricting the number of pockets and banning pleats will have us looking like a bunch of zombies!"

The President's establishment of the Office of Price Administration (OPA) had everyone's approval. "Prices are getting out of hand for everything but alcohol," Leon said. "With beer 5 cents a can and whiskey at $1.50 a quart, we can drown our sorrows and pretend this is the best of all worlds."

In my spare time, I read Ernest Hemingway's "For Whom the Bell Tolls", "What Makes Sammy Run" by Budd Schulberg, "Random Harvest" by James Hilton and "The Keys To the Kingdom" by A.J. Cronin.

On 1 October, I reported to the Commandant, Sixth Naval District, Charleston, SC, and said to the duty officer, "Ensign Jervey reporting aboard, sir. I would like to pay my respects to the Admiral, if I may."

Looking me over, he sharply replied, "There's no need for you to worry the Admiral. Just let me see your orders. The Sterett is not in Charleston. I'll find out where she is. There are no public quarters available, so find a place in town and you'll be reimbursed by the supply officer."

The Sterett was located in Bermuda, and on 4 October, I reported to the Commandant, Fifth Naval District in Norfolk, Va., to await transportation to the Sterett. The Admiral didn't care to see me, and I began to suspect the the protocol of paying a courtesy visit to the Admiral was a lot of baloney.

Hitler was proclaiming to the German people: "Russia has been broken and will never rise again."

The next day, I reported to the USS Mizar for transportation to the Sterett. It was classified as a cargo ship, but looked like the Queen Mary. I was welcomed aboard by the OOD and the messenger escorted me to my quarters. Enroute, he pointed to a small swimming pool on the main deck and said, "That's for recreation."

"What a way to fight a war!" I exclaimed.

My quarters were spacious. After stowing my gear, I was taken to the Captain's cabin. He was a heavy set, white-haired man with a weather-beaten face. After looking at my orders and scratching his head, he said, "Mr. Jervey, you're the first of a kind for me. What is a V-7 E-VG qualified to do?"

I explained and he replied, "We're headed for Bermuda. Get yourself squared away and report to Mr. Turner, the chief engineer." After I passed a few pleasantries with Mr. Turner, he said, "You will stand regular watches with the crew, 4 hours on and 8 hours off."

The officers were a congenial group. I enjoyed hearing about their adventures, homes and families. I relished swimming in the pool. The ride over was smooth and I slept soundly.

After we arrived at Great South Bay, Bermuda, on 8 October, I disembarked. The duty officer at the Naval Base said, "The Sterett is at sea conducting exercises. She'll be back in a few days. The Stack is in her division. You'll report to the CO and remain on board until the Sterett returns." The Captain of the Stack welcomed me and said, "Make yourself at home. You may go on liberty with the other officers."

My roommate was Lt.(jg) Herbert Kabot, Academy '38. He indoctrinated me into shipboard life. The assistant engineering officer was Gordon Jakob, a classmate from the Prairie State. As we shook hands, he noted, "One of the pluses of Navy life is always running into classmates and friends. It's like a big fraternity."

"But the flip side is always knowing someone on board a ship when tragedy strikes," I replied.[6]

I enjoyed the lush beauty of my first semi-tropical islands, which were 700 miles slightly northeast of Charleston, SC. The warm waters of the Gulf Stream kept the temperatures balmy. The islands sat on top of an extinct volcano which rose 14,000 feet from the floor of the Atlantic Ocean. The 20 inhabited islands were connected by bridges and causeways forming a chain 22 miles long and one mile wide. The crystal clear, deep blue water, shading to emerald greens in the shallows, was the most beautiful I'd ever seen. With no springs or wells, fresh water was gotten by collecting rain water from the roofs of houses and storing it in tanks underneath.

In October of 1941, the population of Bermuda consisted of 30,000 people of many nationalities. Hamilton, the capital, had 2,000 residents. I was charmed by the constabulary, who wore white uniforms trimmed in gold with pith helmets, and the pink cottages with white terraced limestone roofs designed to catch the rain water.

Front Street was lined with stores filled with cashmere sweaters, British tweeds, Scottish wools and French perfumes—all at bargain prices. Because of the colorful Poinciana, Bougainvillea, Hibiscus, Poinsettia, Oleander and a large variety of fruit trees, Mark Twain said during his visit, "You go to heaven if you want. I'll just stay here."

Walking down Front Street, I saw a familiar face. I extended my hand and said, "Dr. Livingston, I presume."

With a smile, he exclaimed, "Harold Jervey, it's good to see you." Ensign A.C. Lyles was a classmate at the University of South Carolina. I learned he was in the Supply Corps and had been stationed at the Naval Base for 3 months. He said, "Two other officers and I have a bungalow just out of town on the water. You're welcome to spend the night any time you're free. I've met several girls and can get you a date."

"I'm going to enjoy my stay, with you around."

On weekends, there were dances with big bands at the Elbow Beach, Belmont Manor and Invururie Hotels. Bermuda was an R&R (rest and recreation) area for RAF pilots. Their stirring tales of the air battles over Britain made me eager to get the war started. I even considered joining the RCAF in Canada.

The primary means of transportation were the train, which ran the length of the island, or a bicycle, which I usually rented. My date had her own. This assured me of no drunk driving charges and plenty of exercise. A couple of warnings from the constabulary kept me on the left-hand side of the road.

On 12 October, the executive officer summoned me to his cabin: "The Sterett is coming into port. Get your gear together and I'll send you over." This news I received with mixed emotions. It had been good duty so far.

At 1625 I reported aboard the Sterett and was escorted to the Captain's cabin. Anxiety set in when I entered and saw Lt. Commander Jessie G. Coward, Annapolis, Class of '33. He was a slender, balding man of medium height. He looked me over carefully with steady, grayish eyes and said, "I've been expecting you. Have a seat and tell me

USS Sterett

about yourself." When I finished, he asked me a few questions and said, "I've never encountered a reservist with an engineering-only designation before. I'm going to turn you over to Lt. Luongo, our chief engineer. In the meantime, I'll have the messenger show you to your cabin."

After unpacking, I went to the wardroom for dinner. Cmdr. Coward introduced me to my shipmates. Lt. Everett was executive officer. Next to him was Lt. J.W. Clute, the gunnery officer—a graying, stocky man with the nervous habit of running his hand through his hair. Adjacent was Ensign C.R. Calhoun, communications officer, black-haired with a smile on his bulldog face. Ensign Hugh Sanders, assistant engineering officer, was my cabin mate. He had a small nose, reddish complexion and curly, close-cropped blond hair.

Calhoun's wife, I discovered, was a dietitian at Roper Hospital in Charleston and knew my aunts who worked there. Hugh's wife was from Columbia, and I had known her and her family for several years. Ensign Tom McWhorter, torpedo officer, a lanky, taciturn Texan, was next. All were Annapolis graduates. The remaining two were ninety-day wonders: Ensign H.M. Marver, assistant communication officer, was from Minnesota and his family owned a chain of clothing stores, and Ensign P.G. Hayden was from Chicago.

Lt. Frank Luongo was an engineer by choice. He was swarthy and rarely smiled. After dinner he said, "I want you to know more about this engineering plant than anyone on this ship except me. You will take the correspondence course which the Bureau of Engineering puts out. In addition, I want you to diagram all of the engineering systems: steam, water and electricity. I'll decide when they are satisfactory. While at sea, you'll stand watch in each of the engineering spaces, four hours on and eight hours off. If you run out of something to do, let me know. There is unending work on a destroyer. Any questions?"

"No, sir." Prudence counseled silence.

I mustered daily at 0800 on the fantail with the engineers. Daily inspections were made of the magazines and smokeless powder samples; weekly, the magazine sprinkling systems were inspected; daily, the ship's boats were inspected. Lunch was at 1200, dinner at 1800. When we were in port, movies were shown on the fantail, underway in the crew's mess hall and in the wardroom.

Wow! I thought: 20 years old earning, $125/month with housing, transportation and meals provided at a nominal cost. I was in hog heaven. The tropical island with pretty, friendly girls was a bonus.

My dreams were interrupted at 0530 on 15 October when the PA boomed: "Now hear this! Now hear this! Station special sea details. Make all preparations for getting underway." I reported to my station in the forward boiler room. Throughout the day the Sterett conducted plane guard duty with the aircraft carrier USS Ranger. I sketched the steam lines. As I came up on deck, I asked P.G. Hayden what we were doing. He replied, "Whenever we operate with a carrier, we have two responsibilities: protect her from submarines with our sonar gear, and rescue any pilots who ditch into the ocean. When the planes are taking off, our station is 500 yards off her port bow and on landings, 500 yards off her port quarter."

"Why?"

"The pilots get into trouble shortly after take-off and by being on the bow, we can get to them faster. When they're landing, the reverse is true."

After anchoring in Murray's Bay, the PA boomed, "Now hear this! Now hear this! All men going on liberty, lay up to the quarter deck. The boats will be leaving in 15 minutes." I remained on board and sketched. The next day, I spent the evening dining and dancing at the Belmont Manor Hotel. The following morning, the Sterett was underway, enroute to Hampton Roads, Va., in company with the Stack and the Nashville.

Cal announced, "General Togo has overthrown Prince Konoye's government in Japan. He's itching for war. He has given China an ultimatum: peace talks will begin only if the Dutch East Indies are turned over to Japan. The deadline is 25 November."

Clute snorted, "There's no way the US can accept that. Scuttlebutt has it our military leaders would like to wait until spring before the shooting starts. Personally, I'm ready now. Let's kick their little asses and get it over with. The only thing that concerns me is the Tirpitz, the super battleship of the Germans. I don't want to run into her."

In Europe, the Germans had been advancing steadily and, on 18 October, they were only 80 miles west of Moscow. There was a mass exodus from the city.

During the day, the Sterett conducted drills and I continued sketching steam pipes. At dinner Cal said, "I've just heard that the USS Kearney has been torpedoed northwest of Iceland. I know nothing about the casualties or damage."

"Things are getting serious in the Pacific," Clute exclaimed. "Admiral Harold Stark, Chief of Naval Operations, has sent an alert to our Pacific and Asiatic commanders advising them of the strong possibility of war between Japan and Russia, as well as the US. We're going to be involved shortly."

The next afternoon the Sterett was moored at the Naval Operating Base, Norfolk, Va. The city offered no attractions, so my liberty time was spent at the officer's club, where entertainment and single girls were available. Wives of officers and crew members flew in and rented apartments.

On 27 October, the Sterett began operating with the Wasp, a newly commissioned carrier, with her "green" ir groups. The following morning the formation was enroute to Bermuda.

At supper Hugh told us that exec was having pains in his stomach and wouldn't be in. The pain became more severe and at 0730 the next morning, Lt. G.S. Everett was put on the binnacle list with a diagnosis of kidney stones, and was relieved of all duties. Lt. Luongo succeeded him. Hugh Sanders became chief engineer and I was elevated to assistant. On 31 October, after we moored to the tender USS Melville in Port Royal Bay, Lt. Everett was transferred to the base hospital.

In Europe, conditions were improving. The German advance was halted by a sea of mud and subzero weather. They were still in their summer uniforms and freezing to death. Their supply system had failed and they were almost out of fuel.

We had drills. Captain D.P. Moon, Commander of DesRon 50, had his flag on the USS Wainwright. He was a perfectionist and expected his officers and men to be the best trained in the Navy. At any time of the day or night, a signal might be sent from the Wainwright: "man overboard". The signalman better be alert and sound the alarm. The lifeboat crews got the boats in the water and went through the motions of rescuing the man. The Commodore would be on the bridge with a stopwatch. Poor last-place finisher! That Captain would be summoned to the Wainwright and his ass chewed out.[7]

During our stay, Coward administered punishments for a variety of offenses: absent over leave, a summary court martial; refusing to obey orders and neglect of duty, five days confinement in the brig on bread and water.

I completed my drawings and started on the 10 lessons in the engineering course. When a lesson was completed, it was sent to the Squadron Commander where it was graded. Coward expected me to complete one lesson each week.

On 3 November the Sterett and the Stack played tag all day with the submarine USS 105. We would track her and simulate dropping depth charges. I kept busy crawling through the bilges as my lesson required.

Joseph Grew, US Ambassador to Japan, warned Washington that war might come suddenly. Recent movements of Japanese troops placed them in a position to attack Siberia and/or the southwest Pacific. He also reported the rumors, prevalent in Tokyo, of a surprise attack on Pearl harbor.

The Sterett, in company with the Wasp and Lang, was enroute to Norfolk. Flight operations and gunnery exercises were conducted daily. On 7 November we were moored to Pier 2. Men were transferred to other ships and to training schools. Stores and ammunition were received. I met friends at the officer's club and discussed the war. The battles in North Africa had been see-sawing back and forth with no clear victory by either General Auckinleck or Rommel. The report of the capture of the Odenwald, a German blockade runner, by the USS Omaha and destroyer Sommers was the big news story.

For three days the Sterett did plane guard duty with an unnamed British aircraft carrier and the Long Island. The Captain held mast for five men. I saw the danger of flying when I saw one plane crash coming in for a landing and the rescue party brought in the bruised body of the pilot.

On 13 November the Sterett moved to the outer harbor. Clute held forth in the wardroom, running his hands through his hair and declaring, "Congress has repealed the Neutrality Act of 1939. Roosevelt has wanted us in this war from the beginning, and with no legal restraints, he's going to succeed."

Cal responded, "He still doesn't have the majority of the American people behind him. Congress renewed the Selective Service Act by a vote of 203 to 202. 'OHIO' (over the hill in October) has been written on walls and signs all over the country. It's encouraging draftees not to report for duty." The consensus was it won't be long, so let's get on with it.

On 17 November the Sterett was enroute to Bermuda, and 4 days later was moored to the Altair.

At dinner Luongo said, "Mr. Jervey, because of your demonstrated abilities, I am appointing you movie officer." It was a no win position. My responsibility would be to beg, borrow, trade or steal movies from other ships or the naval base. It was my hide if they weren't exciting. I wrangled from the Altair's movie officer "How Green Was My Valley" with Walter Pidgeon and Maureen O'Hara and "Sergeant York" with Gary Cooper and Joan Leslie. I told the exec, "I don't want any grumbling from the crew. Both of these pictures are up for Academy Awards."

Serious diplomatic discussions were occurring. Togo declared that Japan was willing to withdraw from French Indo-China and parts of China if the US did not interfere with peace negotiations between Japan and Chiang Kai-shek. In addition, Japan wanted the US to support its acquisition of the Dutch East Indies. Even though our military leaders didn't believe the US would be ready for war until spring, they couldn't accede to these demands. The deadline given for an answer was 26 November.

Attack orders were issued to Japanese commanders on 20 November. They were not to strike until the diplomatic negotiations in Washington were completed. On 24 November US Commanders were warned of possible attacks on the Philippines, Guam, Panama, Hawaii and San Francisco. On 26 November the Pearl Harbor strike force, under the command of Admiral Chuichi Nagumo, left its anchorage in the Kurile Islands north of Japan enroute for Hawaii. He had 6 aircraft carriers, 2 battleships, 3 cruisers, 9 destroyers and 8 tankers. On 27 November Japan's Ambassador to the US rejected the demand that it withdraw from China. The talks continued so that Admiral Nagumo could get in position to strike.

At breakfast the Captain said, "Commanders of Pacific Bases have been put on final alert. It's believed Japan will attack at any time. The question is where. The Germans are only 30 miles from Moscow. Things don't look good."

Clute responded, "We're ready to get this damned war over. The sooner it gets started, the sooner all of us can go home."

For the next 3 days various exercises were conducted with the Wasp, Nashville, Wilson and the submarine 157. A major change in shipboard routine occurred when Commander W.W. Warlick, Commodore, Destroyer Division 15, moved his flag aboard on 28 November.

I quickly learned what Commodores do: ride the ship's captain and play acey-ducey with the junior officer. Nothing Coward did satisfied.

He was reluctant to sit around in the wardroom. Warlick was always finding fault. He singled me out to play acey-ducey. He loved it, and it was in my best interests to love it also. While we were playing, he told me about his family, his life and his goals. I shared mine.

I continued working on my lessons and enjoyed my weekend liberty when I stayed with A.C. Lyles.

The fighting in Russia was furious. The Soviets launched a counter attack under General Georgi Zhukov, forcing Von Rundstedt to withdraw. Hitler sacked him.

On 1 December, Admiral Nagumo was ordered to attack Pearl Harbor on 7 December. The Sterett played at war with the Stack, the Nashville and the submarine USS 153. Various exercises and battle problems were conducted. I was envious of the deck officers who talked about how good or poorly an exercise had been performed. It was all Greek to me.

When we anchored at 1534, I announced to the officers in the wardroom, "Fellows, on this day, December 3rd, a fellow with great expectations was born. He is now 21 and can legally vote and hold a commission in the US Navy. To celebrate, the drinks are on me." When I returned to the ship with an empty wallet, I regretted the invitation.

The staff at the Japanese Embassy in Washington was leaving for Japan. "Magic" intercepts alerted President Roosevelt that the code books had been destroyed. He didn't know that the Japanese 25th Army was embarking for Malaya, the Philippine Attack Force was departing from Formosa, the Guam force was enroute and the Wake attack force was ready at Kwajalein.

On Friday afternoon 5 December, the Sterett moored to the Altair. I tried to swap liberties so I could attend the big party being thrown at the Elbow Beach Hotel on Saturday night, but was unsuccessful. I couldn't find a date and spent the night drinking with some unknowns at a joint in Hamilton. When I told Hugh, he said, "Your bad luck is good luck for the Russians. The harsh winter is killing the Germans. The temperature has dropped to 35 degrees centigrade, tank engines won't start, weapons won't fire and hundreds are frostbitten. The German offensive has ground to a halt 19 miles from Moscow. More importantly, Britain has declared war on Finland, Hungary and Rumania."

On Saturday I worked on my lesson and wrote letters to my family and girl friends. The news reported that the Soviets had counter attacked on a broad front and in North Africa, Rommel was in retreat after failing to capture Tobruk.

Through the "Magic" intercept, Washington was able to decipher 13 parts of a lengthy 14-part message sent on 5 December to the Japanese Ambassador. The last part was received the next morning and made it clear that Japan intended to attack, but where or when was not known. Warnings were sent to all US Pacific garrisons except Hawaii, which was delayed due to a snafu in the handling of the dispatch. Roosevelt sent a last minute plea for peace to the Emperor of Japan.

Cal said, "The traffic on the 'skeds' has been exceptionally heavy. Some- thing is going on."

"What?" Sanders asked.

"It's all in top secret code and I can't break it."

As I headed for my bunk, Cal added, "Maybe I can find out tomor-row."

LIST OF OFFICERS

Attached to and on board of the U. S. S. ___S T E R E T T (D D 4 0 7)___, commanded

by ___Lieut-Comdr. J. G. COWARD___, U. S. N., during the period covered by this Log Book, with date of

reporting for duty, detachment, transfer, or death, from ___October 1___, 19 41, to ___October 31___, 19 41

NAME.	RANK.	DATE OF REPORTING FOR DUTY.	DETACHED. Date.	DUTIES.
J. G. COWARD	Lieut-Comdr.	30 Apr 1941		Morale; Commanding
G. S. EVERETT	Lieutenant	28 Mar 1941		Executive Navigator;Courts
F. P. LUONGO, Jr.	Lieutenant	15 Aug 1939		Engineer;Athletics; DamageControl;Welfare
J. M. CLUTE	Lieutenant	15 Aug 1939		Gunnery;Optical
C. R. CALHOUN	Lieutenant (jg)	15 Aug 1939		Communication;Commissary;Tactical
H. B. SANDERS, Jr.	Ensign	2 July 1940		Asst.Engineer; Stores;Movies
P. G. HAYDEN	Ens.D-V(G)USNR	29 Ded 1940		1st Lieut.;Asst.Gun.; Ship's Service
T. O. McWHORTER	Ensign	13 Mar 1941		Torpedo Off.;Asst. "D" Div.Officer.
H. M. MARVER	Ens.D-V(G)USNR	26 Apr 1941		Asst.Communication (Under instruction)
R. J. LETTINO	Ens.D-V(G)USNR	11 July 1941		Asst.Gunnery Off. (Under instruction)
H. E. JERVEY, Jr.	Ens.E-V(G)USNR	12 Oct 1941		Asst.Eng.Officer.

Examined and found to be correct.

F. P. Luongo
F. P. LUONGO, Jr.
Lieutenant, USN, Acting   *Navigator.*

CHAPTER 2

The Battle with the Atlantic
Operating with the British Home Fleet and Reinforcing Malta

Sunday, 7 December, 1941, was rainy, cool, dismal. No topside work could be done. After lunch I was in my stateroom working on my lesson and thinking, "I'll be finished with this damn assignment soon. Maybe the Captain will let me qualify as a deck officer."

Suddenly I heard loud, excited voices in the passageway. Sticking my head out of the cabin, I saw Calhoun waving a dispatch board in his hand and shouting, "It's started! The war has started! The Japs attacked Pearl Harbor this morning."

All the officers ran to the wardroom where Hayden asked, "Did they sink any ships? Was anyone killed?"

"Nothing has been said about the damage. We'll hear about that later."

All of us were stunned. Clute exclaimed, "I'm glad it's finally started. We'll kick their asses and have this thing over within six months."

"I was getting tired of these damn exercises. Let's get the show on the road," Sanders added.

Hayden expressed my thoughts, saying, "I'm not certain you guys are right. From what I've read, the planes of the Germans and Japanese are faster and more maneuverable than ours, and their pilots have had more battle experience. Our torpedoes are pathetic, run off course, broach and fail to explode when they hit the target. This might be one helluva long war."

During the rest of the day scuttlebutt kept everyone edgy. There were submarines offshore ready to bombard us. A German Task Force was enroute to attack.

Cal said, "If the Admirals thought any of this scuttlebutt were true, we'd be at General Quarters and underway."

The Captain instructed me to show the movie. It was "The Maltese Falcon" with Humphrey Bogart, Mary Astor and Peter Lorre. Afterward the talk centered on the war. Hayden expressed the feelings of each: "This won't be the relaxed, peace-time Navy playing games and operating out of Shangri-La. Today paradise has been lost."

There was little sunshine on 8 December. The men were gathered in small groups waving their arms and talking animatedly. In the wardroom, the discussion focused on how badly the Pacific Fleet had been damaged and how quickly we would see combat. Intermittently I worked on my engineering lesson. Suddenly the PA boomed: "Attention all hands! This is the Captain speaking. In a few minutes President Roosevelt will be addressing a joint session of the Congress. The PA system will be connected to the radio so all hands can listen."

I went to the wardroom where the officers were gathered. The familiar, deep, resonant voice of the President rang out: "Mr. President, Mr. Speaker, members of the Senate and House of Representatives: yesterday, December 7, 1941—a date that will live in infamy—the United States of America was suddenly and deliberately attacked by naval and air forces of the Empire of Japan. I regret to tell you that many American lives have been lost. In addition, American ships have been reported torpedoed on the high seas between San Francisco and Honolulu. As Commander-in-Chief of the Army and Navy, I have directed that all measures be taken for our defense. No matter how long it takes us to overcome this premeditated invasion, the American people in their righteous might will win through to an absolute victory. With confidence in our armed forces, with unbending determination to our people, we will gain the inevitable triumph. So help us God. I ask that Congress declare that, since an unprovoked and dastardly attack by Japan on December 7, 1941, a state of war exists between the United States and the Japanese Empire."

There was silence. Then the questions. How many killed? How badly damaged the fleet? Over the next several days, we learned that 2,327 men and officers had been killed, half the aircraft on the island destroyed, 7 battleships sunk or badly damaged, and 3 destroyers reduced to junk. The cost to the Japanese? Only 29 aircraft and 5 midget submarines. However, all oil tanks were intact and our 3 aircraft carriers were safe at sea.

General MacArthur in the Philippines was warned to expect an air attack. At 0400 on 8 December, he was phoned and told, "The Japs are attacking Pearl Harbor."

He went to his headquarters. As a result of snafus, the Japanese planes were able to destroy 18 of the Army's B-17 Flying Fortresses. The Army only had 100, and 35 were stationed in the Philippines.

For us it was anti-climatic to receive a dispatch at 1420 stating, "A state of war was declared by the Congress to exist between Japan and the United States of America."

Cal said, "I'm going to need your help decoding messages. Much of our traffic during peace time has been in plain English. Now everything is going to be in code and we'll be flooded. I'll indoctrinate you as quickly as I can."

The bad news was followed with the good when the Captain said, "We're going to be at sea for longer periods of time and will need more watch officers. Mr. Jervey, I want you to stand Junior Officer of the Deck watches (JOOD) and qualify to stand Officer of the Deck watches (OOD). Finish up your engineering course as fast as possible. Can do?"

"Yes, sir! I've been waiting for this opportunity. Thank you."

There was encouraging news from abroad. German troops, 19 miles from Moscow and within sight of the Kremlin, were counter attacked by 1,000,000 fresh Siberian troops. With the brutal winter and subzero temperatures, the Germans were overwhelmed. They began a panicky retreat.

For the Sterett, the war began at 1536, 10 December, when she got underway with the Wilson, Stack, Wasp and Brooklyn (SOPA). Our first wartime orders read: "Proceed to Martinique. Intercept and destroy any of the French Fleet attempting to leave the harbor."

At dinner the Captain said, "Intelligence has discovered an aircraft carrier, 3 cruisers and several destroyers at anchor in the harbor. It is rumored that Admiral Robert, High Commissioner for the French Antilles, who was appointed by Marshall Petain, is sympathetic to the Vichy French Government. President Roosevelt has warned him through diplomatic circles that if the ships attempt to leave the harbor, the US Navy will stop them. That is our mission."

The news was bad. Japanese troops had landed on Luzon on 11 December. Germany and Italy declared war on the United States. The worst disaster was the sinking of Britain's prize battleships, the Prince of Wales and the Repulse, by Japanese aircraft off Singapore.

When I came off watch and entered the wardroom, Hayden was shaking his finger at Clute and exclaiming, "So the war is going to be over in six months! What happened to that invincibility propaganda we've been filled with? The Japs are first cousins to the apes. Their planes are flying junk heaps. Their pilots can't see with those squint eyes, and their high command is a bunch of nerds. And you say planes can't sink ships! Where is that super-efficient intelligence agency of ours? In my book they're a bunch of arrogant asses."

Running his hand through his hair and cracking his knuckles, Clute replied, "I was wrong like 90 percent of the Navy. We're in for a long haul. I think the sinking of those ships may change the entire strategy of this war."

Our sleeping habits had been changed. With General Quarters ½ hour before sunrise and securing ½ hour after dawn, and the same procedure at dusk, those having the midnight to 0400 watch no sooner got in the sack than it was roll out time. We learned to catnap whenever possible.

At 1800, 12 December, the Captain came on the P.A. System, "Now hear this! This is the Captain speaking. Tomorrow we may be called upon to engage in battle. It will be our first, but surely not our last. You are well-trained. You are prepared. Give your best. Victory will be ours, because our cause is right. God bless you all."

Hayden exclaimed, "It just hit me. Some of us maybe killed. This is the real thing."

I was JOOD with Cal when, at 2323 on 12 December, the Quartermaster of the watch reported, "Caravelle Peninsula Light on Martinique has been sighted, sir."

"Notify the Captain," Cal ordered.

Talk centered on what morning would bring. Would the French Admiral fight? Did he have superior forces? We didn't have the answers. I was relieved of the watch at 2345 by Marver. Sleep was brief and fitful. General Quarters was sounded at 0550. From my station in the after-engine room, I might as well have been entering New York Harbor.

At 0615, my phone talker said, "The Wasp has launched 12 planes." And later, "Pilots report several ships seem to be preparing to get underway. Smoke is coming from their stacks. The Captain says we may see some action."

Admiral Robert had been informed that units of the US Navy were prepared to attack if he attempted to leave the harbor. For two days the discussions went on. It seemed like eternity. The Wasp kept planes in the air monitoring the activities of the French. At 1735 on 14 December, Robert said he would join up with General DeGaulle and the Free French.

With the crisis resolved, we headed home. At 1911 Caravelle Peninsula Light was passed. For the next 4 days, flight operations and various exercises were conducted. One plane crashed and the crew was rescued with only minor injuries. Fish were identified as submarines. A fueling stop was made at St. Thomas, Virgin Islands, and on 18 December, the Sterett was moored to the Altair in Bermuda Harbor. Commander Warlick was congratulated on his promotion to Captain.

For the next 4 days there was routine ship's upkeep. I went on liberty, dated, danced and drank. The Bermudans were warm and friendly. I told A.C., "I'd be happy to spend the war right here. Let's you and me swap places."

Cal cornered me later saying, "I'm getting overloaded. I need your help in decoding." He launched in on Communications Course 101. All messages for sea commands originate from Washington, DC, San Francisco or Pearl Harbor. The Fox Schedule (Skeds) was broadcast 24 hours a day and his men copied it continuously. The Captain and Commodore wanted every message decoded whether addressed to the Sterett or not. Messages to Task Group Commanders were in top secret code and couldn't be deciphered. The codes were changed daily and the books were kept in the safe.

I was kept busy with my engineering course, decoding and indoctrination on the duties of JOOD. Fortunately I was able to get the movies "Suspicion" with Cary Grant and Joan Fontaine, "The Shanghai Gesture" with Gene Tierney and Victor Mature, as well as "Meet John Doe" with Gary Cooper and Barbara Stanwyck. The crew was happy.

Cal reported that a major shake-up had occurred in the Naval command: "On 20 December, Admiral Ernest J. King was appointed Commander, US Navy (Cominch). Admiral Royal E. Ingersoll will take over as Commander of the Atlantic Fleet (CinClant). I understand King is one smart, tough cookie. He's not liked by many, but he's respected by all. We're in for some changes."

On 22 December the Sterett was enroute to Norfolk, Va., with the Stack, Wasp and Long Island. The wind was gusting 15-20 knots and the ship was rolling and plunging into the 5-10 foot waves. My stomach was doing flip flops. I retained no food and little liquid until the Chesapeake Bay Light Ship was sighted on Christmas Eve. With Pilot Davis at the conn, we moored to Pier 7 at 1402. Several females were standing at the end of the dock. Tom McWhorter observed, "Wives must have some sort of psychic ability. They're always waiting on the dock before we're secured. How the hell did they know we'd be in Norfolk?"

Winston Churchill was meeting with President Roosevelt in Washington. They agreed that maximum resources would be focused on the defeat of Hitler and the Axis countries. The Pacific area would be basically a holding action.

The PA boomed: "Now hear this! Mail call for the crew in the mess hall; for officers, in the wardroom." I got letters from my family and girl friends; also a couple of presents. By general agreement, the married officers had liberty. I phoned my mother and my number one girl, whom I discovered had found another guy. Number two was moved up to one.

I spent most of Christmas Day on board decoding and working on my engineering course. The cook prepared a sumptuous dinner with turkey and all the trimmings. After stuffing myself, I went to the officer's club and had a couple of drinks.

The news reported that the Japanese were within 100 miles of Manila. MacArthur's troops were falling back into the jungle peninsula of

Bataan, which was protected at the tip by Corregidor, an underground fortress carved into rock. The troops didn't have time to load the trucks with food and supplies from the warehouses in Manila. As a result, the Japanese ate well and the American and Filipino troops were soon on half rations, 30 ounces of food a day, which quickly lowered their efficiency and hastened their defeat.

On 26 December, the Sterett was underway, along with the Stack and the Long Island, heading north. The Long Island conducted flight operations. After fueling in Casco Bay, the formation was enroute to Argentia, Newfoundland.

Warlick told me, "Even veteran sailors dread the North Atlantic in the winter." I understood why. It was bitter cold. The wind howled at gale force and the waves were mountainous. The ship rolled 30-40 degrees and when headed into the wind, cork screwed into and over the waves, shaking like a dog. On occasion the bow hung over the edge of a wave and plunged 20 feet straight down into the trough. Keeping erect without a firm grip on the rail or bulkhead was impossible. I got a little rest by wedging my leg between the mattress and bulk head. Even with the side rails, I had no sense of security. A few could eat in the wardroom, with guard rails to keep the dishes from sliding, and the chairs tied to the deck. My stomach rebelled. Anything that went down came right back up. I vomited just thinking about food. It was so rough that on 30 December, the motor whale boat on the portside was washed overboard. The battering stopped on New Year's Day when the Sterett entered Placentia Bay, Newfoundland, and moored starboard side to the Stack.

The British had built several military bases on the island, as it was closer to Britain than any port on the Eastern Seaboard. Since the Germans knew convoys heading east made up in these waters, U-boats prowled off shore. Planes being ferried to England flew from the airfield in nearby Gander.

26 nations agreed to form a United Nations to defeat the Axis powers. In the wardroom there were heated arguments over the dismissal of Admiral Kimmel and General Short, the Navy and Army Commanders in Hawaii. Hayden exclaimed, "They're scapegoats. The guys in Washington fiddled around while Rome was burning. The President knew the attack was coming and he didn't give Kimmel and Short adequate warning."

"It wouldn't have made any difference how much time they had. The island was not prepared. They demonstrated incompetence," Sanders responded. "And I'm happy Admiral Chester W. Nimitz has been appointed to command the US Pacific Fleet."

There was no liberty. Several of us were in the wardroom writing letters when Cal came in and asked, "Would you fellers like to hear the Rose Bowl Game?" The vote was unanimous. Each of us put a dollar in the pot and picked his favorite team. I wrote letters, listened and yelled when my team scored. I had Duke, which lost to Oregon 20 to 15. The announcers gave us the scores of the other games which made some happy, others sad: Orange Bowl—Georgia 40, Texas Christian 26; Alabama 29, Texas A&M 21 in the Cotton Bowl and Fordham 2, Missouri 0 in the Sugar Bowl.

German submarines were active all up and down the east coast. In January, Wolfpacks (groups of 5 or more submarines) sank 46 ships. At least 50 U-boats were always on the prowl.

Hayden expressed my feelings when he exclaimed, "It's inconceivable how those submariners survive. The North Atlantic is hell, and I don't mean hot. With the water temperature in the 30's, any one falling overboard would survive only 8 to 10 minutes."

"Submariners don't fall into the water. They cruise under it nice and smooth," McWhorter responded.

I was introduced to "screech". In the early days of the colonies, sailing vessels loaded with rum from the Indies unloaded their cargo in Argentia and St. John's. In the bottoms of the boats was a thick sludge, the concentrate from the rum. The Newfoundlanders would scrape it out, refine it and bottle it. When anyone imbibed, they "screeched ". After one drink, I knew it had been properly named.

On 16 January, the Sterett was enroute to Iceland with the Stack, Ericson and Eberle. The seas to the south were babies compared to what we now encountered. All hands were ordered to wear life jackets except when asleep. I was never warm, even with a heavy jacket, boots, gloves and head gear. Icicles glistened from the rigging and on the beards of the crew after 4 hours watch topside.

I grew a mustache and beard thinking it would help. Hayden laughingly said, "That mustache looks like dirt you forgot to wash off your face, and that gray beard makes you look like an old man who should be retired from the Navy." Thus ended my experiment with the mustache and beard.

Captain Warlick insisted on playing acey-ducey and I had to comply. I said, "I'm not going to give you much competition. I haven't been able to eat since we started this trip. At least I've got company with some of the crew and officers. I feel more comfortable with them than earlier on."

"You're going to discover throughout your life that it makes little difference how brutal the sea, how terrible the wind, your destination or the distance. It's your shipmates that make the difference. Jolly ship-mates will always make the voyage more pleasant."

On 17 January, Cal excitedly reported, "Carol Lombard was killed yesterday in an airplane accident. She had been on a war bond tour to Indianapolis and was returning home to Burbank, California, on a TWA flight. It stopped in Albuquerque for passengers and they tried to bump her party for 3 Army officers. She pulled rank, saying she had been on official government business, and was allowed to stay on board."

Hayden interrupted, "She was married to Clark Gable, wasn't she?"

"Yes, and she still would be if she had gotten off the plane. It landed in Los Vegas to fuel. Shortly after take-off, it crashed into 8,500-foot Mt. Potosi. Everyone was killed and Carol's remains could only be iden-tified by x-rays."

The winds raged from gale to hurricane force day and night. The ship rolled 35 to 40 degrees. At times I felt like I was walking on the overhead rather than the deck. It was always midnight. With only a couple of hours of daylight, it was perfect weather for U-boat opera-tions. We chased them, but never made a kill.

Partial relief came on 25 January when the Sterett moored in Reykjavik Harbor, Iceland. On my first liberty, I felt like the whole earth was moving. I swayed like a drunken sailor as I walked, and in-stinctively wanted to hold on to something for support.

Iceland was an unexpected pleasure. It was equidistant between Moscow and New York and only 500 miles from Scotland. Because of the Gulf Stream, ice was rare in the navigable waters, and the tempera-tures averaged in the 40's year round. The Vikings settled it in 874 AD and it was under Danish rule until granted home rule in 1904. In 1940, British troops occupied the island to protect the sea lanes, and in July, 1941, the United States took over its defenses. The population was 121,474, with 50% of the people living in Reykjavik, the capital. Since the island sat atop a sometimes active volcano, steam rose from cracks and crevices. The buildings and many houses were kept warm with steam heat at little cost. The University of Iceland was a mirage, one enormous hot-house. There were large numbers of fruit trees and flow-ers found only in the tropics. The Hotel Borg was the center of social activities and intrigue. Allegedly, it was frequented by spies, and it was a game trying to identify who they might be.

Clute had told us prior to arrival, "You young fellers are in for a treat. You won't find more beautiful blondes in any one place at night than the Hotel Borg. Nice girls are always chaperoned, usually by their parents. It is perfectly acceptable to go to a table and ask to dance with the daughter."

"And then what?" Hayden asked.

" If you have warm vibrations, you can ask her to sit at your table."

"And then what?"

"That's as far as it goes. I've heard tales of bundling, lying in bed fully clothed under blankets, talking, holding hands and kissing. Maybe one of you can confirm that truth."

I enjoyed dancing and talking with some of the most gorgeous blondes I'd ever seen. Danish pastry was wonderful, just melted in my mouth.[8]

The Japanese were slowly advancing on Bataan. MacArthur withdrew his troops to their final defense position, the Bagac-Orion line. The Japanese captured Sarawak and declared war on the Dutch East Indies, while invading Burma, Rabual and Kavieng in New Ireland. By the end of the month, Borneo was in Japanese hands and Thailand had declared war on Britain and the US.

Rommel was pushing the allies back in Africa and captured Cyrenica with its airfield. This stopped the British bombing of convoys. Churchill proclaimed the Tirpitz, the world's largest battleship, "the most important naval vessel in the war". As a result, the RAF began attacking it at every opportunity, without success.

On 29 January I was enjoying the sights, the clean fresh air and the steady platform. Returning to the dock at 1800, I saw no Sterett whale boat. After waiting for one hour, I went aboard the USS Williamsburg (formerly FDR's presidential yacht) and asked the duty officer, "Do you have any word on the Sterett?"

"The coast guard cutter Alexander Hamilton was torpedoed this afternoon outside of the harbor entrance. Several destroyers were sent to find and sink the U-boat. Your ship was one."

I explained my problem to the Executive Officer who said, "Don't worry about it. We've got an extra stateroom. You can borrow some clothes and toiletries. Just relax and enjoy your freedom. We'll let you know when the Sterett comes in." Borrowing what I needed, I told my cabin mate, "I don't care if the Sterett never returns. Not in my wildest dreams did I think I'd want to spend the winter in Iceland." My pleasures ended at 0500, 31 January, when the messenger woke me: "Sir, the Sterett is in the outer harbor fueling. She has been ordered to the States." I dressed and went topside as though the ship were on fire. The OOD said, "You'd better get out there pronto or you'll spend the war in Iceland."

At 0929 the Sterett, with Task Force 15, was underway for Norfolk, Va. While playing acey-ducey with Captain Warlick, I remarked, "The wind is howling just as much, the waves are just as gigantic and I am just as cold, but I am not as miserable. Maybe I'm becoming a sailor."

"Son, that's only a part of the story. You're going to discover that whether you're 10,000 miles from home or 10, whether the skies are clear or stormy, whether by land, air or sea, the inbound voyage is always better than the outbound. The psychology of heading home does something to our minds and our emotions. The distance is always shorter. You will find that true as long as you live."

The voyage was uneventful. There were shouts of joy when the PA boomed, "This is the Captain speaking. You will be happy to learn our orders have been changed. Rather than Norfolk, we're going to the Brooklyn Navy Yard for upkeep and repairs."

The night prior to our arrival, Marver and I finished showering at the same time. I said, "Let's give the guys a treat, a Broadway show."

"Suits me. Let's pretend we're the Rockettes." We wrapped towels around our hips, intertwined our arms and pranced down the passageway singing, "Give my regards to Broadway. Remember me to Herald Square. Tell all the girls on 42nd Street that I will soon be there." Shipmates stuck their heads out of their staterooms and Cal yelled, "What the hell is all the racket about?"

"Just trying to lift your spirits," I replied. With that there was clapping, whistling and shouts, "Take it off! Take it off!" There were no repeat performances.

On 9 February Ambrose Light Ship was sighted. Cal, who was OOD, remarked, "You'll soon be seeing those girls on 42nd Street. I hope we're here long enough for Ginny to come up."

Pilot Davis came aboard, took the conn and at 1207, the Sterett was moored port side to the USS Dalgreen in the Brooklyn Navy Yard. The North Atlantic had given the Sterett a beating and repairs were needed. 23 new crew members reported aboard, together with Lt. Frank Gould, our new executive officer. He was black-haired, medium build and swarthy.

Lt. Cmdr. Frank Luongo was ordered to report to the new battleship Indiana as chief engineer. Our first medical officer, Lt.(jg) George McInnis, MC-V(G), arrived. For me he was a welcome addition, having graduated from the Medical College in Charleston, SC.

Hayden voiced my thoughts: "New York is the place to be. Everyone thinks we've been battling the German U-boats and we're going to end this war in a few months. What a bunch of crap! We've battled the sea. That's the enemy! It doesn't discriminate. It destroys Germans and Americans alike. If they want to treat me like a hero, so be it."

For six days the war was forgotten. There were plenty of girls at the USO dances. The hotel ballrooms featured big name bands. At the Hotel New Yorker, where Johnny Long was playing, the cover charge was

$.75 during the week and $1 on Saturday. A deluxe dinner was $2 and up. Celebrities were always present at Sherman Billingsley's Stork Club. I was enchanted with "Lohengrin", featuring Lauritz Melchior, Norman Cordon and Astrid Varnay at the Metropolitan Opera.

The officers compared notes. Hayden remarked, "What about these crazy ads! Everybody and everything has gone to war. The Texaco one, 'I'm fighting for my right to boo the Dodgers' and 'Fighting Red—new brave lipstick by Tussey.'"

"And how about the prices! It would pay me to get married," McWhorter added. "Diamond engagement rings $50 and suits $25."

"That ain't even the down payment on marriage," Cal replied.

With Clute's transfer on 12 February, Calhoun became gunnery officer, McWhorter, communication officer, and Hayden, 1st Lieutenant. The Sterett and Stack conducted exercises and moored in Boston on 16 February. Marver and Hayden introduced me to the Copley Plaza Hotel, which was where dates and other entertainment could be found. I visited Scully Square, which was full of honky tonks and strip joints. Girls were available for a price or just a few drinks. Marver said, "Prim and proper Bostonians did not want these places polluting the minds of the young, so they put them all in one location which just made them more accessible to everyone."

Tassel Gertie was the star attraction. She had tassels on her boobs and on her pelvis, fore and aft. She did remarkable gyrations to the tempo of the music. Rotate them clockwise, counter clockwise, reverse them, or have one boob go one direction and the other the opposite. It was fascinating to watch![9]

On 18 February the Sterett was underway with the Stack and at 1414 took station 2,000 yards on the bow of the world's largest luxury liner, the Queen Mary (code name: SS Madam). She had been converted to a troop transport and could carry up to 15,000 men. Hayden, OOD, said, "These seas are running 8 to 10 feet. At 30 knots, she's plowing through them like a knife cutting butter. She just holds her head proudly to the sky and drives ahead. It's remarkable."

"Well, it ain't the same with us. We're taking a beating. I feel like I'm on a submarine with these waves crashing over the bow. I've talked with officers on other destroyers that have escorted her. Their ships looked like they'd hit a brick wall when they returned to port: hulls bent, pilot house windows smashed and whale boats washed over the side."

"It won't be for long. Once clear of the coastal waters, she'll make the crossing alone. No submarine can catch her. British destroyers will pick her up off the coast of Scotland and escort her up the Clyde."

At 1125 the next day, the Queen Mary signaled, "Thanks for your service. Pleasant sailing and good hunting. Until we meet again." No submarine touched her during the many transatlantic crossings.

The news was gloomy. Singapore had fallen on 15 February and the Japanese were now advancing in Burma.

The Sterett headed North and on 21 February anchored in Casco Bay, Maine. Ensign J.D. Jeffery reported on board and was assigned duties as assistant 1st Lieutenant and assistant ship's service officer.

There was anxiety on 24 February when the news reported the shelling of the Richfield Oil Refinery in Santa Barbara, California, by a Japanese submarine.

At dinner the Captain said, "Nothing was damaged but a wooden pump house, but the morale of our people took a hit. It demonstrates clearly that the people of the United States are vulnerable to shelling and bombing."

The talk in the wardroom was the order by the President to relocate all Japanese-Americans from the west coast to inland areas. McWhorter exclaimed, "There are 110,000 of these people who are being uprooted from their homes and friends. They're being put in concentration camps. It ought to be unconstitutional!"

Sanders added, "And what about the statement by Earl Warren, California's Attorney General! He said, 'When we're dealing with the Caucasian race, we have methods that will test loyalty. But when we deal with the Japanese, we are in an entirely different field.' Can you believe any intelligent human being would believe that? He's stupid."[10] Everyone agreed.

I had liberty every third day. Portland, Me., was not New York, but it did have a USO and available girls. When on board, I listened to the radio, played acey-ducey with the Commodore, wrote letters or read "Song of Bernadette" by Franz Werfel and "The Moon is Down" by John Steinbeck. I kept the crew happy with movies: "The Pride of the Yankees" with Gary Cooper and Teresa Wright, "Yankee Doodle Dandy" with James Cagney and Walter Houston and "The Road to Morocco" with Bing Crosby, Bob Hope and Dorothy Lamour.

New men reported aboard and old ones were transferred. The Captain held Mast and awarded various punishments. I continued studying to qualify as a deck officer. My stomach adjusted to the rough seas. The same couldn't be said for Dr. McGinnis. When we were underway, he rarely showed up in the wardroom. He usually could be found huddled on deck outside of the forward engine room. The weather varied from fair to miserable.

On 16 March, the Sterett was underway with the Stack and Wasp enroute to Norfolk, Va. Fog settled in during the night and by 0500 the next morning, visibility had decreased to less than 500 yards. The Wasp could no longer be seen. We dropped back to 1,000 yards and kept station with the sonar gear pinging off her side. At 0603 Hayden, OOD, called the Captain: "We've lost contact with the Wasp, sir."

"When did this happen?"

"Sonar just reported it."

Efforts to regain contact were in vain. The Captain began a retiring search for the Wasp and Stack. It was not until mid-morning when the fog lifted that the Wasp was seen. There was no Stack. The Wasp signaled: "Glad to see you. Had accident last night. The Stack fell across our bow during the poor visibility. Serious damage was inflicted to the forward part of the ship. Several injuries reported. She has retired to Philadelphia Navy Yard for repairs."

The next day the Sterett moored at NOB, Norfolk, Va. I went to the officer's club, had a couple of drinks and shared experiences with fellow officers. Ensign Herbert A. May, D-V(G), USNR, and Ensign Houston I. Shirley, D-V(G), USNR, reported on board. Shirley was slender with sharp facial features. With his glasses, he seemed the scholarly type. He was assigned assistant communication officer, coding, commissary and movies (which I was happy to turn over to him!). Herbie was tall, gangly and brown-haired. He was assigned signal officer, assistant communication and coding. He was a fun-loving guy who always saw the most dismal happening in a positive way. His father was a Congressman from Pennsylvania who had married Mrs. Post-Merriweather, the mother of Dina Merrill and heiress of Kellogg millions.

I asked, "How about getting me a date with your step-sister?"

"I'll do it if we're ever in the Washington area,"[11] he responded.

The headline of the day was the landing of General Douglas MacArthur, his wife, son and key staff members in Australia. President Roosevelt had ordered him to assume command of the new Southwest Pacific Area. PT boats commanded by Lt. Cmdr. Buckley and Lt. R.J. Kelley[12] had carried them south of Luzon where they were picked up and flown out. Before leaving, MacArthur swore to General Wainwright and his troops, "I shall return."

Australia had little to stop the Japanese. Of their 4 field divisions, one had been lost at Singapore and 3 were in the Middle East. Its Navy was scattered all over the world. One US division was due in mid April.

The Japanese were advancing steadily and had landed in New Guinea. The news was bleak. McWhorter cheered us up when he reported, "Aircraft from the Lexington and Yorktown bombed Lae and Salamaua on the 10th. That's going to slow the Japs down for a while. Their aircraft carriers are in the Indian Ocean and they can't advance until they are available. Also our men have occupied New Caledonia and the New Hebrides. That will give some protection to Australia's flank."

I was delighted the following morning when the exec said, "The Captain believes you are qualified to stand OOD watches in port. You'll go on the regular watch list tomorrow. Any questions?"

"None what so ever. I thank you and the Captain."

At 1200 on 20 March, I relieved Hugh Sanders as OOD and stood my first deck watch. The next morning Dr. McGinnis was transferred to the Marine base in New River, North Carolina. As he was leaving, he said, "Life on the ocean is not for me. It hasn't made any difference if the waves were one foot or ten. I haven't been able to eat, sleep or hold sick call. I can serve my country better on terra firma." Dr. A.A. Scharbius, a graduate of Cornell, replaced him. He was a dapper looking fellow, of medium height, black-haired, with a neatly trimmed mustache. At dinner on his first day aboard, Hayden said, "I've heard many stories about Cornell girls. Give us the truth."

"They have one distinguishing characteristic: big muscular legs."

"Why so?"

"The buildings at Cornell sit on the top of hills high above Cayuga's Waters. All day long it's up hill and down dale going from one class to another, which really develops leg muscles."

"If I get a chance, I'll check that out and I'll tell those gals a doctor advised me to do it," Hayden replied.

The next night while I was drinking with a member of the Admiral's staff, he said, "Hitler has decided that Malta must be captured to safeguard his supply lines to North Africa. The air offensive has been intensified. So far this month, the Luftwaffe has flown over 4,000 sorties against Malta. Those people have caught hell. Also this month, a convoy of 4 freighters going to Malta was attacked by an Italian naval group. They damaged one cruiser and sank 3 cargo ships."

"So what's that got to do with us?"

"We're going to have to relieve Malta."

On 24 March Warlick said, "The British Fleet is getting spread thin. The Japanese are planning to establish an air base in the Indian Ocean on Madagascar. This will cut the supply line between the eastern Mediterranean and the Indian Ocean. The British will have to deplete their fleet in Scapa Flow to stop them. Churchill has requested that Roosevelt relieve his forces during April, May and June. Admiral King has agreed. The Sterett will be enroute tomorrow with the first Naval Expeditionary Force to embark for England, Task Force 39, with Rear Admiral John W. Wilcox, Jr., as Commander."

"I heard scuttlebutt about that. I expect tonight will be my last liberty for a long time."

"You better make the most of it," he responded.

Herbie May, Hayden and I picked up our dates, went to a bar and had a few drinks. This was a sign on the wall which was plastered around in all sea coast cities:

A slip of the lip
May sink a ship
Don't blab—the enemy is listening

I took that seriously! Submarine losses in the Atlantic and Arctic areas had gone from 46 ships in January to 120 ships in May. The loss of life was not known.

My head was spinning from too much alcohol when we began eating. I overheard an officer in the adjoining booth saying to his date, "Ours is the first American task force to join up and operate with the British Home Fleet. We're leaving in the morning and I don't know when, if ever, I'll be back."

I jumped up and yelled, "Who the hell are you and what do you mean telling these girls our operation plans? You little bastard! Don't you know you can screw up the entire operation and get us all killed?" I pulled him up by his tie and started to swing. Hayden and Herbie pinned my arms to my side.

"If you don't settle down, you won't be going any where but the brig. It's time to get back to the dock. We'll miss the last launch if we don't hurry," Hayden exclaimed.

Herbie apologized to our dates, bid them goodnight and with him on one side of me and Hayden on the other, they hauled me back to the dock.

I kept mumbling, "I didn't get that officer's name, but I know what ship he's on. I'm going to report him. This whole operation may be in jeopardy."

I continued my ranting and cursing as I climbed aboard the Sterett. The OOD heard me, learned what it was all about and reported it to the Captain.

The next morning, 26 March, the Sterett was underway with Task Force 39 consisting of the new battleship Washington, the Wasp, Tuscaloosa, Wichita, DesRon 8 minus the Stack, plus the destroyers Madison, Ellyson, Plunkette and Liverman. Our course was due east, speed 15 knots.

As soon as we established our cruising disposition, I found myself facing the Captain in his cabin. I was penitent and humiliated. He said, "Now tell me exactly what happened last night and why you were so upset."

I told him as best I could remember. When I finished, he asked a few questions and then said, "This is serious and I'm going to notify the Admiral. You are dismissed." I was disgraced. The message was sent and the reply came quickly: "Have Ensign Harold Jervey report to me as soon as we anchor." For me, the death knoll had been sounded. My navy career was about to end.

The seas were running 10 to 15 feet. The Captain assigned me to the fire control gun platform. It was above the bridge, 60 ft. from the water. I felt like I was doing a high wire act in the circus. When the inclinometer registered 30 degrees, it felt 50. I was sick from the moment I went on watch until I came off. Periodically I would stick my head out of the hatch and vomit. Fortunately, the wind was strong enough to keep the bridge crew from getting showered. I hoped the Admiral would put me ashore for the duration of the war.

On 27 March the wind picked up and the waves became higher. Walking on the decks without support was impossible. It was so rough that the Wasp's flight deck, which was 57 feet above the water line, shipped green water. At 0933 the USS Washington (SOPA) hoisted the signal "man over board". The Wasp launched 4 planes in spite of the foul weather. Clarification came shortly. Admiral Wilcox had told his Marine guard that he was going on deck for his morning constitutional and dismissed him. Shortly thereafter, a huge wave crashed over the fantail and the lookout saw a man being washed overboard. The crew was mustered and all hands were accounted for. When a messenger went to report to the Admiral, he was not in his cabin. The ship was searched and he couldn't be found. It was obvious that he was the man who had gone overboard. 3 of the Wasp's planes landed. One crashed into the sea with no survivors.

In the wardroom I said, "I understand Admiral Wilcox was one of the Navy's most capable leaders. He'll certainly be missed. I feel sorry for his family. However, I'm not going to argue with acts of higher authority."

"Do you think your sins and loose lips will be forgotten?" Hayden asked.

"Yes. Admiral Ike Griffin has more important things to deal with. I hope I've learned my lesson: think before speaking."

At dinner McWhorter said, "The Allies have divided the Pacific into two commands. General Douglas MacArthur has the Southwest Pacific. Admiral Chester Nimitz, the Pacific, which he has split into the North, which he commands, the Central, under Admiral Thomas Kincaid, and the South, under Admiral Robert L. Ghomerly. US troops occupied the Society Islands on 25 March."

On 3 April British Admiral S.S. Bonham-Carter, in the HMS Edinburg with 4 destroyers, joined up with us. He escorted Task Force

39 into Scapa Flow, Orkney Islands. The islands are just north of Scotland and are the anchorage for British Home Fleet. The harbor was full of British ships, and barrage balloons floated overhead to protect against enemy air attack.

I was OOD when Lt. P.J. Wyatt came aboard and said to Captain Coward, "The British Navy is happy to have you aboard and is looking forward to operating with you." He was followed by 10 British seamen. Their mission was to familiarize us with the British communications system and doctrine. They not only read signals, but understood the tactical maneuvers required to execute them. Friendships with our men developed rapidly .

Captain Warlick asked me, "Do you know why Scapa Flow is so important?"

"No, sir."

"It sits astride the Murmansk run and is the shortest route to get American supplies to the Russian armies. It goes over the Arctic circle, around the North Cape of Norway and into the port of Murmansk. We're closer to the Arctic circle than we are to London. The weather is always horrible and the Germans make this one of the most dangerous supply lines in the world. It's not just the subs. They've got airfields close at hand. Major units of their fleet, like the Tirpitz, Hipper, Scheer and Lutzow, hide in the Norwegian Fjords. They've been playing hell with our convoys. Our job is to help the British keep the route open. There should be some action."

"Very interesting," I thought, "but who the hell cares. Why couldn't we sit astride a supply line in warmer weather and calmer seas?"

Clute noted, "There's a bright side to this assignment. Ever since Nelson's time, the British seamen have received a grog of rum daily. You're in for some pleasant surprises."

As I went aboard the destroyer tender HMS Tyne, I was astounded when I saw in the wardroom a well-appointed bar with an experienced attendant. I asked one of the officers, "How do you guys get away with that? Navy regulations forbid any drinking on our ships."

He replied, "Wars have been going on since the beginning of time. If you must do battle, do it with the amenities and creature comforts. Don't you know?"

I didn't know, but I was a quick learner. I found every excuse possible to be on the HMS Tyne when the sun was over the yardarm. I would wander into the wardroom and always an officer would call out, "Won't you join me for a drink, matey?" I never resisted. Only my guardian angel got me home safely.

I was alarmed when I first heard the buzz of a plane overhead. My drinking buddy said, "Don't pay 'im any mind. That's just Sewing

Machine Charlie. He just checks to see what ships are in the anchorage, drops a few bombs and goes home. He's never hit anything. Don't think he means to. Just his way of saying goodnight."

"What a way to fight a war. In our Navy, we'd have gone to general quarters one hour before sundown and stayed there for an hour afterwards, probably would have fired a few shells which might have damaged our own ships. This is a helluva more productive way to spend our time, having a few belts and swapping yarns with gentlemen like you. I'd like to join your outfit for the rest of the war."

"Just remember, mate, when your number comes up on the board, makes no difference if you're home taking a bath, crossing the street or looking down the barrel of a gun. Enjoy the hour and the day. The Lord will provide. Let's drink to that."

The news reported that the Japanese were advancing on Mandalay, had attacked Ceylon and sank 2 cruisers in the Indian Ocean. Along the eastern seaboard, partial convoying known as the "Bucket Brigade" had started on 1 April. The merchant ships stayed underway during the daylight hours and anchored at night. The sinkings were reduced.

At breakfast on 11 April, Tom McWhorter said, "I've got bad news. 75,000 American and Filipino troops on Bataan surrendered. They were malnourished, weak and ravaged by disease. General Wainwright, with the nurses and 15,000 men, are holed up on Corregidor and that won't be for long." We learned the details later. Following the surrender on 9 April, the men were forced to march 65 miles from Mariveles to San Fernando, with little food or water, in the hot sun. Thousands died. This became known as the "Bataan Death March." Of the 12,000 Americans, only 4,000 survived the war.

Our spirits were boosted when Tom came into the wardroom and excitedly said, "We've bombed Tokyo. On 18 April, 16 B-25 bombers under the command of Colonel James Doolittle attacked. The Japanese were taken by surprise. It was a wake-up call for those arrogant bastards."

"What bases did they use?"

"The news said Shangri-La. The consensus is somewhere in China."

There was much discussion and speculation. Weeks later, we learned that the base was the Hornet, sister ship of the Wasp. Only one plane was lost over Japan, but 15 crash landed in China. Most of the crews were rescued, but 6 fell into the hands of the Japanese and were executed.[13] Little damage was done to Tokyo, but it gave the Allies a psychological lift and forced a change in Togo's expansionist plans.

Until 28 April our time was spent conducting various exercises with the British and learning their procedures. From time to time submarines or German ships were reported and we'd search for them to no avail.

Occasionally the dreaded word would be passed that the Tirpitz was on the prowl. Each time, Clute would nervously run his fingers through his hair and say, "I hope we don't find her. We wouldn't have a chance." She was never located and whenever we searched, it was with the entire Home Fleet. The Sterett depth charged many submarines, but could confirm no hits. For everyone, the worst and most frightening experience was doing battle with the North Atlantic, the howling winds, bitter cold and monstrous waves.

To confuse the Germans, the Sterett was called the HMS Steadfast. British procedures gave the gun crews daily practice. A few miles from the harbor entrance, a tug pulling a sled was stationed. Each ship was free to fire on the target on the way out. The tug marked where the shots fell and signaled results.

I was JOOD when we returned to the anchorage, and the signal "scatter" was hoisted. Flank speed was ordered and all of the destroyers raced for the narrow entrance through the antisubmarine nets. The Captain said, "This is one race we're going to let the British win. It calls for good ship handling and a lot of luck. That entrance will accommodate two destroyers and there are frequent collisions. The British treat them as normal operational casualties. If that happened to one of the American skippers, they'd be chewed out and hauled before a review board. The argument that it develops aggressive ship handling wouldn't fly."

Mail caught up with us and the news was shared by everyone. Herbie announced, "A destroyer sank a German submarine just south of Norfolk, Va., and on 18 April, a black-out of lights along the entire eastern seaboard was ordered. The ships were being silhouetted and made excellent targets for the submarines."

"They should have done that at the beginning," Sanders said.

"The reason given for not doing that," Herbie answered, "is they didn't want to ruin the tourist trade. Can you imagine that? Ships were being sunk and men killed just for a few stinking dollars."

Hayden exclaimed, "Just listen to this! The OPA has stopped all car and truck production. Sugar, tire and gas rationing has started. One coupon will entitle a person to buy two gallons of gas a week. For one sugar coupon, you can get one pound of sugar every two weeks. It's going to get worse before it gets better. Maybe being in the Navy is not so bad after all."

"I'll drink to that!" Herbie said. "Let's go ashore."

We went to Lyness, a small town which boasted a couple of pubs. Entertainers came up from London to entertain the servicemen. This night the troupe was performing excerpts from Noel Coward's "Bitter Sweet." The announcer said, "The lead role is being played by the same girl who sang it on opening night in London many years ago." The war was forgotten and I fell in love when she sang:

> "I'll see you again,
> Whenever spring comes through again.
> Time may lie heavy between,
> but what has been is ours forever."

I was transported to paradise: a tropical island, white sandy beaches and warm blue water. I turned to Herbie and said, "No Broadway show has ever moved me like this. I'm going to adopt her song." I did. I needed to believe there was a better world out there and I would see it "whenever spring comes through." I sang it and hummed it on many long, lonely night watches wherever I was. Both home and the girl of the moment became a little closer.[14] On 29 April the Sterett, in company with the Wasp, Lang and HMS Balckmoor, was enroute to Greenock, Scotland, the outer Harbor of Glasgow. The next afternoon the Sterett moored to Pier 4. The Wasp went into Glasgow. On the way down, Captain Warlick told me, "The British are light years ahead of us in antisubmarine warfare. They've got a training school in Glasgow which is unbelievable. It incorporates all of the latest technology. It's so realistic, it's spooky." On 1 May I located it in an old building. Inside I saw the mockup of a destroyer bridge. Climbing aboard and assuming command, I gave orders on speed and course changes just as though I were conning the ship. The sonar man gave me the bearings, course and speed of the submarine. When I thought the ship was in position, I ordered, "Drop depth charges." Afterwards I received a printout which showed me if I'd made a kill or if the submarine's evasive action was successful. It was fantastic. I was ready for any sub.

One-third of the crew and officers went on liberty each day. The Scottish lassies were friendly. On 2 May I received a hand delivered note which said:

"Dear Harold:

Enclosed is the address of an extremely nice girl. At the moment, I'm not sure who the other girl will be as most of my friends seem to be doing something already. Will you please phone Miss Helen Rutherford, who is a Wren driver. The telephone number is Greenock 2280, Extension 45. If you phone sometime after 2:30 today, she should be in.

Sorry I didn't manage to let you know yesterday afternoon. Hope you have a good evening.

Yours Aye,
Margaret"

I phoned and arranged a date with Helen the next day. It was not to be. At 0505 the next morning, the Sterett was underway for Gibraltar with the Wasp, Lang, HMS Echo and HMS Intrepid.

Captain Warlick asked me, "What do you know about Gibraltar?"

"I know it's home to the Barbary Apes and in ancient times, the Pillars of Hercules (Pericles) guarded the straits. From Sunday School, I remember St. Paul was shipwrecked there in 60 AD and converted the people to Christianity."

"I had forgotten that. Today it is of great importance to the British. They took over in 1800 and have remained. The nearest major allied airfield is in Alexandria, Egypt, 1,800 miles to the east. Malta is 1,000 miles from Gibraltar and completely surrounded by axis airfields. It functions as a fueling station for planes being ferried to the Middle East. Also, planes based there have been successfully attacking axis convoys carrying troops and supplies to Africa. Hitler is determined to capture the island[15] or keep it neutralized. The Luftwaffe has been bombing it daily since June, 1940. The attacks were stepped up in January. During April, 6,728 tons of bombs were dropped. With the constant bombing and loss of fighter aircraft, it is rapidly losing its usefulness. Aircraft carriers are the only way they can replenish their supply of planes. The Wasp took on board 47 spitfires in Glasgow. She made this trip in mid-April, but the fighters she supplied have already been destroyed."

"Sounds like we're in for some excitement, but I'd rather be one of those pilots."

At breakfast on 5 May, the talk was of the last message received from Corregidor in plain English and heard by the world: "The jig is up...They are piling the dead and wounded in our tunnel. Arms weak...long hours...short rations...tell my mother how you heard from me. Signed: Irving Strobing, radio operator."

Hayden exclaimed, "What a horrible ending. I can't believe General Wainwright with the nurses and 7,000 troops had to surrender."

Daily the Wasp conducted flight operations and Sterett made submarine contacts. Depth charges were dropped with undetermined results. On 6 May the Sterett was relieved of screening duty and the next afternoon made a fueling stop at Gibraltar. The Captain summoned me to his cabin, "Mr. Jervey, the British Admiralty in Glasgow gave me a dispatch to have hand-delivered to the Commanding General at Gibraltar. I want you to do the job. His car will carry you to the headquarters. It goes to the General or one of his aides." After he handed me the dispatch, I went to the quarter-deck and saw a car, with flags flying, on the dock. After the British officer and I exchanged pleasantries, we rode down several narrow, winding streets and stopped in front of an unimposing building. Inside, I was greeted by an aide to the General. After I handed him the envelope, I returned to the Sterett.

The Sterett got underway and I could soon see the lights of Morocco to the south. At 0220 on 7 May, the Sterett joined the HMS Renown and the HMS Eagle, an aircraft carrier, and the accompanying destroyers. Later the Wasp and 4 destroyers joined the formation and headed east, speed 15 knots.

On 9 May at 0630, the Wasp began launching her 47 spitfires, which took 53 minutes. The Eagle contributed 17. One plane dropped its belly tank. The pilot was granted permission to return and pick up a new one. Upon hearing this, the Captain exclaimed, "A land-based plane has never landed on a carrier. It has no landing hook and it's going to be extremely difficult." After landing successfully only 10 feet from the forward edge of the flight deck, the pilot was given a round of applause by everyone watching. Unfortunately, the Admiral decided the other planes were too far away for the pilot to catch and he remained on board and returned to Scapa Flow, which extended his life by a few months/years.

With mission accomplished, the Task Force headed home. In the wardroom the next morning, McWhorter excitedly reported the news, "The Germans were caught flat-footed this morning when their planes made their routine bombing runs over Malta. Those RAF boys surprised them and knocked down 50-60. Ain't that great?"

Calhoun added, "That's going to be an enormous boost for British morale.[16] The bad news is that General William Sharp, Commanding General of the Central Philippines, has ordered all allied forces to surrender. They held out twice as long as expected and delayed the Japanese advance to the south. More importantly, because of our help, the British were able to land on Madagascar and prevent the Japs from using it as an air base."

"What's happening in North Africa?" Marver asked.

"Rommel is slowly advancing on Tobruk. Churchill has been after Auchinlick to counter attack, but he says he can't until he has more equipment. That won't be before 1 June," Tom replied.

The Sterett and Lang were relieved of screening duties, and at 0036, 11 May, moored to a dock at Gibraltar. After fueling, one long blast was sounded on the whistle as the Sterett backed out from the pier. It stuck in the open position, sounding like a banshee, and woke everyone on the "rock". The excitement made us almost collide with a 4-engine flying boat taxiing across our path. The Captain didn't see an unlighted barge moored at the harbor entrance. The starboard propeller guard made contact with a mooring chain and wrapped it around the shaft. The vibrations felt like a model T running over a cobblestone street. The chain broke and the Sterett passed clear. To insure that there was no damage, she returned to the pier and a diver went over the side to make an assessment. He removed the chain and reported no apparent harm to the hull.

As we passed Cape Trafalgar at 1317, everyone not on watch was in the wardroom talking about the furious naval battle in the Coral Sea. Captain Warlick said, "The Japs have been moving southward and we've established bases in New Caledonia, the New Hebrides and the Society Islands. The Japs have landed on Manus Island and most recently at Tulagi in the Solomon's."

McWhorter interrupted, "Remember those dispatches I showed you? The Japanese had an invasion force heading south. It looked as though they were planning to capture Port Moresby."

" Yes," Warlick responded. "There must have been one helluva battle in the Coral Sea."

Admiral Fletcher, with the carriers Yorktown and Lexington and supporting ships, had been ordered to intercept Port Moresby's invasion force, which was under the command of Admiral Inouye. A two-day battle resulted, in which neither side saw the other. Fletcher's planes sunk the carrier Soho, damaged the Shokohu and sank 3 minesweepers. Of greater importance was the large number of experienced pilots killed.

The carrier Lexington and 2 other ships were lost and the Yorktown badly damaged. The headline in the New York times read "Japanese repulsed in Great Pacific Battle with 17-22 of their ships sunk or crippled."

The Japanese press claimed the sinking of mystical battleships and 2 large carriers. It was a tactical victory for the Japanese and a strategic victory for the USA. Following so closely on the heels of the surrender of Corregidor, it boosted the morale of all allied nations.

The voyage to Scapa Flow was uneventful, and on 15 May the Sterett moored to a buoy in the harbor. The British seamen returned to their ships the next day while I was OOD. Herbie said, "Having those limeys on board is going to change the outlook of our men."

"For better or worse?"

Marver chimed in, "You going to start giving them a portion of rum each day?"

"I'm not talking about that. From the limeys, they've learned more ways to entertain themselves, be more upbeat and realize war is a part of life, so make the best of it. Just live each day to the fullest."

After Captain D.P. Moon inspected us on 17 May, the Sterett was underway for Greenock, Scotland, in company with the Wasp, Wainwright and Lang. After a brief fueling stop, Task Force 38 was underway for Norfolk ,Va.

The voyage home was uneventful. On 27 May the Sterett was moored to a pier at the Portsmouth, Va., Navy Yard. Men were transferred and others reported aboard. Captain Warlick received orders to assume command of Destroyer Squadron 7 on 29 May. I was sorry to see him leave.

The Sterett moved into dry-dock for repairs and installation of the newest gadget, "SC Radar", which the Captain said would permit us to see in the dark.

The news from England was improving. Air Marshall Arthur Harris had issued orders for 1,000 plane raids named "Millennium." They devastated Cologne, Hamburg and Essen.

Hitler went on the offensive with the spring thaw. Turning away from Moscow, his armies began advancing on the rich industrial area of the Ukraine and the oil fields of the Caucasians. The Soviets became upset when the second front was tentatively set for the summer of 1943. An Anglo-Soviet Treaty was signed in which each country pledged to fight until final victory and not make a separate peace.

Our concern was where were we going and when. I listened to Peggy Lee with Benny Goodwin singing "Why Don't You Do Right", Helen Forrest singing "I Had the Craziest Dream last Night", the Mills Brothers in "Paper Doll", and Glenn Miller playing "I've got a Gal in Kalamazoo" and "Chattanooga Choo Choo". The latter sold over one million copies and became the first "gold record", after RCA sprayed gold on one.

I was happy to see Ensign Crawford Clarkson, a classmate from college. He was on a 4-stacker moored close by. Liberty was more pleasant for each of us. We rented a car on 4 June and double dated. We didn't get back to the dock until after midnight.

Crawford said, "We haven't got time to return this car. What do you suggest?"

"There's only one answer. You're sailing in the morning and so am I. Scuttlebutt has it we're heading for the Pacific. Let's just park this car on the dock and put a note on the seat asking the finder to contact the rental company."

We bade farewell to the car and each other.

CHAPTER 3

The Landings on Guadalcanal
The First Battle of Savo Island

On 5 June, the Sterett was enroute to the Panama Canal Zone with Task Force 37, consisting of the North Carolina, Wasp, San Juan and screening destroyers. Our talk centered on what the Pacific would be like.

"Anything will be better than the North Atlantic. I'd rather get eaten by a shark than freeze to death," I said.

At dinner McWhorter announced, "Delos Emmons, Governor of Hawaii, is a guy with guts. He refused to deport Americans of Japanese descent. As a result, over 10,000 of them have volunteered for combat duty. It's a shame Earl Warren didn't take the same position."

On 5 June McWhorter excitedly reported at breakfast, "There was one helluva battle yesterday at Midway. It'll take awhile to decode the messages and get the full story." Gradually the pieces came together. On 4 June at 0500, Admiral Nagumo launched his planes and attacked Midway. Six months earlier, he had stood on the deck of the same carrier when his planes attacked Pearl Harbor. He said, "Once again we will mow the Americans down."

The garrison on Midway had been alerted. Many Japanese planes were shot down and the base suffered little damage. At 0910 Nagumo ordered a second attack. While his planes were refueling and rearming on the flight deck, the Hornet's torpedo planes attacked. All were shot down, including Ensign George Gay. He survived, watched the battle from under a life raft and was later rescued. Most of our next strike force's planes were downed with no damage to the Japanese ships.

At 1025 dive bombers from the Enterprise attacked the carriers Agaki and Kaga. The bombs exploded fuel tanks, bombs and torpedoes. Blazing fires engulfed the ships and the Kaga sank. Dive bombers from the Yorktown attacked the Soryu engulfing her in flames. She was abandoned. The submarine Nautilus was watching and fired a spread of 3 torpedoes. All hit and the Soryu sank at 1920.

Planes from the Hiryu attacked the Yorktown at noon and again at 1430. The damage was so extensive that Fletcher abandoned ship. At 1500 bombers from the Enterprise attacked the Hiryu leaving her in flames and sinking.

To the north, the Japanese attacked Dutch Harbor. They damaged one US Destroyer and many fuel tanks on the island. Yamamoto and Spruance spent the next morning looking for each other. The Akagi was blazing and Yamamoto ordered her sunk. With half of his carriers destroyed, he began retiring. While leaving the area, his cruisers, the Mogami and Mikuma, collided and were left behind. Dive bombers from the Hornet sank the Mogami, and the Mikuma limped into Truk.

On 6 June the Japanese submarine 1-168 fired a spread of 4 torpedoes at the Yorktown. 2 hit the carrier and one hit the destroyer Hammann midship. She sank in a few minutes and the Yorktown quickly followed.

On 7 June, landings were made in the Aleutians on Attu and Kiska.

After decoding all of the dispatches, McWhorter announced, "We had a major victory at Midway. The Japanese lost 4 large carriers, a heavy cruiser, over 300 planes and 5,000 men. We lost one carrier, one destroyer, 150 planes and 300 men.

Captain Coward added, "This is going to be a turning point in the war. Twice within one month the Japanese have been turned back. They can't risk a major fleet action and will have to go on the defensive. Admiral Raymond Spruance has proven himself to be one of our greatest fighting and thinking Admirals."

Frank Gould said, "From what I've heard, Midway was a victory for the intelligence boys. If Nimitz hadn't been forewarned, the ending may have been different."

Before arriving at Panama, the exec spread out a chart on the wardroom table and said, "I want to show you guys what few people realize. Because the canal is so looped, the Pacific entrance is 23 miles farther east than the Atlantic. This is the only place on earth where the sun rises in the West and sets in the East."

At dawn 9 June, I saw the long breakwater jutting out from Toro Point at the Panama Canal Zone. Pilot M. Wallace came aboard, took the conn and at 1030, the Sterett entered the Gatun Locks. Steel cables were thrown on board and secured. The other ends were attached to 4 electric locomotives called "mules". I watched as the 7-foot thick doors closed after we entered the lock. Water was pumped in and the ship slowly rose to the level of the second lock. When the doors opened at 1257, the lines were cast off and the Sterett proceeded across Gatun Lake.

I watched the cattle grazing on the shores, the palm trees and the many floating islands with heavy tropical vegetation. On the bridge I listened to the Pilot: "This lake is 150 square miles in size. About half way across we'll enter Culebra Cut, now known as Gaillard Cut, in honor of

Colonel Gaillard, the engineer in charge from 1907-1913. We'll enter the Pacific slope of the isthmus after leaving the Cut." I was fascinated with his stories. The Sterett passed through the other locks and at 1830 was moored to a pier in Balboa Harbor.

During supper Warlick said, "It took us 8 hours to get from the Atlantic to the Pacific Ocean. Prior to 1914 it would have been a 13,000 mile voyage around stormy Cape Horn and taken 30 days. We'd be in real trouble today fighting a two-ocean war with a one-ocean Navy."

Frank Gould came in and exclaimed, "I've got good and bad news. The bad is that the overhang of the Wasp's flight deck was damaged when it hit stanchions on the dock and we'll stay here until repairs are completed. The good news is you'll have a chance to see Panama City."

It was a wide open sailor's town. As a duty free port, liquor was cheap, so I bought 6 bottles of Black and White scotch. Herbie May, P.G. Hayden and I were introduced to the ubiquitous "B" girls at the bars. They were everywhere! Sexy, pretty ladies who would make us happy "if you buy me a drink." They got colored water and we got sloshed! The high-class cabarets had floor shows, but time ran out.

On 10 June the Sterett was standing out of the Harbor with Task Force 37 enroute to San Diego. The weather was balmy and the seas calm throughout the voyage. On 19 June Santa Catalina Island was sighted, and at 1552 the Sterett was moored to a pier in San Diego Harbor. I was sorry to see Hayden leave to report to BuPers for further assignment.

Cal said, "This is our last stop before heading west. Have fun and drink up. Get some reading material. There aren't any libraries where we're going."

Admiral King had concluded that the Japs must be stopped in their march south. He convinced Churchill that Guadalcanal was the toll gate on the main road from Tokyo. If it wasn't protected, the Japs would sail through to Australia.

Admiral Robert L. Ghomerly moved his headquarters to Noumea, New Caledonia. After learning that the Japanese had captured Tulagi on 3 May, a base was built on Espiritu Santo.

On 18 June Winston Churchill met with President Roosevelt in New York. After heated discussions, they agreed to land troops in Morocco, Algeria and Tunisia behind Rommel's Africa Corps. The Allies could then move into Italy and strike the soft underbelly of Europe. Roosevelt announced that General Dwight Eisenhower would be in command of European operations.

In Russia the Germans were attacking Sevastopol. Rommel was advancing in North Africa and on 21 June, captured Tobruk.

Dr. Alfred P. Scharbies was transferred to the Naval Air Station in Pensacola, Fla., and was replaced by Lt.(jg) Harry C. Nyce, a surgical resident. I kept in touch with my family and girl through phone calls and letters. On 1 July the Sterett was underway. Congratulations were given to Frank Gould on his promotion to Lt. Cmdr., Calhoun and Sanders to Lieutenants and Tom McWhorter to Lt.(jg).

It was with mixed emotions that I watched the skyline of San Diego disappear over the horizon. Task Force 18 consisted of the Wasp, Quincy, San Juan, DesRon 12 and the troop transports Crescent City (SOPA), Ahlena, President Hayes, President Jackson and President Adams. Our course was due west, speed 15 knots, destination point x-ray.

On 2 July Operation "Watchtower", dubbed Operation "Shoe String" due to its limited resources, was put in motion. The landing force was the 1st Marine Division under the command of General Alexander A. Vandergrift. It consisted of 19,000 men who were scattered from New Zealand to San Diego. When reconnaissance planes reported that the Japanese would have an operational airfield on Guadalcanal by 1 August, Admiral King ordered the landings set for 1 August.

The weather was ideal. Sound contacts were investigated, no confirmed hits. In the wardroom we talked about possible objectives and when we'd meet the Japs. The Captain held mast and awarded various punishments. I was JOOD with Tom McWhorter on 13 July when the San Juan signaled "man overboard". His body was not recovered.

I had heard horror stories of the initiation of polliwogs into the lofty order of shellbacks. As we neared the equator, there was much whispering and many snide remarks: "Boy, I can't wait! You'll be sorry you ever came aboard this ship," and "You better eat good. You won't feel like eating for a long time."

"Don't you guys know there is a war going on?" I responded.

"This is a helluva lot more important than a war," was the reply.

On 15 July I was handed a piece of folded paper. The outside read:

SUBPOENA AND SUMMONS
EXTRAORDINARY
THE TRUSTY SHELLBACKS vs CHILDE HAROLD JERVEY, Ens., USNR
ROYAL HIGH COURT OF THE RAGING MAIN, County of Sterett, Vale of Pacificus, Domain of Neptunus Rex
ACTION ON CASE check Ordinary Serious X To be confined awaiting action Short rations awaiting action Double irons awaiting X action Coffin awaiting disposition.

The inside was just as intimidating. It read:

GREETINGS AND BEWARE

WHEREAS, the good ship Sterett, bound southward crossing the Equator, is about to enter our domain; and

WHEREAS, the aforesaid carries a large and slimy cargo of land lubbers, swabs, hay-tossers, beachcombers, cargo rats, sea lawyers, lounge lizards, parlor dunnigans, plow deserters, park bench warmers, chicken chasers, chit signers, soda inhalers, dance hall engineers, four flushers, sand crabs, and all other living creature of the lands, and last but not least, he-vamps and liberty hounds falsely masquerading as seamen, of which LOW SCUM you are a member, having never appeared before us; and

WHEREAS, THE ROYAL HIGH COURT of the Raging Main has been convened by us on board the good ship Sterett in 1942 at latitude 00-00-00 degrees———————————it is high time the said and wandering nautical soul of that much abused body of yours appear before the HIGH TRIBUNAL OF NEPTUNE, and BE IT KNOWN that we hereby summon and command you to appear before this ROYAL HIGH COURT——and to accept most heartily and with good grace the pains and penalties of the awful torture that will be inflicted upon you; and to be examined as to fitness to become one of our TRUSTY SHELLBACKS ———IF NOT, YOU SHALL BE GIVEN AS FOOD TO THE SHARKS, WHALES, FROGS, AND ALL LIVING THINGS of the sea, as warning to any landlubbers entering my domain without warrant.

THEREFORE appear and answer to the following charges:

CHARGE I. In that H.E. Jervey, alias Childe Harold, now an Ensign, USNR, has hereto willfully and maliciously failed to show reverence and allegiance to our ROYAL PERSON, and is therein and thereby a vile landlubber and polliwog.

CHARGE II. Known as Jack the Ripper, he has proven to be a wolf in sheep's clothing, taking unfair advantage of his South Carolina accent. He has played on the sympathies of young females and betrayed them. He is also believed to be using all of his crooked political influence to have the ship sent back to Charleston, where it is rumored he contemplates further conquests.

CHARGE III. Couldn't get near enough with his bucket of water to wash off the egg which sacked a trusty shellback. NOTE: He also threw the egg.

Disobey this summons under the pain of OUR SWIFT AND TER-
RIBLE DISPLEASURE. Our vigilance is ever-wakeful—OUR VEN-
GEANCE JUST AND SURE.

Given under our hand and seal.
Attest for the King:
Davy Jones, Scribe Neptunus Rex

The court and its trusty shellbacks were dressed in outlandish cos-
tumes: mops for hair pieces, eye patches, robes of various hues and
styles. They were a motley group of brigands. They used all of their
imagination for the torture I received: eggs were broken in my hair and
on my face; the concoctions rubbed on my body were vile smelling and
didn't easily wash off. The last insult to my dignity was crawling on all
fours down a double line of shellbacks carrying wet towels and belts
with which I was beat until my butt was blistered, at the conclusion of
which I was declared a worthy shellback.

As the Sterett was passing through the 180th Meridian, I received an
impressive document attesting to the fact that we had lost one day of
our being, in the CELESTIAL Realm of the Golden Dragon. It stated:
"A Royal Welcome is granted to your crew and the Army who are joining their Down Under Comrades-in-Arms in driving the Nipponese
from the jungles of Java, the Roads to Mandalay, Burma, and Baquio.
Roll your tanks through Singapore's Raffles Square and the Bund of
Shanghai; climb the Peak of Hong Kong and march into Tokyo to plant
the Stars and Stripes and, returning victorious, fight your battles once
again across the tables of Tom's Dixie Kitchen or dance at the Santa
Ana and Manila Hotels."

The Tonga Islands were sighted on 18 July and at 1645, the Sterett
was anchored in Nuku'alofa Harbor, Tongatabu. Herbie exclaimed,
"After 18 days at sea, any land would look good, but this is paradise. We
must be the first large group of Navy ships the Tonganese have ever
seen. Look at the greeting. We're surrounded by bumboats."

Sanders said, "Those canoes are hewn out of logs by hand and
they're loaded to the gunwales with bananas, mangoes, papayas and
fruits I can't identify. And look at the beautiful shells and necklaces."

I asked a petty officer, "What are all of our men doing on the fantail?"

"The natives want to swap their goods for clothes, any kind. We've
been having one helluva time keeping our guys from stripping down to
their skivvies and giving everything away. I've had to threaten to put
them on report," he replied.

Before the day was, out the Sterett looked like a Greek fruit stand. Stalks of bananas hung everywhere, including my stateroom.

I saw Frank Gould looking at a chart on the bridge. "Let me show you where the day begins. The 180 degree meridian of longitude bends around these islands. We're in time zone 12."

"Why doesn't the meridian run straight down?" I asked.

"It was a political decision. It would have been awkward for dawn to be the beginning of one day for part of the Tonga group and the end of the previous day for other islands."

Tonga was Polynesia's oldest and last remaining monarchy and the only Pacific nation never brought under foreign rule. Captain Cook visited in 1773. The natives were so outgoing he named them "Friendly Isles". It was of volcanic origin. Legend proclaimed that the god Maui yanked the island from the sea with a fish hook acquired from the Samoans. In truth, the original Tongans came from Fiji over 3,000 years ago. Queen Salute Toupee III, whose grandfather, King George Toupee I, had unified the islands, was the constitutional ruler.[17] The crown owned all of the land, which was the source of its power. At age 18, each male Tongan was entitled to 1½ acres of land.

On liberty I took in the sights. Everyone was warm, friendly and spoke understandable pidgin English. Their dress was the ta'ovala, a skirt made of a finely woven pandas. Some went barefoot. Others wore sandals. They were a handsome people. The bars were palm-covered and open-aired. Rum was the drink and music filled the air. Men with ukuleles played alone or in groups. The females danced slowly and gracefully with elaborate hand and arm gestures. The men's movements were more vigorous with stomping and swirling.

I swam in the warm waters of the lagoon and met a roly poly youngster on the beach who, I discovered, was the youngest son of the Queen. He acted like any ordinary boy of his age.[18] In the wardroom as we compared notes, McWhorter said, "Everywhere I went, kids no older than 7 or 8 had outstretched hands assuring me that for 'one dahlah' I would receive a most beautiful girl and the best lay on the island," Harry Nyce responded, "You better be careful. Venereal disease is rampant. So far none of the crew has shown up at sick call with VD. I guess they aren't willing to risk an hour of pleasure for my needle and maybe months of misery."

While we were enjoying Tonga, General MacArthur was trying to build an airfield on Papua to capture Rabual and support the operations in the Solomon's. He landed two Australian Infantry and one Papuan battalion at Port Moresby in June. He expected them to cross the Owen Stanley Mountains via the Kokoda trail. During the first two weeks in

July, they moved up the trail and on 15 July reached the village of Kokoda. On 21 July the Japanese landed troops at Gona, who arrived at Kokoda on 23 July and forced MacArthur's men to withdraw.

Our golden days ended with the Sterett getting underway with Task Force 18. Three days later the "Watchtower" Expeditionary Force was sighted with ships reaching to the horizon.

"Where are we?" I asked the quartermaster.

Pointing to the chart, he said, "400 miles southeast of the Fiji Islands."

Admiral Fletcher conferred with Admirals R. Kelly Turner, Thomas Kincaid, Leigh Noyes, McCain and Major General Vandergrift to finalize plans for the operation. Admiral Turner had been told on 30 June, while he was in San Francisco, that he'd be in charge of the Amphibious Force. Flying to Pearl Harbor, he drafted plans and on 18 July flew to Wellington, New Zealand, to assume command of the first amphibious landing of World War II.

Admirals King and Nimitz had scraped together 3 carrier groups: the Saratoga under Fletcher with 2 Cruisers and 5 destroyers; the Enterprise under Admiral Kincaid with the new battleship North Carolina, 2 cruisers and 5 destroyers; and the Wasp under Admiral Noyes with the cruisers San Francisco and Salt Lake City plus DesRon 12 under Captain Robert Tobin, consisting of Lang, Sterett, Stack, Laffey, Farenholt and Aaron Ward.

Amphibious Group TF 62, under Kelly Turner in the McCawley, was escorted by 4 cruisers and 9 destroyers. The 18 transports carried Major General Alexander Vandergrift with 959 officers and 18,146 enlisted men. In addition, 4 converted destroyers, the Calhoun, Little, McKean and Gregory, carried Lt. Col. Merritt Edson's 1st Raider Battalion.

McWhorter, OOD, remarked, "Admiral Fletcher is a smart cookie, but he lost a carrier at Midway and in the Coral Sea. I wonder if that is going to affect his judgment?"

"It would mine," I replied.

"This whole setup is screwy. Admiral Ghomerly has overall command and he's sitting down in Noumea. He's never going to see this fleet. How the hell can he issue orders?"

"Sounds pretty awkward and inefficient to me."

The next morning Tom said, "The news from home is depressing. FDR announced that 395 ships have been sunk off the Atlantic Coast since the beginning of the year. 5,000 men have been lost. Churchill concluded that we're losing ships faster than we can build them."

"Is that it? Nothing else?" Cal asked.

"This may interest the single men. The President signed a bill setting up a female naval group called 'Waves', which stands for Women Appointed for Various Emergency Services. There will be 1,000 officers and 10,000 enlisted personnel."

Herbie gleefully rubbed his hands and said, "I've got several emergency services they can perform on me right now. One will do, but I'd prefer several."

"Sorry about that. They're going to stay stateside for the duration. The WAAC's (Women's Army Auxiliary Corps) was established in May and I still don't know what they're doing."

At dinner on 29 July, the Captain said, "I just received operation plan 'Watchtower'. It's lengthy and complicated. I expect each of you watch officers to study and commit the pertinent parts to memory. You've got little time. D-Day is 7 August." After receiving it, I exclaimed to McWhorter, "How the hell does the Captain expect me to memorize this thing? What with standing watch, General Quarters, drills and my studying the deck officer manuals, I've got no time. I'm going to recommend that a hypnotist be put on board each ship in the next war. He can do his thing, read to us while we sleep and presto, we'll know it perfectly."

Fortunately the plan was padded with background information. Don Alvaro Mendana, a Spaniard, discovered the Solomon Islands in 1568 while looking for the lost continent of Terra Australia and King Solomon's Ophir. Guadalcanal was named after Ortega's hometown in Valencia. There was little gold. Nobody wanted the islands. Britain finally annexed them. They were wet, hot and steamy. They were 6,000 miles southwest of San Francisco in two parallel columns like a strand of pearls, running southeasterly some 600 miles from Rabual. On the north side of the column were Choiseul, Santa Isabel and Malaita; on the south side were Villa Lavella, New Georgia and Guadalcanal. Both lines merged on San Cristobal. Sealark Channel to the north and Lengo Channel to the south led from Indispensable Strait directly into what came to be known as "Ironbottom" Sound.[19] It was 20 miles wide and shaped like a ship. At the bow was Savo Island. On the right side was Tulagi; close by was Florida Island. On the left, and the point of our attack, was Guadalcanal. It was 90 miles long and 25 miles wide with an 8,000 foot range of mountains on the southern side. The tropical rain forest was filled with thousands of malaria- carrying mosquitoes which would inflict more casualties on the Marines than Japanese shells. In 1942 Tulagi was the capital of the Solomon's. It was a one-street town with Chinese shops, a small hotel, a wireless station and a few bungalows which British officials used. The waters were uncharted and infested with sharks.

Farewell party in San Duyer before heading out for first D-Day bombing on Guadal Canal, 7 August 1942.

On 4 August the Farenholt came alongside to pass mail. There were shouts of joy when the PA boomed: "Now hear this! Mail call for the crew in the mess hall; for the officers, in the wardroom." I shared information: "College girls are wearing slacks, jeans and long skirts. It's no use to dress up when there are no men on the campus. Zippers and metal fastenings are taboo so skirts are wrap around."

"That ought to make them more accessible," Herbie exclaimed, "especially since there are no silk stockings and they're having to use eyebrow pencil to draw lines on their legs to give the illusion of stockings."

"Ginny tells me they're having periodic blackout drills, and pennies are now zinc coated to save copper. More interesting is the decree that no one can have a salary over $25,000. I fail to understand how that will contribute to the war effort, or how it will be enforced." Cal said.

"How does this grab you? I've got an ad for Big Ben clocks which says 'Victory won't wait for the nation that's late'. My girl says if I have any spare time I might listen to Bob Hope, Jack Benny and the Chase and Sanborn Hour," Herbie added.

"I wonder if they are trying to cheer us up, or if they just think we're bored?" Sanders asked.

The news reported that the RAF had destroyed a large convoy departing from Naples with supplies for Rommel. He believed there was a spy in Naples and was furious.[20]

All talking stopped when the PA boomed: "This is the Captain speaking. All ships have received this message from Admiral Kelly Turner: 'On August 7th, this force will recapture Tulagi and Guadalcanal which are now in the hands of the enemy. In this first forward step toward clearing the Japanese out of conquered territory, we have support from the Pacific Fleet and from air, surface and submarine forces in the South Pacific and Australia....I have confidence that all elements of this armada will, in skill and courage, show themselves fit comrades of those brave men who have already dealt the enemy mighty blows for our great cause. God bless you all.' "

I kidded Shirley, "You won't have to worry about what movie to show for awhile. You're probably starting to repeat them anyway."

"You're right. I haven't been able to get any new ones. I thought I'd have the crew vote on which ones to repeat."

At 0527 on August 7, the Wasp commenced launching planes to cover the 11,000 Marines in landing crafts headed for the beach. Little opposition was encountered. A weather front covered our approach and surprise was complete. Only Japanese working brigades were present, no combat troops.

Task Force 61 remained south of the island. The planes of the Wasp landed and took off in a steady stream. The bridge radio was jammed with pilots talking about bombing this area and that. Numerous false submarine contacts were made. We were at GQ most of the day. In the after engine room, I knew little of what was happening. The Japanese attacked with 2 waves of bombers. Kelly was forewarned by a coastwatcher on Bougainville, and the carrier aircraft beat them off. No transports were hit, but the destroyers Mugford and Jarvis were damaged. By 1600 the next afternoon, the Marines had captured the partially completed airfield and about 1,000 Japanese. All others retreated into the jungle. Combat experienced troops guarded Tulagi and the fighting was fierce. It wasn't secured until midnight 8 August.

All ships received a dispatch from Admiral Ghomerly declaring, "Results so far achieved make every officer and man in the South Pacific area proud of your achievement." Admiral Mikawa, Commander of the Japanese Eighth Fleet headquartered in Rabual, didn't agree. When he received the last message from his Tulagi garrison ("We pray for enduring fortunes of war, promising resistance to the last man."), he stormed down the slot on the Chokaiand with 6 other cruisers and one destroyer. His plan was to torpedo those ships anchored off Guadalcanal, attack those on the Tulagi side and retire to the north.

On 8 August his force was sighted and his course and speed were reported. All were misdirected and incompetently interpreted. Admiral Turner did not suspect a night attack. The last sighting was made by a plane only 350 miles away. The message went to Canberra and then to Pearl Harbor. It was put on the skeds. This took 8 hours to reach Turner. If radio silence had been broken,[21] Admiral Mikawa could not have made his approach undetected.

To delight the Japanese even more, I decoded the dispatch from Admiral Fletcher to Admiral Ghomerly: "Fighter plane strength reduced from 99 to 78. In view of large number of enemy bombers and torpedo planes in this area, I recommend the immediate withdrawal of my carriers. Request tankers be sent forward as fuel running low."

"That's a lie," I mumbled. We were not that low on fuel. The truth was, Fletcher, having lost the Lexington at Battle of the Coral Sea and the Yorktown at Midway, was not going to take any chances with his carriers. Our Task Force headed south.

Admiral Turner continued unloading the transports and freighters throughout the night. For protection, the sound was divided into 3 sectors. The Eastern approach through Sealark Channel was guarded by Admiral Norman Scott with the San Juan, HMAS Hobart and 2 destroyers, Monssen and Buchanan. The Southern Force, patrolling between Cape Esperance at the northern end of Guadalcanal and Savo Island, was under the command of Admiral Crutchley with the cruisers Australia and Chicago and the destroyers Patterson and Bagley. The Northern Force, patrolling the entrance between Savo and Florida Island, was under the command of Captain Frederick Riefkohl in the Vincennes, together with the HMS Astoria, HMS Canberra and the Quincy with the destroyers Helm and Wilson. For early warning purposes, the destroyers Blue and Ralph Talbert, with SC radar, were stationed to the west. Turner did not believe Mikawa could approach undetected.

Mikawa arrived off Savo Island the night of 8 August. Our men, seeing flares dropping from his scout planes to identify our ships, reported them as friendlies. For almost two hours his planes sent information on our ship movements to the Admiral. At 0045 the Japanese were at their battle stations. The Patterson sounded the alarm at 0143 when they were separated by only 5,000 yds: "Warning: strange ships entering harbor."

The Japanese opened fire with deadly accuracy. The Canberra was put out of commission in 5 minutes. The Chicago got off a few shells, but the Japanese hit her with gunfire and torpedoes. Her bow was blown off. Neither the Bagley nor the Patterson got into the fight.

The Vincennes group was following in line. Their Commanding Officers were in their bunks asleep. Each arrived on the bridge with droopy eyes asking, "Who are we shooting at?"

It was a wild melee and the skippers never knew what hit them. In minutes, the Astoria was a blazing shambles and went to the bottom. The Quincy and Vincennes quickly followed her. In 32 minutes Mikawa's forces sank 4 heavy cruisers, disabled a fifth and sank one destroyer. His ships received only minor damage with only 35 men killed and 57 wounded. With 1,270 of our men killed and 709 wounded, it was one of the worst defeats ever suffered by the US Navy.

With the transports unprotected, Mikawa could have destroyed them all. Fortunately, he believed our carriers were close at hand and that by daylight, his ships would be under attack. With no more torpedoes, at 0240 he ordered them to bend on full speed for Rabual.

Seeing the dispatches reporting on the Battle of Savo Island, I moaned, "I can't believe it. I spent a month on the Quincy. I know many of the men. How could it happen? They were well trained and now they're dead. It isn't possible."

Sanders replied, "War gets personal. Our superior mindset was just so much ignorant propaganda. The Japs aren't stupid barbarians. They're damn capable fighters."

"You're right and it's going to be one long war. Many of us are not going to be around to go home," I replied.

At breakfast, the Captain observed, "We can't stand to lose any more ships. We were already out-manned and out-gunned in the beginning."

Admiral Ghomerly must have agreed. The dispatches to his Commanders clearly indicated a holding action, and our Task Force stayed well south of the Islands. The Sterett did plane guard duty while the Wasp pilots pounded the Japanese daily.

At dinner Tom exclaimed, "The war is getting close to our folks at home. Germans loaded with explosives were sent ashore on Long Island and Florida beaches. They were going to blow up Army installations. They were captured and yesterday 6 of them were executed."

Daily drills and flight operations were conducted. On 13 August a plane crashed and Ensign Cleland and his 2 crewmen were rescued. They had multiple lacerations. R.A. Wolverton, AMN 3/c, dove off the Wasp to assist the men and was recommended for a gold life-saving medal.

While life was boring for us, the 16,000 men on the island were suffering. McWhorter reported, "From what I read in the dispatches, those guys on the island are catching hell. Turner pulled out his transports on 9 August when they were only half unloaded. The Marines are on two meals a day, much of it the rice left behind by the Japanese. They're being bombed all day long and Yamamoto sends his ships to shell them unmercifully at night. They're getting no sleep."

To the Marines' good fortune, General Hayakutaka at Rabual had estimated there were only 3,000 on the island. As a result, he repeatedly sent in the "Tokyo Express", with only 1,500 men on the destroyers to augment his troops. Captain Coward commented, "As fast as the Seabees repair Henderson Field, the Japs tear it up again. We've got no ships to prevent the Tokyo Express from coming down the slot and shelling it every night."

Yamamoto didn't know that the carrier groups stayed well south of the island. His ships hightailed it before dawn believing they would be attacked as soon as the sun came up.

When the Sterett fueled on 19 August, Ensign Cleland, with his two men, were transferred. The Lang came alongside and almost dumped Lt.(jg) Gordon Hanna out of the breeches buoy. He was reporting aboard as 1st Lieutenant. He was from Virginia, married, 6 ft. tall, weighing 230 lbs. Appropriately, he was called "Tiny".

The news of the day was the raid on Dieppe, France. 6,000 troops, primarily Canadians, went ashore to probe the German defenses. 3,600 were killed, demonstrating that the Allies were not ready for a major channel crossing. However, lessons were learned which were invaluable 22 months later.

The Germans were attacking Stalingrad and were already occupying the oil fields in Markop. Stalin sent in reinforcements and ordered his Commanders to hold Stalingrad at all costs.

Closer at hand, MacArthur reinforced his Marouba Force with the 7th Australian Division, which had recently returned from the Middle East. Kokoda was retaken and, on 18 August, the Japanese landed 11,500 troops at Buna.

On 27 August, sonar made a submarine contact. 9 depth charges were dropped. In the wardroom Cal exclaimed, "This is a losing battle. I don't know if we have ever hit one of the Jap subs. The Marines are getting shelled every night and the Japanese are building up their troops. Where are the reinforcements?"

Little did we know.....

CHAPTER 4

The Campaign for Guadalcanal;
Second Battle of Savo Island and Battle of Santa Cruz

The Captain replied, "The only troops available to reinforce the Marines is the 7th regiment on Espiritu Santo. There has been nothing in the dispatches indicating they are being sent," Tom exclaimed, "More than reinforcements, those guys need food, gas and ammunition. They're hurting."

On 1 September the PA boomed, "This is the Captain speaking. I've got good news. We have been ordered to Noumea, New Caledonia, for liberty and repairs." There were shouts of joy. Jeffrey asked, "What the hell is in Noumea?"

"Who cares?" responded Herbie. "I just want to get on dry land and have a beer."

September 3 in Noumea Harbor, the Sterett was moored to the Whitney, a destroyer tender, with the Stack and Buchanan. This was Admiral Ghomerly's headquarters. It was first inhabited by Papuans who came from Asia 30,000 years ago. When Captain Cook arrived in 1774, the pine trees reminded him of the Scottish coast, so he named it New Caledonia. Emperor Napoleon III annexed the island in 1843. A constant battle had been going on between the French settlers and the native Kanaks. In 1940, after the fall of France, New Caledonia expelled the pro-Vichy Governor and joined forces with the Free French. It was now a major allied naval base.

When Herbie, Shirley and I went on liberty, we saw the city square, with duty free shops offering Paris imports, the one hotel and several bars. Herbie said, "This reminds me of New Orleans."

"More like Paris from what I've heard," remarked Shirley. "Everything is French, including the 11a.m.-2p.m. lunch break, and the Cafe de Paris looks like something on the French Riviera."

"Enough chatter!" Herbie exclaimed. "Let's get a drink." The bar was crowded with Americans. There were "B" girls of various shades offering to share their personalities and bodies for a drink. In one corner an Aussie named Digger, with crutches and a cast on his leg, was holding forth. "What's going on?" I asked.

"This guy is a coastwatcher. He's been on Malaita. Broke his leg and was evacuated by submarine."

"What have you learned?" asked Herbie.

"He says Australia has had coastwatchers stationed in the Solomons and up into New Guinea since World War I."

"Why?"

"To protect Australia from a surprise invasion. A Lt. Cmdr. Eric Feldt was put in charge in September of 1939. He has lived in the islands since 1922, knows the people and they trust him. He established over 100 coastwatching stations, extending 2,500 miles from the western border of Papua, New Guinea, to Vila in the New Hebrides. Feldt's headquarters are in Townsville, Australia."

"Where do they get these guys?" Shirley asked.

"Some are planters who came out here to get lost from civilization, some are priests spreading the word of God, and some are members of the Royal Australian Navy assigned here."

"What is their job? How do they function?"

"They're observers. They are to run and not fight. Each coastwatcher has a cadre of loyal natives who know the jungles and can hide him from the Japs. They're equipped with 'teleradios'. Feldt taught them a simple cipher system which is easy to learn, but not very secure."

Herbie said, "Let's go over and listen."

Digger was waving his arms, "You should have seen them blokes on Tulagi on 8 February. The Morinda was sailing for the last time to Australia. The dock was a mob scene. There were piles of luggage and nowhere to put it. A Japanese flying boat showed up and made a couple of bombing runs; didn't hit anything. In the midst of this bedlam, this bloke, Martin Clemens, dressed in a white suit, arrives in a small boat."

"How come you didn't leave?"

"I'm in the Australian Navy, mate. I had spent some time in the islands in the thirties and volunteered for the assignment."

"So what's with this guy Clemens coming in when everyone is heading out?"

"He was appointed District Commissioner to over see the activities of the coastwatchers. He set up housekeeping on the eastern end of Guadalcanal. Ashton 'Snowy' Rhoades was assigned the western end and Lt. D.S. MacFarland, being new to the islands, the middle. Kenneth Hay, an old-timer, is helping him."

"So where were you?"

"I stayed with Clemens to learn the ropes. When the Japs started bombing Tulagi in April, I had a front row seat from the top of a Banyan tree at Aola. The morale of the fellahs was sagging a bit, and believe it or not, Martin staged a cricket match, which helped temporarily."

"What happened in early May when the Japs started invading the island?" Shirley asked.

"They bombed Tulagi and swarmed ashore, led by T. Ishimoto, a Japanese who had worked on Tulagi as a carpenter. All of us on Guadalcanal packed and headed for the bush. Martin tried to contact Tulagi, but heard only a faint voice calling, 'Steak and eggs, damn it. Steak and eggs.', which were the code words for 'We're shutting down'. We thought they were through, but on 3 May an ancient coastal vessel arrived with all of them. After getting some grub, they took off, heading south." He paused, drank some beer, wiped his mouth and said, "Any more questions?"

"Hell, yes. How did you guys survive with the Japs on the Island?"

"We took to the bush. Ken Hayes and MacFarland moved to Gold Ridge, 15 miles inland and 2,800 feet high. It had a five bedroom house to live in and a great view of the harbor. Hayes even had the natives haul up an Electrolux refrigerator."

"Was everyone that well off?"

"No. Clemens and Rhoades went deeper into the bush. Martin organized his 18 loyal native constables and put Cpl. Andrew Langelesca in charge. He scouted the island for information. One guy even rowed a canoe back and forth to Tulagi every day to report on activities. Refugees showed up from everywhere. The Catholic Bishop brought in rescued American pilots looking for a ride to Pearl Harbor. In late May, when the Japs sent larger patrols to the island, Clemens sent me to Malaita with a group of natives. In late June Martin realized the Japs were building an air strip and notified Eric Feldt who sent word to Admiral King. Hayes and his people were discovered by patrol planes on 12 July and had to get off Gold Ridge and move deeper into the bush. Food was running out, batteries were low and the natives were getting hostile. On 15 July Feldt radioed, 'Keep radio silence. Stick it out. I'll have you rescued in 4 weeks.' That was hard to believe with Japs swarming all over the place. On 4 August Clemens got an urgent request for information on troops, ships and gun emplacements. Three days later Martin alerted us, 'Ships are bombarding the island and carrier planes are overhead.'"

Herbie chimed in, "Who broadcast in the clear on 7 August that Jap planes were headed your way?"

"That was Paul Mason. He's stationed on the southern end of Bougainville. Jack Read, a tough ole bloke, is on the northern end. For 12 years he was with the Foreign Service on New Guinea. Moved over to Bougainville when the war started. Both have excellent views of the slot and can give two hours warning to your fellers at Guadalcanal."

"What happened to your guys after the Marines landed on Guadalcanal?"

"They're being used as scouts. Lt. Cmdr. Hugh MacKenzie set up 'Ken', the coastwatchers headquarters on Guadalcanal, and coordinates all activities. He's a tough old bastard and does a good job."

We left shaking our heads, "Those guys are fantastic. They're deep in enemy territory, living on the land and depending on the loyalty of the natives for support. That's real courage. They are the unsung heroes of this operation," Herbie exclaimed.

"Or the most stupid," Shirley added.

"No matter. It sure makes things easier for us."

The news reported that Glen Miller would soon be Captain Glenn Miller, USA Air Corps. When he announced his retirement, the orchestra was playing "I'll Be Home for Christmas". Herbie said, "I'll never forget listening to him late at night while studying. His broadcasts started at 11 o'clock with his theme song, 'Moonlight Serenade'. He was playing at Frank Dailey's Meadowbrook on the New Jersey turnpike. I'd hoped to see him one day."

"You still might," Shirley responded.

General Rommel was attacking El Alameen, Egypt, and unless he was stopped, would soon be at the Suez Canal. From dispatches, we knew plans were being made for operation "Torch" with General Eisenhower in command.

All was forgotten with the arrival of mail. Jeff exclaimed, "I don't know which I prefer the most, liberty or mail from home."

"Right now I'll take the beers. Just listen to this, my first and, I hope, my last Dear John letter:

'Dear Harold,

I hope this letter finds you safe and in good health. I think of you often and friends are always asking how you are.

I wanted you to be one of the first to know that I have become engaged to Lt. Cecil Burbage. He is stationed at Fort Jackson. You and he have much in common and I'm sure you'll like him. Our wedding plans have not yet been finalized.

I will always cherish the memories of the good times we had together. I look forward to the day when you'll come home to stay.

With all my love,
Caroline'

"Now how do you like them apples?" I asked.

"All of us have gotten at least one letter like that," Herbie responded. "Don't sweat it. She wasn't meant for you."

"It reconfirms a basic belief of mine. No permanent liaisons until this war is over. I've seen the anguish and tears when guys are leaving wives and children. Also the guilts when they went out and had a good time. My motto is eat, drink and be merry. So let's hit the beach this afternoon." I tried to drink up all of the alcohol in Noumea and got lost from Herbie. The Sterett's last whale boat had left when I found the dock. It was swim, spend the night and catch hell from the Skipper, or find a ride.

A 4-striper stumbled down to the dock and I said, "Captain, sir, I've got a problem. The last boat for my destroyer has gone. Could you possibly give me a ride?" He put his arm around my shoulders and mumbled, "Sure, son. Come on with me. You tin can sailors are the real Navy. We'll lick them damn Japs. Where's your ship?" We staggered over and into his boat. With no help from me, the coxswain found the Sterett and I climbed aboard with assistance from my shipmates.

On Sunday 6 September, the Sterett was underway with Task Force 18. The next day we rendezvoused with the McCawley and Guadeloupe, which had the 7th Marine Regiment on board.

Admiral Ghomerly knew the Japs would be waiting with submarines and planes. He ordered the Wasp and Hornet to take station 100 miles to the east to act as decoys. The Japs would think the transports were with the carriers.

The Sterett was ordered to proceed independently and on 11 September, rendezvoused with the Brastagi (SOPA), Betelgeuse and Hercules. At 1430 the PA boomed, "Now Hear this! All hands not on watch prepare for Captain's inspection of all compartments and holds below the main deck."

The bitching started, "We're supposed to be fighting a war and the Captain is holding an inspection. He's got a hole in his head."

"He's looking for that liquor you guys have hidden," another added.

"And if you guys don't shut up, you're going to end up in the brig on bread and water."

Arriving in Espiritu Santo, we fueled and headed for "Sleepless Hollow."

On 14 September the Sterett was patrolling the entrance of Tulagi Harbor. The cargo ships entered, and began unloading supplies. At 1753 while I was JOOD, the familiar voice of John Read was heard, "18 twin engine bombers, 23 fighters now enroute. Yours." General Quarters was sounded and the Sterett proceeded out of Tulagi harbor with the Fuller. At 1825 Russell, my talker in the engineer room, said, "The shore batteries on Guadalcanal have opened fire on the planes as they are making bombing runs. Bridge reports one has crashed into the water." He paused and at 1830 exclaimed, "One is heading for us. The Captain has given the order to commence firing." I could hear the guns and feel the ship recoiling from the salvos. Russell excitedly jumped up and down, "We hit him! Scratch one Jap plane."

The next afternoon the Sterett joined up with the troop transports in TF 65. The Wasp and Hornet were 100 miles to the east. At 1420 the Wasp launched an anti-submarine patrol. Simultaneously a Jap submarine fired a spread of 4 torpedoes. 2 hit on the starboard side igniting gasoline and engulfing the Wasp in flames. Another sub fired a spread at the Hornet, which missed, but one hit the North Carolina on the port side killing 5 men. The damage was controlled and the North Carolina was able to maintain her speed of 25 knots. The O'Brien, a few hundred yards on the quarter, had its bow blown off. The fires on the Wasp couldn't be contained and Captain Sherman ordered "abandon ship". At 2100 15 September, the Wasp sank slowly below the waves.

Captain Coward said, as he was reading the dispatches, "This is the only time since the Wasp was commissioned that we haven't been with her. She survived the subs in the Atlantic and the Mediterranean. Makes me feel like I've lost one of my best friends. We now have only one carrier in the entire Pacific Ocean."

At dinner Herbie exclaimed, "If those stupid Admirals had let us stay with the Wasp, she wouldn't have been sunk. We'd have gotten that submarine first."

The Sterett was detached and the following afternoon was in Second Channel at Espiritu Santo, moored portside to the Buchanan. At 1635 Ensign Perry Hall reported aboard. He was assigned to the First Lieutenant's Department.

The island of Espiritu Santo was first visited by Pedro Fernandez de Quiros in April 1606. He thought he had found the "lost" southern continent and named it Terra Australis del Espiritu Santo, after the Holy Ghost. In 1774 Captain Cook explored the islands and named them New Hebrides after the Scottish Islands of his homeland. The natives were Melanesians, mixed with French, Chinese and Vietnamese. Cannibalism was rampant and a man didn't wander far from his village. Pigs created bonds which held groups together. To become a "big man," one had to supply pigs to be slaughtered at clan festivals.

Missionaries came. Many were eaten, others spread measles, influenza and dysentery. They were considered evil sorcerers. Eventually they were able to stop cannibalism and village warfare. The planters grew bananas, coffee, and copra. It was rumored that a French planter lived in the hills with a cacao beautiful daughter.[22] I never found anyone who had seen her.

On 20 September, with a couple of men and several canvas bags, I was foraging for fresh fruit in the jungle: bananas, papayas, oranges and mangos. Rounding a bend in the narrow path, I saw a Naval officer asleep under a tree. Recognizing him, I yelled, "Claude Sapp, what the hell are you doing here? The last time I saw you was in Columbia, SC."

He pushed back his cap and said, "Well, I'll be damned if it ain't Harold Jervey. I'm on one of those 4-stackers converted into a troop transport. We haul Carlson's Raiders around. So what's your excuse for being in this God-forsaken spot?" We shared experiences and I learned that Carlson's Raiders were an elite group of Marines. They had landed behind the Japanese lines several times and had built up an outstanding reputation for their successful operations. When I left, he was still sitting under the tree.[23]

On 22 September the Sterett was enroute to Guadalcanal with the Betelgeuse. From dispatches, I knew the fighting on New Guinea was see- sawing back and forth. When the US 32nd Division arrived to reinforce the Aussies, they were advancing slowly along the Kokoda trail. The jungle was destroying General Horii's troops. They had malaria, dysentery and no rice. He knew there would be no reinforcements and was ordered to return to Buna and hold the beach.

Cal commented, "The savage Russian winter is beating the Germans. Here, the jungle has been protecting the Japs. Now it has turned against them. In North Africa, the British have been successfully attacking Rommel's supply convoys. He is short of gasoline, ammunition and food. Supplies are winning this war, not men."

Tom McWhorter added, "Churchill sacked Auckinleck. Montgomery is now in command of the 8th Army and the morale of the troops has soared. They're ready to move out."

On 25 September the Sterett was patrolling off Lunga Point while the Betelgeuse unloaded. There was little to do on the bridge except talk. I said to McWhorter, "Aren't these nights magnificent? It's remarkable how quickly it cools off once the sun goes down. Just look at the stars twinkling and those white clouds drifting by. The one thing I will never forget is this fragrance. It's a combination of honeysuckle, gardenias, wisteria and other flowers. It fills the air and hangs so heavy it envelopes you. Whenever I smell it, I will be reminded of the tropics."

Tom said, "Strange how each of us reacts to the same thing in a different way. The Marines on that island complain of the overpowering fecal stench, like an outhouse which hasn't been cleaned in a month. Here on the water, the smell is heavenly. If I were transported here with my eyes closed, I would know where I was. What are you going to do when the war is over? I'll probably put in 20 years and retire."

"I don't know. I considered medicine at one time, but the money wasn't there, and I'm not certain I'm cut out to be a doctor." We continued philosophizing until we were relieved by Herbie May.

After the Betelgeuse finished unloading, the Sterett was enroute to Espiritu Santo. The talk in the wardroom was the World Series. Herbie said, "I'll bet you $2 the New York Yankees win. With Joe Dimaggio, they're a sure thing."

"That ain't what the bookies are saying," I exclaimed. "They're picking the St. Louis Cardinals because of Stan Musial. I'll take your bet."

Although the Sterett anchored in Noumea harbor on 1 October, I didn't get ashore until the next afternoon. Herbie, Tom and I got in the gig and Herbie said, "Let's go to the bar at the Grand Hotel du Pacifique. That's where the action is."

Tom responded, "There'll be plenty of 'B' girls and guys from other ships, but no datable females."

"Any girls are better than none," I replied.

The place was packed. The men were either just returning or heading up to Guadalcanal. Their tales brought the war home: ship sunk and waiting reassignment; saw buddies blown to bits or eaten by sharks; plane shot down; crewmen killed. Sharing experiences was a catharsis for everyone. For the officers fresh from the States, it was frightening to realize what lay ahead.

"The limeys and Aussies have the right attitude," Tom said. "Let's get a couple of those girls over here and drink up. We're on a beautiful South Pacific island. To hell with the war."

"I'll drink to that," Herbie said.

Two girls came over. We couldn't understand their pidgin English. "No matter," Tom exclaimed. "They sure smell good."

On our next visit we ran into Digger, and Herbie asked him, "How are your coastwatcher buddies faring?"

"They're doing fine except for the damn Bishop with his priests and nuns. They won't leave. The Japs don't have much use for their God. Sooner or later they're going to dispose of them, Bishop or no Bishop. It's causing a problem for some of our fellahs. McKenzie has decided there's a need to expand the network. Henry Josselyn is going to Vella Lavella and Nick Wadell to Choiseul. Both of them know the area and the natives. They're going to be sent in by submarine."

For the next 9 days it was routine upkeep work. I started reading "Inside Latin America" by John Gunther and "The Just and Unjust " by James Cozzens. I won $2 when the Cardinals won the World Series 4-1 with Whitey Kurowski's home run in the top of the ninth inning.

Conditions on Guadalcanal were improving. The air was controlled by our pilots during the day, but the nights belonged to the Japanese. Prior to dawn the Japs hightailed it up the slot. Gasoline remained a problem. A submarine fitted with special tanks carrying 9,000 gals of aviation gasoline helped.

On 9 October the Sterett was enroute to "Sleepless Hollow", with the McCawley and Zeilen carrying the 164th Infantry Regiment of the American Division. On 11 October sonar reported a sub contact and depth charges were dropped. It was a big fish.

The morning news reported that German troops had surrounded Stalingrad and its fall was eminent. Tom commented, "Hitler told his Generals 'take Stalingrad, or don't come back.' "

"I wouldn't bet the family jewels on their success just yet. With the Russian winter setting in, the Germans are going to have the same problems they had outside of Moscow last year," Gould said.

When I reported to the Captain in the afternoon, I was relieved to see him smiling as he said, "I've got good news for you, Mr. Jervey. This dispatch from the Bureau announces the promotion of all Ensigns with a date of commission prior to 1 October, 1941. Do you know of any reason why you shouldn't be promoted?"

"No, sir."

"Consider yourself now a Lieutenant, junior grade. Have the yeoman and paymaster square away the paper work. I'll sign whatever is required and swear you in."

"Thank you, sir, " I said and left. Several of the other officers also received promotions.

200 miles south of the island, I knew from the flurry of messages that a big battle was brewing. General Hyakutake was determined to retake Guadalcanal. He was throwing 25,000 men at Vandergrift and told his superiors, "I'll have him appear with a white flag by 15 October."

To stop his advance and protect our troop convoy, Admiral Nimitz had assigned 3 Task Forces: Admiral Murray's Hornet group, Admiral Lee's Washington group and Admiral Norman Scott's Task Force 64. His orders were "To search for and destroy enemy ships and landing craft".

Admiral Mikawa had been landing up to 900 men each night on Cape Esperance. On 11 October Mikawa sent down 3 heavy cruisers and 8 destroyers to harass the Marines while much larger numbers of his troops were landing. Admiral Scott learned of the Japanese forces shortly before midnight and quickly closed on them. His ships were in an unwieldy column. The best SC radar was on the Helena and messages were garbled and misunderstood.

Admiral Goto had no radar and never knew where Scott was. At 2345 he inadvertently crossed the tee at the same time Scott ordered "commence firing". From then on it was a wild melee. Both Scott and Mikawa were confused and uncertain as to who was firing at whom. When it was over at 0028, the Salt Lake City had received 2 hits, the

Boise was in flames but still able to make way, and the Farenholt was dead in the water. The Duncan was abandoned and sank at 0200.[24]

Goto's losses were greater. He was killed and his ship severely damaged. The Fubuki and Furutaka were sunk. The Hatsuyuki and Kimugaza were hit many times and the Japs were in full retreat up the slot. In spite of this, troops were landed, together with supplies, ammunition and, most importantly, heavy artillery. Admiral Scott was the hero of the Battle of Cape Esperance.

Americans were happy to get good news for a change. The papers erred in reporting that 4 cruisers and 4 destroyers had been sunk. It was a victory and partial revenge for the first Savo Island debacle. The tactical errors made were not recognized and were repeated in later engagements.

The Sterett was to the south, and at 0541 on 13 October, was patrolling off Lunga Point while the transports unloaded the much needed 164th Infantry Regiment. "Cactus Airforce" had 90 operational planes. At 1155 coastwatchers reported 22 Mitsubishi bombers heading our way. At 1202 the Nicholas opened fire and the Sterett followed. No hits were made and the bombers made mince meat of Henderson field. There was another air attack with 15 bombers two hours later with the same result.

At 1830 the Sterett was directed to take under fire "Pistol Pete", a large Japanese artillery piece, which was tearing up Henderson Field. The Sterett, Gwin and Nicholas commenced firing at 1835. Firing was intermittent until 1906 when "Pistol Pete" was silenced after expending 370 rounds of 5"/38 ammunition.

The Sterett, with the McCawley and other ships of Task Unit 62.6, was soon enroute to Espiritu Santo. From reports of coastwatchers and scout planes, we knew the Japs were coming down the slot with 2 battleships, one cruiser and 4 destroyers under the command of Vice Admiral Kurita. At 0100 they were on station and commenced firing. The Marines had another sleepless night and Henderson Field was left in shambles, blazing from one end to the other.

Only 42 planes could fly, aviation gas was almost gone and the field was inoperable. "Pistol Pete" was again firing away. Two air raids followed. In the afternoon a Colonel from headquarters told the aviators: "We don't know whether we'll be able to hold the field or not. There's a Japanese task force with cruisers, destroyers and transports headed our way. We have enough gasoline for one mission. Load your planes with bombs and hit them. After the gas is gone, the ground troops take over. You officers and men will attach yourselves to some infantry outfit. Good luck and goodbye."

At 2200 Admiral Kelley ordered the Sterett and Gwin to proceed independently to Espiritu Santo, while the Marines and Henderson Field caught hell from Mikawa's bombardment group. At dawn the transports began unloading the troops at Tassafaronga while the Marines watched.

The Seabees made Henderson field operational and gasoline was flown in from Espiritu Santo. By noon planes were in the air, bombing and strafing. 3 of the Japanese transports which had not finished unloading were so severely damaged they had to be beached. By 1550 the Japanese commander withdrew with his other 3 transports. None escaped damage; no troop unit landed without casualties and loss of equipment. The Marines lost 3 dive bombers and 3 fighter planes.

The Sterett anchored in Second Channel, Espiritu Santo. I went to the Captain's cabin with a dispatch from Admiral Nimitz: "It now appears we are unable to control the sea in the Guadalcanal area. Thus our ability to supply these positions will be done at great expense to us. Situation not hopeless, but it is certainly critical." The Captain signed the dispatch and asked, "Is there anything else?"

"No, sir. You've seen everything. Those Marines are desperate."

He said, "We've lost too many ships. We can't afford to lose any more. Getting gasoline to the fliers with twin engine Douglas Sky Troopers is a clever idea, but it's only a drop in the bucket."

"The irony of it all is, while the Marines are desperately hanging on, the crew and I are complaining about the poor liberty facilities here in Espiritu Santo." There weren't any females. We had beer, whiskey and soda and partied under a palm tree. The talk always focused on the plight of the Marines. Tom said, "The Japanese are throwing everything they have at us in an attempt to recapture Henderson Field. Fortunately they hold our pilots in high regard. Rarely do they bring their ships down during daylight hours. That limits the number of reinforcements they can land." The discussions ended with some version of, "Put me in charge and I'll end this war in a hurry."

On Sunday 18 October, the Sterett was enroute to rendezvous with the Bobolink in the Coral Sea. At the same time Vice Admiral William F. Halsey was landing in Noumea. His orders from Admiral Nimitz read, "You will take command of the South Pacific Area and South Pacific Forces." Our reaction was immediate. "The high command is making a scapegoat of Ghomerly," Herbie said. "He did the best he could with what he had. He ain't no miracle worker."

Frank Gould replied, "That's not the whole picture. Ghomerly is not an aggressive leader. Bull Halsey is. He has a reputation of 'damn the torpedoes, full speed ahead'. I'm pleased with the change."

"From my perspective, I don't see what difference it makes who's in charge. We'll follow orders—good or bad. If the past is any way to judge, some will be reasonable and others irrational. Only the name of the Commander will change," Herbie added.

The Sterett rendezvoused with the Bobolink. The next day Admiral Lee's group was sighted. As we closed, Herbie announced, "I just received a dispatch saying that the heavy cruiser Chester was hit yesterday in the forward engine room by a torpedo.[25] Her maximum speed is 6 knots. You are to rendezvous with her tomorrow." The next afternoon the Chester and her escorts were sighted. The formation crawled to Espiritu Santo at 6 knots and arrived on 23 October.

There was momentary excitement on 25 October when General Quarters was sounded. I asked Russell, my talker, what the hell was going on. He said, "Bridge reports the President Coolidge was blown apart while shifting berths. It was first thought to be a torpedo. It wasn't. She ran into one of our mines."

To the north a battle was brewing. The arrival of the carrier Enterprise with the new battleship South Dakota was good news. Admiral Halsey now had 2 carriers, 2 battleships, 9 cruisers and 24 destroyers. He divided them into 3 groups: TF 16 under Admiral Kincaid, TF 17 under Admiral Murray and TF 64 under Admiral Lee. The 2 carrier groups were ordered to take a position by the Santa Cruz Islands and intercept Japanese forces approaching Guadalcanal.

Admiral Yamamoto instructed his army counterparts to capture Henderson Field immediately, as fuel was running short. A report was sent to Yamamoto at 0126 on 25 October that Henderson Field was taken. At 0623 this was corrected; the Marines were holding fast.

Admiral Kondo, with 4 carriers, was to the north when, shortly before midnight, Yamamoto ordered him to seek out and destroy the enemy fleet. B-17's and Catalinas sighted Kondo's ships through out the day. Kondo turned away to await the outcome of the battle for Henderson Field. Admiral Kincaid headed for Kondo at 20 knots. At 0011 a PBY reported the enemy fleet 300 miles to the northwest. Three hours later another PBY reported one large carrier and 6 other ships 200 miles away. When Tom came to the bridge waving his dispatch board, he exclaimed, "Admiral Halsey has sent out an order to Kincaid, 'Attack-Repeat-Repeat-Attack.' There's going to be some action."
The reaction was immediate. "Hooray! That's the way to go. Let's go get them."

At 0630 Enterprise planes sighted Admiral Abe's vanguard group of battleships and cruisers. They were searching for the carriers and didn't attack. The carriers were picked up at 0650, 200 miles northwest of Kincaid. Dive bombers hit the Zuiho, opened a hole in her flight deck and started numerous fires.

The Hornet was sighted at 0630 and a 65-plane strike was launched by the Japanese. The Hornet and Enterprise launched another strike and the 2 groups of planes saw and passed each other. The question in the minds of the pilots was, "Who is going to have a flight deck to land on when we return?"

The Japanese attacked the Hornet at 0906. Kincaid's fighters, stationed 10 miles out at 22,000 feet, were of little help. The Japanese attacked with bombs and torpedoes. Many hits were made and the Hornet was soon in flames and dead in the water. At 0930 her planes attacked the carrier Shokaku. Bombs ripped holes in her flight deck and many fires were started.[26] Another group of planes attacked the cruiser Chikuma, killing most of the bridge personnel and sending her to Tokyo for repairs. The Japanese were left with the carriers Zuikaku and Junyo intact. The fires on the Hornet were extinguished and the Northhampton took her in tow. At 1002 a Jap sub fired a salvo and hit the destroyer Porter in the fire room. She was abandoned and sunk by gunfire.

The 44 plane group from the Japanese carriers found the Enterprise. The bombers made 3 hits: one close to the bowl, one abaft the forward elevator and the third penetrated to the third deck before exploding. Many men were killed and wounded. The torpedo planes which followed hit the Portland and a suicide plane crashed into the destroyer Smith. The Japanese lost most of their planes. The strike from the Junyo arrived and hit the South Dakota, causing minor damage. The San Juan was struck by an armor-piercing bomb which caused considerable damage. Several enemy planes were destroyed.

The flight deck of the Enterprise was congested. The forward elevator was handling her planes and also the Hornet's. Many had to ditch in the water since they were low on gas. Others were ordered to Espiritu Santo.

Admiral Kondo sent his 2 damaged carriers north. The Zuikaku and Junyo took off after Kincaid. After losing over 100 planes, Kondo had only 15 planes left. At 1515 they attacked the Hornet's group. Torpedoes missed the Northhampton, but one hit the starboard side of the Hornet, flooding the after engine room and causing a 14-degree list to starboard. 6 Kates attacked and one bomb hit the after starboard corner of the flight deck. She was ablaze and abandon ship was ordered. One man sliding down into the water asked another, "Are you going to reenlist?" The reply was, "Yes, Godammit—on the new Hornet!" The destroyers completed their rescue work by dark. The Mustin and Anderson were unsuccessful in sinking the Hornet. Their 16 torpedoes either ran erratically or didn't explode. Admiral Abe's group, in hot pursuit of Kincaid, came upon the blazing Hornet. His destroyers fired 4 torpedoes and at 0135 she sank.

An hour later two "Black Cats" from Espiritu attacked Abe's group with torpedoes and one hit the destroyer Teruzuki. Abe continued steaming around looking for targets. He retired to Truk in the early afternoon.

Kincaid's ships were enroute to Noumea when the Mahan and South Dakota collided. Admiral Lee had a close call when the sub I-15 fired a spread of fish, barely missing. This convinced Halsey that capital ships should not operate in submarine infested waters. From the dispatches, Coward had a feel for what was going on and said, "That action once again demonstrates our inferiority with torpedo attacks and long range search. The fighter direction was poor. The Japanese have lost so many experienced pilots, it's going to change their strategy."

The Japanese won a tactical victory at the Battle of Santa Cruz, but had to retreat. The assault on the Marines had fizzled out. Even so, Tokyo claimed "3 carriers, one battleship, 3 cruisers and one destroyer were sunk." Our papers acknowledged the loss of the Hornet.

Gould said, "We're getting low in carriers. Sooner or later there's going to be a slugfest between our battleships."

He was right. It wouldn't be long.

CHAPTER 5

The Third Battle of Savo Island;
Turning point of the war in the Pacific

The news reported that Admiral Nimitz had publicly declared: "The general situation at Guadalcanal is not unfavorable," Gould said, "That's a much more optimistic comment than he made 2 weeks ago. Obviously he believes the Battle of Santa Cruz gave us more time to reinforce and prepare for the next engagement."

On 30 October the Sterett was anchored at Efate, capital of the New Hebrides, where 115 languages and dialects were spoken. Melanesians and Polynesians settled the island. When the British arrived, the French moved up from Noumea. A unique entity was formed: an Anglo-French condominium some said was an Anglo-French pandemonium. Each country maintained its own militia and legal, educational and health systems for its citizens. The Melanesians were judged by whatever law they ran afoul of.

After fueling, the Sterett was enroute to Guadalcanal with Task Force 65. Tom reported, "During the last 10 days, the Japanese haven't captured Henderson Field and they've lost about 103 planes and one cruiser. We've lost only 14 planes."

"What about personnel casualties?"

"About 300 Marines have been killed. The number of Japanese casualties is unknown, but much larger."

"Do we still control the area from sunup to sundown and the Japanese after dark?" Cal asked.

"The Tokyo Express is running full tilt. Once the troops and supplies are unloaded, they bombard the Marines and head home," Tom replied.

Admiral Yamamoto had under his command 5 carriers, 5 battleships, 14 cruisers and 44 destroyers. He was frustrated and determined to recapture the island. He ordered his commanders to apprehend and annihilate any powerful forces in the Solomon's area, which meant us.

On 2 November the Pensacola, Cushing, Preston, Anderson and Mustin joined our formation. When San Cristobal Island was sighted the next morning, the Task Force was split into 2 groups. Ours consisted of the San Francisco, Helena, Gwin and Buchanan. Coward said, "This is going to be an interesting mission. We're going to bombard the Japanese shore positions and give the Marines some relief."

On 4 November our Task Group was off Kokumbona Point. The San Francisco fired its main batteries at Japanese positions for one hour. At 1005 the Sterett took position off Koli Point and commenced firing. A spotting plane directed our fire. The pilot would order Cal to lift fire 100 yards, down 50 yards, to the right and to the left. Firing ceased at 1048. The pilot reported that many fires were started. Gould said, "To the best of my knowledge, this is the first time supporting bombardment has been given to troops in WW II. Before, it has always been pre-invasion fire support."

Cal exclaimed, "It's not going to be the last. I don't know how much damage we did, but it boosted the morale of the Marines."

The Task Group returned to Lungo Point to screen the transports while they were unloading. At 1616 the Sterett, together with the transports, headed east through Lengo Channel. The same routine continued for the next 2 days. When the sun went down, the ships departed through Indispensable Straits.

In the wardroom there was bitching. Herbie said, "This is no way to fight a war. When night falls, the ocean belongs to the Japs. Let's stay and fight them. Winner take all. What the hell is happening in the rest of the world?"

Tom replied, "In North Africa, Rommel has returned, but he's out of fuel and had to retreat. MacArthur's troops are slowly advancing over the mountains toward Buna. Winter has stopped the advance of the Germans in the Caucasus."

"Isn't it ironic," Jeff remarked. "We're advancing everywhere in the world because the enemy lacks supplies. At Guadalcanal, we're losing because we can't get gas, food and ammunition to the Marines."

The transports completed unloading on 6 November, and Task Group 65.4 headed south for Espiritu Santo. General Quarters was sounded several times, but only friendly planes were seen.

From dispatches, we knew that from 2 November until 10 November, the Japanese had landed 65 destroyer and 2 cruiser-loads of troops. At breakfast Tom said, "Secretary Knox is not too optimistic about our chances. In the New York Times he told the American people, 'It is a bitter, tough fight and the whole Japanese Navy is involved.' "

"He should have told them we haven't got enough ships to stop them," Herbie added.

On the morning of 9 November, Tom excitedly said at breakfast, "There is great news from Europe. At El Alamien, Egypt, General Bernard Montgomery is advancing rapidly. With Rommel having little fuel and few tanks, Montgomery has overrun him and captured or killed

59,000. More importantly, our troops under the command of General Dwight Eisenhower have invaded North Africa.

Landings were made simultaneously at Casablanca, with troops under the command of General George Patton, at Oran, under the command of General Fredendali, and at Algiers, under the command of General Ryder. He captured Pro-Vichy Admiral Francois Darlan, the High Commissioner in Algiers, who ordered his troops to cease firing and agreed to switch his alliance to DeGaulle."

"That's unbelievable," Gould exclaimed, "The war in Europe is going to end quicker than anyone thought. What about the Russian front?"

"Winter is setting in. General Zhukov is getting fresh troops and replenishing his supply of tanks and planes. He's on the offensive around Stalingrad."

"I'm happy for those guys in Europe. We've got a date with the Japs at 'Sleepless Hollow'. I hope we can send our people some good news when this mission is finished," Gould added.

On 10 November the Sterett was enroute to Guadalcanal with Task Group 67.4, consisting of the San Francisco (SOPA), Helena, Cushing, Laffey and Buchanan. The next morning the Portland and Juneau joined the formation.

At midnight we were patrolling the western entrance of Sealark Channel. On Thursday 12 November at 0425, the formation sortied into Iron Bottom Bay. The Laffey and Buchanan made a submarine contact and attacked, results unknown. At dawn the Task Group was off Lunga Point patrolling while the transports unloaded. At 0725 the Helena, Barton and Laffey commenced firing at enemy shore batteries.

At 1320 the familiar voice of Jack Read on Bougainville was heard, "21 twin-engine bombers now enroute yours." General Quarters sounded. At 1406 Russell exclaimed, "21 Japanese torpedo bombers have been sighted, bearing 055 degrees, distance 10 miles." At 1413 sledge hammer blows could be felt and heard as the Sterett commenced firing. Russell yelled, "Those planes are close aboard. Bridge says we splashed one, 2, 3 and maybe 4. What a sight! 2 more have been hit. What a day!"

"How about the others?" I asked.

"Bridge reports only one got away and one crash-dived into the fantail of the San Francisco. Fires have been started. There are a lot of casualties."[27]

In the wardroom Sanders said, "This afternoon's air show is only the first act of the main production. Yamamoto and the Japanese high command are determined to retake this god-forsaken island."

"You're right," Tom replied. "Intelligence and coastwatchers reported that the Tokyo Express is coming down the slot tonight with the

Kirshima and Hei, together with one heavy cruiser and 14 destroyers under the command of Vice Admiral Abe."

" We're no match for them," Gould said. "Admiral Callahan has orders to stop the Japanese from bombarding the Marines and landing reinforcements. I don't see how it can be done with only 8 destroyers and 3 heavy and 2 light cruisers.

"He's a good man, but he doesn't have the horses," Cal replied. "We're coming up on Friday the 13th and that's going to be an unlucky day for one of us."

After escorting the transports south of the island, Task Group 67.4 reversed course. General Quarters was sounded at 2007. Admiral Callahan ordered the ships to form up in a single line with the destroyers 500 yards apart.

Captain Coward cussed when I showed him the dispatch from Admiral Willis Lee: "Sorry! Unable to make rendezvous. Good luck and good hunting."

"Callahan is going to be unhappy when he sees this. Lee has the Washington and South Dakota, our two newest battleships. Their firepower is needed badly. We're in trouble. Any other information?" he asked.

"That's it."

The Cushing was leading the column followed by the Laffey, Sterett, O'Bannon, Atlanta, with Admiral Norman Scott second in command, San Francisco, Portland, Helena, Juneau, Aaron Ward, Barton, Monssen and Fletcher. Iron Bottom Sound was entered from the southeast at 2353.

On Friday 13 November at 0124, Russell said ,"Bridge reports radar contact has been made with 2 groups of ships. One is bearing 312 degrees, distance 27,000 yards. The other bearing 310 degrees, distance 32,000 yards. The right looks like 3 destroyers and 2 cruisers; the center, 2 battleships and 2 destroyers." With Task Group 67.4's course due west, speed 18 knots and Abe on an easterly heading, the 2 forces were approaching each other at almost 40 knots. The distances closed rapidly. Admiral Abe thought we had retired to the south at sundown as always. His men were at their battle stations in preparation for the shore bombardment of Henderson Field.

Admiral Callahan's flagship, the San Francisco, did not have SC radar, as did the Helena, and the closing distances had to be relayed by TBS. Russell exclaimed, "The Captain says he doesn't understand why the order to commence firing has not been given. We're within firing range." He paused and at 0140 said, "Fire Control reported to the bridge that enemy ships have been picked up, distance 14,500 yards."

Soon afterwards, the Cushing reported over the TBS, "Japanese destroyers sighted crossing dead ahead—port to starboard, distance 3,000 yards." The Japanese saw us at the same time and surprise was lost. Russell said, "The Cushing has requested permission to fire torpedoes and this has been granted."

He continued, "The Cushing made a turn to port to unmask torpedoes and all ships are having a helluva time avoiding a collision. It's a mess. The Captain is complaining he has no maneuverability with 500 yards between ships." There was silence and at 0145 he said, "Admiral Callahan has ordered 'standby to commence firing'." At 0150 he excitedly exclaimed, "The Japs have turned on their searchlights and the place looks like Times Square. Callahan has ordered, 'Odd ships fire to starboard, even to port' "

It was too late. The Atlanta, only 1,600 yards from the Japs, received multiple salvos, wiping out the superstructure and killing Admiral Norman Scott and his staff. It began sinking. The Cushing fired 6 torpedoes at the Hiei; no hits. In return, salvo after salvo crashed down on her, and by 0152 she was sinking. The Laffey almost collided with the Hiei and launched torpedoes so close they didn't arm. She sprayed the bridge with 20mm shells and in turn was hit by large caliber shells and one torpedo. She began sinking immediately.

All Russell could say was, "Looks like the Cushing and Laffey are finished."

Salvo after salvo hit ships in each formation. It was impossible to miss at such close range. I could hear and feel the recoil as the Sterett opened fire. Russell said, "We're firing at a cruiser 4,000 yards on our starboard bow. Hits have been made on the bridge and superstructure."

At 0151, I felt the Sterett shudder as hits were received on the port quarter. Russell reported, "The starboard cable to the steering gear has been cut. The rudder is jammed. The Captain is steering with the engines. Several men in Gun Control have received shrapnel wounds from near misses."

At 0155 I asked, "Why have we ceased firing?"

"It's impossible to identify friend from enemy. The O'Bannon has come up on our starboard quarter and is getting in our line of fire. The Captain thinks the San Francisco may have been firing on the Atlanta."

He continued, "The San Francisco has been illuminated by searchlights and is being hit repeatedly with salvos of 5" and 14" shells. The bridge is in shambles.[28] The Portland must have been hit by a torpedo. She is going around in circles, but still firing."

The Helena opened fire on a cruiser and destroyer. In return she received only minor damage to the superstructure. The Juneau had difficulty identifying targets, and before getting off effective salvos, a torpedo exploded in her forward fire room putting her out of action. The Captain's main concern was keeping her afloat and he cleared out.

Friendlies got in the way of the Aaron Ward and she was unable to get any salvos off until 0200. Firing at various targets, she received many hits. By 0235 she was dead in the water with a flooded engine room.

The Barton, immediately behind the Aaron Ward, was able to launch a spread of 4 torpedoes and fired several 5" salvos. At 0157 she was hit by 2 torpedoes, one in the fire room and the other in the engine room. She broke in two and sank.

Russell exclaimed, "The Monssen has been illuminated by star shells. She has turned on her recognition lights, which was a mistake. She is getting hit repeatedly. My God! She's nothing but a burning hulk." In a few minutes he continued, "Captain Hoover in the Helena has been unable to raise Callahan or Scott and has assumed tactical command. He has ordered a cease-fire, but everyone is disregarding it."

"Why in the hell did he do that? What's going on out there? I might as well be in a broom closet."

"There is a lot of confusion. Nobody knows who is firing at whom. No one can identify enemy ships from friendlies. The Captain doesn't know where the rest of our Task Group is," Russell replied.

The skipper of the Fletcher, at the rear of the ship, saw all of the burning ships and the disintegration of the Barton and Monssen. He fired at several targets. He retired to evaluate the situation and was unscathed. Admiral Abe was also confused and ordered his battleships, the Hiei and Kirshima, to retire to the north. They were slow in turning and the Sterett was in their path.

At 0205 I felt a giant sledge hammer hitting the hull on the port side.

Russell said, "The foremast has been hit. The SC radar, emergency identification lights and the TBS antenna have been knocked out. We are deaf and blind." At 0208 I felt the ship tremble and Russell said, "We've fired a salvo of torpedoes to port at a battleship of the Kongo class, range 3,000 yards. The order has been given to open fire with the 5" guns." He jumped up and down exclaiming, "At least two hits were made with the torpedoes. The 5" salvos are raking the bridge. Several fires have been started in the superstructure. They're getting hit by shells from other ships. Some of the crew are jumping over the side. We're giving them hell." At 0215 Captain Hoover ordered all ships to follow him and retire. The Sterett didn't hear the order.

At 0220 Russell reported, "A destroyer of the Fubuki class is on the starboard bow, range 1,000 yards. Hell! I could spit on her. 2 torpedo hits have been made and have lifted her out of the water. Our 5" salvos are hitting her head-on. She's exploded and is sinking." He added, "The fire from the destroyer has lit up the whole area like the Chicago Loop. The Captain thinks the Japs are firing at each other."

I felt the ship shudder as hits were received on the port quarter at 0227. Russell said, "No. 3 and 4 guns have been knocked out. Hits have been made in the handling rooms. Powder tanks have exploded. At least 2 men looking like flaming torches have jumped overboard."

"Jesus Christ," I mumbled, "and here we sit unable to do a damn thing."

I felt another sledge hammer blow. Russell continued, "A salvo has hit amidships, right over our heads. One pierced the corner of the port torpedo tubes. Other shells have passed through the midship shipping room. Damage has been reported to the starboard torpedo tubes. The magazine and handling rooms of No. 3 and No. 4 guns have been flooded and power cut. Repair parties are fighting the fires on the fantail. Bridge reports there are burning ships all around us and we are steering various courses to avoid them. There is no way to identify who they are."

Cal was ordered by the Captain to come down from Gun Control and assess the damage. He wrote: "Topside the ship was dark. I groped my way down to the main deck and went aft on the starboard side. The upper handling room for the No. 3 gun was in shambles. Three 14" shells had struck the port side bulkhead and detonated on impact. Thousands of shrapnel fragments had made a sieve of the compartment, killing everyone inside. Ignited bins of 5" ready service powder were deflected upward through the gun mount itself, killing all but 2 of the gun's crew. Hodge and Keenum were removing cans of powder from the room when I arrived. Hodge entered through one of the holes gouged by the 14" projectiles, scooped up the hot powder cans in his arms and hurried through the washroom door to dump them overboard. Keenum played a fire hose on him during the early part of this procedure, but eventually gave up and joined in the unloading process. Several cans of powder actually detonated in the air with low-order explosions after Hodge tossed them overboard. Keenum also operated the magazine's sprinkler system on his first trip into the compartment. A single 5" hit also penetrated the mount of No. 3 gun without detonating. It mortally wounded V.R.E. Martin, the gun captain, who insisted the doctor attend to others because he was sure he would die anyway. I found what was left of the crew, dead at their battle stations. Gann, the young first shellman of gun No. 4, had dived overboard with his clothing on fire. No doubt he was one of the 2 men I had seen from the gun director. Hodge and I moved aft on the main deck, leaving Keenum to fight the fire. Opening the hatch to the ladder, the two of us descended into the No. 4 handling room. Here the casualties were also heavy. The scene was similar to what we had encountered on the deck above. Shrapnel fragments had ignited ready service powder and started searing fires. The crew's quarters forward of the handling room were still ablaze. Ensign Perry Hall was single-handedly fighting the fire with a hose and appeared to have the situation under control. He assured me he needed no assistance. Electrical, steering and degaussing cables had been severed by shell hits. Gun mounts, ammunition hoists, bulkheads and frames were twisted and distorted. Our watertight integrity was intact, and no machinery was damaged, other than instruments and electrical steering control devices. I marveled at the ship's ability to take punishment. I left Hodge to assist with the firefighting and made my way back up to the bridge to make my report to the skipper."

Perry Hall was JOOD when the engagement started. Sensing he could be of greater help at his damage control station on the main deck, he asked for and was granted permission to go below. This is his account of what transpired from the time he arrived on the main deck after our encounter with the battleship: "First I checked my 20mm crew, who were watching intently the havoc around them. As we stood there, the starboard torpedo tubes released 2 torpedoes at a ship only 1,000 yards away. The 5" battery commenced firing at the same ship. Then what had been a ghostly gray shape became a brilliant orange ship from stem to stern. It was as if a huge star shell had burst and illuminated the sea. It was like noon on a bright, sunny day. The next thing I knew, I was thrown violently to the deck. I landed in a sitting position and momentarily blacked out. I got up, dazed but with no apparent physical damage, except cuts and bruises. I realized we had been hit, and I could see men jumping over the side with their clothes ablaze. I dashed to the wardroom looking for Tiny Hanna. He was assisting Doc Nyce with the wounded. I asked him what he wanted me to do. 'Take charge of the after-repair party.' As I turned to leave, he noticed I had been cut and asked if I needed attention. It was minor compared to the carnage around me, so I left. By the time I got out on deck, the repair party had hoses playing on the fires. Unfortunately, shrapnel had pierced a number of the hoses and pressure wasn't what it should be. The decks were slippery with blood, and potatoes were scattered everywhere. The ship was turning to avoid gunfire and other ships. Maintaining footing was a problem. The screams of the wounded pierced the night and mingled with orders directing the firefighting. I continued aft. The No. 4 handling room was a holocaust. Bits of burning bedding smoldered on bunks, burnt bodies were scattered about the deck, and water poured into a shell hole just above the water line whenever the ship heeled over. The stench of burning flesh and powder made breathing difficult. Men and I stuffed mattresses into the holes and used shoring to hold them in place. A fire hose extinguished the burning materials that had fallen into the powder room. Water was streaming over the hatch coaming, helping to flood the magazine. Bodies, mattresses and other debris sloshed back and forth with the movement of the ship. Battle lanterns provided the only light. I had no idea of the time or where the ship was. I knew we were maneuvering with the screws because I couldn't hear the rudder. Finally the fires were out and the holes plugged. I made my way topside. The sudden burst of fresh air into my lungs made me feel faint. I suddenly realized the battle was over and I was still alive. The horror of the last hour hit me like a punch in the stomach and I retched."

At 0327 Russell said, "The rudder has jammed at full right. All engines full astern. We're running into Guadalcanal." The Captain successfully maneuvered the ship out of danger. Russell continued, "The Captain thinks all of our ships have retired. We've got no torpedoes and only the forward 2 guns are operational. He has told Mr. McWhorter, OOD, to head east."

Russell had given me as clear a picture of the action as anyone had. From time to time, I stuck my head out of the hatch. All I could see were incendiaries filling the sky, like fireworks on New Year's Eve Night. I could see burning ships all over the horizon.

At 0345 the Sterett entered Lengo Channel, speed 23 knots. Cal relieved McWhorter as OOD.

The Sterett had received 11 direct hits including three 14' shells. She had been so close to the Japs, they could not depress their guns so as to hit us below the water line. Fragments from near misses were evident in the hull, superstructure and crew. 4 men had jumped over the side.[29]

When Tom was relieved of the watch he wrote, "I went below to the wardroom thinking how good it would be to get some sleep. When I opened the wardroom door I was aghast at the bloody assemblage of the wounded. I saw 3 of my torpedo gang who had performed so well only a few minutes earlier. They were seriously wounded, but in high spirits. Rhodes called out, 'There's that man from Texas!' Shrieves said, 'We sure gave 'em hell, didn't we? Did you see us get that tin can?' Rhodes added, 'Yeah, and we sure knocked the hell out of that battleship.' Hawkins was silent and I replied, 'You guys were wonderful.'

"I asked Harry Nyce how I could help. I was handed a jar of sulfathiazol cream and told how to use it. My first patient was a youngster with multiple shrapnel wounds. I managed to get him to my bunk by some means, laid him out and started cleaning the wounds with warm water, spreading sulfathiazol over them and bandaging them up. Jansen, a radioman, came in and helped me. After fixing up one man, we went back into the wardroom and got another. Some were suffering from shock, some from burns and others had horrible wounds of all descriptions. There was not a whimper out of one of them. Solloway told me almost the entire crew of the after guns had been killed. This was the first indication I had of the extent of our casualties.

"In a short while, Harry sent for me to come back to sick bay. It was the first time I had been near the heaviest damage, and because the sick bay was only a short distance from the No. 4 handling room, there was a putrid odor all about, the result of a combination of burned flesh, blood and death. It was unbearably hot. Harry was stripped down to his shorts and I followed suit.

Hawkins was brought in and laid on the operating room table. His right leg had to be amputated. Doc stuck a hypodermic needle into Hawkins wrist, then gave it to me. He said, 'If he starts to pull out of it, give him another cc, Mac.' Hawkins quickly passed out as the sodium pentothal took effect. He had a wound of his left eye where he had been hit by shrapnel, a deep wound of his cheekbone and numerous other wounds over his body. Harry patched him up as best he could and called for the next patient. We thought Hawkins might die, but some spirit pulled him through.

"Next came Shrieves with a shattered leg but in good humor. 'You're not going to have to cut it off, are you Doc?' he asked anxiously. 'I don't know, old man,' Harry replied. 'I'll do all I can to save it.' This was just small talk because Harry knew it was hopeless. 'I'll keep my fingers crossed, Doc,' and as Shrieves went under from the anesthesia, his fingers were still crossed in a futile gesture. They remained crossed throughout the operation. His leg had to be amputated.

"The next man on the operating table was L.A. Martin. He was on a morphine jag, and in spite of his multiple wounds, was singing out his name 'L-A-A-A Martin.' He had a shattered left leg, injuries around his head and chest and ominous shrapnel holes in his abdomen. We got to work on his leg first.

"Doc and I were smoking one cigarette after another throughout this time. He was doing a masterpiece of first aid surgery—not a slack or hesitant motion throughout the ordeal. He was fighting hard for the lives of our shipmates. There was one incident which caused him to stop temporarily. He spilled some alcohol on the front of his shorts and it flowed down to his crotch. He howled with pain and danced around until he washed it off. Everyone laughed at him at the most unfunny time of our lives.

"Red Spaulding was brought in next. He was in such bad shape that Doc held him until almost last. Red was one of the most unforgettable men in my life. He was a red-headed, freckle-faced kid that I had known since he came aboard as an apprentice seaman. He was courteous and hard working with a personality that made me want to run him as I would a plebe at the Academy. There was no doubt that I liked him and he liked me. I had personally given him his semaphore and blinker tests a couple of months before when he was going up for his rate of coxswain. A little coaching and he made it in a breeze.

When we had begun carrying men from the wardroom back to sick bay for surgery, Red had remarked, 'I wonder why they don't take me now?' After a few moments he said, 'Well, I guess those other fellows need it worse than I do.' Although he was being given large amounts of plasma, he didn't realize the real reason was his case was hopeless. When he was stretched out on the operating room table, he was still conscious and in good humor. At that moment depth charges were dropped on a submarine. The ship shook as the charges blasted away.[30] It was unexpected, and since we were jittery from our recent surface action, I was afraid it would disturb Red. To reassure him I remarked, 'We're just kicking hell out of their submarines now. Just routine. Nothing to worry about.' He might well have been trying to calm me when he replied, 'Sure, Mac. We'll get 'em the same way we did last night.' We passed a few more remarks. When I was trying to inject morphine into his arm, he said, 'That arm is a tough one, Mac.' I agreed. 'Just like iron, Red. When old Doc Nyce gets through fixing you up, you'll be like a new man, Red.' 'I hope so, Mac.' The anesthesia took effect and Red passed out with a faint smile on his lips. It was the last thing he ever said."

Some time during the period when Perry Hall was fighting the fires and Tom McWhorter was assisting Harry Nyce, I received permission to come topside and help with the wounded. It was gruesomely incredible. It was difficult to maintain my footing with the deck awash with blood and human parts. The salvo which hit above my head had wiped out the torpedo crew. A few inches lower, and I and everyone else in the after engine room would have been among the casualties.

George Jackson, the chief torpedoman, a kindly, competent man, was dead. Next to him was Smitty, a 17 year old who had volunteered for Navy duty. Smitty's station was in the forward part of the ship. He had become frightened and sought out the chief. If he had stayed at his station, he would have survived.

All around the horizon were burning ships. It looked like Dante's description of hell. I saw a stretcher bearer heading for the stern. "Can I help?" I asked. "There's a wounded fellow on top of No. 3 gun. We'll probably need help in getting him down." I followed and heard someone crying in pain. I climbed up on the gun mount and recognized Huger, a 19 year old from Charleston, SC. We had talked about the

"Holy City" on several occasions. His right leg was shattered and was loosely attached to his body. He had shrapnel wounds all over and was bleeding profusely. "Just hang in there, Huger. We're going to get you to the doctor. He'll get you fixed up. It's going to hurt getting you down. Yell if you feel like it." We got him to the main deck with difficulty, put him on the stretcher and carried him to the passageway by the wardroom. The dining table was being used to dress wounds and treat those patients that didn't require surgery. Harry Nyce came by occasionally to check the new patients.[31] After examining Huger, he took me aside and said, "He's lost too much blood. The little plasma we have is for the men I can help. Just keep him comfortable. Here's a styrette of morphine." It was my first exposure to triage. I was shocked! Passing judgment on who lived or died! Barbaric!

My attitude changed later when I went to sick bay and watched as Doc Nyce calmly and competently put another mangled body back together. I suddenly realized neither he, nor hundreds of his colleagues around the world, had asked for the awesome responsibility of deciding how their limited resources should be used. How ironic, I thought. The whole world is going up in flames. In this hell hole, everyone is trying to kill everyone else. In their midst, this guy is trying to repair the damage the rest are doing. Truly amazing and inspiring. For the first time I knew what I wanted to do if I got back home in one piece.

Surrounded by the dead, dying and wounded, there was no joy in learning. The Third Battle of Savo Island was described as the most furious naval engagement since Jutland, when major war vessels slugged it out toe to toe. In summing it, up CinCPac said, "This action was a turning point in the Solomon's campaign. Had the powerful enemy fleet succeeded in its mission, the task of preventing a major enemy attack and landing large-scale reinforcements would have been difficult if not impossible. The well-directed fire and courage of our personnel merit the highest praise."

Cominch said, "This desperately fought action, the Third Battle of Savo, is believed to have few parallels in naval history. We have come to expect and count on complete courage in battle from our officers and men of the US Navy. But here in this engagement, we have displayed, for lasting respect and admiration, cool and eager gallantry that is above praise. These splendid ships and determined men won a great victory against heavy odds. Had this battle not been fought and won, our hold on Guadalcanal would have been gravely endangered." In speaking of the Sterett's part in this action, Cominch said, "The Sterett appears to have had a grasp of the situation and to have taken advantage of every opportunity. She appears to have done a magnificent job. She was fought boldly and with determination."

ComSoPac cited the actions as "another splendid example of the fighting spirit of our destroyer force. Only after all offensive armament, except forward 5" guns, were put out of action, and being completely ablaze, did the Sterett retire. Fire control and damage control are considered outstanding."

The Sterett received the Presidential Unit Citation which stated: "For extraordinary heroism against a Japanese Task Force on the night of November 12-13, 1942. Fighting boldly, the Sterett successfully engaged 3 Japanese vessels at close range, scoring numerous hits on a light cruiser; fired a full salvo of torpedoes to cause large explosions and assist in sinking a battleship with 2 torpedoes and two 5" salvos; exploded and sank destroyer 1,000 yards on starboard bow...A gallant fighting ship superbly handled by her officers and men..."

Neither I, nor over 50% of the crew, could testify to the accuracy of those statements. Physically, we had been present, but had seen nothing, only the ghastly results. From my standpoint and that of my shipmates, we hadn't won. Admiral Hiroaki Abe had lost. Several of his ships had been hit, but only 2 of his destroyers had been sunk, with one battleship mortally damaged. There had been nothing to prevent him from carrying out his shore bombardment and landing reinforcements.[32]

Many medals were awarded. Captain Coward received the Navy Cross. Four men received the silver star and 13 the purple heart. When we later heard that Admirals Callahan and Norman Scott had been decorated, Herbie exclaimed, "For what? Stupidity? Sure they were competent, decent guys, but they made one snafu after another. We were in the wrong formation. All of our guns and torpedo tubes couldn't bear on the Japs. The Fletcher and Barton, with the most modern SC radar, should have been leading the formation. Callahan should have been on the Helena. The San Francisco had only SC radar which was of no help. He was confused and didn't know what the Japs were doing. Why in the hell did he delay giving the order to commence firing until the Japs sighted us? We could have blasted them out of the water before they opened fire. If he had lived, he should have been court martialed."

Tom, rubbing his chin, said, "The moral to this story is: sometimes you get awards, not for merit, but for dying at the right time and the right place."

-

CHAPTER 6

The Horror Of War; The Joy Of Home

When the sun rose on Friday, 13 November, 1942, only the dead slept. Wardroom country was a hospital. In every bunk lay the amputees, together with other mangled and burned bodies. Men were putting the dead in canvas bags. I overhead one remarking, "I don't know who the hell these pieces belong to." The response came quickly, "Don't worry about it. God knows and that's what counts."

Temporary repairs were made to our TBS. The Captain knew from overhearing conversations that some of our ships were afloat and heading south. At 0615, the Sterett took station in the screen with the Helena, San Francisco, Juneau, Fletcher and O'Bannon. Jeffrey exclaimed, "My God! Only five ships left out of thirteen. It's incredible."

Only the Fletcher was unscathed. The others were damaged and filled with dead and wounded. Captain Hoover of the Helena was the Senior Officer Present Afloat (SOPA). Only after all hands on the Sterett were mustered at 0825 did I learn the names of the 28 dead, 4 missing, 13 seriously wounded and 8 with minor injuries.

We learned that planes from Henderson Field sank the Hiei. The Portland was towed into Tulagi Harbor for repairs. Although the Atlanta and Aaron were not salvageable, many men were rescued.[33]

At 1101 while I was standing outside the radio shack trying to read a message being sent by blinker light from the Juneau, the Japanese sub I-26 fired a spread of torpedoes. One hit a magazine on the port side. In horror I watched as the Juneau disintegrated and disappeared in one big, black pillar of smoke. Believing the Task Group was under air attack, I dived into the radio shack. When I got the courage to look again, 600 men and officers were dead, including the five Sullivan brothers. They were serving on the same ship so they could look after each other.[34] [35] A B-17 in the vicinity was requested to notify Admiral Halsey of the sinking and send a rescue team. Due to a snafu this was not done.[36]

I was in the wardroom when a radioman came in and asked, "Guess what the news headline is?"

"Peace has been declared," I responded.

"Nope. Henry Kaiser is turning out one Liberty ship every seven days."

Herbie exclaimed, "He better make that five or six at the rate we're losing them."

Throughout the day, bodies were identified and sown up in canvas bags with a 5" shell as a sinker. At 1700 the PA boomed, "Now hear this! All hands not on duty, muster on the fantail." The flag was at half mast. The bodies of the dead were stacked up by No. 4 gun. The Captain faced aft with the crew lined up on either side. Two men held a plank of wood hanging over the stern as a body was placed on it. Four others were holding the American flag over the body.

The Captain began reading: "God is our refuge and strength, a very present help in trouble. Therefore will we not fear, though the earth do change, and though the mountains be shaken into the heart of the seas. He will be our guide even unto death. If God is for us, who is against us? He who did not spare his Son, but gave him up for all of us, will he not also give us all things? For I am sure that neither death, nor life, nor things present, nor things to come, nor powers, nor height, nor depth, nor anything else in all creation, will be able to separate us from the love of God in Christ Jesus our Lord."

The Captain then said, "Let us bow our heads in prayer. O God, whose days are without end, and whose mercies are not numbered, make us, we beseech thee, deeply sensible of the shortness and uncertainty of human life, and let Thy Holy Spirit lead us in holiness and righteousness all our days. Oh God, we pray thee that the memory of our comrade, George R. Jackson, may be ever sacred in our hearts, that the sacrifice he has offered for our country's cause may be acceptable in Thy sight, and that an entrance into Thine eternal peace may, by Thy pardoning grace, be open unto him, through Jesus Christ our Lord, Amen."

The Captain said, "All hands will stand at attention and salute as the body is released into the sea."

"Unto Almighty God we commend the soul of our brother George Jackson, departed, and we commit his body to the deep, in the sure and certain hope of the resurrection unto eternal life, through our Lord, Jesus Christ."[37]

Coward repeated the Committal and Benediction for each of the 28 men. With the propellers churning at 15 knots, there was barely an audible splash as the bodies entered the water. There was no expression on the face of anyone. We each looked like a robot, with eyes staring blankly at the body. We were physically and emotionally exhausted. We now knew war was personal and hell.

That night the dispatches described the severe bombardment Mikawa was giving the Marines. There was no sleep for them. I crawled up on the after deck house, with a life jacket as a pillow, and dozed and ignored the tropical showers .

Saturday 14 November was a beautiful day in the South Pacific: puffy, white clouds and a 6-knot breeze. The formation limped into the harbor of Espiritu Santo and at 1635, the Sterett was moored to the tanker Tappahannock. At 1800 our most severely injured men were transferred to the base hospital. The news reported that General Rommel's Africa Corps was shattered and retreating. Hitler was sending in reinforcements.

Tom McWhorter said, "Search planes discovered Mikawa's ships at 0700 this morning, 150 miles up the slot. Fighters and dive bombers attacked. Two cruisers were damaged. They attacked again at 0950 and two other cruisers and a destroyer were hit. They found Admiral Tanaka's reinforcement group with the transports, and struck at 1150 with torpedo planes and dive bombers. Another group attacked with B-17's from Espiritu and everybody claimed hits."

"So where was Kincaid all this time?" Cal asked.

"Because he was out of range, he flew some of his planes from the Enterprise to Henderson Field, and they joined in the fray. 7 transports were sunk with troops and supplies. Tanaka had his destroyers take off as many men as they could from the burning ships. Tanaka still has 4 transports afloat and 11 destroyers. Kondo is up north with a helluva force, so the action is not yet over."

The next morning we moored to the Tangier, a destroyer tender. Coward said, "Get your essential repairs done. We're going down to Noumea, and a decision will be made as to whether we go to the States or Pearl."

At 1100 the other wounded were transferred to the hospital ship Solace. They were in high spirits and taunted their shipmates: "The war is over for us."

"Get a Jap for me." "I'll think of you guys while drinking and entertaining the girls." The bantering continued, but each of us knew they would carry the scars for the rest of their lives.

Afterward in the wardroom, I asked Tom what was going on up North.

"There was one helluva battle last night. Admiral Lee was waiting to intercept Admiral Kondo's bombardment group, which consisted of the battleship Kirshima, 2 heavy cruisers, 2 light cruisers and 8 destroyers. Lee had no battle plan. The Walke, Gwin, Benham and Preston were in the lead. Two of Kondo's destroyers and one cruiser attacked them before being seen. By 2335, Lee's destroyers were out of action without inflicting any damage. Admiral Lee had so many targets on his radar screen, he didn't know which one to take under fire. All power was lost on the South Dakota, and Captain Gatch became confused. He didn't know where Lee was and turned into Kondo's path. He was illuminated by searchlights, and shells plowed into the South Dakota's superstructure, causing numerous fires and casualties. With radar and TBS destroyed, Captain Gatch retired at full speed."

"So what was Lee doing all this time?"

"He began firing on the Kirshima and hit her repeatedly with 16" and 5" salvos. In a few minutes she was burning and out of the fight. Admiral Tanaka retired to the north. Lee, knowing from his radar that there would be no troops landing that night, also retired."

"What happened this morning?" Shirley asked.

"Two battleships and a couple of destroyers were sunk; other ships were damaged. The 4 transports which had been beached were bombed and strafed unmercifully."

"So who won?"

The Captain came in and said, "We achieved our objective of holding Henderson Field. The Japs landed only a few troops and little food and supplies. We dominated the air. The Japs are going to think twice before coming down here again. I believe we're going on the offensive."

The news was full of the great battles fought at "Cactus." Some stories were accurate, others pure propaganda to boost the morale of the American people.

When Herbie, Tom and I went on liberty, we took beer, found a vacant spot on the beach and got soused.

The news reported that General Patton had captured Casablanca and French Morocco. Admiral Jean Darlan had been appointed Governor of French North Africa.

On 18 November the Sterett was enroute to Noumea. On three occasions, submarine contacts were made and depth charges dropped. Results were unknown.

President Roosevelt announced to the American people, "It would seem that the turning point of this war has been finally reached."

Tom exclaimed, "Tell that to the Marines up at 'Sleepless Hollow'".

Gould added, "Vandergrift and the 1st Marine Division are getting a well- deserved rest. They are under-strength and most of the men have malaria. General Alexander Patch is taking over with the US Army X1V Corps and the 5th Marine Division."

On 20 November the Sterett moored to the USS Whitney in Noumea. The next day at 1415, the PA boomed, "Now hear this! All hands will stand at attention when Vice-Admiral William F. Halsey,

Commander of the South Pacific Forces, and members of his staff come aboard to inspect the battle damage."

When Halsey was leaving at 1430, Shirley said, "That has to be the quickest inspection on record."

Hugh Sanders, Herbie and I went on liberty at 1600 and relaxed at the Cafe de Paris bar. Digger, now attached to Halsey's staff, was surrounded by men. I listened in. "Our blokes have been doing terrific—bang-up job. They've kept Ken on Guadalcanal warned of every ship and plane heading down the slot. Paul Mason and Jack Read have been playing hide and seek with the Japs on Bougainville. They alerted you blokes when that large bunch of Navy ships headed down the slot on the 12th of November. There are still several priests, nuns and planters who need evacuating."

"Any plans to pick up your friends?"

"Nope. They are there for the duration."

We found a table with friends from other ships and exchanged stories. Each had a gruesome tale to tell.

After repairs were completed on 24 November, the Sterett got underway for Pearl Harbor with Task Group 66.7, consisting of the San Francisco, Mahan and Connyham. The talk was of home, family and girl friends. At breakfast the Captain said, "No decision has been made about whether we'll get repaired at Pearl or San Francisco."

The news reported that the President had signed a bill authorizing the drafting of 18 and 19 year olds. More importantly, the Russians were on the offensive and had trapped a couple hundred thousand Germans in Stalingrad.

The entry in the Deck Log on 27 November at 1400 noted: "Sighted Samoan Islands, bearing 030 degrees, distance 27 miles." The only other entries made were: "Lighted ship.....observed sunset .....Darkened ship.....No remarks..... steaming as before." There was one exception: At 0819 on 30 November, "Crossed equator at longitude 163-49.3 west."

MacArthur's troops had taken the offensive at Port Moresby. The jungle and starvation were defeating the Japs.

The talk in the wardroom concerned the news head line: "487 killed in fire at the Coconut Grove Night Club in Boston." Herbie said, "I've been there. It's a nice place, but I can understand why it went up in flames. It was decorated with colored paper."

"I stuck my head in the door when we were in Boston, but spent most of my time watching Tassel Gertie in Scully Square," I said.

The days passed uneventfully until 1 December, when Tom reported, "There was a tremendous fight at Guadalcanal on the night of

30 November. Admiral Tanaka came down the slot with 8 destroyers loaded with supplies and troops. Admiral Carlton Wright, with 5 cruisers and 6 destroyers, intercepted him, with the Fletcher leading the van. Tanaka passed west of Savo preparing to release floating drums of food and supplies. Radar alerted Wright of the Japanese ships and Tanaka was unaware of Wright's presence until all 11 ships commenced firing. It was a wild melee. From what I can understand, the Japs let fly with torpedoes which hit the Minneapolis, the New Orleans, the Pensacola and the Northampton. At 0130 Tanaka retired up the slot."

"Those Japanese torpedoes always hit something. Sounds like a repeat of our fiasco," Shirley remarked.

"You're right," Tom replied. "The Battle of Tassafronga was a victory for the Japanese. They lost only one destroyer. On the other hand, their starving troops didn't get the food they needed. Even with radar giving us an early warning, we can't seem to get our act together."

At breakfast 3 December, I announced, "Fellers, this is my 22nd birthday and I'm buying the drinks."

"Are you sure you can afford them?" Herbie asked.

"Nothing is too good for you guys. My offer expires at midnight."

It was a good thing. The next morning at 0742, the Sterett arrived at the entrance to Pearl Harbor. As the Task Force passed through the narrow entrance, I recognized the docks on the port side known as "battleship row".

Admiral Nimitz, anticipating our arrival, ordered the crews and officers of every ship in the harbor to be topside in dress whites and salute us as we passed. Upon seeing this, Captain Coward came on the PA: "This is the Captain speaking. All hands not on watch, muster on the forecastle and fantail. You are to stand at attention and acknowledge the salutes from the ships as we pass."

What a sight! I was overwhelmed with the emotional impact. I had never experienced anything like this in my life. On the large ships, bands were playing the "Star Spangled Banner" and "Anchor's Aweigh". We were heroes! It was a thrill that defies description.[38]

At 1000 the Sterett was anchored. I heard the men clapping when the first provisions received on board were 20 gallons of ice cream. Herbie, Shirley and I left on liberty at 1600. After we had caught a taxi, we quickly discovered that Honolulu was a small town and street cars provided the primary transportation.

Waikiki was a disappointment. The only hotels were the Royal Hawaiian, which the Navy used as a rest and recreation habitat for the submariners, and the Moana, with a huge Banyan tree in the front courtyard. Between them was the Waikiki Outrigger Beach and Canoe Club, a private club for wealthy Hawaiians. The beach was narrow compared to SC beaches, and the coral sand difficult to walk on. However, Diamond Head was an impressive sight. The water was a rich blue, but too chilly for a southern boy. These failings were offset by the warm and friendly natives. The enchanting lilt of Hawaiian music was everywhere. We had dinner at the Moana. Joining friends at the bar afterwards, we shared experiences. Curfew was at 2300, and our celebration was short.

At lunch the next day, there were smiles when the Captain announced, "We are heading for San Francisco. Pearl can't handle our repairs. That should make the crew happy. The married men can have their wives come out."

My eyes moistened when I sighted the Golden Gate Bridge at midday on 11 December. It represented what the war was all about: home, friends and family. I thought, "Just like the Statue of Liberty in New York harbor."

The San Francisco moored downtown where the city could throw out the welcome mat, while the Sterett sneaked up to Mare Island Navy Yard at Vallejo, California. One-third of the crew and officers were getting 20 days leave. At 1530 I left the ship with Cal and Herbie and boarded a Navy transport plane for Washington, DC. There was no heat, and the bucket seats felt like we were sitting on a block of ice. Running up and down the aisle was the only way to keep warm. Herbie left in Pittsburgh, and the weather roughened. Everyone got airsick except a Navy nurse, Cal and me.

Cal transferred in Washington, DC, to a flight for Winston-Salem, NC. I went to the American Airlines ticket counter to get a flight into Columbia, SC. The pretty reservations agent said, "We had a cute girl working here who was from Columbia. She was personable and liked by everybody. Her sister has leukemia, and with two brothers in the service, her mother needed her at home. She had a thick southern accent and we called her 'Little Miss Magnolia Blossom'."

"Do you remember her name?"

"Lil Hair."

"Small world. I dated her several times and will probably see her when I get home."

"Give her my regards and tell her we miss her."

The flight down was uneventful. My parents met me in their newly acquired car.

The next day while I was in Melhman's Music Store on Main Street, I heard a familiar voice call out, "Harold! What are you doing home?

It's good to see you." Looking around, I exclaimed, "Well, if it isn't Little Miss Magnolia Blossom. How is Myrtie doing?"

"You must have visited American Airlines in Washington."

"I did, and they send their regards."

"Myrtie's doing about as good as can be expected. I am working at the ration board. Interesting work, but frustrating. The bigwigs always think they're entitled to more gas than anyone else. You're authorized an extra allotment while you're on leave. If you need any help, let me know. How long are you going to be home?"

"I have 20 days leave and I want to go to Charleston to visit my grandparents. I might need some extra gas."

"That's no problem. Come by anytime and I'll fix you up."

"I'll give you a ring and see if we can get together."

As I was leaving, I wondered if she was still going steady with Carroll Crouch, who was on a destroyer overseas. Dating her behind his back would be cheating.

With the Christmas season in full swing, there were parties and dances. Bing Crosby's rendition of "White Christmas" was heard everywhere, as well as Frank Loesser's "Praise the Lord and Pass the Ammunition". The popular movies were "The Maltese Falcon" with Humphrey Bogart and "The Man Who Came to Dinner" with Betty Davis and Monty Wooley. The front page of "The State" newspaper carried a picture and write up on the USS San Francisco and its exploits. Another told of Admiral Darlan's assassination and his replacement by General Giraud. The romance of Mickey Rooney and Ava Gardner, and Cary Grant with Barbara Hutton were the gossip items of the day.

I went to the ration board and Lil greeted me saying, "I was planning to call and ask you to be my date for the Spinster's Christmas Dance.[39] There'll be lotsa people you'll be happy to see. Some of our new members are Pat Salley, Betsy Walker, Francis Sawyer and Edith Bateman."

"I'd love to. What is the day?"

"Christmas night at the Columbia Hotel, ten until two. Melvin Hemphill is playing."

"Sounds like fun to me. Do I need to rent a formal outfit, or will my uniform do?"

"Whatever suits you will be all right."

Detecting a slight hesitancy, I quickly responded, "You're the secretary. I'm going to dress up in white tie and tails. I'll give you a ring when I get back from Charleston."

My blond bombshell in Charleston greeted me with a big smile and kiss. She was smart and knew what appealed to men. She was good company and I enjoyed being with her.

I asked her, "How about a date for the Citadel's Christmas Hop on 17 December? Tommy Dorsey is playing."

"I'd love to, but I have a prior commitment."

I went alone. I knew the chairman of the Hop Committee, who could get me in without a ticket. Greeting me with a smile, he said, "It's good to see you, Harold. I wish I could get you in, but it's against the rules. If I do it for you, I'll have to do it for everybody. I sure am sorry. Glad you're doing OK."

"You SOB," I thought. "Where do you get off with that crap?"

Ralph Bagnal overheard the conversation, and as soon as we were alone he exclaimed, "He's a bastard. I'll get you a ticket. Wait here."

He did. I had a wonderful time dancing cheek to cheek with beautiful girls and Tommy Dorsey's music. I sang and hummed the songs "When the Lights Go on Again All Over the World", "That Old Black Magic", "You'd Be so Nice to Come Home To" and others. Visiting with friends who would be heading overseas within the next year was exciting. When Tommy struck up his theme song, "I'm Getting Sentimental Over You", I knew the end was at hand. To the girl in my arms I said, "I can't believe it's over, but 'we'll meet again, don't know where, don't know when'...."[40]

On Christmas night I pinned a corsage on Lil's dress. She looked beautiful. The officers led the Grand March, and walking around the ball room with her on my arm was like old times. I was once again in college. I knew many of the girls and their dates. There was no war.

As I said goodnight on the corner of Laurens and Senate Sts., I gave Lil a brief embrace, a chaste kiss and promised to keep in touch. I thought, "I sure wish you weren't spoken for by a friend."

I had long talks with my father about the war and learned of the adjustments civilians had made. Most consumable goods such as tin, metal and paper were collected and recycled. Tuesdays and Fridays were meatless days. The work week was 48 hours. The speed limit was 35 miles/hr. Almost everything was rationed: butter, 4 oz/week and meat, 28 oz/week. I now understood the motto I'd seen: "Use it up, wear it out, make it do or do without."

Time ran out. I had no plane reservations. Flying standby, I was successful in getting flights to Chicago, St. Louis, Denver and into Los Angeles, where I had a layover on New Year's Eve. I found a room at the Beverly Hills Hotel in Hollywood, and discovered a big, lavish party in progress with many celebrities. One man in a white tie and tails said, "Lieutenant, you look lost. Join us and celebrate the New Year. We'd love to have you."

"You're very kind, but I'm dead tired. I've been flying cross-country for what seems like an eternity. I'd be lousy company. Thanks for the invitation and my best wishes to you and your friends for a Happy New Year."

In the morning paper I read that Frank Sinatra, a skinny 27 year old crooner, had opened at the Paramount Theater in New York. Thousands of squealing, fainting, entranced teenagers had turned out and crowned him King.

Reporting aboard the Sterett at 1600, I saw many new faces and several of the old ones were missing. Welcoming me, the Captain said, "The Bureau has approved your request to change your designator to DE-VG USNR. You will be on the regular watch list underway and in port."

"That's great. Now I can qualify for a command."

On 5 January I was sorry to see Tom McWhorter leave after receiving orders to new construction.

On liberty days I went into San Francisco and stopped first at either the Top of the Mark Hopkins Hotel or the Fairmont, which was across the street. Always I'd find friends and girls.

On 8 January I left the ship as officer in charge of the shore patrol, a first for me. The exec had said, "You have only one responsibility: keep the peace. How you do it is up to you." Lucky me, I thought. A contingent of Marines from Guadalcanal has just arrived. They'll be ready to have fun, which meant raising hell! Like breaking a few jaws and busting up some furniture. I had a potentially explosive problem which I'd better defuse quickly. My petty officers were big and experienced. As I explained my game plan to them, they agreed it was worth a try.

Going into the first bar, I yelled, "Fellers! Listen to me for a minute. You guys want to have a good time. You're entitled to it. I know you've just gotten back from Guadalcanal and you've been through hell. Me, too. I was there on August 7 and was there until my ship got shot up on the night of 12 November. I don't want the responsibility of keeping the peace, but I was ordered to do it. I'd much rather be drinking with you. Get out of line and you're going to end up in the brig. Let's make a pact! Get as drunk as you want. Raise hell! Don't start fights with civilians and don't destroy private property. Look after each other. If you see one of your buddies is getting out of line, slip him a mickey, put him in a cab and send him back to the base. I don't want to see any of you in the brig in the morning. Enjoy yourselves."

I visited every bar and made the same pitch. Something worked. I was real proud of the Marines. Only a couple passed out and had to be taken to the brig for their own safety. I returned to the Sterett at 0330.

There was little sleep to be had. Rosie the Riveter didn't respect the time of day. She banged away throughout the night. In addition there were the fumes from the paint scrapers, the hammers and acetylene torches.

In the morning the men were gathered in groups sharing their experiences. I listened in. Hayes, a machinist mate, said, "Those Marines were telling some wild stories. One was talking about how the graves were marked with wooden crosses and the Star of David. Mess kits were used as plaques with the names of the dead scratched on them. One said, 'Cpl. C.H. Meglin killed in action 8/20, one swell guy. God Bless him.'"

"You guys must have had a great time with the Marines," I interjected. "Did you learn anything else?"

"Yes, sir. For those guys, Guadalcanal is not a place. It represents anger, hate, despair, frustration and, above all, they felt deserted by family, friends and country. The nightly bombardment, the naval battles with the skies filled with exploding shells, the Banzai charges. Always there was the overpowering stench of the jungle. Clothes soaked with sweat, rain or swamps; little food or fresh water. In addition they had to contend with dysentery, malaria and jungle rot. The epitaph on the grave of Pvt. First Class Cameron, buried at Lunga Point, expressed the feelings of every one:

> And when he goes to Heaven
> To Saint Peter he will tell
> Another Marine reporting, sir.
> I've served my time in hell.[41]

There was silence and then, "I was right there and I can't begin to comprehend or empathize. You won't hear any more bitching from me unless I don't find a date tonight."

The San Francisco Chronicle reported that the British were advancing in North Africa and closing in on Tripoli. The RAF and US 8th Airforce were successfully bombing German industrial cities. General Eichelberger had captured Buna. For me it was occurring on another planet.

One morning Herbie asked me, "Where did you get lost last night?"

"I had a fantastic time. A community group was performing Verdi's "La Traviata". The cast were friends of everyone in the audience. When the opera ended, everyone went up on the stage and had a party, with wine and great food. I was treated like a member of the family. One of the best times I've had in Frisco."

Throughout our stay, new crew members kept reporting aboard. At 1300 on 18 January, Frank Gould relieved Cmdr. J.C. Coward as Commanding Officer of the Sterett. Upon hearing this, Herbie remarked, "He's a known quantity, a nice guy and a competent officer. I'm even happier that Calhoun has been made executive officer."

Roosevelt and Churchill were meeting in Casablanca from 13-24 January. Stalin couldn't leave Russia, and sent his regrets. They reaffirmed their agreement that the war would not end until Germany, Japan and Italy surrendered unconditionally, which prevented them from making peace with one of the Allies and not all. The US agreed to a Mediterranean operation in '43 and a Normandy landing in '44. The British agreed to let the US run the war in the Pacific if it didn't interfere with its European commitments. They agreed to these objectives:

(1) Continue operation "Watch Tower" up from Guadalcanal and New Guinea until Rabual was taken and the Bismarck's Barrier was broken.
(2) Advance westward toward Truk and Guam.
(3) Make Aleutians secure.
(4) Advance along New Guinea-Mindanao axis as far as Timor.
(5) Recapture Burma.

On 28 January the Sterett conducted dockside trials. There was excitement over the new radar systems. Cal said, "With the new SG radar, there'll be no problems navigating at night in the islands. It'll pick up a taxi cab at 20 miles."

"And how about the Fire Control radar?" Jeffrey added. "It'll pick up a gnat on the water at 10 miles."

"Just remember one thing," Gould said. "None of that stuff is any better than the man operating it. Get your men trained so we can get the best results possible from all of this high tech equipment."

On 29 January Admiral Doenitz succeeded Rader as Commander-in-Chief of the German navy. Believing the Allies knew the locations of his submarines by radar rather than suspecting his codes were being broken, he began concentrating his U-boats on the loaded eastbound traffic rather than the empty westbound shipping.

We rejoiced on learning that General Patch had radioed Admiral Halsey on 9 February, "Total and complete defeat of Japanese forces on Guadalcanal effected 1625 today. Tokyo Express no longer has a terminus on the island."

From 2 February through 7 February under the cover of darkness, the destroyers of the Tokyo Express had successfully evacuated over 11,000 troops. General Patch was unaware of it until his men found only empty boats and abandoned supplies at Cape Esperance. Admiral Nimitz praised the Japs, "Only skill in keeping their plans disguised and

bold celerity in carrying them out enabled the Japanese to withdraw the remnants of the Guadalcanal garrison."
The total losses would never be accurately known. Iron Bottom Sound was covered with the remnants of 24 Japanese naval vessels and a like number of our own.

On 10 February Ensigns O.L. Griffin, Robert Hightower and Dan Poor reported aboard for duty. At 1650 the Sterett was underway for Pearl Harbor. I looked out from the after engine room as the Sterett passed under the Golden Gate Bridge. I thought, "Which of us will never see it again? Will I be one?"

On the trip to Pearl there were daily drills. For the engineers, some were exercises in futility. If a shell ruptured a main steam line, there was only one thing any of us could do—pray. With the temperature of the steam at 850 degrees and the pressure at 600 lbs. per square inch, no one would survive.

On 15 February the Sterett was moored at Pearl Harbor. For the next week, gunnery practice on sleeves pulled by planes and targets pulled by tugs was conducted. Shore bombardment was practiced on Kahoolawee, an island inhabited only by goats. The Captain remarked, "How those goats survive this bombardment I'll never understand."

Cal responded, "From what I hear, they're multiplying. Our aim must not be too good."

On 21 February the Sterett was underway for the South Pacific. Orders, which made no sense to anyone, were that we were not permitted to write anything in the Deck Log except "steaming as before" or "no remarks". There was one exception. At 1900 24 February, Davy Jones and his court came aboard. The next morning at 0940, the log noted, "Hoisted Admiral Davy Jones Flag. Began initiation of Polliwogs. 1115 Executed Admiral Davy Jones Flag." 25 February: "Completed initiation of Pollywogs."

On 2 March the Sterett was moored in Noumea, New Caledonia. In the afternoon, Herbie, Shirley and I went to the Cafe du Paris. Digger was at the bar with a group of men. "The Japs have moved north and now have an airfield on Munda, 150 miles from Tulagi. MacKenzie sent Dick Horton to New Georgia, where he has an excellent view of the airfield. Others have moved to get a better view of the ship and plane movements in the slot."

"What happened to the priests, nuns and planters who wouldn't leave?" Herbie asked.

"After a couple of planters had their heads cut off, they yelled for help. Jack Read rounded everyone up from the outlying islands and put them in Tsipatavi, a little village in the mountains. On Christmas Eve the Japs were close by. Amazingly, Father de Klerk held midnight mass, with 400 people in the congregation at his mission church. The Japs were closing in, but this didn't stop the carol singing on Christmas day."

"Where the hell was the rescue team?" I asked.

Digger scratched his head and said, "MacKenzie didn't think it proper to ask Halsey for help, but Father Lebel and Bishop Wade, an American, were given the okay to send a message: 'Urgently request immediate evacuation of American women from Bougainville stop Fear repetition of crimes on Guadalcanal stop Teop and Tinputz Harbors safe and convenient stop eternally grateful. Wade' He got immediate action. The submarine Nautilus arrived off Teop Harbor on New Year's Eve night. On 1 January the Nautilus submerged, carrying 17 women, nuns and wives of plantation owners, 3 children, together with 2 priests, 5 planters and one Austrian. A message came in from SoPac, 'Congratulations, Nautilus. You were just ahead of the Sheriff. Jap destroyer entered Teop Harbor shortly after you left.' The journey to Tulagi was uneventful, and they were put on board a schooner for Noumea."

"Is there anybody else up there needing to get out?"

"There's a couple of priests and nuns who should, but God has told them to stay and that is what they're going to do.[42] Our guys will be there for the duration."

On 11 March the Sterett was anchored in Tulagi Harbor. Gould met with ComTaskForce 61. After he returned, he called a meeting of the officers and said, "The Japanese are sending in reinforcements to the central and northern Solomon's. Air fields have been built on Munda and planes are being ferried into the fields at Buin and Kahili on Bouganville. Togo is determined to make us pay dearly for any advance to the north."

"What are we doing?" Herbie asked.

"We're building a new landing field in the Russell Islands, 60 miles west of Tulagi. We're going to be escorting supply ships and amphibious craft to the Russell's."

On 20 March, sonar reported a submarine contact. General Quarters was sounded. Russell said, "The Captain is on an attack course." He paused and exclaimed, "The exec has told the skipper that a twin engine aircraft is over taking us." I could feel the "thump" as the depth charges were fired. At the same time Russell yelled, "A stick of bombs just exploded in our wake about 100 yards astern. No one knows how that guy missed us."

Later in the wardroom, Jeff said, "With all of these new gadgets, Fire Control and SG radar, I don't understand how a plane sneaked in that close without being detected."

"Gadgets have their weaknesses and it proves the Japs can strike without warning," Gould responded.

The Tokyo Express continued to send in troops and supplies. Jack Mason and other coastwatchers reported a massive buildup of air strength by Yamamoto on Buka, Kahali and Balale. In the Atlantic the Allies lost 315,000 tons of shipping in February and 540,000 tons in March.

On 7 April the Sterett was patrolling off Lunga Point while several troop transports unloaded. Learning about this from his scout planes, Yamamoto ordered 67 bombers and 110 fighters to attack. Adequate warning was given by the coastwatchers, and 76 fighters were scrambled from Henderson Field.

I was OOD when the Japs arrived. Gould came to the bridge and asked what was going on. "The Japs are bombing Henderson Field and some of them have peeled off to attack our formation." He ran from one side of the bridge to the other getting oriented. Planes from Henderson Field intercepted the Japs, and one helluva dog fight was taking place. We could see burning planes falling and parachutes floating in the sky.

"We'd better pick up some of those fellers, don't you think?"

"No, sir. Our primary responsibility is to protect our transports. There's plenty of people on the island who can pick them up. They're in no danger."

Herbie relieved me and I went to my battle station. Russell said, "Bridge reports Japanese planes are all over the sky. They're diving on ships in the anchorage. One has been hit and is smoking badly. Several planes are heading toward our formation. We've knocked one down. One is coming up our port side. Bombs are exploding close aboard. Several men have received shrapnel wounds."

Going topside after the battle, I saw Harry Nyce probing a wound under Cal's arm. He said, "You've severed the radial nerve and you're going to need a neurosurgeon to repair it. This is going to take several months of rehabilitation and the States is the place for you to get treatment." Cal found it difficult to believe such a small wound was going to take that much treatment.

Our Task Force headed south and on 10 April, the Sterett was fueling at Espiritu Santo. I was summoned to the Captain's cabin. Captain Gould greeted me with a smile, "Look what I just received." I read the dispatch with amazement. It said in effect that I was being ordered back to the States for new construction. BuPers would give me the details after I reported to the nearest Naval District on the west coast.

"Somebody has made a mistake," I exclaimed. "Hugh Sanders should be getting transferred to new construction. He's not going to be happy when he hears this."

"Forget it," Gould replied. "Get yourself packed. We're going back to Guadalcanal and you'd better be off this ship when we weigh anchor."

The word got around quickly and my cabin filled with shipmates. All had various tasks for me: call this one, mail this letter, have a drink for me. It was with mixed emotions that I picked up my orders. I liked, trusted and felt comfortable with my shipmates. On a new ship I'd be having to prove myself one more time.

At 1200 I saluted the flag and the OOD saying, "Request permission to leave the ship."

"Permission granted and good luck. We'll keep the war going until you get back."

Cal, Harry Nyce and Tiny Hanna got in the Captain's Gig with me. At the dock, I wished Cal a speedy and complete recovery.[43] At mid-afternoon I reported on board the Mormachawk, a troop transport carrying combat- fatigued Marines to the states for R&R. I was pleased to discover Lt. Bill Davis, a classmate of mine at the University of SC, now a B-17 pilot. His plane had been shot down and he was returning to the states for R&R.

The ship was heavenly. I had a large private stateroom. Being able to sun on deck with a balmy breeze and the gentle roll of the blue Pacific was a dream come true. For reasons unclear, I had a copy of Tolstoy's novel "War and Peace." If fame related to length, this book qualified.

While I was reading on 20 April, the communications officer excitedly came up and said, "Admiral Yamamoto has been killed. Mitscher's fliers ambushed him. Several of his key staff members were shot down as they were landing at Kahili airfield at Buin."

"This is going to change the plans of the Japs. He was highly respected by Nimitz and the others," I responded. Later I learned that intelligence discovered that Yamamoto was leaving Rabual at 1100 on 18 April to boost morale and inspect bases in the upper Solomon's. Mitscher sent 16 Lightnings from Henderson Field to intercept him. They arrived over Buin at 1135, just as Yamamoto's planes were approaching land. Surprise was complete. The Admiral's plane crashed into the jungle and his chief of staff's into the sea.

After Yamamoto's death, the Emperor appointed Admiral Minlichi Koga Commander in Chief of Combined Fleets. He ordered the Japanese garrisons stationed in the Bismarck Archipelago to delay the Allied offensive. A Japanese leader later said, "The southwest area was changed from a crucial battle front to a holding front by decision of Imperial Headquarters."

While the Japanese were making these momentous decisions, I continued with "War and Peace". It took 6,000 miles and almost 3 weeks to finish it. On the morning of 2 May, I again saw one of the most beautiful sights in the world: the Golden Gate Bridge.

CHAPTER 7

The Dortch: Commissioning and Shake-Down Cruise

Settling into my room at the St. Francis Hotel, I made a few phone calls and then visited with friends at the Top of the Mark Hopkins. The next morning the duty officer at the Twelfth Naval District Headquarters said, as he endorsed my orders, "Check in daily."

That afternoon at a bar, I saw a group of officers huddled around a civilian. He was saying, "This is a real picture. A friend got a copy from the photographer who took it while Carmen Miranda was dancing. It wasn't until she swirled her skirt that everyone realized she had on no underwear." I verified that when the picture reached me. For the next while, the discussion revolved about Carmen, her well-displayed attributes and how they would like to test her abilities to use them. "She is a real 'Brazilian Bombshell'. I understand why she's been wowing them at the Waldorf Astoria Hotel in New York. Bet they'd like to see her as we do," someone remarked.

July 1943—Chief Engineer USS Dortch DD 670.

The next day my orders instructed me to report to the Kearny, NJ, Shipyard for duty as engineering officer on the Dortch DD670. I was authorized 15 days leave. My flight home was uneventful. When I walked through the terminal at Owens Field, I was surprised to see Lil Hair. "What in the world are you doing here? I thought you were with the ration board."

Laughing, she replied, "I could ask you the same thing. I got fed up with the bureaucracy. It was a losing battle, and I really enjoy working with the airlines. In a small station like this, I sometimes act as radio operator and give the pilots instructions. Once when a stewardess got sick, I substituted on a flight to Charleston. Never a dull moment."

"How's Myrtie doing?"

"We're keeping her comfortable, but it's just a matter of time."

USS Dortch DD 670

"I'm sorry to hear that. I've got two weeks leave before reporting to my new assignment. I'll try to get by and see you."

When I arrived home, my brother Herbert greeted me saying, "You'll be happy to learn I've joined the Navy as an apprentice seaman."

"Why in the hell did you do that? You must be off your rocker."

"I was going to be drafted and I didn't care to be a private in the Army."

"With your college credits, you're eligible for Officer Candidate School. Why didn't you apply?"

He had no appropriate answer. Two days later we were in the district recruiting office in Charleston. The Chief Petty officer on duty looked at me like I was crazy when I said, "The Navy can't use my brother effectively as a seaman. With his college credits, he's eligible for Officer Candidate School. The Army has a far greater need for officers than enlisted men. He signed those papers under duress. Let's just tear them up and forget it."

Taking off his hat and scratching his head, the Chief said, "Sir, your brother has already signed up. I can't get those papers back. It's not possible."

"Chief, nothing is impossible for you guys. My brother's knowledge and ability would be wasted as an enlisted man. The services need competent officers."

Commissioning of USS Dortch—author second on left

Mumbling, he replied, "I've never done anything like this before, but I'll try."

"Thanks. You won't regret it."

Herbert was accepted into Officer Candidate School.

My mother told me about life on the home front. "Like all housewives, I collect rubber, metal and paper for recycling. Kitchen fats can be exchanged for ration points. Everyone receives 28 ounces of meat per week, 4 ounces of butter and 4 pounds of cheese. Each of us is allowed 3 pairs of shoes per year. Sneakers can't be bought because of the rubber shortage."

"From now on I won't be complaining about shipboard chow. I'm living high on the hog. I've a better understanding of the billboard sign:

STAMP OUT
Black markets with your ration stamps
Pay no more than legal prices."

I dated Ann, whom I had known in college. She was a beauty and fun to be with. She lived close by in an apartment with two of her classmates. We saw "The Phantom of the Opera " starring Nelson Eddy and Claude Rains and "For Whom the Bells Toll" starring Gary Cooper and Ingrid Bergman. Sometimes we went dancing with friends. I spent more time at her apartment than I did at my home. We liked the same type of people, the same foods, the same music, had similar aspirations, and liked each other. I took her to visit my family. I was tempted to ask her to marry me, but we agreed the future was too uncertain to make a commitment. The closest I came was saying, "I hope you'll be around when I come home." We exchanged pictures.

I didn't see Lil, but I talked with her on the phone. I heard she was engaged to a high school beau.[44]

I talked with my father and told him I'd like to study medicine after the war. I asked him to get the application forms from the Medical College in Charleston and fill them in. He said he'd be happy to. I knew that he, as a frustrated doctor-to-be, was pleased. He was enrolled in Medical School when his National Guard unit was activated due to a border dispute with Mexico. Upon his return, his anatomy professor insisted he repeat the freshman year. He refused, and although he never admitted it, I knew he had regretted this decision all of his life.

On 11 May General Alexander notified Churchill, "We are master of the North African shore". Roosevelt and Churchill agreed that the channel crossing would have to be delayed until May 1944, angering Stalin. The bombing of Germany would continue around the clock, the RAF at night and the US during the daytime.

There was an uprising by the Jews in Warsaw due to hunger and persecution. Although they fought desperately, the Warsaw Ghetto was razed and all resistance ended on 16 May with the death of 56,000 Jews.

Time ran out on my leave, and on 29 May, I was settled in my room at the Astor Hotel in New York City. I found friends at the bar, who urged me to see "Oklahoma" with Alfred Drake and Celeste Holm. They declared that it was the best show ever to hit Broadway. "I don't know Rogers and Hammerstein's music.[45] There are others I'd rather see," I replied.

I quickly discovered that New York had changed. With the dim out, it was no longer the Great White Way. The brilliant multicolored neon signs were gone. There was a 20% amusement tax. This didn't bother anyone, since cocktails were only 25-50 cents and show tickets $4. Tuesdays and Fridays were meatless days even in the most exclusive restaurants.

The Stage Door Canteen had opened in an old theater on 44th St., giving enlisted men a place to relax. Bette Davis, Greer Garson, Ethel Merman, Gene Kelly, Ronald Coleman and others could be found entertaining them on any given night.

When I reported in at the Brooklyn Navy Yard, I was told to sit tight until my orders arrived. I called my old girlfriend Martie and said, "This is your former beau, Harold Jervey. I've got tickets for the 'Ziegfield Follies' tonight. How about joining me?"

"I'd love to." The show was wonderful and afterwards we stopped by the Stork Club for a night cap. Sitting at his table by the door was Walter Winchell, one of the most widely read gossip columnists in the country. At other tables were celebrities we recognized.

German submarines were having a field day with our shipping in the North Atlantic. 12 ships were sunk in one convoy in early May, with only two U-boats in return.

The exciting news from the Pacific was the landing of US Troops on Attu on 11 May and the securing of the island on 30 May.

On 4 June the duty officer said, "You're being assigned two weeks duty on the Kimberly for indoctrination on the engineering plant of a 2100-ton destroyer." I moved to the Henry Hudson Hotel by Central Park which had weekly rates. This gave me more spending money. My days were spent on the Kimberly. In off hours it was difficult to decide whether to join friends at the Astor bar, attend a show or go dancing with a date. Occasionally I went to Radio City Music Hall to see the Rockettes or to a USO-sponsored dance at a hotel. I saw Ethel Barrymore, the first lady of the theater, in "The Corn is Green" and was enchanted with her acting.

On 14 June I was ordered to report to the Dortch at Kearney, New Jersey. Arriving by bus, I found the Dortch and introduced myself to the skipper, Lt. Cmdr. R.C. Young. He was 6 ft., slender, blond-haired, with a reddish glow to his face. This was his first destroyer command. The executive officer, Lt. Ed Gibson, was of medium build. Both were academy graduates, married and living in apartments. I was the combat veteran of the group.

I met Ensign Phil Williams,[46] a handsome, black-haired Harvard graduate, who said, "I've located a 3-bedroom apartment at 166 East 66th Street. It's in an excellent location, only a couple of blocks from the subway and the Barbison Hotel,[47] where you can always find cute girls. Charles Sedwich has already signed on. Are you interested?"

"Sounds like a winner to me. When is it available?"

"As soon as you're ready." I moved in that afternoon.

During the day I familiarized myself with the engineering plant, my men and the other officers. One was Rocky Rothschild, 1st lieutenant, from North Adams, Mass., married with one child. He was always bitching about the paper work and Young kept telling him to put it into writing and he'd forward it to Admiral King.

Returning to the apartment in the afternoon, Charles, Phil and I usually relaxed before going out. "What do you guys think of Bonita Granville's quote?" Charles asked.

"What did she say?"

" 'I know how easy it is for a girl to be tempted to forsake her chastity, especially in these times when human life is so uncertain, especially if the boy is in uniform. Our salvation lies within us, in a hard-boiled code of wartime morals.' How do you like them apples?"

"I hope the girls I date either disagree or can't read," Phil exclaimed.

On Sunday I usually went to The Cathedral of St. John the Divine at 112th St. and Amsterdam Ave., the largest gothic church in the world, or to Trinity Church at the foot of Broadway and Wall Sts.

One night while Reed Boyd, a close friend from SC, was visiting and having his eye prosthesis checked, we were on the Astor roof listening to Harry James. He was engaged to Betty Grable, who was voted the armed forces No. 1 pin-up girl, a blue-eyed, curvaceous blonde. A commotion was heard in the back of the room, and all heads turned in that direction.

"What's that all about?" I asked. Reed stood up and said, "Somebody important must be arriving. Well, what do you know! It's Betty Grable herself. How nice of her! She must have known I was here on a visit." Threading her way through the crowd and speaking to various people, we were delighted when she sat at the table adjacent to ours. "Miss sex symbol herself. She is one beautiful doll. And what a figure!" Reed exclaimed. The rest of the night was spent ogling her and humming as Dick Haynes sang "Fools Rush In", "The Nearness of You", "You Made Me Love You" and others. Reed expressed my feelings, "I don't know what she sees in Harry James. Either one of us would be a better catch."

Deciding where to go at night was difficult. Count Basie was at the Blue Room in the Hotel Lincoln, Les Brown and his Band of Renown in the Green Room of the Edison Hotel, with Doris Day singing such hits as "Sentimental Journey", and Xavier Cugat on the Starlight Roof in the Waldorf Astoria.

"A Stairway To the Stars" will always remind me of the Gaiety Theater, the premier Burlesque theater in New York. At the closing, the statuesque show girls with fancy head dresses, flowing, flimsy, colorful garments, a "G" string and bare, large, perfectly formed breasts, would slither up the stairs, which reached to the heavens, singing "We'll build a stairway to the stars..." Unforgettable.

Reality returned in the morning. The news from North Africa was encouraging. On 11 June British Troops landed on Pantelleria, an island between Tunisia and Sicily. The garrison of 11,000 Italians surrendered without firing a shot. This gave the Allies airfields from which to support the invasion of Sicily.

I kept in touch with my family and Ann. Heading out one Saturday, I exclaimed, "I just hope Ann is having as good a time as I am. These USO dances bring out the prettiest and smartest girls from Wellesley, Vassar, Sarah Lawrence and all colleges in between. If anyone calls, I'm at the Waldorf Astoria." The dance floor was crowded. I cut in on a well-built, pretty brunette and said, "You ought to be in show business."

"How did you guess?"

"Those flashing eyes and that warm smile."

"For the moment I'm unemployed. I played one of the leads in 'Babes in Toyland'. I'm trying out for a couple of parts now."

"That's one of my favorite Victor Herbert operettas."

It was mental telepathy. The orchestra began playing "Toyland." As we danced cheek to cheek I began singing and she quickly joined in:

"Toyland, Joyland, little girl and boy land,

Once you've left its borders,

You can never return again."

I got goose bumps.[48]

On another occasion the girl in my arms exclaimed, after hearing my name, "Are you any kin to Professor Huger Jervey? He's the Dean at Columbia Law School and his classes are the most popular on the campus."

"I've heard of him. He's from Charleston, SC. We're probably cousins of some sort."

"Give him a ring. He'd like to see you."

"On advice of legal counsel, I will."

When I called Professor Jervey and identified myself, he insisted I join him for supper. Two nights later I was at his Eastside apartment. He was of medium build, a nice looking man of indeterminate age. His maid and man servant cleaned his apartment and prepared and served his meals. After listening to my background, he decided we were 5th cousins.

He said, "I was Professor of Greek at Sewanee for several years and enjoyed teaching, but I needed more of a challenge. I wanted to be of greater service to my fellow man and turned to law. I have thoroughly enjoyed it, plenty of excitement and very rewarding."[49] It was a memorable visit and I promised to keep in touch.[50]

On 20 June the Dortch was christened by Miss Mary Clare Dortch, daughter of the late Captain Isaac Foote Dortch, who had distinguished himself in anti-submarine warfare in World War I. Our sister ship, the USS Gatling, was christened a few minutes later. Captain Young remarked, "It's incredible! It only took four months to build these ships."

I quickly came to know Lt.(jg) John Burt, gunnery officer, married from New York City, and Lt.(jg) John Gommengenger, communication officer, single from Rochester, NY, both Academy graduates. My assistant engineering officer was Lt.(jg) Robert Dickey, E-V(G), from Pennsylvania and single. Lt.(jg) Claire Wible, from Pennsylvania and married, was the doctor. Lt.(jg) Carl Drake, assistant 1st Lieutenant, married, was from St. Paul, Minn.[51] The others I got to know during the next several weeks.

The Dortch moved to the Brooklyn Navy Yard, where our days were spent assembling machinery, obtaining spare parts and putting together the basic records necessary to maintain the ship while operating for sustained periods in the Western Pacific.

On 20 June General Walter Kruger of the US 6th Army set up his headquarters at Milne Bay, New Guinea. From here he could control land operations through out the Southwest Pacific. Halsey issued orders for landings on New Georgia in the Solomon's.

While I rested at the apartment, I read Wendell Wilkie's "One World", a runaway best seller. In it he expressed his hopes for the post-war world. I enjoyed "Victory Through Airpower" by Alexander deSeversky, which advocated winning the war by precision bombing. Both "Guadalcanal Diary" by Richard Tregaskis and William White's "They Were Expendable" took me back to the Solomon's, which I wanted to forget. I much preferred Ilka Chase's "Past Imperfect."

The ads in the subways amused me:

"Pass the Ammunition
Oldsmobile workers have been doing it for nearly two years.
Backing up our fighting men with volume production of fire-power."

Or:

"Well—Shut my Mouth
I shut my mouth on a Kleenex tissue
To give my lipstick that neat, natural look.
These days it's a crime to stain a towel."

The 21 Club had a sign over the bar: "Be courteous to our help; customers, we can always get."

One night I stopped by the Astor Bar before going to the Metropolitan Opera, where Lawrence Melchior was singing the lead in "Lohengrin". I was introduced to Enid Butler, a pretty brunette. She couldn't understand my going to the opera alone.

"It'll be over by eleven o'clock," I said.

"And what am I suppose to do until then?"

"Go to a movie and I will meet you back here."

This suited. I was entranced with the performance. The audience stopped the production several times with prolonged clapping and loud bravos .

I met Enid at the bar. After a drink, we went to the Stork Club where we joined friends, danced and ogled the celebrities, among whom was Maureen O'Hara.

On 28 June I was ordered to Boiler School at the Philadelphia Navy Yard. My residence became the Bellview Stratford Hotel.

In the Pacific the Marines were landing at Segi Point on the southern tip of New Georgia and to the north, landing in the Trobiand Islands. Bombers flew in looking for transports. They found only Admiral Kelly Turner's flag ship, the Wacky Mac. One torpedo flooded the engine room. He shifted his flag to the Farenholt and the crew was transferred to the McCalla. That night torpedoes hit the McCawley sending her to the bottom.

The next morning Lt. Cmdr. Robert B. Kelly[52], arriving at Rendova with his PT Boats, reported the sinking of an enemy transport in Blanche Channel. He misidentified the Wacky Mac to be Japanese. After this disaster, all PT boats were placed directly under Admiral Turner's command.

I attended USO dances and listened to the Philadelphia Symphony under the stars at the Robin O'Dell Theater. Sarah Gist invited me to her palatial home in the suburbs. I enjoyed the meal and meeting her parents.

Marines landed at Munda, New Georgia, on 3 July. On the nights of 5/6 July, Admiral Ainsworth, with the Helena, Honolulu, St. Louis and accompanying destroyers, picked up the Tokyo Express by radar shortly after midnight. Commence firing was not given until after Japanese lookouts had spotted his ships and surprise was lost. In the melee the Japanese destroyer Niizuki was sunk. Torpedoes hit the Helena blowing off her bow and sending her to the bottom. The battle was over within the hour and the Japanese landed troops at Vila.

When I returned to New York on 10 July, the news reported that US and British troops were invading Sicily and the landings had gone well.

There were new faces at the dances. Gloria Crosswell, a statuesque brunette, became my steady. She lived with her parents on Park Avenue and introduced me to a new group of people.

The New York Times ran a story on the Battle of Kolombangara the night of 12/13 July. Admiral Ainsworth had little success intercepting the Tokyo Express at Vila Gulf. The Japanese succeeded in landing reinforcements, sinking the Qwin and seriously damaging the Honolulu and St. Louis. Admiral Izaki's flagship, the Jintzu, was sunk. I exclaimed to

Dickey, "We don't learn. The order to commence firing is never given until the Japs see us. Our torpedoes run erratically and if they hit, they don't explode."

The British and General George Patton were on the offensive in Sicily. With the Allies bombing Rome, Mussolini's spirits were sagging. When Patton reached Palermo on 23 July, the Fascist Grand Council was losing confidence in him. On 25 July Mussolini was arrested and King Victor Emanuel asked Marshall Pietro Badoglio to form a new government. Hitler sent German troops into Northern Italy to rescue Mussolini.

Life for the crew changed at 1206 on 7 August when Admiral Monroe Kelly, the Commandant of the Brooklyn Navy Yard, placed the Dortch in commission. I moved aboard and the apartment on East 66th St. was closed.

When Gommengenger came into the wardroom the next morning, he exclaimed, "I've got a friend at Headquarters. Listen to this dispatch, "ComDesDiv 12 with DesDiv 15...depart Tulagi 1230 August 6. Proceed to Vella Gulf south of Russell's and Rendova, to arrive Gizo Strait 2200 and make sweep of Gulf. If no enemy contact made by 0200, return down slot. Kelly's PT boats will operate in southern Kula Gulf..."

"So what happened? The Sterett and the Stack are in DesDiv 15."

"This was the first time destroyers had a chance to go it alone. The Japs came down the slot with 4 destroyers loaded with troop reinforcements. Our ships were in two columns and picked up the Japs at 2342. The Japs were surprised when torpedoes hit the Hagikaze and Arashi. Both ships burst into flames and were knocked out of action."

"There was no gun firing?" I asked.

"Not at first. As soon as the Jap ships exploded, the sky lit up like New Year's Eve. The Kawakaze was hit with several salvos. The Stack fired a spread of 4 torpedoes, and one more Japanese destroyer went down. The remarkable part is, we didn't have a single casualty! There's going to be some celebrating when they get back to Tulagi."

"Reports I've seen say the Japs lost over 1,500 men. Many were in the water and the stupid jackasses refused to be rescued," Gommengenger added.

With the Germans retreating from Sicily on 12 August and the Italian government declaring Rome an open city, they sent General Castellano to Madrid to meet the British Ambassador and discuss terms of surrender.

On 19 August, the news reported that the Eighth USAAF met with disaster on a raid of ball-bearing manufacturing plants in Schweinfurt and Regensburg, Germany. 60 out of 376 bombers were shot down. The high command considered switching to nighttime bombing.

Sir Arthur Harris attacked Berlin on the nights of August 23/25 with 719 planes and lost 57. During the next 3 nights, 127 were lost. This was too great a price and he decided to concentrate on other targets.

In Europe General Castellani was told that the Allies would accept only unconditional surrender. The news also reported that New Georgia in the Pacific had been cleared of all Japanese and they were now concentrating their efforts on Bougainville.

The Dortch moved to Boston, and on 27 August all guns were test-fired.

"You guys ought to go up on deck and relax. You're at ole Cape Cod Bay surrounded by history. To the southwest is the light house at the end of the island, and to the northwest is Pilgrim Monument where the Pilgrims first landed," Gibson said.

"I'll drink to that," Rocky responded.

There was no chance for drinking. The Dortch was soon underway, arriving at Casco Bay, Maine, on 29 August. For the next week, gunnery exercises were conducted. The Captain held mast for 13 men absent over leave for varying periods of time. Punishments varied from summary and deck court martials to extra duty hours.

On 3 September the Italian government signed an armistice and the invasion of Italy began at the Strait of Messina.

At breakfast Young said, "You'll be happy to know that our shakedown will continue in Bermuda. Chief, you are designated tour guide. It ought to be old home week for you."

On 4 September the Dortch anchored in Hamilton Harbor, Bermuda. For the next ten days I enjoyed showing my shipmates the island and renewing friendships. Each morning, the Dortch was underway, conducting antisubmarine exercises with the USS Young, Cogswell and submarine R-9, and usually returned by 1600.

The Pacific strategy was changing. Rabual was to be by-passed and MacArthur, with assistance from Halsey, was to continue clearing the New Guinea coast. Nimitz was to begin an island-hopping operation, ending with landings in the Philippines. Air bases were to be established in southern China, from which Japan could be dominated and her supply lines strangled.

The news reported that a USAAF raid on Stuttgart, Germany, lost only 45 bombers. Accompanied by P-38 fighters with a range of 450 miles and a nose turret in the B-17G, the pilots were regaining their confidence.

At dinner on 12 September the Captain said, "For reasons I can't explain, we've been ordered back to Casco Bay."

"We've been missed," Rocky exclaimed.

The news reported that Mussolini and his wife were rescued by the Germans and taken to Bavaria where Hitler was waiting. The fighting in Italy was fierce.

On 15 September the Dortch was anchored in Casco Bay, Maine, and conducted gunnery exercises for the next four days. On 20 September the Captain said, "Chief, today is your test of fire. We'll have a full-speed run at 35 knots, reverse throttle and crash astern."

"I'll be holding my breath. Every rivet in this ship is going to rattle when we go full astern."

At 0922 the Dortch had worked up to 27 knots when Sam, my phone operator, exclaimed, "Lubrication has been lost to the after main engine."

"Order them to shut down the engine. I'm coming back. Tell the Captain what has happened. I'll give him a status report as soon as I can." Angel, the chief machinist mate, greeted me saying, "The lub pump to the main engine stopped for several minutes. There's no way to tell if the bearings have been damaged without pulling off the casing, and we can't do that until the engine has cooled down."

With my face glistening with sweat, I went to the bridge to tell the Captain what had happened. He stared at me, stuck out his chin and, with a flushed face, bellowed, "What do you mean you can't start the engine? We're supposed to be conducting full power runs. What am I to do? Return to port and tell them I've got an engineering officer that's afraid to start the engine? If I order you to get it moving, you damn well will."

"Captain, with all due respect, you'll have to give that order directly to the men. I can't. Navy operating procedure states clearly that whenever lubrication is lost to an engine, the bearings must be inspected. If we screw up an engine, you can explain to the Admiral."

After a few moments' reflection, he relaxed and said, "You know what you're doing. I trust you. We'll return to port and you can explain what happened to the squadron commander." At 1325 the Dortch was anchored in Berth Item. Angel reported, "Those bearings were starting to wipe. If we hadn't secured the engine, we'd have been in serious trouble."

The Squadron Commander came aboard and I gave him a full report. He said, "You are to be commended on taking such decisive and proper action."

He told Young he was fortunate to have such a competent chief engineer. Later I remarked to Dickey, "I've learned a valuable lesson: do your homework and stand your ground."

On 21 September the Dortch was underway for New York, and two days later we moored in the Brooklyn Navy Yard. Our shake-down cruise had revealed several defects and repairs were needed. Rosy the Riveter, with many helpers, hammered during the day and night. I did paperwork.

A commissioning party for all hands was held in the Biltmore Hotel. There was excellent food, a good band and pretty girls. For the next week various exercises were conducted and all machinery was checked out.

We were happy to learn that the Japs had evacuated Kolombangara in the Solomon's and an airfield was now operational.

Talk in the wardroom was about plays seen during the summer. Everyone except me had been to "Oklahoma". Rocky said, "We'll be singing those songs for the rest of our lives."

"Not me," I said. "I'm going to be singing 'Golden Days' and 'Deep in My Heart' from Sigmund Romberg's 'Student Prince.' I won't forget Rudolph Freml's 'Vagabond King' and Franz Lehar's 'Merry Widow.'"

"I'll bet you didn't miss Gershwin's 'Porgy and Bess'," Rocky continued.

"Sure didn't. I didn't want to leave the theater. It was magnificent."

Everyone had a favorite, but all agreed that 15 year old Joan Caulfield was destined for stardom, and the best picture of the year would be "Casablanca" starring Humphrey Bogart and Ingrid Bergman.

The talk ceased when Ed said, "We're heading for Casco Bay in the morning, so it's sack time for me."

On 2 October the Dortch was anchored at Casco Bay. Carl Drake said at dinner, "The seaman who left under guard this afternoon was sentenced to solitary confinement on bread and water for 30 days. That's the most severe punishment I've heard of. He must have robbed the Captain of his family jewels."

For the next two weeks it was gunnery exercises, torpedo firings with submarine R-16 and battle problems with other ships. On 6 October the engineers were put to the test. At 1330 the Dortch reached maximum speed of 36 knots. Anxiously I awaited the signal. At 1426 it came: crash back, full speed astern. The ship shook like a dog shaking off fleas. In 61 seconds, the Dortch came to a full stop and started moving astern. I breathed a sigh of relief.

After we docked, I was summoned to the Captain's cabin. With some anxiety, I knocked. "Come in. I've got good news for you. This dispatch states: 'All Lt.(jg)'s with a date of rank of 1 October 1942 or earlier are eligible for promotion.' I consider you qualified and I'll have the yeoman get together the necessary papers."

The Dortch was ordered to Hampton Roads, Va. As we passed Buoy "CH," a tremor was felt throughout the ship. The bottom had scrapped on a submerged wreck and the sound dome gear was stripped, putting water in the dome. Repairs were made and the Dortch moored to Pier 2.

The Dortch was ordered to Trinidad and on 28 October, was moored to Pier #1 in Trinidad, BWI. The following morning the Captain conferred with the base commandant regarding our training schedule. In the afternoon Gommengenger and I left in search of dates. We discovered that US bases had girls from the States to fill the clerical billets. We found their barracks and arranged dates. The Trinidians were friendly and arranged guest privileges for the officers at some of their exclusive clubs.

The news reported that landings were made on Bougainville[53] at Cape Torokina, Empress Augusta Bay, under General Alexander Vandergrift. Since General Hyakutake's 17th Army was concentrated to the south, little opposition was encountered.

Gunnery exercises and plane guard duty were conducted with the Langley, who was on her shake-down cruise. Chief machinist mate Angel said, "Mr. Jervey, we've got a problem. With the temperature of the water in the 80's, our evaporator tubes are salting up and we're down to 300 gallons an hour. To scrape the salt off the tubes, we'll have to secure the evaporator for several hours. We're going to the South Pacific and the water temperature is not going to get any colder. To provide adequate water for the boilers, cooking, drinking and bathing, we need 500 gallons/hour. No one, including me, is going to be happy if we have to restrict water."

"So what do you propose?" I asked.

"A ship in the Navy Yard has jury rigged a starch injector on their evaporator. This has improved the efficiency markedly. Rather than pulling the tubes every few weeks, it's now several months between shut downs."

"Do you know how to do it?" I asked.

"Yes, sir."

"Requisition whatever you need and put it on the evaps."

On liberty days I usually went to a private club on the ocean, found a date, drank and danced. While on board, I read "A Tree Grows in Brooklyn" by Betty Smith, Ernie Pyle's "Here is Your War" and Marion Hargrove's "See Here, Private Hargrove."

One night the Captain invited the Commanding Officer of the Naval Base to be his guest for dinner. Ed Gibson, Gommengenger and I headed into town. The only transportation available was a bus. As we were leaving the ship, we saw the base commander's car and driver close by. Ed walked over and asked the driver if he was going to wait there all night for the Captain. He replied, "Them's my orders, sir."

"Do you have any idea what time he'll be finished?"

"He didn't say, but probably not before 11 o'clock."

"We need a ride into town and I am sure he won't mind if you take us in. He told me he'd help us any way he could. You'll be back long before he needs you."

Scratching his head he replied, "I jus don know whether I should or not."

"Of course you should. I'll be responsible. We'll pay you well and your boss will be pleased that you helped us."

We did the town. Time was forgotten and we didn't get back to the ship until after midnight. The petty officer of the watch exclaimed, "The Captain wants to see you in the wardroom immediately." We were soused, but had an overdose of the guilts. As we arrived in the wardroom, the base commander looked us over and said to the Captain as he stalked out, "Give me a report on your findings and how you handle them." We mumbled our reasons for our irresponsible behavior in an irrational way. The Captain's face flushed as he bellowed, "All of you ought to be put in hack. How the hell can I run a ship if my executive officer, communications officer and chief engineer are confined to their staterooms? You embarrassed the hell out of me! Just get out of my sight. I'll concoct a reasonable story to give to the base commander."

Dr. Claire Wible said to us, "I can fix you up if you've got other troubles. Sulfathiazole is doing a remarkable job curing gonorrhea and chancroid."

Gommengenger responded, "You're not going to get a chance to see if it works 'cause we weren't exposed."

On 15 November the Dortch was underway for Delaware Bay, in company with the Gatling and Langley. Various drills were conducted enroute. The news reported that the Battle of Berlin had begun. Over 400 planes attacked the city and a similar number bombed Mannheim and Ludwigshafen.

After we moored to a dock at Norfolk, Va., on 19 November, Angel said, "I've got the starch rigged to the evaporators. It's going to be the answer to the water problem."

In the Pacific, landings were made on Tarawa and Makin Islands. The fighting was fierce and the islands were secured on 23 November.

On 26 November I was awakened by a violent tremor which shook the entire ship. Michaelsen reported, "We've ruptured the sound dome and it's back into the dry-dock."

Gommengenger exclaimed, "We're well-off compared to our friends in the Solomon's. On the nights of 24/25 November, Captain Arleigh Burke, with 5 US destroyers, was ordered to destroy any enemy he had contacted."

"So what's unusual about that?" Gibson asked.

"Captain Yamashiro, with 5 destroyers, was heading south to evacuate troops at Buka. Burke's group made radar contact after midnight. His destroyers attacked, and torpedoes were launched from 6,000 yards. Several Japanese ships were sunk. None of our ships were lost and there were no casualties."

"Sounds like we're finally learning from our past mistakes. It's going to be an unforgettable Thanksgiving Day for those men," Gibson added.[54]

On 30 November the Dortch was in dry-dock #6 for repairs to the sound dome. The next morning a dispatch was received from ComDesLant: "Prepare all ships for extended sea voyage. Check spare parts and report findings." I called McHenry, who was in charge, and said, "Mac, take whatever men you need and check out the spare parts. There's not going to be a spare parts store on every South Pacific island. Do it quickly and let me know the results."

"I've been checking for the past two weeks. I'm almost finished," he replied. At 1700, McHenry, with hat in hand, showed up at my stateroom and sheepishly said, "All spare parts are accounted for except the rotor for the main feed pump."

"Are you certain? The Captain will have to report this to the ComDesLant and this might delay the sailing of our Task Force."

"I'm positive it's not on board."

I reported to the Captain who passed it on to the Admiral. His dispatch followed immediately, ordering us to search more diligently. It had to be on board. I showed McHenry the dispatch. "The Admiral believes the rotor is on board. Go through those boxes with a fine tooth comb." The next morning he was back. "We've looked all over. The rotor is not on board." Within hours, a dispatch was received from the Bureau of Engineering, Washington, DC. It read: "We have reasons to believe the rotor is on board. Check spare part box #35 on port bulkhead of after engine room. Report findings." I had a feeling I was in trouble. Summoning McHenry, I asked, "Did you look in this box?"

"I certainly did," he said emphatically.

"Well, you and I are going to take a trip to the after engine room." Crawling down the ladder, he had two men pull box #35 off the bulkhead. As I opened it and reached in, I pulled out a familiar part. "What would you say this is, McHenry? You sure as hell didn't look in here. If you did, you were too damn stupid to recognize it." I knew I shared the blame. I should have personally checked after the second dispatch. I would have to confess my guilt and let the chips fall where they may. The Captain reported the finding. Quickly, the response came: "Investigate matter thoroughly. Report action taken to me."

I told Gibson and the Captain I was responsible. Later Gibson said, "The Captain knows you aren't personally to blame. Tell him who is and you'll be off the hook."

"Sorry, Ed, I can't do that. The blame is mine. I should have personally checked and I didn't. Tell the Captain I appreciate his concern. I'll accept whatever punishment he considers appropriate." I received a letter of reprimand which was put in my permanent record.[55] It hurt, but in the long run, it paid off in a positive way. The crew knew who was responsible. Now they realized I would stand by them even if I were penalized. From that time on, they worked their butts off and sang my praises.

There was the usual transfer of personnel and on 2 December, the Dortch was moored at Pier #3 NOB, Norfolk. In the wardroom Rocky announced, "Our shake-down cruise is over and it's back to the war."

"For me this has been a shake-up cruise. Reports I've seen say our friends in the South Pacific have done well with out us," I responded.

The news reported that the Teheran (Eureka) conference with Stalin, Churchill and Roosevelt had started on 28 November and concluded 1 December. Each one agreed to "Overlord" occurring in May 1944, with concurrent landings in the south of France. Stalin would mount an offensive on the eastern front to prevent the Germans from switching troops to the west. He also agreed to join in the fight against Japan as soon as Germany was defeated. How the democracies would work with the dictatorship government of Russia in the postwar world was not mentioned. This proved to be a grave mistake.

For the first time in 3 months, when the crew mustered at quarters, there were no absentees. At 1414 the Dortch was enroute to Panama with the Gatling, Haradan and Intrepid.

UNITED STATES SHIP _DORTCH (DD670)_ _____   _31_   _October_   , 19 _43_
                                             (Day)   (Date)   (Month)

ADMINISTRATIVE REMARKS

Robert C. Young, Lieut-Comdr., USN, Commanding
    Mrs. Robert C. Young, wife, 7009 E. Sea Side Walk, Long Beach, Calif.
    Sandra Elaine Young, daughter, age 4½ yrs., same as above.

Edward Isham Gibson, Lieutenant, USN, Executive Officer
    Mrs. Betty Barco Gibson, wife, 2534 Flamingo Drive, Miami Beach, Fla.

Robert Isaac Rothschild, Lieutenant, D-V(G), USNR, First Lieutenant
    Mrs. Mary Alice Rothschild, wife, 49 Ashland Street, North Adams, Mass.
    Barbara Anne Rothschild, daughter, age 1 yr., same as above.

Harold Edward Jervey, Jr., Lieutenant, DE-V(G), USNR, Engineer Officer
    Mrs. Harold E. Jervey, mother, 2906 Duncan Street, Columbia, S.C.

John Andrew Gommengenger, Lieutenant, USN, Communication Officer
    Mr. Roman W. Gommengenger, father, 63 Holcroft Road, Rochester, N.Y.

John Haugh Burt, Lieutenant, USN, Gunnery Officer
    Mrs. Mary L. Burt, wife, 155 E. 52nd Street, New York, N.Y.

Robert Ross Dickey, Lieutenant(jg), E-V(G), USNR, Asst. Engineer Officer
    Mr. John O. Dickey, father, Friedens, Pennsylvania.

Austin Lee Detweiler, Lieutenant(jg), USN, Asst. Gunnery Officer.
    Mr. Milan H. Detweiler, father, 201 S. Main Street, Zeigler, Ill.

Carl Bigelow Drake, Jr., Lieutenant(jg), D-V(G), USNR, Asst. First Lieutenant
    Mrs. Frances Louise Drake, wife, #2 Lambert Road, Belmont, Mass.

Gerald Eugene Wise, Lieutenant(jg), D-V(S), USNR, M.G. & Recognition Officer
    Mrs. Frieda M. Wise, wife, 3226 W. Grace Street, Richmond, Virginia.

James Everett Campbell, Lieutenant(jg), D-V(S), USNR, Ship's Secretary
    Mrs. Dorothy L. Campbell, wife, 119 Joliet St., S.W., Washington, D.C.

John McLay, Jr., Ensign, E-V(G), USNR, Asst. Engineer Officer
    Mr. John McLay, father, Midland Avenue Wortendyke, N.J.

Orville Hamilton Roberts, Ensign, D-V(G), USNR, Torpedo Officer
    Mrs. Ora Lee Roberts, wife, 1690 Bodenger Bl'v'd., New Orleans, La.

Edward Earle Tietz, Ensign, D-V(G), USNR, Radar Officer
    Mr. Edward Earnest Tietz, father, 67 Alta Drive, Mt. Vernon, N.Y.

Phillip Lewis Williams, Ensign, D-V(G), USNR, Asst. First Lieutenant
    Mrs. Eugene J. Williams, mother, 2413 N. Bay Road, Miami Beach, Fla.

James Christian Michaelsen, Ensign, D-V(G), USNR, Sound Officer
    Mrs. Eloise Friestedt Michaelsen, wife, 108 S. Sycamore Ave., Lansing,Mich.

Charles Miller Robbins, Ensing, C-V(S), USNR, Asst. Communication Officer
    Mrs. Marguerite Cook Robbins, wife, 30 Pierce Street, Kingston, Pa.

Leon Douglas Netter, Jr., Ensign, D-V(G), USNR, Asst. Gunnery Officer
    Mr. Leon D. Netter, father, 21 Beechmont Avenue, Bronxville, N.Y.

Richard Milton Gray, Ensign, D-V(S), USNR, Asst. Communication officer
    Mrs. Josephine Herbert Gray, wife, Park street, Nacozdoches, Texas.
    Duke Herbert Gray, son, age 4 yrs., same as above.

Examined:

          E. I. GIBSON, Lieutenant, U.S. Navy,
                                        Navigator.

To be forwarded direct to the Bureau of Naval Personnel at the end of each month.

☆ U. S. GOVERNMENT PRINTING OFFICE : 1943   16—33079-1

UNITED STATES SHIP _DORTCH (DD670)_____   _31_ October_____ , 1943
                                              (Day) (Date)   (Month)

ADMINISTRATIVE REMARKS

Ross Moore Lockhart, Machinist, USN, Asst. Engineer Officer
    Mrs. Frieda Lockhart, wife, General Delivery, Cornville, Arizona.

James William Porter, III, Ensign, SC-V(G), USNR, Supply & Disbursing Officer
    Mrs. Elizabeth Walsh Porter, wife, 1846 Spruce Street, Berkeley, Calif.

Claire Edgar Wible, Lieutenant(jg), MC-V(G), USNR, Medical Officer
    Mrs. Sara Edna Wible, wife, 961 Davis Avenue, Northside, Pittsburgh, Pa.

Examined:

E. I. GIBBON, Lieutenant, U.S. Navy.
Navigator.

To be forwarded direct to the Bureau of Naval Personnel at the end of each month.

☆ U. S. GOVERNMENT PRINTING OFFICE : 1943   16—23079-1

Name	No.	Name	No.
MENARD, JJohn F,, BM.1c	299 91 07	MIKLOVICH, Gustave A., S.2c	807 49 47
MILLER, Elias W., S.2c	820 98 75	MILLS, Joseph C., S.2c	821 49 16
MINTER, Ray, S.1c	268 98 23	MIRANDA, John D.C., S.1c	375 65 83
MONTGOMERY, Owen E., MM.2c	238 57 87	MOORE, James "C", EM.2c	669 71 01
LOGAN,,Woodrow W., MM.1c	262 28 28	MORROW, Joseph F., S.2c	245 68 28
MOSKOWITZ, Samuel, S.2c	821 83 97	MOULTON, Clifford C., Y.1c	638 05 83
MULIGAN, Edward J., S.2c	249 92 34	MUMMA, Lewis W., S.2c	821 89 03
MURRAY, Raymond W., S.2c	810 66 90	NADIN, George T., F.2c	668 90 98
NAPOLITANO, Salvatore G., S1c	709 37 34	NIEZGODA, Stanley I., S.2c	249 92 37
NOWRY, Arthur E., S.2c	821 84 06	NUSS, John E., S.2c	249 82 63
O'BRIEN, Lester D., QM.3c	368 56 36	OLSON, Robert P., SoM.3c	851 37 67
OREO, Charles C., Jr., S.2c	817 56 89	OSHMAN, John, S.2c	821 13 92
OSIEJA, Eugene H., S.2c	245 68 37	PARENTE, Louis R., S.2c	646 72 20
PARKER, George L.O., CY	201 44 26	PEARRE, John A., CBM	267 82 43
PERRY, Novie L., WT.1c	274 24 00	PETKO, Andrew J., S.2c	821 89 13
PINASKY, John, EM.3c	285 09 45	PIZZO, Alfred F., S.2c	810 66 95
PLATT, Thomas M., F.1c	244 35 56	PLONA, Chester T., S.2c	821 00 36
PLOUCHER, John F., S.2c	817 59 84	POFFENBERGER, Frank J.,SC3c	612 35 78
POLSELLI, Benjamin, S.2c	823 56 84	POTTS, Roy G., TM.3c	621 42 77
PRESTON, Claude R., MM.1c	287 10 30	PRIOLA, Pasquale S., FC.3c(M	603 58 20
PULVER, Milford J., Jr., S.1c	312 90 05	RADICAN, Waino W., SK.3c	666 89 94
REBSTOCK, Christian J.C.,F1c	405 48 81	REBSAMEN, Cruitt B., SK.1c	630 01 09
REESE, Henry L., S.2c	249 82 68	REGER, Waldon C., S.1c	337 84 75
REILLY, Ward R., M.2c	279 75 89	REVELLA, James A., F.2c	238 67 99
RICE, "F" K., S.1c	608 54 34	RICHVALSKY, Michael, S.1c	402 78 74
RIDGE, Morton J., S.2c	205 45 28	RIDGE, Robert L., RM.3c	496 00 29
ROBER, Lawrence A., S.1c	810 58 84	ROBERTSON, Ralph C. Jr.,F3c	244 60 81
ROBILLARD, Roland F., RM.2c	607 11 00	ROBITAILLE, Wilfred H., S.1c	201 65 43
ROGERSON, Mack G., MM.1c	266 20 98	ROHLFING, Raymond W., CMM	336 32 50
ROSA, Christopher C., F.1c	400 54 93	ROSS, Dewey, S.1c	291 84 38
RUBIN, Morris L., S.1c	414 91 92	RUDOLPH, E., S.1c	305 37 97
SADDELL, Charles A., TMM.3c	651 42 40	SALTER, Edward M., S.2c	817 60 14
SAMMON, Roger B., MM.1c	403 02 87	SCHOFFSTALL, Luther Jr.,S2c	245 68 21
SAVINO, Salvatore Jr., S.2c	817 59 83	SEWARD, William T., F.1c	555 62 01
SCZESNIK, Stanley F., S.2c	810 59 10	SHAW, Thomas J., RM.2c	403 87 47
SHANNON, Robert B., SoM.3c	560 53 44	SIFFORD, Carl W., CPhM	261 88 82
SHEARS, Herbert M., EM.1c	560 12 50	SIRAGO, Domenic, TMM.3c	618 87 03
SIMS, Edward L., MM.1c	346 71 09	SLATTING, Robert J., S.2c	761 81 11
SKIPPER, George R., S.2c	245 68 33	SMITH, Harold T., S.2c	245 68 34
SLESS, Leonard J., S.2c	810 67 01	SMITH, Warren D., F.3c	342 43 48
SMITH, Joseph M., Ck.3c	725 12 07	SNYDER, Donald E., S.2c	819 12 92
SNEAD, Howard LaV., GM.1c	356 28 83	SPHAR, Charles F., F.1c	562 59 33
SPENCE, John W., S.1c	337 53 08	STEFANCIK, P., S.2c	821 84 32
STANFORD, Walter M., F.1c	625 49 33	STEPP, William A., M.1c	261 00 97
STELLRECHT, Earl R., S.1c	608 78 73	STEWART, George P., S.1c	244 00 73
STEVENS, Harold D., S.1c	329 04 62	STIDHAM, Harold W., F.1c	562 56 26
STEWART, John A., GM.3c	725 70 48	STOWERS, Millard McN.,FC1c(M	356 22 67
STONESIFER, Joseph E., Jr.S2c	249 82 65	SYLVIA, Alfred W., Jr., Y3c	202 44 83
SURDERSKI, John F., S.2c	817 60 27	THOMPSON, Calvin, StM.2c	826 86 14
THOMAS, John E., StM.2c	832 04 51	TRAYFORD, Edward, TMM.2c	647 16 40
TORREY, Creighton E., F.2c	640 35 09	TROTTER, Ernest J., S.2c	817 59 72
TRIDENTI, Ernest, S.2c	823 59 21	TURNER, William M., StM.2c	835 36 20
TUCKER, James C., StM.2c	832 04 53	VAN NAME, Robert V., S.2c	810 67 03
UNGER, Richard J., SoM.3c	710 53 90	WALSH, William E., S.2c	205 45 30
WALKER, Jacob D., StM.2c	830 12 07	WARE, Alex R., FC.3c	272 95 90
WALTER, Forest H., S.2c	249 82 67	WEBB, Oliver H., SM.3c	271 95 98
WATSON, Eugene F., S.2c	245 68 20	WELLS, Albert I., F.2c	600 92 23
WEINHOLD, Percy A., S.2c	245 68 32	WEST, Edgar H., S.1c 95 74	224 55 74
WESSON, Glen D., S.1c	311 39 23	WHITTEN, Maurice J., EM.3c	400 32 61
WHEELHOUSE, Franklin T.Jr.SoM3c	266 35 68	WILSON, William S. Jr.,S.1c	603 77 61
WILLIAMS, Joseph B., S.2c	821 00 29	WOOD, Earl S., S.2c	810 58 93
WITTIC, Walter A., S.2c	821 13 79	WORKMAN, Joseph W., RM.3c	648 49 74
WOLF, Harold E., SC.3c	311 70 86	WRIGHT, Guy F., F.1c	669 60 83
WORTLEY, William L., F.3c	700 08 05	ZAKIDWICZ, Edward, S.1c	234 41 25
ZAINO, John W., S.1c	607 30 20	ZIMA, Donald V., F.1c	305 43 86
ZARCUFSKY, Edward L., S.2c	245 68 31		
MEEHAN, Louis J., EM.3c	245 15 98		

Name			
ABBOTT, Joseph H., S.2c	823	59	34
AGNEW, Richard R., Bkr.3c	316	53	90
ALLCROFT, Harry, F.1c	709	57	61
ANDERSON, Charles W., S.1c	300	92	13
ANNS, George W., Jr., S.2c	821	14	16
ARTHUR, Richard T., TM.3c	603	72	36
BANKO, Amos W., S.2c	821	14	15
BARRETT, Everett L., S.1c	875	36	68
BEACH, Robert D., Cox	382	27	95
BEAUDET, Robert H., S.2c	205	45	47
BELAK, John P., S.2c	821	14	35
BERGILOSKY, Walter, S.2c	819	16	80
BERTRAND, Donald J., SF.2c	201	82	90
BLALOCK, William W., S.1c	263	57	06
BOYCE, Curtis L., S.1c	266	67	62
BRUNO, John C., F.1c	710	27	75
BULLEN, Thomas E., QM.3c	615	89	98
CADY, Charles H., F.2c	300	84	92
CHRISTIAN, Ishmael L., TMM.3c	555	74	31
COLLINS, Richard G., S.2c	249	82	78
COOK, Carlton H., BM.2c	265	76	05
CORDEIRO, Edwin A., F.2c	607	05	92
CROWLEY, Robert S., S.2c	653	21	56
D'AREZZO, Edward F., S.2c	823	59	40
DEHART, Robert H., S.2c	821	14	11
DEMUTH, Francis L., S.2c	205	45	54
DEPINO, Frank R., Jr., S.2c	807	53	56
DI CARLO, Joseph A., SoM.3c	836	35	51
DI MARTINO, Carlo A., S.2c	225	30	73
DOLBY, Charles W., S.2c	667	00	42
FARMER, Hugh W., Jr., Y.3c	560	33	54
FAUSER, Warren, MM.2c	244	72	89
FIRICH, Sam B., FC.3c	652	16	66
FOWLER, Richard G., SC.1c	381	42	02
FUERSICH, Edward B., EM.1c	411	44	75
GENOVESE, Joseph R., S.2c	810	66	79
GERAGHTY, John T., GM.3c	708	84	25
GOEBEL, Willard C., Jr., S.2c	601	28	74
GRAFFY, Anthony R., F.2c	224	09	03
GREENBERG, Morton B., RM.3c	224	03	98
GUINDON, Noel J.A., MM.2c	204	75	55
HALAS, John S., S.2c	817	59	70
HANSELMAN, Robert B., PhM.2c	300	45	38
HARROD, Eugene B., FC.3c(M)	669	62	23
HARVEY, Kenneth W., QM.3c	602	49	54
HAWKS, John B., S.1c	393	35	61
HELANDER, Hutson M., F.2c	269	12	85
HIRKALA, J., SM.1c	223	94	67
HOPKINS, Quentin D., GM.3c	669	15	25
HRNCIREK, Steven, S.1c	238	85	59
HURLEY, James F., S.2c	810	67	27
IMMEDIATO, Julius, S.2c	810	66	83
IRISH, Richard J., CM.1c	201	56	91
JOHNSON, Dan H., SM.2c	670	04	65
KASTINA, Anthony, GM.3c	602	72	62
KELLER, Francis A., S.2c	245	68	29
KENNEDY, John A., S.2c	810	66	84
KINNE, Morse N., FC.3c	600	60	78
KULPINSKI, Charles H., S.1c	627	77	17
LAMM, Loyd E., TMM.2c	620	75	09
LAWRENCE, Memory N., WT.1c	385	61	64
LEIGH, Frank, S.1c	264	50	52
LEYBICK, Michael, F.1c	652	03	23
LYNCH, Charles W., CGM	341	84	95
LYNCH, Robert E., MoMM.1c	341	92	61
MANSON, James B., S.2c	563	29	79
MARSHALL, William L., S.2c	249	82	64
McALLISTER, John C., CTMM	606	94	36
McCALL, Francis E., S.1c	204	56	87
McCOY, Daniel J., CTMM	133	19	99
McCULLOUGH, John R., TMM.2c	403	48	93
McMILLAN, Howard T., F.3c	602	40	29

Name			
ADAMS, Robert I., StM.2c	846	48	35
AIREY, Robert E., MM.2c	250	50	92
ALLMAN, Clifford L., S.1c	628	36	44
ANDERSON, Roy W., S.2c	807	42	93
ARNETT, Alfred, CM(AA)	371	55	69
BAILEY, Robert G., QM.1c	393	24	18
BARKER, John "F""D", WT.2c	292	01	62
BAXTER, Robert Jr., EM.3c	709	30	87
BEATON, Glendon D., FC.3c	666	58	14
BECKSTEAD, Lee A., Cox	368	51	87
BENEDICT, Delbert D., F.2c	620	52	16
BERTELSEN, Henry F., SC.3c	224	07	75
BINETTE, Robert, F.2c	208	65	58
BOONE, Brantley J., S.1c	258	55	78
BROWN, Francis W., S.2c	821	14	28
BRYAND, Edward T., S.2c	205	45	51
BURKS, Odell H., CWT(AA)	265	72	29
CHMIELEWSKI, A. J., SC.2c	606	05	68
CIARLONE, Dominick A., S.2c	807	53	61
COLLINS, Roy E., S.2c	823	59	48
COOPER, Milford H., SC.1c	311	09	84
CORDORA, Tony M., S.2c	821	00	58
CUFF, Richard M., GM.3c	725	73	55
DAVIS, J., WT.1c	130	44	25
DEMPSEY, John J., S.2c	810	40	68
DINICHOLAS, William, F.2c	202	09	91
DE ROSE, Anthony J., S.2c	807	53	62
DICE, Jerry T., PhM.2c	325	05	31
DI MEO, Joseph W., S.2c	817	60	15
EVANS, Ronald C., S.2c	245	68	18
FARRELL, Thomas J., Jr., S2c	810	67	19
FERRIS, Philip, SC.3c	205	29	92
FISHER, Clyde E., S.2c	245	68	27
FREEMAN, Jack "R", F.2c	311	39	96
FUERSICH, William F., S.2c	855	24	56
GEPHART, Jacob J., Jr., S.2c	817	59	80
GILL, Rodney I., Cox	385	83	49
GOOD, Fred J., Jr., S.2c	810	67	24
GREGORY, Arthur A., S.1c	563	32	45
GRIEGER, Alvin E., F.1c	305	49	03
GUNDERSON, Roy E., S.1c	725	16	13
HAMMOND, William C., WT.2c	244	53	92
HARFORD, William J., S.2c	810	67	26
HARROLL, Charles T., MM.2c	405	79	34
HAWK, Willard J., MM.2c	244	91	61
HEATH, Ashwell B., MM.1c	212	53	70
HINRICHS, Robert H., F.2c	299	80	06
HOLLAND, David L., SoM.3c	855	21	17
HORAN, Edward F., S.2c	817	59	75
HUBBARD, William T., SoM.3c	629	69	46
HUSSMAN, Ralph B., F.1c	562	96	43
INCUDINE, Charles F., S.2c	817	59	88
JAMES, Charles C., S.1c	262	74	96
JOINER, Robert L., SK.2c	639	29	70
KEITH, Ernest L., FC.3c	627	40	33
KELLY, Vorus C., Y.2c	616	23	34
KERMAREC, Leon H., WT.2c	214	95	30
KROHN, George A., S.1c	305	59	96
LAMAC, Richard, FC.3c	707	60	14
LANHAM, Albert E., WT.2c	265	92	27
LAXTON, Claude D., S.2c	830	08	88
LEMAY, David M., MM.1c	201	62	85
LOONEY, John M., S.1c	203	75	09
LYNCH, John J., EM.3c	710	22	26
MALONEY, William J., S.2c	817	60	21
MARINO, Thomas, S.2c	821	13	90
MATUS, Frank J., S.2c	821	84	00
McBRIDE, John A., S.2c	800	40	54
McCLELLAN, Eldon O., SK.3c	356	47	72
McCUE, Robert L., S.2c	810	53	43
McDANIELS, John "B", MM.1c	287	09	04
MEEHAN, John J., EM.2c	205	27	19

-

CHAPTER 8

Securing of the Marshall Islands; Neutralization of Truk;
Attacks on Saipan and Tinian

Flight operations started at dawn. There were plane crashes almost daily. The crews usually suffered minor injuries. On one occasion when no survivors were found, Young said, "That's one unlucky pilot. They can't walk on water, but most can make a safe landing. We don't need the Japs. We're our own worse enemy."

The Allies agreed that the Anzio landings would proceed on schedule. Mark Clark was advancing and the German 10th Army was slowly withdrawing.

Roosevelt appointed Eisenhower as Supreme Allied Commander for "Overlord", to appease Churchill and Stalin, who did not want General George Marshall, Roosevelt's first choice.

At dinner on 7 December Gibson said, "Chief, we'll arrive in Panama tomorrow. What should we see?"

"Liquor is cheap and girls are plentiful. They make the best Planter's Punch in the world," I replied. At 0759 on 9 December, the Dortch was underway to transit the Panama Canal, with Pilot C.W. Celti at the conn. The trip through was uneventful. At 1845 the Dortch moored to Pier 18 at NOB, Balboa, CZ.

Gommengenger and I went to a night spot, where we enjoyed the band and "B" girls. The next time, I went alone to a private club and ordered a Planter's Punch. The officer on the adjacent bar stool looked vaguely familiar and I asked, "Don't I know you from somewhere?" In a slow drawl he replied, "Don't think so."

"Well, your face is familiar."

Laughing he replied, "You've seen me. I've been in a few movies. Does Van Heflin ring a bell?"

"Sure does. I last saw you in a western. Can't remember the name, but I enjoyed the picture."

He asked, "Do you recognize this fellow next to me?"

Looking carefully, I replied, "Vaguely, but I can't give him a name."

"I'm not surprised," he chuckled. "He's a second rate actor, but he's got a first class wife. He's Richard Ney. His wife is Greer Garson. If you don't know him, you certainly know her."

"You betcha. I saw her in her academy award performance of 'Mrs. Miniver'. She's one beautiful gal and a helluva actress."

Over several drinks, we got to know each other. As I left, I said, "When this war is over, I'm going to visit you in Hollywood. I expect you to get me a date with a beautiful starlet."

"That's a promise," Van Heflin replied. "Richard and I are going to hold you to it."

The following day I heard a crew member saying, "I can't believe how plentiful and beautiful the girls are. I went to the Blue Moon and the Coconut Grove. The entertainment was fantastic." Another added, "And did you catch those whore houses? One street was lined with them. There was just a flimsy curtain covering the doors and windows. What a floor show, and for free."

On 14 December the Dortch was underway for San Francisco with the Intrepid, Haradan and Gatling. Enroute, various drills and flight operations were conducted. There were plane crashes and some of the crews were rescued.

On the morning of 22 December, the Dortch passed under the Golden Gate Bridge. At 1552 we moored to the Gatlin at Pier #54, San Francisco, California.

I went to the Top Of the Mark Hopkins, found friends, drank and reminisced. At breakfast the next morning, Ed Gibson was bemoaning his fate. "One of our buddies thought he had caught 'VD' from one of his Panamanian consorts. His wife showed up on the dock and he didn't want her exposed. He wouldn't let me leave his side. He got soused and insisted I carry him back to the ship on my shoulders. I did. I had a miserable time, but I might have saved a marriage. I hope we're not going to spend another night here."

At 1605 the Dortch was enroute to Pearl Harbor with the Gatling and Sullivans. Rocky remarked, as the Golden Gate Bridge disappeared from view, "I wonder when we'll see that bridge again?"

I replied, "For some, never."

The usual exercises were conducted enroute. When I relieved Rocky at 2345 on 24 December, he said, "It's been a quiet watch. The lookouts haven't sighted Santa Claus. If you see him, tell the old boy all I want is to go home."

The talk on the bridge was of Christmases past and what their families and friends might be doing now. I led the watch in some familiar carols. Santa Claus didn't appear, but there was turkey with all of the trimmings for dinner.

For many, this was their first Christmas away from home. The sadness could be felt. When they learned the 1st Marine Division had just landed on Cape Gloucester, New Britain, and the casualties were heavy, they realized how blessed they were.

Midday on 28 December, the Dortch was moored to the Gatling and the Sullivans, Berth X-4, Pearl Harbor.

In Europe, General Rommel was ordered to defend the coast from Holland to the Bay of Biscay. General Montgomery was put in charge of General Bradley's First Army. When he saw the plans for "Overlord", he complained that the Normandy landing area was too small. It would allow the Germans to contain the beachhead and create congestion on the beaches. Eisenhower agreed and it was revised.

Our next objective was Micronesia, consisting of the Gilbert's, Marshall's, Caroline's and Mariana's. They sprawled across the main sea lanes between the US and China.

The Dortch remained moored for the next week. Men were transferred to schools and other duty. On New Year's Eve and New Year's Day, the radios were tuned to the bowl games. Each of us bet on our favorites. Georgia Tech beat Tulsa in the Sugar Bowl 20-18. It was Randolph Field 7—Texas 7 in the Cotton, Louisiana State 19—Texas A&M 14 in the Orange and Southern California 29—Washington O in the Rose.

Knowing this to be my last contact with civilization for months to come, I went to the officer's club to get soused. I was pleasantly surprised to find Dave Baker, a friend from Columbia and a shipmate from my Quincy days. After we embraced, he said, "I'm on the Cimmaron, a tanker. We're shoving off in the morning. I've been in and out of Pearl over the past few months and been dating Audry Houvner, a cute brunette whose father is a dentist. They moved from the States before the war. I'm one of the family. They're nice people and I'll introduce you to them by phone before I leave in the morning."

He kept his word and assured the Houvners I was a reliable, responsible friend who would take good care of Audry. At breakfast I shared the news, "Am I the lucky one! I'll be a member of Honolulu's upper crust. The Houvners are members of the Waikiki Beach and Canoe Club. I've heard they have excellent floor shows and Hilo Hattie is performing there next week."

"Well, don't forget your buddies," Gommengenger said.

On my first date with Audry, the Houvner's car was placed at my disposal. It was fancier than anything I'd ever seen. I found the ignition, started the engine, pushed down on the clutch and put it in gear. The car lurched forward like it had the hiccups. Audry said nothing, but I sensed she was apprehensive. I took my foot off the gas pedal and pushed down gently on the gas. As we moved forward with increasing speed, I was so pleased with my success I took my eyes off the road and almost ran into a stop sign. As I came to an abrupt halt, Audry was thrown against the dash. I explained, "Just getting the feel of the car. They all react differently. I wanted to be certain the brakes are in good shape." She said nothing. With a few more lurches, we arrived at the beach club. The night was memorable. We danced, talked and enjoyed Hilo Hattie.

The days were filled with routine maintenance, paperwork, gunnery exercises and fighter direction drills, with planes making simulated torpedo attacks.

In Europe, the RAF attacked Berlin and Leipzig. Damage was extensive. General Spaatz took over command of the US Strategic Air Force in Europe, General Eacker, the Allied forces in the Mediterranean, and General Doolittle, the US Eighth Army Air Force.

Both Montgomery and Eisenhower relinquished their field commands and moved to Britain. On 3 January Montgomery held his first "Overlord" conference and recommended that 5 divisions land on a 50-mile front from the River Orne to the east side of the Cherbourg Peninsula. Airborne divisions would protect the flank and the Second British Army would tie down the Germans in the Caen area.

For us, it was plane guard duty with the Yorktown, a new carrier. There were plane crashes, but only once were there no survivors. Shore bombardment was practiced on Kahoolawee Island, which was still inhabited only by goats. After one bombardment Burt said, "Those goats should be schizophrenic from the shelling they've been getting, but apparently they're thriving."

The Captain attended meetings with Admiral Nimitz's staff, where he was briefed on the organizational structure of the Pacific Fleet and the upcoming operations. He told me, "Chief, this is a different Navy and war from the one you left 9 months ago. We were just hanging on. Now we have 10 Essex Class carriers, 7 escort carriers, 9 new battle wagons and countless cruisers, destroyers and supply ships. It's mind boggling."

"Who's in charge of what?" I asked.

"There are two fleets. When Admiral Raymond Spruance is in command, it's the Fifth Fleet. When Halsey takes over, it's the Third Fleet. The players are the same. Only the Captains change."

"What's the purpose of that?"

"To maximize the time of Spruance and Halsey. One staff can be back in Pearl planning the next operation while the other is carrying one out."

"Who's in command of the carriers?"

"Admiral Marc Mitscher. He's a little guy, but a highly respected aviator. He's in charge of the Fast Carrier Task Forces. Nimitz has thought of everything. If a fleet action is a possibility, Spruance and Halsey have designated specific ships to be the battle line. They will drop out of the formation and attack the Japanese Fleet."

While we were conducting flight operations in the afternoon on 8 January, the ship shook convulsively. Rocky investigated and reported, "The starboard section of the bilge keel between frames #85 and #110 has broken loose from the shell of the ship. No leaks have been found in the hull, but it's back into the dry-dock."

"We're getting a message from a higher authority," Dickey said. "This is the third time we've tried to sink this ship. Maybe we should return to the States."

After repairs were made on 15 January, the Captain said, "You'd better enjoy this night. We're leaving tomorrow."

In the afternoon I went to Audry's house and was given the keys to the car. This time I drove confidently. We dined and danced the night away at the Moana Hotel. Time got away. I didn't catch a taxi for the base until 2330, thirty minutes after curfew. The cab was stopped by the shore patrol and I was given a summons to appear at the Honolulu Police Station the next morning.

On 16 January the Dortch was underway, and as I watched the heavy ships sortieing from the harbor, I said to Dickey, "Right now I'm supposed to be in the Police Station. Hopefully my citation is going to gather dust and be forgotten by the time I get back."

At 1400 Task Group 58.1, consisting of DesRon 50, Cotton, C.K. Bronson, Dortch, Gatling, Healy, Cogswell, Ingersoll, Knapp and Caperton, formed up. The carriers were the San Jacinto, with Ensign George Bush on board, the Yorktown (CTF58), Enterprise (CTG 58.1) and Cowpens. Accompanying us were the oilers Cimmeron and Ashtabula, with the cruisers Wichita and Oakland.

When we joined up with Task Groups 58.2, 3 and 4, forming the Fifth Fleet, there were ships as far as the eye could see, 375 with 700 carrier planes. The industrial might of the United States was beginning to assert itself.

At dinner Young said, "The basic strategy is to proceed on schedule. General MacArthur's forces are moving up the Solomon's, Bismarck's and the New Guinea axis to the Philippines. Admirals King and Nimitz are striking directly across the Pacific through the Marshall's, Gilbert's and Mariana's. Air bases will be built on Guam and Saipan so B29's can bomb Japan directly. To minimize the loss of life, the Japanese strongholds are going to by-passed."

The Marshall Islands were named after a shipmaster who discovered them in 1788. Germany possessed them prior to WWI. The Japanese captured them, and when Japan seceded from the League of Nations in 1935, she kept the Marshall's.

No foreign ships were allowed to enter any of the harbors or lagoons. By 1941, airfields, together with supply bases, were established on many of the islands. With Guadalcanal 1100 miles distant, none of our search planes could reach them.

Kwajalein was number one target. It would protect MacArthur's flank as he moved through the Bismarck's. The two-pronged attack would confuse and deceive the Japanese. The planes based on Tarawa and Makin supplied us with pictures of the beaches and fortifications.

At dinner Burt said, "I just heard Italy and Sicily have been secured and the submarine menace in the Atlantic is under control."

Rothschild chimed in, "The number one priority is still Europe. We get what's left over. It blows my mind to think how large the Atlantic Fleet must be when you see the size of the Fifth Fleet."

Our course was westerly, speed 15 knots. Everyone studied silhouettes of Japanese planes and ships. No garbage or trash could be thrown over the side or the bilges pumped until one hour after sunset. The tactical formations which would be used in enemy territory were practiced. Destroyers were sent out on night picket duty for early warning purposes. I was OOD on 17 January when the Dortch took up station 14,000 yards from the guide. Sonar reported a sound contact. I attacked and dropped depth charges. Results unknown.

On 22 January the PA boomed, "Now hear this! Now hear this! Today we will be crossing the Equator and the International Date Line. The Captain has granted a temporary reprieve to all of you slimy pollywogs. We're too close to enemy territory. The reprieve is only temporary. You will be properly inducted into King Neptune's Realm in a few days."

The news reported that landings were made at Anzio, surprising the Germans. Only two battalions were in the area and a beachhead was quickly established. General Lucas failed to exploit his early success, which allowed the Germans to bring in reinforcements.

The battleships Washington, Indiana and Massachusetts joined our formation. The Dortch fueled and the crew loaded up on ice cream and porgy bait.

In the afternoon of 28 January, the PA blared, "Now hear this! Now hear this! This dispatch has been received from Admiral Reeves: 'You are courageous and superbly trained men. Tomorrow we attack the enemy. I expect you to strike them hard. Victory will be ours, and then on to Tokyo.' "

At dawn on 29 January, "Flintlock" began, with planes attacking targets on Taroa and Maloelap Atoll, Marshall Islands. The Yorktown lost one pilot on take-off and had one rescued. By 1110 all planes on the ground were destroyed, and at 1635 our planes had safely returned to the carriers. I was outside of the forward engine room when 6 B-25's approached from the stern. I was shocked as I saw shells exploding around them. I exclaimed to Dickey, "Some guys have made a bad mistake. They think they're Japanese."

Dickey exclaimed, "Our combat air patrol is attacking. My God, one is going down in flames. It's a horrible tragedy."

When I relieved Rothschild as OOD at 1800, he said, "You saw how those B-25's were misidentified. Somebody is going to catch hell. There's no excuse for that. The Gatling and Bronson have been unable to locate any survivors."

The formation headed northwest, and on 31 January the carriers launched strikes against Kwajalein Atoll, the world's largest, 66 miles long and 20 miles wide. There were 97 islands and islets strung around it. Roi-Mamur at the southeast corner had military installations manned with 3,500 Japanese troops.

The Washington, Indiana and Massachusetts with DesDiv 100 left the formation to shell the Jap positions. They effectively pounded the beaches all day and reduced them to rubble. It was fortunate, because the rains came and the air strikes had to be stopped.

On 27 January the Japanese had 150 serviceable planes in the Marshall's and none on D-Day, 31 January.

When Burt relieved me at 0345 on 1 February, I said, "The Indiana[56] is to drop out of the Task Force to fuel destroyers during your watch. She will slow down and leave the formation from the rear." At breakfast Burt said, "The Indiana didn't follow operating procedure. I was looking at her through my binoculars and saw her crossing the bow of the Washington, which was on her starboard side. Her OOD had obviously increased speed rather than slowing down. The Washington's OOD, trying to avoid a collision ordered, 'Hard right rudder. Full speed.' With us on the starboard side of the formation, both of those monsters headed straight for us at full speed, I ordered, 'Full right rudder. Bend on maximum speed. Notify the Captain on the double.' It was eternity before the Dortch started turning away and picked up speed. I could imagine those ships ripping us apart. You guys asleep below decks would never have known what hit you. The radar operator kept calling out the distances, '1,000 yards, 800, 500.' The Captain came out of his cabin in his skivvies rubbing his eyes. He ran from one side of the bridge to the other trying to get his bearings. He yelled at me, 'What are you doing? We're going to be run down.'

"He saw those mountains bearing down and could hear the distances closing in. I thought the end had come. I shouted, 'I've got all the speed I can get. We're gaining slowly. The Captain yelled, 'This is one helluva way to die. Run over by your own damn ships.'

"I heard the sound of an enormous explosion. The Washington collided with the Indiana on her starboard quarter. At the same time, the radarman yelled out, '600 yards. We're pulling away; 700 yards.'

"I ordered the helmsman, 'Steady as you go.' It just wasn't our time."

The Cotton, Knapp, Healy and Gatling left the formation to screen the damaged vessels. The Sterett and Stack joined our formation. The Washington lost most of her bow, and many men were seriously injured on both ships. Two of our modern battleships were put out of action for several months because of one asinine mistake.

On 31 January the men on the transports scrambled into the landing craft and headed for the beach. Admiral Turner had 41,000 troops, with the 4th Marine Division in the northern attack group and the 7th Infantry Regiment in the southern. When they landed on the beaches at 0930, resistance was met in both sectors. Naval gunfire softened the Japanese resistance, and by 2 February, the islands were secured. We had 372 killed and 1,582 wounded. The Japanese lost 7,870 because they fought to the last man.

By 2 February the Kwajalein lagoon was ready for use and airstrips were started so land-based planes could support operations throughout this area.

250 miles to the southeast, Rear Admiral Hill with the Majuro Attack Group landed without opposition. In the afternoon Gommengenger reported, "It's unreal! When the Marines landed this morning, they met no resistance. The stars and stripes were raised at 0950. This amounted to free real estate and is the first Japanese Territory held before WW II which we have recaptured."

Our Task Group headed south, and on 5 February after 3 weeks at sea, the Dortch was anchored in Majuro Atoll Lagoon, Marshall Islands. We fueled from the Cimmarron and I visited with Dave Baker via megaphone, who sent over ice cream and porgy bait.

It was the picture-book tropical island: coconut palms waving in the warm breeze, lush, green undergrowth, pink and white coral sand beaches, crystal clear blue water. For recreation the crew was permitted to swim from the ship. One man circled the swimmers in a boat, with a submachine gun to protect against sharks.

Drake commented, "I'm not certain how much good he's doing. If he ever had to fire that gun, he'd probably hit our men rather than the sharks. He does look intimidating and maybe that'll scare the sharks away."

I enjoyed swimming and sunning in the lagoon. At night there were movies on the fantail. The men enjoyed "Cover Girl" with Rita Hayworth and Gene Kelly as well as a repeat performance of "Casablanca".

Repairs, general maintenance and paperwork kept everyone busy. On 11 February the Dortch was underway with the Minneapolis, New Orleans and accompanying destroyers and 6 tankers. On 14 February we joined up with Task Groups 58.1, 2 and 3. All ships fueled and changed course to 248 degrees, enroute to the Caroline Islands. Task Group 58.4 was left behind to cover the landings on Eniwetok. The Captain announced at dinner, "Our objective is Truk, the Japanese Pearl Harbor of the Western Pacific. It is 696 miles from Rabual, which MacArthur is now encircling, and 669 miles from Eniwetok, where D-Day is 17 February."

The next morning the PA system boomed: "This is the Captain speaking. Admiral Mitscher has sent a dispatch to all hands, which reads: 'You are a magnificent group of fighting men. Our job is to find the Japanese navy and sink it. With the help of Almighty God, we will succeed.'"

Truk was the anchorage for the main body of the Japanese Fleet and a vital staging area between Japan and the Bismarck's. The US high command had two schools of thought. One considered a take-over essential, the other preferred neutralizing and by-passing Truk.

Admiral Koga, CinC of the Japanese Combined Fleet, was warned by reconnaissance planes that the Fifth Fleet was enroute. On 16 February, 72 fighter planes were launched from 5 carriers to destroy the Jap planes. 45 enemy planes attempted to intercept and 30 were knocked down. The Hellcats proceeded to Moen, Eten and Param Fields, where 40 more were destroyed. Only 4 US planes failed to return. The pilots reported only 2 light cruisers and 8 destroyers in the anchorage. The rest of the Combined Fleet had fled to Palau. There were 50 merchant ships and auxiliaries in the harbor, which dive bombers and torpedo planes attacked throughout the day.

At 1955 the Dortch rescued Lt.(jg) L.E. Richardson. He had only minor injuries. General Quarters was sounded. Sammy said, "Radar has picked up unidentified planes coming in from the west. Our Commander is maneuvering the formation to keep the planes astern."

For the next hour with nothing happening, the men told stories and talked about home. Sammy excitedly interrupted, "Two planes passed close by on the starboard side. Several ships have commenced firing. No hits were seen."

At 2345 with the radar screen, GQ was secured. Night-trained pilots on the Enterprise took off and made the Navy's first nighttime bombing attacks. Air strikes continued the next day until a pilot reported that Jap ships were escaping to the west through the North Pass. Admiral Spruance ordered the battleships New Jersey and Iowa, the cruisers Minneapolis and New Orleans, the carrier Cowpens and several destroyers to "search for and destroy the enemy ships". He led the search in the New Jersey. They found and sank the cruiser Katori, the destroyer Maikaze, the trawler Shonan Maru and the Sc-24. Only the destroyer Nowake escaped.

At 1900 GQ was sounded and Sammy said, "7 torpedo bombers are attacking." Through evasive maneuvering, they were kept at bay for two hours. At 2211 Sammy exclaimed, "A Kate got through. It's heading for the Intrepid. It has crashed on the starboard quarter."

When GQ was secured I learned 11 men were killed and 17 were wounded. The Intrepid, accompanied by 2 cruisers and 4 destroyers, retired to Enewetok for repairs.[57]

The formation retired to the east the next day. The two days of air strikes resulted in the sinking of 2 auxiliary cruisers, one destroyer, 2 submarine tenders, one aircraft ferry, 6 tankers and 17 other ships. Approximately 365 enemy planes were destroyed. Most of our pilots who were shot down were rescued, either by destroyers or the 10 submarines stationed in the area.

This strike affected the Japanese morale more than any of our previous ones. Radio Tokyo declared that the United States was unsuccessful in landing troops, but on 18 February broadcast, "A powerful American Task Force suddenly advanced to our Caroline Islands Wednesday morning and repeatedly attacked our important strategic base at Truk. The war situation has increased with unprecedented seriousness—nay, furiousness. The tempo of enemy operations indicates that the attacking force is pressing upon our mainland."

Admiral Nimitz announced, "The Pacific Fleet has returned at Truk the visit made by the Japanese Fleet at Pearl Harbor on December 7,1941, and effected a partial settlement of the debt." Truk was no longer useful as a fleet anchorage or an advanced naval base.

During this time, landings occurred on Eniwetok and Parry Atolls. After heavy fighting and 1,200 casualties, these atolls were secured on 22 February.

On 19 February I was OOD at 0400 when the radar man yelled, "There are enemy planes bearing 233 degrees, distance 29 miles."

"Notify the Captain and sound General Quarters." I ran to my battle station and at 0500 Sammy exclaimed, "A ship on the port side has shot down one plane." In a few minutes he added, "The carriers are launching planes. That will probably take care of the Japs." It did. At 0918 the Dortch went alongside the Enterprise and transferred Lt.(jg) Richardson.

At lunch Gibson said, "We've received a dispatch from CTF 58 directing us to join Task Group 58.2 and TG 58.3. We are to conduct air strikes against Saipan and Tinian in the Mariana Islands." In the afternoon we joined Admiral A.E. Montgomery's Task Force 58.2. Flight operations were conducted throughout the day. The Captain said, "Tinian and Saipan are heavily fortified and the Japanese have air fields on many of the surrounding islands. There is going to be some excitement."

On 22 February Admiral Spruance learned that the Fleet had been spotted and sent a dispatch to all ships: "We must be prepared to fight our way in." He was right. GQ was sounded at 2045. Sammy said, "Bridge reports many enemy planes approaching. Some of the ships have commenced firing. White flares are being dropped all around us. It looks like Market Street in San Francisco on New Year's Eve. Bridge reports torpedo bombers are attacking from the rear. The South Dakota has one under fire." He paused and yelled, "They got him. He's gone up in flames. Increase speed to 25 knots." I could feel the ship tilting from one side to the other as emergency turns were made to keep them astern.

"What's going on?" I asked.

"The Yorktown just missed a torpedo. It looks like the attack is over. The bridge can see 7 planes burning. Must have been some show."

General Quarters was secured at 2217. No one was asleep when GQ was again sounded at 2245. Sammy reported, "Bridge says there are many planes. Looks like they're attacking the South Dakota. 2 planes have burst into flames. The anti-aircraft fire is so intense there's no way to tell which ships made hits."

I felt the shock as our guns fired repeatedly.

"Any more news?" I asked. At 0024 Sammy yelled out, "We just knocked one down. Others are in flames. Bridge doesn't know the number. Radar says screen is clear of bogeys."

When GQ was secured at 0305, I took a life preserver as a pillow and lay down under the torpedo tubes outside of the forward engine room. At 0535 it was back to GQ. Sammy exclaimed, "10 torpedo planes are coming in at masthead height. There's another group dropping bombs from high altitudes. The anti-aircraft fire is hellacious. None are getting through. Several planes have been splashed."

Emergency turns were executed to keep the planes astern. At 0815 Sammy reported, "The carriers are launching their first air strikes against Japanese bases on Tinian and Saipan." At 0828 he shouted, "We just got another one."

Attacks continued throughout the morning. The carriers kept launching and recovering planes. In the afternoon when GQ was secured, 14 additional Japanese planes had been shot down and not one of our ships was hit. At 1642 the Fleet retired eastward, speed 25 knots. Although photographs and reconnaissance were major objectives of the attack, much more had been accomplished. Planes, shipping and buildings were destroyed.

By mid-day on 26 February, the Dortch was anchored in the lagoon at Majuro Atoll. The crew was smiling and discussing what they were going to do on liberty. One said, "We've got paradise, but without girls, it's more like hell."

The crew took beer and swam off the beach. The officers took the Captain's Gig with ice, beer and scotch and cruised around the lagoon. Rocky spoke for all, "I hear there is a war going on, but you can't prove it by me." By late afternoon we were pretty drunk and Gibson, who had been on the Annapolis swimming team, exclaimed, "I'll bet you guys $5 I can beat you back to the ship."

"You're nuts," Rocky responded. "We're a mile away and you're so drunk you can't see straight."

" Anybody take my bet?" Ed persisted.

"You're on," Gommengenger said. Removing only his shoes, Ed dove overboard and headed toward the ship with a powerful crawl. He was no match for the gig, but was only a few yards behind when we reached the gangway. He stumbled up as the men on the quarter-deck watched in astonishment. Never had they seen the executive officer fully clothed, drenched, weaving from side to side and mumbling incoherently.

The fighting in Italy was furious throughout February. The Germans counter-attacked at Anzio and almost threw the Allies into the sea. General Lucas was replaced by Lucian Truscott. Due to the superiority of Allied airpower, on 3 March, the Germans stopped their assault on Anzio. To the north Russian attacks continued throughout the winter. The Germans had looked forward to the spring thaw to give them some relief, but Stalin was determined to drive them out of the Ukraine. Zhukov started his offensive on 4 March and advanced 25 miles in two days on a 100 mile front. Hundreds of tanks, guns and thousands of trucks were abandoned by the Germans.

While I was doing paperwork, Angel appeared at my door, hat in hand, and asked, "Mr. Jervey, can I speak to you a minute?"

"Come in. What's on your mind?"

"The men are bored and need some entertainment."

Since he was fidgeting with his hat, I knew I was in for trouble, "So how do you propose to entertain them?"

"Well, you did some boxing in college and the men thought you'd be willing to give them some excitement."

"I'm supposed to give them some excitement by getting my head knocked off? Come off it! Who dreamed this up? How the hell am I going to get them to obey orders after that?"

"You've got it all wrong, sir. The fellow you'll be boxing can't touch you. The men will respect you even more. You'll be a hero. Most of the men are betting on you."

"Bets have already been made? You're off your rocker," I shouted.

The bottom line was: am I a chump or a coward? I opted to be a chump. I discovered everything was set. The men had boxing gloves, headgear and mouth pieces. The ring was to be roped off on the fantail. The referee and my opponent, H.H. McFalls, MM1c, were designated. He was stocky and heavily muscled with a face like a bulldog. He kept in shape using wrenches on the steam pipes and other heavy machinery; I, by pushing a pencil and running to my General Quarters station.

When he heard about the match, the Captain exclaimed, "In all of my years, I have never witnessed anything like this. I must be dreaming."

"I wish I were," I responded.

There was little I could do to get ready with only two days to prepare. Angel and the men made life uncomfortable with remarks like, "I discovered McFalls won his weight in the Golden Gloves." Another added, "With knockouts."

The afternoon arrived. The ring was roped off. With all of the officers and crew as spectators, the fantail was crowded. I put the headgear on, the mouth piece in, my hands were wrapped in gauze and the gloves were put on. McFalls looked bigger and meaner than I had ever seen him. I was sweating. He was loosening up by jumping around in his corner. The referee called us to the center of the ring. "No hitting below the belt. No rabbit punching. When I say break, break. The rounds will be 3 minutes with one minute rests. Go to your corners and when you hear the bell, touch gloves and fire away. May the best man win."

The bell rang. I was sweating profusely. We touched gloves. McFalls immediately started throwing punches. I backed up to protect myself. Seeing an opening, I led with a left and followed to the head with a right. Moving in and ducking, I started punching away at his stomach. Trying to protect himself, he dropped his gloves and leaned over me. I pulled my head up suddenly and bone crunched on bone. Blood started gushing over me. The referee stepped between us. "Stop the fight. I want the doctor to check this cut." Doctor Wible carefully examined the 2" cut over McFalls' right eye and declared, "The fight has to be called. Serious damage could be done to this eye if it continues." It was pronounced a draw. Thus ended my Navy boxing career.

The Marshall's campaign was proclaimed a spectacular success. The outer perimeter of the Japanese defenses were broken. This campaign restored the American people's confidence in the Navy. The pundits declared that it demonstrated our mastery of the art of amphibious warfare and the unlimited potential of aircraft carriers. Walter Lippman wrote in the New York Herald Tribune on 21 February: "In the Marshall's and at Truk, the Navy has done more than win a good victory over the enemy. It has won a resounding victory in the hearts and minds of our people over anxiety and doubt, which have, since the close of the other war, divided and confused us."

Of greater importance to the men in the service was the good feeling and respect developing between the Navy, Army and Marines. Many laudatory messages were received. Typical was the one received from General Holland M. Smith, USMC: "The cooperation and coordination at Kwajalein was the most satisfactory ever experienced." Admiral King was most succinct: "To all hands concerned with the Marshall Islands operation: well and smartly done. Carry on."

We knew MacArthur was ready to isolate Rabual. The US 1st Cavalry landed on Los Negros in the Admiralty islands and seized the airfield. The news reported on 4 March that 600 USAAF bombers attacked Berlin in a daylight raid; only 30 were lost.

The ten days spent in the lagoon were wonderful. It came to an end on 7 March. The Dortch with TG 58.1 departed for Espiritu Santo. The next day the PA boomed, "Now hear this! Now hear this! All you slimy pollywogs, prepare to meet King Neptune. Say your prayers. Your time has come. Tomorrow the Dortch will officially cross the equator."

The night before the crossing, several unscrupulous pollywogs attempted to evade the humiliation by chaining several shellbacks to their bunks. This was to no avail. Despite the humid, hot weather, dawn found two junior officers clothed in blue uniforms and topcoats, peering vainly ahead on the bridge through two Coke bottles taped together as binoculars. They were looking for King Neptune as he rose from the sea to greet the pollywogs. The majority of the crew were uninitiated, including Ed Gibson. He was given the honor of being introduced to the mysteries of the deep first. The privileges of rank and rating were forgotten in the spirit of fun. The watch was relieved so all pollywogs could receive the biased sentence of the shellback judges. This consisted of a foul-tasting mouth swab, Southern Cross haircuts and a rather severe beating administered to their butts. This converted the pollywogs into shellbacks, which permitted them to administer the rites of Neptune to future pollywogs crossing the line.

For a short time the war was forgotten, but flight operations continued during the ceremony.

MacArthur and Nimitz were told that the next major objective would be Luzon with a target date of February 1945. Prior to that, Emiru Island was to be seized and a landing made on Hollandia in New Guinea.

On the afternoon of 11 March, the Dortch moored portside to the Cotton in Second Channel. Admiral Halsey assumed command and the designation of the Task Force was changed from 58.1 to 38.1. The date changed to 12 March, as we were now in east latitude.

Standing on the forecastle with Burt, I reminisced, "It's been one year since I left Espiritu. Seems like yesterday. The island had only a few Quonset huts. Now it looks like the Brooklyn Navy Yard. There are buildings as far as the eye can see. The harbor is jammed with ships. The lush, green jungles haven't changed, and I'm certain there are bananas, papayas and mangoes to be had for the picking. That was my job on my last visit. This time, I'm looking for girls."

Burt said, "And I bet you didn't have a USO Group, or show movies topside."

"We showed movies, but we were interrupted some of the time by Wet Dream Charlie. I'll be interested in knowing if anyone has dated the daughter of the French planter who lives on the top of that mountain. There was one hospital ship. Now Army and Navy nurses are all over the place. Any girl of any skin color will look beautiful to me. Makes no difference if they are short, tall, skinny or fat."

"Me being married, I want to look, but not touch. I bet you're going to get no closer than studying them through a pair of binoculars."

The PA boomed, "Now hear this! Now hear this! Mail call in the mess hall. For the officers, in the wardroom." There were loud shouts of approval. It was the most welcome news we'd had in 58 days. Everyone had letters and packages. One of the crew received over 100 letters. I heard from my family, friends and Ann. I remarked to my shipmates, "Seems like I'm about to lose one more girl. Her letters aren't quite as loving and she isn't missing me like she used to. I'll bet she's found someone to take my place."

"Don't sweat it, Chief," Gommengenger said. "At least you didn't get a 'Dear John' letter like I did."

Our stay was brief, only long enough to provision and do limited maintenance work.

-

CHAPTER 9

The Battle Of The Philippine Sea;
Mariana's Turkey Shoot

On 15 March the Dortch sortied from Espiritu Santo with Task Group 36.1 to support the Army's landings on Emiru Island in the Admiralties.

The Captain explained, "This landing will permit us to by-pass the Japanese base at Rabual and cut off over 100,000 combat troops together with their supplies and weapons. General MacArthur will continue to push up the New Guinea-Netherlands East Indies-Mindanao axis to the Philippines. He wanted the carriers under his command, but was refused, as the area provides little maneuverability for the ships and the Japanese have airfields on most of the islands."

He went on to explain, "MacArthur will land on Hollandia on 15 April. Nimitz will start landings on Saipan, Tinian and Guam on 15 June, and the Palaus beginning 15 September. The occupation of Mindanao by MacArthur should start on 15 November. Admiral Koga is committed to using the Japanese Navy to protect their Army's supply and communication system. He believes the Army wins wars. Their Navy will not fight an all-out battle until the US Navy comes within shooting distance of Tokyo."

At breakfast on 16 March Gibson announced, "In keeping with Article 1222 of Navy Regulations, today you'll start the annual inventory of all equipment on board." Rocky exclaimed, "That's got to be the stupidest damn regulation I ever heard of. Who the hell cares what we've got on board if we are sunk tomorrow. Those desk Admirals don't know what war is all about." At 1515 the annual inventory was commenced.

On 20 March the carriers began launching air strikes on Emiru Island. The Japanese, being warned of our coming, had few planes on the ground. At 1535 flight operations were completed.

While we were chatting in the wardroom after dinner, the PA boomed, "Now hear this! The chief engineer is wanted in the forward engine room immediately."

When I arrived, Angel said, "We've had to secure the port engine. The lub pump is acting up."

"How long will it take to fix it?"

"45 minutes to an hour," I told the Captain, "There won't be any problem keeping station unless speeds of over 20 knots are required." At 2025 the engine was repaired and back on line.

On 26 March the Third Fleet became the Fifth Fleet under the command of Vice Admiral Raymond Spruance in the New Jersey. At dinner Young said, "Our next objective will be to neutralize the bases on Palau, Yap, Woleai and Ulithi prior to MacArthur's assault on New Guinea. It will be difficult, as Palau is 2,000 miles west of Majuro. More importantly, it's only 500 miles from major Japanese bases in the Philippines."

We rendezvoused with Task Groups 58.2 and 58.3 the next day. Nearing enemy territory, the Task Group exercised at emergency maneuvers. At sundown, enemy planes were reported in the area and GQ was sounded. Sammy said, "We're being attacked by torpedo planes. They can't get through the anti-aircraft fire. It is massive. We've also got fighter planes in the air." At 2105 Sammy reported, "A fighter plane has landed a few hundred yards on our starboard side and we're looking for the pilot." I waited anxiously. Sammy added, "Bridge says with the darkened conditions, it's hard to see anything, but the pilot fired his revolver with tracer bullets and yelled 'Hoy, can.' We swung about, came alongside, threw him a line and pulled him aboard. He's one lucky guy."

Sammy yelled, "The Japs aren't finished. A plane is attacking from our stern. Commence firing has been given. He's turned away. There's another one coming in on our port quarter." I could hear the giant firecrackers exploding and didn't need confirmation when Sammy said, "He's gone."

At 2250 General Quarters was secured.

I drank coffee in the wardroom until I relieved Rocky at 2345. When Burt relieved me at 0345, I said, "Air strikes against the Palau Islands will commence at dawn." Hundreds of planes bombed and strafed the islands. The Japanese flew in help from outlying islands to no avail. Our only excitement was picking up Lt.(jg) C.W. Smith, pilot of a crashed plane from the Bunker Hill.

GQ sounded at 1953. Sammy said, "There's a group of bogeys high overhead. The cruisers are firing at them. Bombs are straddling the Belleau Wood." Later he exclaimed, "Flares are dropping. The night has been turned into day. Torpedo planes are attacking from all sides." There was a pause and he continued, "Bridge reports several planes have been shot down. There are burning hulks all over the ocean. No hits have been made on any of our ships."

GQ was secured at 2130.

Task Group 58.1 under Admiral Reeves headed north. At dawn air strikes were launched against Yap. No planes or ships were found because Admiral Toga had sent his ships to Singapore.

On April Fool's Day, the planes hit Woleai, 350 miles south of Guam. Few Jap planes were found, but two ships were sighted. The Hunt and Hickox went to investigate. They found Japanese patrol vessels and sunk them with gunfire.

Air strikes continued throughout the day, with extensive damage to the ground installations. When I relieved Drake at 2000, he remarked, "This wasn't much of an April Fool's Day for the garrison on Wolaie, but it will be long remembered."

"No, it won't. They've all committed Hari Kari."

The following morning the destroyers fueled and the Dortch transferred two men from one ship to another. Rocky remarked, "We're running a taxi service and we don't even get tips."

There were smiling faces on 5 April when the PA boomed, "Now hear this! Task Group 58.1 has been detached and we're proceeding to Majuro." In the afternoon of 7 April, the Dortch was moored to the tender Markab in a nest with other destroyers. The crew enjoyed the beer busts on the beach, returning with coconuts. Doctor Wible said, "I wish they hadn't gotten so cut up on the coral. They're going to be sick cookies for a few days."

There were movies on the fantail: "Going My Way" with Bing Crosby and Barry Fitzgerald and "Gaslight" with Charles Boyer and Ingrid Bergman. The most excitement came when the PA boomed, "Now hear this! Mail call for the crew in the mess hall; for the officers, in the wardroom." The bonanza of news from home boosted the spirits of everyone including myself.

Drake got a laugh from an ad his wife sent:

> "The more women at war,
> The sooner we'll win."

Rocky's wife reported, "Because of gas rationing, neighborhood groceries are expanding rapidly. I've had to switch to Chesterfield cigarettes because you guys like Camels so much."

Doc Wible exclaimed, "What good news! We've been on the verge of running out of quinine and a synthetic form has been developed which will alleviate the shortage."

Every one got a chuckle hearing about the new fashion in the States, broad shoulders and pointed lapels. Men and women looked like football players.

The bar at the Majuro officer's club now had bourbon and the tables were boards laid across barrels. The seats were planks laid across smaller barrels. The roof had palm branches on top of two by fours.

On 12 April at 0815, the Captain held meritorious mast and awarded letters of commendation to Mast, J.M., CMM; McFalls, H.H., MM1/c; and Gaffney, W.E, S1c. An hour later, when two men were sent to Majuro for solitary confinement on bread and water for 30 days, Chuck Robbins said, "That's just to even things out. For every good, there has to be a counter balancing bad. That's known as Robbins 12th Commandment."

At dinner Rocky said, "At the bar some of the airdales were talking about Air Group 51[58], which has just arrived from the States and is on the San Jacinto. During the shake-down cruise, 2 pilots were killed, 9 injured and 50% of the planes were involved in crashes. The Captain of the San Jacinto considers them a sorry air group."

Gibson added, "They've already lost more planes than our group did attacking Truk and the other islands. It'll be interesting to see how they operate under fire."

On 13 April, TG 58.3, consisting of the carriers Enterprise, Lexington, Princeton, San Jacinto and screening ships was underway for Hollandia, New Guinea, to support MacArthur's landings. Strikes were launched on 21 April. No enemy planes met them, only anti-aircraft fire. General Kennedy's Army air force had destroyed them. The troops which landed the following day met with little opposition. The base was so pulverized, the Japs had withdrawn inland.

Bogeys were reported, but none were seen until 26 April at 1245, during my watch. While acting as a fighter director picket, a "Betty" was shot down by our CAP 15 miles to the south. A dispatch from Admiral Reeves ordered us to search for survivors and report findings. At 1400 a lookout yelled, "There's a life raft off our starboard bow with 3 men in it." Lowering a boat, 3 Japs were brought aboard. I exclaimed, "In 2½ years of war, this is the first time I have eye-balled the enemy. They're not as sinister looking as I imagined."

The Captain replied, "The Doctor says one of them is badly injured and you won't be seeing him for long." He died at 1900 and was buried at sea. His name was never known. The other two were placed in the potato locker. Since they spoke no English, the crew just gawked at them. They were transferred to the Lexington the next day.

Mail was picked up from a tanker and when the PA boomed, "Now hear this! Mail call!" there were shouts of joy. Everyone shared the news. I mourned, "I've still got a few girl friends, but my one and only has taken up with a Marine. If any of you can spare one, send her over to me."

The Fleet was 150 miles from Truk and air strikes were launched at dawn. The Japanese put up 62 fighters and 59 were shot down. An additional 34 were destroyed on the ground. All of the small ships in the harbor were sunk. Task Force 58 lost 26 planes, and of the 46 airman shot down, half of them were rescued by submarines. The Fleet retired to the east.

Stalin told Roosevelt and Churchill he would start an offensive in the spring which would coincide with "Overlord".

On 4 May we were anchored in Majuro Lagoon. When I entered the wardroom Gibson was cussing, "This paperwork is absurd. 3 men have their enlistments expiring today. I've got to discharge them and have them reenlist for 4 more years tomorrow. Where in the hell would they go? I can't just throw them over the side."

"That's just to keep executive officers on their toes. Washington doesn't want you to get sloppy," Chuck remarked.

At dinner Gommengenger asked, "Did you guys see the Relief anchored close by? It's got real live American nurses on board and I'm going to make contact."

"It's also got doctors on board and I'm tired of seeing this war from a broom closet. The airdales are having all of the fun. I'm going to get into flight school. Being around the nurses will be a bonus," I remarked.

The next morning I joined Oliver Webb and Harold Stevens, who were going to the Hospital Ship for treatment. Although the nurses were the most beautiful females I had ever seen, l went straight to the sickbay. "Doc, I want to go to flight school. I've been on destroyers for 3 years and I've seen everything there is to see in the Atlantic and Pacific! I've had my share of excitement, chased submarines and exchanged salvos with Jap battleships. Sitting in an engine room is boring as hell and I want out."

The Doctor asked, "Have you applied for flight school before?"

"Yes, a couple of years ago. Everything was fine except for my eyes. I'll sign a waiver. Just give me a chance."

"OK. Let's take a look."

He went over me with a fine tooth comb and when he finished, I asked, "What's the result?"

"You're in excellent shape and should live forever if you don't catch a stray Jap shell."

"So how about flight school?"

"You have astigmatism and your depth perception is off. I'll pass you if you really want to be a pilot, but I wouldn't wager a thin dime on your making more than a couple of landings on the deck of a bouncing carrier."

"You've answered my question. I've seen too many dead pilots and rescued others mangled for life. I'm not for a burial at sea unless I have no other choice. I'm not going to question your judgment or test fate. Thanks for your willingness to help." Returning to the Dortch I told my shipmates the results and said, "That finishes my flying career, but I'll always envy those lucky suckers. They have all of the fun." I drowned my sorrows at the Majuro officer's club. Somehow the nurses were never present when I was there.

Scuttlebutt was rampant about our next operation. When two officers reported aboard at 2200 on 6 May for transportation to Pearl Harbor, speculation ended. The next day the Dortch was underway with the Cotton and Boyd and the carriers Barnes and Petrof Bay.

On 13 May the Dortch moored to the Cotton at Pearl Harbor. As I was watching the men handling the lines, I heard a voice saying, "Toy down dem fawd loin. Wen ya get done, yuh kin go below." The speaker was a slender, blond lieutenant. When the gang plank was secured I went aboard and asked, "Is that a geechie accent I'm hearing?"

"Sure is." I introduced myself and learned he was Augustine T. Smythe, Jr., a member of a prominent Charleston family. We had many friends in common and agreed to continue our conversation over a drink at our earliest opportunity.

There was no end to the repairs and maintenance work. On 14 May Gibson was promoted to Lt. Cmdr.

On liberty days I went to the Moana Hotel and watched the girls walking the beach. Always there were former shipmates and friends to be found. Audry Houvner was busy with final exams, but I saw her twice and her father took me to a party as his guest.

The Sterett was in port and I enjoyed visiting my former shipmates. I reminded Herbie May, "Don't forget the date I'm having with Dina Merrill if she is still free."

"It's a done deal. Here in Hawaii it's hard to imagine there's a war going on. If that's what I believe, how in the hell can our families in the States empathize with us?" This was discussed with no conclusion reached.

While I was enjoying the islands, final preparations for the Normandy landings were taking place. The channel needed to be crossed in darkness, and only at the beginning of the month would there be no moon. Eisenhower selected 5 June as D-Day. The roads in southern England were filled with vehicles as the troops assembled in the channel ports. German agents who had been "turned" reported the landings would occur in southeast France and Norway. As a result, the Germans thought the Normandy landings were a feint.

On 24 May the Dortch, with Task Group 12.1, consisting of the Washington, North Carolina, Vincennes and several accompanying destroyers, was heading west. Gunnery practice, radar tracking and tactical drills were conducted enroute.

On 30 May the Dortch was moored port side to the tanker Quiros in Majuro Lagoon. Gommengenger said, "I learned in Hawaii that Admirals Spruance and Kelly Turner have been drawing up plans for 'Tattersalls', 'Tearaway' and 'Stevedore', sporty code names for Saipan, Tinian and Guam. This will be Turner's fifth major amphibious assault."

"How lucky can one get. I've been with him on all landings except Tarawa," I exclaimed.

At dinner the Captain said, "Saipan has been chosen for the first landing. It has the best airfield in the Mariana's and is 100 miles closer to Japan than Guam. Turner has developed an Underwater Demolition Team to help with the landings. Each member has to be able to swim two miles. He is given a fish line for measuring distances and a stylus and piece of waterproof plastic for taking notes. Beside inspecting the reefs and beaches prior to D-Day, he is supposed to clear out anti-boat mines and other obstacles. If necessary, he can blast passages through the reef."

"Sounds like exciting duty," Drake remarked.

"And dangerous," the Captain responded. "These operations have to be undertaken during daylight. The LCI's will open fire with their 20mm and 40mm guns to distract the Japs."

"If our close support aircraft drop a bomb in the water, it will be goodbye to some of the UDT."

"That's not supposed to happen. They're guarding an emergency radio frequency and the spotters in the LCI's should call them off."[59]

The next day the Captain announced, "There's going to be a reshuffling of jobs. Rothschild will relieve Gibson as navigator. Gommengenger, you'll take over as first lieutenant and Chuck Robbins will relieve you as communication officer."

The weather for 5 June was predicted to be overcast and stormy, so "Overlord" was postponed for 24 hours. In Italy Mark Clark broke out of the Anzio beachhead and was advancing along a broad front. On 5 June the 5th Army entered Rome.

The next day TG 58.3 was enroute to the Mariana's.

While we were eating dinner on 7 June, loud noises were heard in the passageway. "What's that all about?" Gibson asked. Robbins came in shouting, "The Allies hit the beaches of Normandy at 0630 this morning. The first assault waves had 176,000 troops."

"So how did it go?"

"The planning was excellent, except no one realized the large number of men that would get seasick, or the many who would jump out of their landing crafts into water over their heads and drown. In addition, the Russians have attacked Finland and Minsk and are advancing into the Ukraine."

Later we learned that the gunfire on Omaha Beach had been especially murderous because of ineffective bombing. On the other hand, the Luftwaffe was so badly beaten up, they were ineffective. Allied planes ruled the skies and prevented the Germans from bringing up replacements.

Later we saw the personal message Eisenhower sent to each man in the invading force: "You are about to embark upon the Great Crusade toward which we have striven for many months. The eyes of the world are upon you. Your task will not be an easy one. Your enemy is well trained. He will fight savagely. The tide has turned. The free men of the world are marching together to Victory. I have full confidence in your courage, devotion to duty and skill is battle. Good luck! And let us beseech the blessing of Almighty God upon this great and noble undertaking."

We were faced with 30,000 Japanese troops on Saipan who had received few supplies after April, 1944. All were not armed. No reinforcements could be sent in, even from the nearby islands of Guam and Tinian. The troops on the island were sitting around, rather than putting in place the hundreds of anti-boat mines, bales of wire and tons of building materials on hand. They never thought they would have to defend the island. General Saito's plan of defense was "destroy the enemy on the beach".

This was an emotionally charged operation. Admiral Ainsworth expressed it well in this dispatch: "Today a large United States Naval Force, of which your ship is a unit, is on its way to take the islands of Saipan and Tinian away from the Japs and make them give up Guam to its rightful owners. I promise you days and nights of hard fighting, as we must make the sea safe for our transports and pave the way for our Marines. We are trained and ready. I have the utmost confidence in your ability to put the Japs where all the good ones are."

At dinner the Captain said, "From the dispatches I've seen, it looks like the Japanese might commit their capital ships to this action. From the movement of their fleet, it appears that a second Battle of Midway maybe shaping up."

On 8 June the battleships joined the formation, followed by Admiral Spruance in the Indianapolis. Our CAP shot down several snoopy planes during the next three days.

On 12 June air strikes were launched against Saipan. Bogeys were picked up on radar, but never got close. The pilots destroyed 36 planes and several small ships. The strikes continued over the next two days. At night the Japs sent over high-flying planes which dropped bombs but hit nothing.

While we were fueling from the South Dakota, Q.D. Hopkins fell over board. Fortunately, the Gatling lookouts saw this and rescued him uninjured.

At dinner Robbins said, "I heard one of our Task Groups intercepted a Japanese convoy and sank 5 supply ships and damaged 6 others. The battleships have been pounding the fortifications with 16" shells which should make the landings tomorrow a little easier."

Flight operations commenced at dawn. The amphibian tractors followed with men from the 2nd and 5th Marine Divisions. The Japs sent up planes from Truk which harassed our formation, but all were shot down.

At dusk, 9 torpedo bombers penetrated the screen. When General Quarters sounded, I was in my stateroom. When I came out on the deck, I was scared to move as tracers and star shells filled the sky. Each shell seemed to be headed directly at me. For a moment I panicked. It didn't seem possible that I would survive running down the unprotected deck to the engine room. I took a deep breath, turned my eyes away from the sky and ran as fast as I could. I felt secure only after sliding down the ladder into the engine room.

Sammy reported, "Bridge says torpedo bombers are attacking from the port and starboard sides. All ships are firing." I could hear and feel the salvos from our 5" guns.

Sammy exclaimed, "We've knocked down one on the starboard quarter. Others are in flames all around us. Some of our ships are firing on others.[60] There is one helluva mess."

Coming topside I saw six planes burning on the water.

At dinner Robbins said, "B-29's from the 21st Bomber Group in China attacked an iron and steel mill at Yawata yesterday. The results weren't too good. We lost 18 out of 70 planes." Rocky exclaimed, "That's no way to win the war even if those suckers can carry a full bomb load for over 3,000 miles. We can't keep that up for long." General Hap Arnold, in command of the 21st Bomber Group based in southern China, agreed that high level daylight raids were not productive and ceased them.

On the beaches of Saipan, the fighting was intense. The shore bombardment damaged only a few of the pill boxes. As a result the Japanese mortar and artillery fire was devastating. It took 3 days to secure a 100-yard line of beach. The US 27th Division landed to assist. General Saito was confident his men could hold up until Admiral Ozawa arrived from Tawi Tawi.

Ozawa had been ordered to annihilate Spruance, and he planned to lure Spruance into the waters between the Palau's, Yap and Woleai where both land- based and carrier-based planes could slaughter the Fifth Fleet. He had 9 carriers, 5 battleships, 7 heavy cruisers and 34 destroyers. In addition, he had 25 submarines. Lt. Cmdr. Robert Riser, Captain of the submarine Flying Fish, spotted Ozawa's fleet coming through San Bernadino Straits. He dispatched Spruance, "This is the largest group of enemy ships I have ever seen." He kept the Admiral informed of its movement. As a result, Spruance refused to be lured into the trap. He calculated how long it would take Ozawa to cross the Philippine Sea and gave Admiral Jocko Clark's Task Group 58.1 permission to strike Iwo Jima and Chichi Jima. Dozens of planes which were waiting to attack Saipan were destroyed.

I had the watch at 0230 when Spruance signaled, "Two unidentified surface contacts have been picked up on radar. Investigate." The radar man said, "I have them on the screen bearing 259 degrees, distance 8 miles."

GQ was sounded. I asked the Captain, "How about letting me stay on the bridge during this investigation? Dickey can handle the engineering department."

"OK."

At flank speed the distance quickly closed and at 0240 the Captain ordered, "Illuminate the targets with the searchlights."

I saw two Japanese fishing boats, each about 70 feet long.

The Captain asked, "Is the gunnery officer prepared to open fire?"

"He's ready."

"Commence firing." The first salvo straddled the boats. The next were on target. Both boats were hit repeatedly, and by 0303 they were sinking rapidly.

The Captain ordered, "Cease firing and tell the gun crews that deserves a 'well done.'"

Progress was slow in Europe due to the terrain and tenacity of the German troops. On 17 June Generals Rommel and Rundstedt advised withdrawal, as they had no defensive line set up to contain the Allies. Hitler refused. His scientists had developed rockets and jet-propelled bombs. Rather than use them on advancing troops, he terrorized the civilians in London. The first buzz bombs hit on the nights of June 13-14. During the summer, they killed over 6,000 Londoners and wounded 40,000. Even with a speed of over 400 miles per hour, the RAF learned to intercept and destroy them. The V-2's had a speed of 2,000 miles per hour at a height of 60 miles, and nothing could be done with them until the launching sites were captured.

With a major battle looming, on 17 June Admiral Spruance had the fleet rendezvous 160 miles west of Tinian. His battle plan for Admirals Mitscher and Lee was simple: "Our air will first knock out enemy carriers, then attack enemy battleships and cruisers to slow or disable them. Our battle line will then destroy enemy fleet by fleet action if enemy elects to fight, or by sinking slowed or crippled ships if enemy retreats. Action against enemy must be pushed vigorously by all hands to ensure complete destruction of fleet. Destroyers running short of fuel may return to Saipan, if necessary, for refueling. Desire you proceed at your discretion selecting dispositions and movements best calculated to meet the enemy under most advantageous conditions. I shall issue general directives when necessary and leave details to you."

The Japanese had 473 planes; the Fifth Fleet, 956. Admiral Ozawa possessed 3 tactical advantages: (1)He intended to do battle within range of his 100 land-based planes at Guam, Rota and Yap. (2)Japanese planes lacking armor and self-sealing gas tanks had a search range of 560 miles; Mitscher's only 325 miles. (3)The easterly tradewind gave Ozawa the lee, which enabled him to launch and land planes as he approached. In addition, Spruance's movement was restricted, as his primary duty was to cover and protect the invasion of Saipan.

The majority of the Jap pilots had only a few months training and limited flying time. The veterans were killed in earlier actions. Our pilots had two years training, over 300 hours flying time and most were veterans. In addition, Lt. Charles Simmons, Mitscher's communicator, was able to get on the radio circuit with the Japanese air coordinator, translate his commands into English and tell Mitscher precisely where the Japanese planes were being vectored.

In the afternoon Task Group 58.7, consisting of battleships and destroyers under the command of Admiral Willis Lee, left the formation in preparation for the engagement with the Japanese fleet. A message from Admiral Nimitz to Spruance was received: "On the eve of a possible fleet action, you and your officers and the men of your command have the confidence of the Naval Service and your country. We count on you to make the victory decisive."

At dinner Rocky asked, "How come all these laudatory messages always originate from someone thousands of miles from danger? I'll bet he had a drink in his hand as he wrote it."

On 19 June the Fifth Fleet was on a north/south line of bearing. Task Group 58.3 was 110 miles SW of Saipan. 12 miles to the north was TG 58.1 and 12 miles to the south was TG 58.2. The battle line, TG 58.7, was 15 miles to the west, and TG 58.4, with the responsibility for air cover, was deployed within signaling distance.

Although Spruance and Mitscher followed Ozawa's movements

from submarine reports, our scout planes had not seen him. Mitscher set a course to take him within air strike range in the morning. Spruance didn't concur, believing protection of the Saipan invasion force was his first priority.

Ozawa was planning to use the airfields on Guam to refuel his planes and also get help from the land-based planes. Mitscher foiled his plans by sending in a strike which destroyed the airfield and planes.

A scout plane of Ozawa's reported the location of the Fifth Fleet at 0730. Within an hour he launched his first strike. At 0940 radar reported a large group of bogeys 150 miles to the west. GQ was sounded and planes were launched. Ozawa's group of 69 were intercepted west of the fleet. Sammy said, "Some on the bridge can see vapor trails made by the planes, but none of the action."

45 Jap planes were shot down. Ozawa launched 150 more planes at 0900. Radar picked them up 130 miles to the west. Sammy reported, "Torpedo bombers are coming in low from astern. There is heavy anti-aircraft fire from ships on the starboard side. One bomb exploded close aboard the Enterprise. No hits have been made, but several planes have been shot down." The official count was 98.

The third raid of 47 planes was fortunate. It couldn't find our ships, and all of our planes returned to base safely.

The fourth raid of 82 planes was launched at 1100. They got lost, but unfortunately ran into our Hellcats and only 9 returned to their carrier.

Throughout the day bombers had been working over the airfields of Guam and Rota. When the Japanese attempted to land, the fields were so torn up, they crashed and many were killed.

At dinner Robbins said, "The submarines have had a good day. The Sokaku, a surviving carrier from the attack on Pearl, was sunk by the Cavella. At 1552 the Albacore made a hit in a magazine of the Taibo, the fleet flagship. It exploded and sunk so rapidly it took most of the crew to the bottom. Ozawa transferred his flag and got the hell out of there."

Gibson yawned and said, "I'm going to get a little sack time. We've been at General Quarters all day and still haven't found the Jap fleet. Some war!"

On the Lexington, Simmons asked if he could vector out fighters and have the Japanese communicator shot down. Mitscher replied, "Hell, no. He has done us too much good. He's entitled to get home safely."

Ozawa was as confused as we were. He didn't know the location of our ships, or how many planes he had lost. His destroyers needed fueling, but he decided to put it off until the next day.

The Captain remarked, "I don't understand why Mitscher doesn't send out search planes to locate the Japanese fleet so he can attack at dawn."

The Fifth Fleet headed west, and at 1600 Burt was relieving me when the TBS boomed: "Attention all ships. An Enterprise pilot has reported sighting the Japanese fleet, bearing 290 degrees, distance 215 miles, on course 270 degrees, speed 20 knots. It consists of 4 carriers, several cruisers, many destroyers and two tankers."

"Wow! This shapes up to be one of the greatest carrier battles of the war. There are four times the number of ships that were engaged at Midway. Sure wish I could see it from the bridge," I exclaimed.

"If Mitscher is going to order an all out strike at this distance, recovery won't occur until after sundown. It's going to be a dark night. You're going to be better off in the engine room than in a plane," Burt replied.

At 1640, 216 planes were launched. Ozawa was sighted at 1810. The dive bombers attacked the oilers and sank two. The carrier Hiyo was torpedoed and sank. The carriers Ryuho, Zuikaku and Chiyoda were strafed and bombed. Hits were made on the battle ship Haruna as well as other ships, but none were sunk. 65 of Ozawa's surviving 100 planes were destroyed.

With the distance involved, many of our planes failed to make it back. The pilots were tired and fuel ran out. The planes began arriving at 2045. Mitscher ordered the fleet to turn on all lights as well as spotlights. Ships were ordered to fire star shells. It looked like New Year's Eve in Times Square. The lightning flashes to the south from a thunder storm distracted some pilots and were mistaken for star shells. Half of the planes landed on wrong carriers. There were numerous deck crashes and even more water-ditching when fuel ran out. It was rumored that a couple of Japanese planes landed on our carriers, but this proved to be untrue. The last plane landed at 2252.

Throughout the night the destroyers investigated all reported lights and sounds. At 2200 the Dortch rescued Lt.(jg) J. Gagnan Harmon and his crewmen, L.H. Harris, AMM 3/c, and A.C. Kitchen, ARM 2/c, who had a dislocated shoulder. Thirty minutes later, Lt.(jg) C.B. Collins, G.C. Ehemann, AM 1/c, and W.V. Langworthy, ARM 2/c, were picked up. At breakfast the Captain said, "It was a tough night, but we've been handsomely rewarded." The pilots responded, "You can say that again. I'd hate to think what might have happened if you hadn't found us."

At dawn air strikes were launched, but the pilots were unable to find Ozawa.

The Dortch picked up Admiral McCain from the Indianapolis and almost dumped him into the Pacific Ocean while hauling him over by breeches buoy. At 0850 he was transferred to the Lexington. In the afternoon the rescued pilots and crewmen were delivered to the Enterprise.

When Ozawa anchored at Okinawa on 22 June, he had only 35 serviceable planes. 92% of his carrier planes had been destroyed. He also lost the 80 planes based on Guam. 3 of his largest carriers had been sunk and 445 of his pilots killed. This was the third time his carrier air groups had been wiped out. We lost 50 planes to enemy action and 80 had crash landed. All but 16 pilots and 33 crew men were rescued.

"The Great Mariana's Turkey Shoot" was over. Historians proclaimed it to be the greatest carrier battle of all time.

The Task Force spent the afternoon fueling. Admiral Jocko Clark with TG 58.1 was given permission to work over Iwo and Jico Jima. When he struck the next morning, his pilots shot down 66 Jap planes and destroyed many on the ground.

The Battle of the Philippine Sea was a disaster for the Japanese. Their planes could never again engage on any terms other than suicidal. Without pilots, the Japanese could only use their carriers as decoys. When Ozawa anchored in Nakagasku Bay, Okinawa, he submitted his resignation. This was rejected by Admiral Toyoda.

Mitscher reported, "Enemy escaped. Damaged, but fleet not sunk."

Young said, "I'll bet the desk Admirals in Pearl Harbor are doing their usual Monday morning quarterbacking and complaining about placing a non-aviator in command over carriers. In my opinion, Spruance was justified in staying close to Guam and covering Saipan. The troops needed air support. We couldn't have destroyed any more Jap planes and we might have lost some of our ships."

"That's true, but Mitscher's failure to send out searches for Ozawa after sundown on 19 June could be justifiably criticized. The air battle on the 20th could have been delivered in the morning with better results," Gibson exclaimed.

"True, but Mitscher felt his pilots needed rest after flying all day. No matter, the Battle of the Philippine Sea will go down as one of the most decisive of the war." This had been predicted by Admiral Toyoda's announcement on 15 June: "The fate of the Empire rests on this one battle."

The Japanese forces on Saipan, Tinian and Guam could not be reinforced. They were doomed. Victory in the Mariana's made an American victory over Japan inevitable.

The Marines on Saipan weren't convinced at first. When they saw the Fifth Fleet leave, they thought they had been abandoned just as at Guadalcanal. On the other hand, General Saito assumed the Japanese navy had destroyed our forces when Tokyo Rose broadcast: "11 American carriers have been sunk."

The battle for the Mariana's was not over. On 25 June, strikes were launched against Rota and Guam. At 1942 the starboard engine broke down and wasn't repaired until 0252. We fueled in the morning and spent the afternoon delivering mail.

Chuck Robbins commented at dinner, "From dispatches I've read, the Marine Generals have been unhappy with our reconnaissance to date. H.M. 'Howlin' Mad' Smith is angry because of the criticism he received for the high casualty rates in the Mariana's invasion. To counteract his complaints, Admiral Nimitz has ordered Task Force 58 to conduct a massive photo mission called 'Operation Snapshot'. The San Jacinto has been given prime responsibility for getting pictures of every nook and cranny of Peleliu Island so the casualty rate can be reduced. The First Marine Division is scheduled to land on 15 September."

"So how is that going to affect us?"

"Admiral Montgomery has sent this dispatch to all ships: 'The primary objective of this mission is the photographic coverage of assigned area. Unless complete and thorough coverage is obtained, the entire operation will have been a failure."

"So far as I can see, it's business as usual for us," Rocky exclaimed.

On 27 June the American flag was raised on the top of Mount Tapotchau. In the end, Saito and Admiral Nagumo, the admiral who in 1941 led his carriers to the successful attack on Pearl harbor, committed suicide. It was a costly operation. We had over 3,000 killed and over 13,000 wounded. Japanese losses were unknown, but over 23,000 bodies were buried. Hundreds committed suicide jumping off the cliffs. Men, women and children cut each others throats; parents dashed their babies brains out; children tossed grenades at each other. Over 14,000 internees, including Japanese, Koreans and Chamorros, were captured. Feeding them became a problem.

General Holland Smith wrote; "I have always considered Saipan to be the decisive battle of the Pacific offensive. It was Japan's Pearl Harbor. Its loss caused greater dismay than all of her previous defeats put together."

Tojo and his entire cabinet resigned. General Kuniaki Koiso formed a new cabinet with Admiral Shigemitsu as his Deputy Prime Minister. This was interpreted as an admission of defeat and a desire for peace.

On 2 July at 1326 while I was OOD, a wrecked Japanese bomber was sighted. I was directed to investigate. I went close aboard, but could see no sign of life. "We need to check and see if there are any code books or important papers on board," the Captain said. "Let's get a volunteer to swim over."

"I'll go. I'm as good a swimmer as anyone on board. Besides, I might be able to identify something of value better than others."

"Forget it. I need you right here. I'll get a volunteer." W.J. Hawk, MM2c, was selected. With a lifeline tied around his waist, he swam over. Upon returning he said, "The cockpit door was open and there was no sign of life. I could see no bodies. I found nothing. The plane had been stripped of all military equipment and publications."

"Thanks for your help. I guess we'll never know what happened to the crew," the Captain said.

At 1807 a raft with 6 Japanese was sighted, survivors from the downed bomber. They gesticulated, waved their clenched fists and kept shouting words we couldn't understand. Someone remarked, "They're probably cussing us in Japanese." One aimed a pistol at the men on the forecastle. He was killed immediately. All of the others except one jumped off the raft and swam away. At 1841 the remaining Japanese clamored aboard. He spoke no English. His name and rank remained unknown.

The next morning the prisoner was transferred to the Lexington. Fueling and flight operations were conducted throughout the day.

The Allies were advancing in Europe. On 29 June Hitler met with Rommel and von Rundstedt at Berchetesgaden and demanded containment of the beachhead. The Generals proposed evacuation of Normandy. Hitler refused. Von Rundstedt resigned and von Kluge replaced him.

For us the fourth of July was just another day of lifeguard duty ten miles west of Orote Point. In the afternoon we rescued the crews of two downed bombers. They were transferred to the Lexington the next morning .

Following lunch on 6 July, there was a loud blast and the Dortch shook like it had been hit by a shell. Burt left to investigate. Returning in a few minutes he said, "Believe it or not, the torpedoman on duty swears a 300 lb. depth charge set on 'safe' accidentally fired. Fortunately no damage was done."

The Captain disagreed and at 1340 held Mast for the TM3c on duty and gave him a warning for being negligent.

There were smiling faces on 9 July when Enewetok Atoll was sighted. The name meant "Land between the East and West". It had been a resting and refreshment stop for the primitive Micronesians in their long voyages from west to east. The Japanese navy took it over and built an air strip on Engebi Island and used it for staging purposes. The lagoon was the second largest in the Marshall's, covering 388 square miles. There were fewer than 100 natives. It was only lightly defended, and when the landings were made on 22 February, only 195 Americans were killed. The Japanese fought to the last man and lost 2,677.

There was liberty for all. The men enjoyed beer busts on the beach and swimming in the crystal clear waters of the lagoon. There was the usual officer's club: coconut palm branches over a few limbs with a bar of planks on barrels. The beer and tongues flowed freely. The pilots gave their version of the big battle and we gave ours.

I was sorry to see Phil Williams leave, at 1402 on 10 July, for Fleet Gunnery and Torpedo School on Oahu. New men reported aboard.

In Italy Mark Clark was advancing slowly until the River Arno was reached on 15 July. The Germans had established a heavily fortified position and he was forced to halt.

On 14 July TG 58.3 was underway for Guam. The next morning I was summoned to the Captain's cabin. I thought, "What in the hell have I done now?" Young had a dispatch in his hand and a scowl on his face. "Chief, what have you been up to? You been talking with some of your friends in the Bureau?"

"What's he talking about?" I thought. There was no way I could contact anyone in Washington. "You've got me this time. I haven't the foggiest idea of what you're talking about."

When he handed me the dispatch, I read:
ORDERS 15 July 1944

Lt. Harold E. Jervey, Jr., hereby detached from such duties as may have been assigned. Proceed immediately and report to Commanding Officer USS Ingersoll (DD 652) for duty.

"I'm shocked and puzzled. I don't even know what my job will be. I know Bob Dickey is fully qualified to take over as engineering officer. There won't be any problem in my proceeding immediately, with the Ingersoll only a few thousand yards away. Very strange."

"Not really. I suspect the chief engineer on the Ingersoll is being transferred and there is no replacement aboard. I'll miss you. We've had some exciting times together. Get your things together and we'll transfer you in a breeches buoy as soon as you're ready." I met with Bob Dickey, went over all of the records and had him officially relieve me.

At dinner I said, "I don't know whether I'm lucky or unlucky. I ought to be heading back to the States, but instead I'll still be in the same squadron. I'll buy you a beer on our next liberty."

On 17 July at 0930 the lines were rigged from the bridge of the Dortch to the bridge of the Ingersoll. My luggage was transferred. I stood on the bow with mixed emotions. I recalled the saying I had heard many times: "The only two good ships are the one you're leaving and the one you're going to." That's how I felt as I saluted the quarter-deck, looked up at Burt, OOD, on the bridge and asked, "Request permission to leave the ship."

He returned my salute and replied, "Permission granted. Good luck and good hunting."

-

CHAPTER 10

Securing the Mariana's, Peleliu and Morotai;
Bombing of the Bonnins, Luzon, Formosa and Okinawa

I climbed into the breeches buoy and waved to my shipmates who lined the rail. Arriving at the Ingersoll, I was greeted by the OOD whom I immediately recognized. "Tack Townsend!" I exclaimed, "I haven't seen you since graduation day at the University of South Carolina in June '41. We've been operating in the same destroyer division, sharing liberties and yet our paths have not crossed."

"True," he replied. " Maybe we don't frequent the same bar."

"No matter. I already feel at home."

He escorted me to the bridge where I met Commander A.C. Veasey, USN, balding, slender and of medium height. He was the second honor graduate in his class at Annapolis.

"Good to have you aboard, Lieutenant. Our chief engineer has orders to attend MIT for more schooling. I think you'll find everything in order."

We chatted briefly and I went to the wardroom, where I met Lt. J.W. Mitchell, gunnery officer, from Natick, Mass., Ensign Fusfield, radar officer, Sioux Falls, SD, Lt.(jg) W.G. Wheeler, torpedo officer, from Dedham, Mass., and Lt. C.C. Wright, engineering officer, who greeted me with a smile and said, "This is a miracle. I was resigned to wait a couple of weeks for my replacement."

During the next two days he introduced me to key petty officers, my assistants, Lt. Will Pardee, USN, and Ensign Piper, who had been commissioned from the enlisted ranks. Checking the paperwork and finding everything in order, I relieved him.

The Ingersoll was named for Admiral Royal Rodney Ingersoll, a distinguished veteran of the Civil War, Spanish American War and World War I. His son, Admiral Ingersoll, Jr., was distinguishing himself in WW II. He also had a son who was killed at the Battle of Midway.

The planes of TG 58.3 continued strafing and bombing the island of Guam in preparation for the landings on 21 July. At 1400 the Ingersoll left the formation with DesDiv 100 and the battleships New Jersey, Alabama and Iowa. At 2345 I relieved Will Pardee, my bunk mate from Atlanta, Ga. He said, "Everything is quiet. We're on course 045 degrees, speed 18 knots. The guide is the Iowa. There are no special orders or course changes."

I replied, "I have the deck. Sleep good." During the next four hours I learned something about my watch members. At 0345 Lt. Hollander, assistant gunnery officer, relieved me.

On 20 July, while the Ingersoll was fueling from the New Jersey in Saipan Harbor, Captain Veasey discovered a cousin of his wife's whom he had not seen since his wedding 11 years earlier. The two enjoyed catching up via megaphones. I watched the bombardment of Tinian 3 miles away, where the sky filled with spectacular fireworks when ammunition dumps exploded.

Entering the wardroom, I found Lt.(jg) Jack Elliott, the communication officer from Newark, Ohio, exclaiming, "Our guys in Europe have been having a tough time. General George Patton was reassigned to the Twelfth Army under General Omar Bradley. His armored divisions captured St. Lo on the 18th. We're going to start moving now. The Russians are at the Polish border and Rommell was wounded when his car was strafed by an RAF plane."

Lt.(jg) Robert "Stinky" Davis responded, "I've heard of Patton. They should have put him in charge earlier." Stinky was from Harrison, New York. He had finished his freshman year at Columbia University Law School when he was called up. He was a tall blond with short-cropped curly hair.

"Stinky! Where do you get all of your information? There is no subject that you aren't an authority on," Fusfield exclaimed.

Without hesitation Davis replied, "I travel in the best circles. I was having a drink on the beach with Mitscher's chief of staff and he gave me an update on the war in Europe. Just stick with me, fellows. I won't lead you astray."

At 1210 Lt. C.C. Wright was detached to report to SOPA for transportation to the First Naval District.

In the afternoon DesDiv 100 with the battleships sortied out of the harbor during my watch. Will relieved me. As I entered the wardroom, Stinky corralled me, "Are you related to Professor Huger Jervey, former Dean of Columbia Law School?"

"He's a distant cousin. I had dinner with him when I was putting the Dortch in commission."

"You'd better study law, then," he exclaimed. "You'd have it made. He's one of the most respected and popular teachers at Columbia. His classes always have a waiting line, and he's a senior member of one of the most prestigious law firms in New York. In addition, three of the present US Supreme Court Judges were his students and admirers. They still turn to him when they have difficult legal problems."

" That's great! But what if law isn't my cup of tea?"

"So what do you plan to study?"

"Medicine for the moment. There are a lot of ifs however. Keep talking. You might convince me law is my bag."

Doctor H.H. MacGilpin from Massachusetts said, "You're nuts if you even consider law. We've got too many lawyers now. They're a bunch of crooks chasing the dollar."

When I relieved Hollander on 21 July at 0345, he said, "We're supposed to rendezvous with Task Force 58.3 during your watch. TG 58.4 is being left behind to support operations on Guam. With 58.1 and 2 we will launch strikes against Palau and Yap."

At 0659 the Ingersoll was on station in TG 58.3. When I was relieved of the watch and went to the wardroom, I found Tack in a heated discussion with the executive officer, Lt. Cmdr. I.J. Superfine, an academy graduate. He operated by the book, and if it wasn't in Navy Regs, he made up his own. Tack had said, "He's a super pain in the butt, par for executive officers."

From Superfine's expression I knew he was getting pleasure telling Tack how poorly his men handled the lines when docking.

I said, "Fellows, is this a closed discussion or can I be included?"

Superfine glared and Tack laughingly said, "Join in. The Exec has just been singing my praises, or rather plans to just as soon as I demonstrate my competency in line handling."

Without a word Superfine, stalked out. Tack and I reminisced. Elliott came in exclaiming, "An attempt to assassinate Hitler was made by some of his Generals. He was conferring with them at Wolf's Lair in Prussia. A bomb was placed under his table and exploded. It did him no harm since he was seated at the other end of the table."

"I'll wager every one of the conspirators will face a firing squad or be hung," Tack responded.[61]

The Combined Joint Chiefs of Staff were debating strategy. Admiral King and General Marshall wanted to by-pass the Philippines and land on Formosa and Okinawa. General MacArthur was outraged at the idea. He had promised those 16,000,000 Filipinos he would return. It was a matter of honor. Moreover, he believed land-based planes were necessary to assist in occupying Formosa and Okinawa. His plan called for landings on Mindanao on 15 October, Leyte on 15 November and Luzon on 15 January. King and Marshall disapproved. No decision was reached.

When I relieved Pardee at 2345, he said, "We are heading for Palau. Our goal is to prevent the Japanese from using these islands as staging areas to bomb Guam and Tinian. Hopefully the pictures taken of the fortifications on Pelelieu will reduce the casualty rate when the landings start on 15 September."

The Palau Islands were discovered in 1543 by Villabos, a Spaniard. In 1919 they were taken over by Japan as spoils of World War I. No pictures of the islands were available. The major mission of Ensign George Bush and the other pilots on the San Jacinto was to get aerial photographs of the fortifications.

On 25 July planes began bombing Palau. Few enemy planes rose to intercept. Many were destroyed on the ground. The Japanese were unable to attack our troops landing on Tinian. With the extensive shore bombardment prior to the landings, the fighting was over by 2 August. General Holland Smith announced, "Tinian stands as the perfect amphibious operation of the Pacific War."

Roosevelt arrived at Honolulu on 26 July. With Admirals Nimitz and Leahy present, General MacArthur gave such a convincing argument that the President said, "We will occupy the Philippines before moving north."

Our planes pounded Palau and continued doing photo reconnaissance work through 27 July. The formation then headed east.

Paul Watson, assistant gunnery officer, was getting the latest news from Jim Elliott when I entered the wardroom. Tack had said, "Paul is the token Texan on board. All destroyers are required to have one. He's from Dallas, and when you get him upset, you won't be able to understand a thing he says."

Paul asked, "So is the war ending in Europe?"

"Hell, no! But General Patton's armored divisions broke through the enemy lines on July 25. They are advancing up to 40 miles a day, sweeping westward through Brittany. Other divisions are moving south and north to trap the Seventh Army of Field Marshall Kluge. The war isn't over, but progress is being made."

"So what's happening with the Italians?"

"After Rome was captured, the going was slow. Some of Alexander's troops were needed elsewhere. On 19 July the advance came to an end at the River Arno. It's heavily defended and until Alexander gets more troops, he's going no farther."

I knew I had been accepted when Chief Machinist Mate Simpson asked, "How would you like a drink of the finest hooch this side of the States?"

"And how am I going to get that?"

"One of our shipmates is a chemist of the first order. The last time we provisioned, he got a large quantity of raisins. With sugar, fresh water, a few glass jars and several helpers, he has ready the finest raisin liquor you could hope for."

"I'm going to pretend I didn't hear you and I suggest you don't repeat what you said. However, on the next liberty, I'm going to find you on the beach and verify how good that hooch is."

For the next two days the Dortch patrolled the entrance to Saipan Anchorage. We joined the formation when they sortied out enroute to Iwo Jima, which was only 600 miles from downtown Tokyo.

On 2 August the Cogeswell delivered mail and the PA boomed, "Now hear this! Mail call for the crew in the mess hall; for the officers, in the wardroom."

Elliott came in and said, "The Poles in Warsaw have revolted against the Germans and Hitler has sent in reinforcements. Stalin is angry because he wasn't told. His troops are outside of Warsaw and ordered to stay put."

At dinner on 3 August, Veasy said, "We're in for some excitement. Intelligence has reported much shipping in and around Iwo Jima and Chichi Jima. Plans call for DesDiv 100, DesRon 46 and CruDiv 13 to form up on 4 August and destroy aircraft, shipping and other installations on Iwo Jima."

"My men will be happy to hear that," Mitchell said. "They're getting tired of target practice with no live targets."

The next morning during my watch, air strikes began against the Bonnins. At 1240 the Ingersoll left the formation to form up Task Unit 58.1.6. Our planes found a convoy off Muko Jima and sank one destroyer, 2 destroyer escorts and 5 freighters.

At sundown radar picked up an unidentified ship, bearing 300 degrees, distance 12 miles. GQ was sounded. At 1900 George, my talker, said, "We have a Sampan in sight and have taken it under fire." George excitedly added, "The sampan is burning and sinking." At 1925 he yelled, "There's a convoy ahead consisting of 5 merchant ships, 3 destroyers and maybe a cruiser. We're going after them." The van destroyers and cruisers closed and commenced firing. George said, "Hits are being made on several of the ships. We've been ordered, with the rest of DesDiv 100, to close on the cruiser and deliver the coup de grace." At 30 knots the distance closed rapidly, and George said, "A ship 9,200 yards away is dead in the water. The destroyers have been ordered to sink it."

I could hear and feel salvo after salvo pounding away. George exclaimed, "They're firing at us, but the shells are off target and falling short." At 2145 George yelled, "It's burning and sinking. The Captain believes it is a destroyer of the Mutuki class."

The Ingersoll rejoined the formation at 0352. GQ was set as Chichi Jima was neared. At 1007, spotting planes were overhead and the first bombardment run was started. No salvos were fired because 15,000 yards was out of our range. On the second run, George said, "We've taken under fire a large transport near the seaplane base. Visibility is so poor fire control doesn't know if hits have been made." In a few minutes he excitedly added, "A spotter plane reports we've inflicted heavy damage on the ship." On the next run George said, "We're firing on a shore battery. This is going to be our final run. Carrier planes have been called to mop up." Chichi Jima was left in shambles. Only 3 enemy planes took to the air and 25 were destroyed on the ground.

On 9 August the Ingersoll joined up with the Iowa, Indiana, Alabama, Washington (OTC), CruDiv 13 and DesRons 50 and 52. We stayed at GQ most of the day while battle problems and gunnery practice were conducted. There were smiles when Superfine announced, "Everyone can relax. We're enroute to Enewetok for a little R&R."

Entering the harbor on 11 August, the men started bitching, "This place is a hell hole with more water and less land than Majuro. It sure ain't no Panama, or Boston. I miss Tassel Gertie who could twirl the tassels backwards and forwards on her boobs. We need her to boost our morale."

At lunch on 13 August Doc MacGilbin came in exclaiming, "Every time we come into port I have a patient to transfer to a larger ship. Just

USS Ingersoll 652

took one of our fellows over to the Prairie with a diagnosis of appendicitis." Horton remarked, "Better that way than having to dump them into the ocean."

It was a happy occasion on 14 August when representatives of ComDesPac presented Frank J. Passenant, FC3\c, and Donald Mosher, GM3/c, the Bronze Star medal. Captain Veasey got a letter of commendation for distinguished service during the operation at Tinian, Saipan and Guam.

The next day the news reported that the Allies had made an amphibious landing in Southern France between Cannes and Hyeres. With little resistance they advanced to Marseilles, Toulon, Cannes and Nice.

On 18 August Superfine said, "War or no war, Chief, Navy Regs require a semi-annual inspection of the hull and fittings. You're the senior member of the Hull Board." After we entered the floating dry-dock the next morning, I inspected all outboard sea valves, propellers and shafts. Tack inspected the other underwater fittings. I reported to the Captain, "Conditions are satisfactory. No repairs are necessary."

The crew enjoyed loading up the whale boat with iced-down beer, swimming and shooting craps on the beach. The torpedo men were always welcomed with their refined 180 proof alcohol which they removed from the torpedoes. The officers went to the primitive officer's club and drank or swam on the beach. At night we saw "Since You Went Away" with Claudette Colbert, Jennifer Jones and Joseph Cotton as well as "Laura" with Gene Tierney, Dana Andrews and Clifton Webb. On one occasion when the projector was acting up, someone sang out, "Send for the doctor. This projector needs an operation." Another yelled, "Hell, no, send for Lt. Jervey. This is an engineering problem." The problem was quickly resolved.

The Allies were on the move in Europe. Russian troops advancing into Rumania trapped 20 German divisions. King Carol, on 23 August, declared hostilities over and then Finland asked for a truce.

There were loud cheers on 25 August when General DeGaulle made a triumphant entrance into Paris with French and American troops.

With Halsey now in command, we became the Third Fleet. On 30 August the Ingersoll was underway with TF 34. At lunch Veasey said, "We're enroute to Palau to destroy Jap planes and to deceive them as to our next landing. The San Jacinto and other carriers are enroute to Chichi Jima to do the same."

Stinky responded, "Admiral Jocko Clark's Task Group 38.1 has bombed the Bonnins so many times his air groups have issued shares in the 'Jocko Jima Development Corp'. The forms have printed on them: 'Choice locations of all types in Iwo, Chicho, Haha and Muko Jima.

Only 500 miles from Downtown Tokyo'. I saw them at the Enewetok officer's club."

"Are they legal?" Will asked.

"Who knows. Everyone had a good laugh from the wording on the stock certificates."

Strikes were launched the next morning. The bombing was so successful that the Japanese moved their radio operations into hillside caves where the men and equipment would be safer from attacks.

On 6 September a high speed run was begun to the Palaus. At breakfast Elliott announced, "Brussels has been liberated and Bulgaria has surrendered. No one knows what the hell is going on in Greece. There's been a civil war between a group that supports the deposed King, another one who call themselves Republicans and another who are Communists. The German troops now occupying the country are just watching these people kill each other."

The Ingersoll was on station as ordered and commenced its first firing run on Pelelieu Island. I asked George what we were firing at.

"Bridge says we're firing at an airfield, which can't be seen because it's too far inland. Some one spotted several Japanese sitting on the beach. They scurried for cover as soon as our shells passed over their heads."

I heard and felt steam close by. McDuffy yelled, "The plug on a drainpipe of the evaps has blown off." I saw the main switchboard getting drenched with salt water. Sparks were everywhere. McDuffy shouted, "That's the end of the board. There's no power for the ventilation system and a couple of the pumps. We're going to have to shut down the boilers in the forward fireroom." I grabbed the phone and reported the damage to the Captain and assured him that we could keep up with the other destroyers as long as flank speed was not required and that it would take about two hours to repair. The temperature rose, but was tolerated while the repairs were being made.

The bombardment runs continued. Each had a specified target. George said, "Control reports our fire has been deadly. Several gun emplacements, anti-tank traps and a pillbox have been pulverized."

When firing ceased I asked, "What's happening?"

"We're heading south to work over Anguar Island."

When the firing resumed, George said, "There's a phosphate plant, a village and a tall light house. We're firing at the phosphate loading docks. Control reports they have been destroyed and we've completed our assignment."

The Combined Chiefs of Staff, with Prime Minister Churchill and FDR, met in Quebec on 11 September. They agreed on future landing dates in the Pacific and overall strategy for Europe. Post-war Germany would be occupied in the north by the British, in the south by the US and Russia in the east. There would be no zone for the French.

At dinner on 9 September, Veasey said we were headed for Leyte and on the way we would make air strikes on Mindanao, Leyte and Luzon. 200 planes were shot down, many ships sunk and numerous installations destroyed. Halsey and his staff believed the Japanese air force was finished. They didn't realize the Japanese were holding back waiting for the major landings.

On 13 September Halsey recommended the Palau, Yap, Morotai and Mindanao landings be canceled and the troops with Task Force 38 be made available to MacArthur for an immediate assault on Leyte with D-Day 20 October. Within two hours the President and the Combined Chiefs of Staff agreed with Halsey's recommendation. However, the Morotai and Pelelieu operations were too far along. Some believed these islands would be necessary for air bases and a fleet anchorage in the attack on Luzon. Veasey announced that D-Day for Morotai and Pelelieu would be 15 September.

TG 58.3 headed south to support the landings on Pelelieu, where 10,000 Japanese troops were dug in. Colonel Nakagawa, with the aid of professional miners, had excavated a system of interlocking caves in the coral which were too deep for naval or air bombardment to reach. The only weapons which could cope with them were the flame throwers which could penetrate 40 or 50 feet and lick around corners. Our troops were only momentarily stopped at the beach. The Colonel's main line of defense was so far back that naval bombardment couldn't reach the troops. He also had adequate forces in reserve to mount counter-attacks at opportune times. The island took a pounding for 5 days prior to the landings. On D-Day carrier strikes continued in support of the troops. Halsey expected an attack by the Japanese Navy and had Admiral Lee form TF 34. To the north at Morotai the Marines encountered no opposition.

By 24 September the harbor could be used and the first transport plane was able to land on 1 October. Resistance didn't cease until 25 November. Colonel Nagawa committed suicide. We had over 10,000 killed and wounded, the Japs about as many.

At dinner on 19 September, Veasey said, "With our mission completed, we're on our way to Luzon. We'll see some action there."

When I relieved Stinky on 20 September, I saw everyone staring to the port side. Stinky pointed and exclaimed, "Look at that monstrosity. Have you ever seen anything like it?" I was shocked. The creature was 60 feet long and was swimming with its head held high on a long neck. I gasped in disbelief. It acted like it owned the ocean. We soon passed and lost sight of it. Veasey said, "It looked like a sea serpent to me. We're near the Philippine Trench where the water is 6,000 fathoms deep. No one knows what lives in those depths." The 1145 deck log entry read, "Sighted a sea serpent close aboard to port, approximately 60 feet in length."

At breakfast Elliott announced, "We're on the move in Europe. Mark Clark's 5th Army has broken through the Gothic Line in Italy and is heading for Bologna. Finland has signed an armistice with Russia."

"What about Warsaw?"

"It's a mess. The Poles are holding part of the city and being supplied by air drops. The Germans are giving them a tough time and the Russians are still sitting on their butts a few miles from the city."

"If they keep that up, we still might get to Tokyo first," Paul exclaimed.

At dawn on 22 September GQ was sounded when the Essex reported enemy air craft approaching. George said, "The planes seem to be circling around." At 0745 he exclaimed, "They're 11,000 yards away and commence firing has been ordered." No hits were made and GQ was secured.

Manila and the surrounding airfields were bombed and strafed for the next two days. The Japanese were surprised. Our pilots destroyed 375 planes, sank 40 ships and did major damage to both Nichols and Clark Airfields.

On 27 September the fleet was anchored in Kossol Passage, Palau Islands. The weather was miserable with rain and fog most of the time. We could hear the gunfire ashore. Superfine remarked, "Aren't you guys glad you're in the Navy? Those poor Marines are catching hell." There was a resounding yes.

Elliott reported the news that the Allies had crossed into Germany at Stalzemburg, fought their way into Arnhem and seized the bridge across the Rhine. The Germans had counter-attacked and pushed them back across the river.

"Even with most of France liberated," Horton said, "it's going to be slow going with our supply lines over-extended."

"Well, the Greeks have finally gotten their act together. All forces have been placed under the command of Papandreou. They can now contribute to the war effort," Superfine said.

"General Mountbatten has been ordered to clear the Japanese from Burma. There's no way he can do the job without more troops and supplies," Elliott added.

Over the next two days supplies were replenished. On 30 September the Ingersoll was underway with TG 38.3. The doctor was kept busy with the crew's eye problems. The boiler tubes were routinely blown after dark. The soot came out like black hail. Eyes became inflamed and painful. Many had bronchitis.

"Why don't you guys quit blowing those tubes?" the doctor asked. "I'm getting more work than I need."

" If we stopped, it wouldn't be long before this ship would stop. Why don't you tell those fellows to cover their noses and mouths with a wet handkerchief and wear sun glasses?" I replied.

At breakfast Veasey announced that the Ulithi landings were on schedule. The Marines had encountered little opposition. The Fleet would have an advance base when landings start in the Philippines, and we'd have an anchorage for recreation.

Ulithi was sighted on the afternoon of 2 October. The atoll was discovered in 1526 by the Portuguese navigator Diego da Rocha and is inhabited by Micronesians. The Japanese established a radio and weather station, but after being bombed a few times, the Japs evacuated it. The lagoon could accommodate up to 700 ships. It was halfway between Guam and Pelelieu, 900 miles from Leyte and 3,660 miles west of Pearl Harbor.

In the afternoon the Ingersoll anchored. During the night the wind picked up, the waves grew in size and the rain poured down. At 0550 a typhoon was reported close at hand and all ships were ordered out to sea. The waves became gigantic. The Ingersoll rolled and plunged. Everyone received K-rations. There was no sleep, and negotiating the decks to watch stations even with the life lines was hazardous. No damage was suffered, but one LCT was sunk, 3 others beached, 14 LCM's and 65 LCVP's were destroyed. Midday on 4 October, the Ingersoll was anchored in the lagoon.

The news reported that the British had landed at Patros on Greece and Mark Clark was closing in on Bologna.

On liberty I went to the islet Mog-Mog [62], where the officer's club known as "Crowley's Bar" was located. It was similar to those on the other atolls. The beer was green and the vile-tasting scotch had been nicknamed "Australian Death". As I hoisted a beer, Tack said, "It ain't the Ritz, but it don't move and it don't bite."

Mitchell mumbled, "Who said it don't move? I can't stand up straight. Everything is topsy turvy and I'm about to fall on my face." Horton muttered, "That stuff bites worse than that ole moonshine I had in college." We returned safely to the Ingersoll.

With little sleep and big headaches, there was loud bitching at 0230 when the PA boomed, "Now hear this! Set special sea details. Make all preparations for getting underway." As the Ingersoll got underway at

0318, the PA boomed, "This is the Captain speaking. We've been allotted 1¾ hours to get our provisions and supplies. I expect all hands to turn to. This may be our last chance for awhile." Superfine told me and the other department heads, "The South Dakota is moored alongside the supply ship Aldebaren. We can't handle those large cargo nets so we'll use the battleship as a loading dock. Normally this job would be Tack's and his deck gang, but I want all hands involved, which also means the black gang." Everyone turned to. We got our provisions and an additional 25 crates of fresh fruit left behind by less efficient ships. The crew of the Aldebaren yelled, "You guys are nuts. With all those crates topside, you're going to capsize in the first heavy sea." The reply rang out, "If we do, we'll die happy."

In the afternoon Admiral Mitscher sent a message, "All ships and personnel have extended themselves to the limits. The past ten months have included the most constant and intensive operations of the Pacific War. I am aware that tens of thousands of men have only set their feet on a barren coral reef for an hour or two at a time. No other naval force has ever been subjected to such a period of constant battle operations. The most crucial period of fighting lies ahead. I caution you against relaxing your intensity and personal readiness. There will be trying days in the weeks ahead. With the help of Almighty God, we will prevail!"

The sky turned black on Saturday 7 October as TG 38.3 sortied out enroute to Okinawa and our afternoon rendezvous with the other Task Groups. With a typhoon nearby, the waves were running 10-15 feet the next morning when the Ingersoll went alongside the Massachusetts to fuel. The hoses kept parting and the men held tightly to stanchions to keep from getting washed over the side.

My talker excitedly exclaimed, "The oil king wants to see you in wardroom country immediately." I ran forward and found the oil king standing outside the hatch leading to officer's country. "We've got a mess." He pointed. Sloshing back and forth was two inches of black oil. "I've already shut off the valves to the forward tanks. A bubble of air got trapped in the tank and when it escaped through the vent, it carried a couple hundred gallons of oil with it. Your stateroom is covered with the mess."

"Well, this isn't my first experience and it won't be my last. It's not your fault. I'll tell the Captain and when we get through fueling, have all hands turn to with buckets, mops and rags. Wardroom country won't smell the same for a while, but we can live with it." The oil was cleaned up in a couple of hours, but the stench remained for several days. I took a ribbing about the incompetence of my men.

The voyage to Okinawa was uneventful. At dawn on 10 October, air strikes took off for Okinawa. During the morning CTG 38.3 dispatched a cruiser and two destroyers to annihilate the shipping. Bogeys were reported over the other Task Groups in the afternoon, and General Quarters was sounded off and on all day. The pilots reported destroying a submarine tender, 12 torpedo boats, 2 midget submarines, 4 cargo ships, several sampans and 111 planes.

The radioman tuned in Tokyo Rose. Music was being played, interspersed with comments aimed at the 3rd Fleet, "Of the two or three million men overseas, only one in ten will ever become involved in actual combat. You men in the US Fleet, you are the one in 1,000 Americans fighting for the other 999. Why do you waste your time and your lives when your wives and sweethearts are sleeping with other men?" The comments were loud and lewd.

Admiral Toyoda heard of our attack while he was on Formosa. Guessing this was the start of something big, he alerted the Japanese Navy's air bases for Sho-1 (meaning Victory, Leyte) or SHO-2 (Victory, Formosa). He believed his Navy needed only one decisive victory to wrap up the war. His carriers Zuikaku, Zuiho, Chitose, Chiyoda and the converted battleship carriers were ordered to stand by to transfer their planes to land bases. Admiral Toyoda stayed on Formosa to direct the battle. Vice-Admiral Mikawa in Manila correctly guessed the next strike would be against Formosa.

Veasey said, "Prior to hitting Formosa, Halsey is going to divert attention from our objective by striking northern Luzon. This may backfire because it will give the Japs an extra day to prepare." The air strike was launched at dawn on 11 October, 323 miles from Luzon. There was no opposition and 15 planes were destroyed on the ground. We lost 7. Throughout the night, unidentified planes were reported. At dawn the planes were launched 90 miles east of Formosa. They destroyed one third of the Admiral's air strength while we lost 42 planes.

Elliott announced at dinner, "In Italy Mark Clark has crossed the Rubicon and the Germans have evacuated Corinth and Athens."

"Sounds like you're reading from the Bible. I thought that river was Caesar's downfall," Tack responded.

"You're 2,000 years too late."

The discussion ended when General Quarters was sounded. Our Task Group Commander signaled that radar had made contact with enemy aircraft, bearing OOO degrees, distance 16 miles.

At 1902 George said, "We're under attack. Several ships are firing at planes. None are close to us." At 2232 George exclaimed, "Enemy planes are close aboard. Firing has commenced." I could hear and feel the salvos exploding. Just after midnight George said, "There are high flying planes dropping flares all around us. It looks like Times Square.

Captain orders us to lay down a smoke screen." All destroyers did this 4 times during the next 4 hours. Sooty air made breathing difficult topside, especially aft of the stacks. Throughout the night the formation was harassed by Bettys. No damage was done and Fukudome lost 42 planes.

The next morning, Friday 13 October, the fleet was 70 miles east of Formosa and strikes were launched. Our pilots found 15 airfields in our sector as opposed to the 4 shown on the charts. Enemy planes attacked Task Force 38.4 to the south. Fighters from the Belleau Wood intercepted and shot down 11. At dusk while the Franklin was recovering planes, 4 Bettys got through the screen and headed for the Franklin. Three were shot down. The fourth crashed on her flight deck, but did no major damage.

TG 58.3 was attacked and GQ was sounded. At 1850 George excitedly exclaimed, "Several Bettys are attacking the Wasp and Monterey. The flack is extremely heavy. Gun Control doesn't understand how they are still flying. 3 have exploded. Several are heading straight for the heavy cruiser Canberra. She has scratched 3 more. Wow! A torpedo has hit in the area of the after engine room. That might put her out of action. Planes are coming in from all directions."

With the ship going at flank speed and executing emergency turns, I was having a problem keeping my feet, even holding on to a rail. Suddenly, George yelled, "A plane is attacking from our starboard quarter. We've made a hit. It has crashed astern."

The attacks ceased as suddenly as they had started. The Canberra reported that a torpedo had hit between fire rooms. Water was rushing in and way was lost. 23 men were killed. Halsey instructed the Wichita to take her under tow. With the heavy seas and the darkness, the Wichita had a difficult time. Several men were injured and the lines weren't secured until 2022. At 1930 the Ingersoll, with other destroyers and CruDiv 13, was ordered to screen the Canberra. TG 30.3 formed a circle 5 miles in diameter around the Canberra and Wichita. Our course was 133 degrees, speed 15 knots. The forward speed of the formation was only 4 knots. Elliott announced at dinner that Halsey had ordered additional strikes on Formosa to divert attention from us. Enemy planes were reported off and on the next morning. In the afternoon they attacked over a three hour period. No damage was inflicted.

The fleet tug Munsee arrived on 15 October and took the Canberra in tow. At 1155 the Houston, towed by the Boston and escorted by several destroyers, joined the formation. The day before, a group of Frans had attacked TG 38.1. The Houston was hit by a torpedo which severely damaged and flooded the engineering spaces. All power was lost.

Initially Captain Behrens ordered all hands to abandon ship, but changed his mind, and at 2020 requested a tow. Within the hour the Boston secured a hawser and was underway at a speed of 5 knots. Halsey ordered them to join our group. The tug Pawnee arrived the next morning and took the Houston in tow. Everyone laughed when Elliott said, "We've acquired a new name. Dispatches now refer to our Task Group as "Crippled Div 1'."

On the basis of his pilots' reports, Admiral Toyoda sent Admiral Fukudome a message saying that the Third Fleet was retiring in defeat. "Annihilate the remnants," he ordered. Fukudome, on 15 October, believing a pilot's report that the Third Fleet was striking Manila, sent planes to attack. They struck at 1045. It was only Admiral Davidson's TG 38.4. One hit was made on the carrier Franklin and many Jap planes were shot down.

Midday, as the formation was crawling through Luzon Strait, Fukodome's strike of 107 planes attacked. Only 3 managed to penetrate the screen. George said, "A Frances has gotten through. She has released her torpedo and it's heading straight for the Houston. She's been hit in the stern. God! There's been an explosion. Flames and debris are everywhere. Another plane is making a run on the Santa Fe. The torpedo missed. We just hit a Kate. It's in flames and has crashed."

When GQ was secured at 1358, we learned that water had flooded the Houston's compartments. Her damage control parties did an exceptional job keeping her afloat, but she had to be abandoned. At 1500 the PA boomed, "This is the Captain speaking. Station special sea details and rig for rescuing personnel from the Houston." She looked as though she would capsize at any moment. Our stanchions were removed and lifelines dropped over the side. A cargo net, extra life jackets and swimmers were readied. At 1540 the Ingersoll was in position and men from the Houston began entering the water, some jumping, others sliding down ropes and a few walked in off the fantail. Herman Crumpler and his shipmate Lee, nicknamed "Rooster", disembarked through the large torpedo hole in the side. Herman floated and paddled until he reached the Ingersoll. Rooster couldn't swim. Seeing his failure to make any progress, someone yelled, "Can't you swim?"

"I'm learning now," he replied. Fulton dove in and found Rooster disoriented and uncooperative. With a life jacket under him, Fulton was able, with much pushing and cursing, to get him to the net where 3 men pulled him aboard. By 1551 we had rescued 91 crew members. The Stephen Potter and the Sullivans recovered 200 more.

My men relayed some of the stories told by the Houston crew. Alex McCaw, an electrician, was on the number 3 turret when the torpedo hit. He said, "I saw the torpedo drop from the plane and followed its wake. After the explosion, I went over the side fully clothed, with an inflatable life belt. I was bushed and dozed off. I heard rifle shots and saw them splashing around me. I didn't realize your guys were shooting at sharks until after I was pulled out of the water."

Richard Johnson, a machinist mate, said, "I had just finished loading ammunition in a forward gun and was heading aft when the hit was made. Two days before when the first torpedo exploded, I was in the after engine room and saw one of the propulsion shafts fly by me in the air. This time I jumped into the water with an inflatable belt around my waist. I was glad to see you guys show up." Others had similar stories.

I had the 16-20 watch when a Japanese search plane found "Crip-Div 1". GQ was sounded. Fukudome sent in 3 strikes. One failed to make contact. His second was intercepted by planes of TG 38.1 and most were shot down. His third returned to base when the flight commander's plane developed engine trouble.

When I got off watch, Radio Tokyo was putting out reports saying the Third Fleet had been annihilated. The Japanese pilots were under the delusion that "Crip-Div 1" represented the remnants of Task Force 38. Halsey, hoping to spring a trap using the Canberra and Houston as bait, stationed TG 38.3 to the north and Task Groups 38.1 and 2 to the east. We acquired the new name "Bait-Div 1". The ruse almost worked. Vice Admiral Shima's Second Striking Force sortied from the Inland Sea to knock off the crippled cruisers. When he was attacked by Bunker Hill planes while fueling on 16 October, he decided there was more to the remnants than reported and reversed course.

We all got a laugh at this interchange of messages: Halsey to Dubose: "Don't worry." Dubose to Halsey: "Not worrying. Just wondering." Captain Inglis of Birmingham to Dubose: "Now I know how a worm on a fishhook must

Our group joined TG 38.3 at dawn on 18 October. When I relieved Samony at 0745, he said, "The Captain has the conn. We've been ordered to go alongside the Ruyard Bay and transfer the Houston personnel." The transfer took 1½ hours. The Dortch came alongside to deliver mail, and I had a brief but pleasant visit with my former shipmates. Cheers rang out when the PA boomed, "Mail call in the mess hall for the crew; for the officers, in the wardroom." I had mail from my fan club and shared it with my shipmates.

During the 3-day Formosa air battle, 500 planes were destroyed, 20 freighters and small craft were sunk, together with the destruction of ammunition dumps, hangars, barracks, shops and industrial plants. The Japanese made 3 hits. Our losses were 79 planes, 64 pilots and an unknown number of seamen killed. Of more importance was the demolition of the myth that carriers could not stand up to land-based planes. These had been the heaviest air attacks since the Battle of the Philippine Sea.

The Japanese broadcast and stated in official communiqués that their "eagles" had sunk 11 carriers, 2 battleships and 3 cruisers. Japan was swept by a wave of exhilaration. Mass celebrations of the "Glorious victory of Taiwan" were held throughout the country. The Army for the moment assumed the invasion would be given up and started planning accordingly. Everyone had a good laugh when the PA boomed, "Attention all hands! This is the Captain speaking. I believe you'll enjoy this dispatch. Admiral Nimitz has received from Admiral Halsey the comforting assurance that he is now retiring toward the enemy following the salvage of all of the Third Fleet ships recently reported sunk by Radio Tokyo. The Ingersoll is one of the ships that has been sunk. Thought you'd be interested in how it feels to be at the bottom of the ocean."

This had been a tough week, but a bigger one lay ahead.

LIST OF OFFICERS
ATTACHED TO AND ON BOARD THE U. S. S. INGERSOLL (DD652)
_____, COMMANDED

BY A. C. VEASEY, Commander, _____ U. S. N. , DURING THE PERIOD COVERED BY THIS LOG BOOK, WITH DATE OF

REPORTING FOR DUTY, DETACHMENT, OR DEATH, FROM 1 August ,19 44 , TO 31 August ,19 44

NAME AND FILE NUMBER (Show file No. below name)	RANK	DATE OF REPORTING ON BOARD DATE OF DETACHMENT (Show detachment date below reporting date)	PRIMARY DUTIES	NAME, RELATIONSHIP, AND ADDRESS OF NEXT OF KIN (Show address at which BuPers may most readily communicate with next of kin in an emergency)
A. C. VEASEY. 70301	Comdr. USN.	8/31/43	Command	Mrs. Frances Guy Veasey, Wife, 1328 Graydon Avenue, Norfolk, Virginia.
I. J. SUPERFINE 81037	Lt.Comdr. USN.	8/31/43	Executive Officer.	Mrs.Majorie Elizabeth Superfine, 3121 16th St., N.W.,Wife, Washington, #10, D. C.
MITCHELL, J. W. 97459	Lieut. D-V(G)	8/31/43	Gunnery Officer.	Mr.Alexander J.Mitchell,Father, 11 High Street, Natick, Mass.
H. E. JERVEY,Jr., 102461	Lieut. DE-V(G) USNR.	7/17/44	Engineer Officer.	Mr. H.E.Jervey, Father, 2906 Duncan Street, Columbia, S.C.
J. A. HOLLANDER, 166656	Lieut. D-V(G) USNR.	9/15/43	Assistant Gun. Off.	Mr. J.A. Hollander, Father, 3427 Palmer Street, Chicago, Illinois.
W. McK. PARDEE, 165760	Lieut. USN.	8/31/43	Assistant Eng. Off.	Mrs. Emily P. Pardee, Mother, 1041 Oakdale, Road, Atlanta, Georgia.
J. S. ELLIOTT, 160842	Lt.(jg) C-V(G) USNR.	8/31/43	Communication Officer.	MrsBeth Ann Dugan Elliott,Wife, 121 Rugg Avenue, Newark, Ohio.
R. H. DAVIS, 189421	Lt.(jg) D-V(G) USNR.	8/31/43	Navigator	Mr. A. N. Davis, Father, West Street, Harrison, New York.
R. T. SWARTZ, 266244	D-V(G) Lt.(jg)	8/31/43	MG Officer.	Mr. Albert A. Swartz, Father, 1834 Union Avenue, S. E., Grand Rapids, Michigan.
J. I. TOWNSEND, Jr. 226520	Lt. (jg) D-V(G) USNR.	8/31/43	1st. Lieut.	Mrs. Emma Cothran Townsend, Mother, 118W. 31st. Street, Norfolk, Virginia.
STALNAKER, Z. W. 226851	Lt.(jg) D-V(G) USNR.	8/31/43	Assistant Comm. Off.	Mrs. Doris Dean Stalnaker, Wife, Seffner, Florida.
W.G. WHEELER, Jr. 227992	Lt.(jg) D-V(G) USNR.	8/31/43	Torp. Off.	Mrs. Warren G. Wheeler, Mother, 34 Willow Street, Dedham, Mass.
SAMONY, C. J. 276849	Lt. (jg) D-(G) USNR.	11/26/43	Assistant 1st. Lieut.	Mrs. Delores Ann Samony,Wife, 234 Fallowfield Avenue, Charleroi, Pa. _R4D_
HORTON, P. B. 256178	Lt.(jg) D-V(G) USNR.	11/26/43	Assistant MG. Off.	Mrs. Joyce Carolyn Horton, Wife, 3460 Purdue Avenue, Dallas, Texas. _R4D_
LANG, P. W. 283082	Ensign USN.	9/9/43	Intercept Officer.	Mrs. C. D. Lang, Mother, 509 North Beverly Drive, Beverly Hills, Calif.
FUSFIELD, C. W. 311236	Ensign D-V(G) USNR.	11/26/43	Radar Off.	Mr. David Fusfield, Father, Fusfield's Inc. Sioux Falls, S. D. _R4D_
PIPER, E. E.	Ensign E-V(G) USNR.	7/9/44	Assistant Eng. Off.	W. E. Piper, Father, 1518 West 9th. South, Salt Lake City, Utah.
FEIGHNY, R. E. 356118	Ensign D-V(G) USNR.	8/11/44	Assistant 1st. Lt.	Mrs. Helen Feighny, Wife, 277 Jayne Street, Oakland, California.
MacGILPIN, H.H.,Jr. 143246	Lieut. MC-V(G) USNR.	8/31/43	Med. Off.	Mr. H. H. MacGilpin,Sr.,Father, 15 Hanna Road, Worcester, Mass.
BAUGH, L. R. 193022	Lt.(jg) SC-V(G) USNR.	12/27/43	Supply & Disb.	Mrs. Phyllis Baugh, Wife, Robert Lee Route, (c/oC.A.Bowen) San Angelo, Texas.

EXAMINED AND FOUND TO BE CORRECT:

R. H. Davis

R. H. DAVIS Lieut. (jg) _____ U.S.N.R. NAVIGATOR.

TO BE FORWARDED DIRECT TO THE BUREAU OF NAVAL PERSONNEL AT THE END OF EACH MONTH

CHAPTER 11

Leyte Gulf; The Greatest Naval Battle in History

At dinner on 18 October Veasey said, "The air strikes and shore bombardment of the Jimas, Formosa and Northern Luzon have been highly successful. The Japanese air force in these areas has been destroyed. MacArthur's heading north to the Philippines."

"I understand why we need the Philippines, but why do the Japanese?" asked Mitchell.

"It's a source of minerals. More importantly, it allows them to protect their supply lines to the south where much needed oil is located."

"Scuttlebutt has it the British Navy is going to join us," Elliott said.

"Apparently that was discussed in September at Quebec. King and MacArthur were opposed because the British ships are short-legged, needing upkeep every 2 or 3 weeks. We stay at sea for months, and our operations would be restricted," Veasey replied.

"So what's going to happen?"

"To keep peace with Churchill, Roosevelt overruled his advisors. We'll be seeing the British ships within the next few weeks," Veasey responded.

The puppet government the Japanese setup to appease the Filipino people didn't work. A dispatch was sent to Toyoda: "Current of pro-American sentiment remains ....something steadfast that cannot be destroyed....Guerrilla activities are gradually increasing." Field Marshal Terauchi, Commander of the Southern Army headquartered in Manila, had 260,000 troops, but estimated he needed an additional 15 divisions to hold Luzon. The guerrillas had been harassing the Japanese since 1943 and MacArthur had kept in touch with them. Commander Chick Parsons, USNR, stayed in Manila after the war started, and MacArthur placed him on his staff. He returned to Leyte several times coordinating the guerrillas' activities with MacArthur's plans. He set up coastwatcher stations and delivered supplies.

D-Day for Leyte was 20 October, and MacArthur's Forces began assembling at Manus Island and along the coast of New Guinea early in the month. More than 700 ships were involved, and with 1,250 miles from Hollandia to Leyte, the ships began moving northward on 10 October. By 17 October the mine sweeping units were clearing the mines off the entrance to the gulf. Rangers began securing the outer islands on the 17th, and underwater demolition teams were clearing away barriers.

Toyoda, believing the landings would be in the southern Philippines on 18 October, gave the order to execute Sho-1 (Victory in the Philippines) with the engagement to be on 25 October. The Combined Fleet at the time was scattered in the Inland Sea Of Japan, Singapore and Borneo.

Vice Admiral Ozawa with his Northern Force sortied from the Inland Sea undetected. Our submarines were chasing merchant shipping rather than guarding the entrance at Bungo Suido. Always Toyoda intended for the Japanese Navy to destroy the US Navy in a "general decisive battle." D-Day occurring earlier than he expected gave us an advantage.

While I was relieving Stinky, Veasey said, "Our intelligence doesn't believe a fleet action will occur. They believe there'll be Tokyo Express runs to Leyte just as in the Solomon's."

"I'd hate to bet the family jewels on that," Stinky responded. "They're going to throw the book at us. We'll probably see new weapons and tactics never seen before."

When Will arrived at 0745, I gave him the pertinent information and added, "You'd better get all the sack time you can, 'cause I believe we're going to be busy when the landings start."

At breakfast the talk was about the forthcoming battle and the disorganized command structure. Veasey said, "General MacArthur is the Supreme Allied Commander. He has under him Lt. General Walter Krueger, Sixth Army Commander, and Vice Admiral Kincaid, Commander of the 7th Fleet. Each of these has northern and southern groups under him. In addition, Kincaid has the Escort Carrier Group under Rear Admiral T.L. Sprague.[63] His forces are divided into Taffy 1, commanded by Admiral Sprague, with 4 baby carriers (CVE), 3 destroyers and 4 destroyer escorts; Taffy 2, commanded by Rear Admiral F.B. Stump with 6 CVE's, 3 destroyers and 4 DE's; and Taffy 3, commanded by Rear Admiral C.A.F. Sprague with 6 CVE's, 3 destroyers and 4 DE's. I just don't see how they can coordinate their efforts effectively."

Superfine responded, "And that's not all. MacArthur is in command of the landings, but no one person is in charge overall. Admiral Chester Nimitz is Commander of the Pacific Fleet with Admiral Halsey under him, who in turn has Vice Admiral Mitscher with 4 carrier groups under him. Who dreamed up this command structure?" No one had an answer.

Later we learned that the orders to the 7th Fleet under Admiral Kincaid stated: 1. Transport and establish landing forces ashore in Leyte Gulf-Surigao Strait area as arranged with General Krueger, Commander of 6th Army. 2. To support the operation by: (a) Providing air protection for convoys and direct air support for landings and subsequent operations, including anti-submarine patrol of gulf and combat air patrol over the amphibious ships and crafts from his escort carriers; (b) Lifting reinforcements and supplies to Leyte; (c) Preventing Japanese reinforcement by sea of its Leyte garrison; (d) Opening Surigao Strait for Allied use; (e) Providing submarine reconnaissance, life guard service and escort of convoy.

Orders from Admiral Halsey stated: to cover and support the Leyte landings by: (a) Striking Okinawa, Formosa and northern Leyte on 10-13 October; (b) Striking Bicol Peninsula, Leyte, Cebu, Negros and supporting the Landings on Leyte 16-20 October; (c) Operating in "strategic support" of the Leyte Operation by destroying enemy navies and air forces threatening the Philippines area on and after 21 Oct.

Also, Admiral Nimitz's Operation Order contained this gem: "If opportunity for destruction of a major portion of the enemy fleet is offered, or can be created, such destruction becomes the primary task."

Since Admiral Halsey regarded this as his primary task, his operation order to us read: "If opportunity exists, or can be created, to destroy a major portion of the enemy fleet, this becomes the primary task."

Veasey, seeing this dispatch, exclaimed, "This is new! It hasn't been present in any op-orders before and it's going to cause problems. Halsey and the British believe the Fleet's primary duty in landings is the 'destruction of the enemy fleet'. Spruance is convinced the paramount function of a covering force is to prevent interference with the landing. Why don't those damn eggheads learn from history. If the Japanese had lured us away in the Marina's, the casualty rate would have been ten times higher."

"Only time will tell," I responded.

"Chief, that's what frightens me. Halsey will be the sole judge as to when to execute his primary duty. MacArthur, who is in overall command, doesn't even have to be notified. This is one screwed up operation."

On 20 October Sprague's carrier planes flew 472 sorties in support of the landings. Task Groups 38.1 and 4 also gave air support. Our Task Group stayed off the entrance to Leyte Gulf, steaming in circles. I had the mid-watch, and the talk was about home, interspersed with how the landings would go.

Will relieved me at 0345 and said, "I can't believe the Japanese won't contest this landing with everything they've got. If they don't, it's the beginning of the end for them."

"I agree. They'll come up with something we haven't seen before. They always do."

At breakfast, Elliott was holding forth. "Something is going on. The traffic is unreal. Most of it is Top Secret and we can't break it." Each of us had ideas.

At 1000 the landings began at Talcoban by the north forces. The troops met little resistance. Colonel Frank Rouwelle, having kept in touch with the guerrilla forces from the start of the war, landed on a beach south of Talcoban. He immediately spread the word of the impending bombardment and invasion to the civilian population. The beach areas were evacuated and not one Filipino died.

Colonel Kangleon, Commander of the Guerrilla Forces, deployed his troops so they could kill the Japanese as they retreated from the beaches. The other landings were equally successful, and by noon Dulag had been captured. Within two hours, the American flag was raised.

When I relieved Stinky at 1145, he said, "Just another beautiful day in the Pacific while the Army and Marines are catching hell on the beach."

"Right you are. So what's going on?" I responded.

"The guide is in the Lexington, bearing 159 degrees, distance 7,500 yards. We've been going around in circles, but for the moment we're on base course 263 degrees."

During my watch President Osmena and General MacArthur waded ashore at Leyte, where he proclaimed to all the world: "People of the Philippines, I have returned. By the grace of Almighty God, our forces stand again on Philippine soil. At my side is your President, Sergio Osmena. Rally to me. Let every arm be steeled. The guidance of divine God points the way. Follow in His name to the Holy Grail of righteous victory."

General Yamashita, the "Tiger of Malaya", refused to believe MacArthur had landed on Leyte. He thought the photographs flashed around the world of MacArthur wading ashore were mock-ups done in New Guinea. He told his staff, "I can't imagine so important a General going to the front lines. If I had known he was wading ashore, I would have avenged the death of Admiral Yamamota with a massive suicide attack on his headquarters."

Will relieved me at 1545. In the wardroom everyone was discussing how well the landings had gone, when over the PA came the familiar voice of President Roosevelt, "Citizens of the Philippines, you have endured suffering, humiliation and mental torture for 3 long years. On this occasion of the return of General MacArthur to Philippine soil, we renew our pledge to you. We and our Philippine brothers in arms with the help of Almighty God will drive out the invader. We will restore a world of dignity and freedom, a world of confidence and honesty and peace."

Japanese land-based planes began attacking in the afternoon. The Honolulu was put out of action. It began raining heavily, making flying treacherous, but the Japs hit the Australia, forcing her to retire. Minor damage was inflicted on other ships.

At supper the talk centered on a dispatch sent to Halsey by MacArthur's headquarters: "An approach by the Japanese Fleet through Surigao or San Bernardino Straits is impractical because of navigational hazards and the lack of maneuvering space." As usual, Stinky argued, "That is a bunch of crap! When are our leaders going to wise up? The Japs have consistently done the unexpected, and I'll bet my next pay check they will this time." Some of Halsey's staff continued believing MacArthur's assessment even after Japanese vessels were sighted on the early morning of 23 October. Toyoda and his staff had guessed that the two prongs from the southwest and central Pacific would converge on the Philippines. Without knowing the exact time or place, he was unable to have his fleet in a position to attack.

We remained to the east and our planes continued attacking the air fields of central Luzon. On 22 October the Task Group fueled in the morning and the Ingersoll spent the afternoon delivering mail to the other ships. I received several letters and my girls told me about friends who'd been home on leave, movies they'd seen, how tough rationing was and how much I was loved and missed.

Elliott got a laugh when he announced, "Congress has passed a GI Bill of Rights. That means any of you survivors will have your education paid for by Uncle Sam. Chief, send in your application to Medical School. Stinky will be back in law school. Anyone want to be a preacher?"

General Kenney's Far Eastern Air Force was also bombing and strafing. By 25 October the beach was consolidated. To the north 80,000 men and 102,990 tons of supplies had been landed; to the south 51,500 men and 85,000 tons of supplies. The amphibious assault phase was essentially over.

The Japanese weren't idle. They still hoped for a "general decisive battle." Sho-Go 1 was a well thought out plan. They had 3 forces, northern, central and southern. Vice Admiral Ozawa's Northern Force consisted of the carriers Zuikaku, Zuiko, Chitose and Chiyoda. His 116 planes weren't much of a threat. He also had 2 converted carriers, Ise and Hyuga, together with 3 cruisers and 8 destroyers. He was a decoy and intended to lure the Third Fleet to northern Luzon away from the action. This wouldn't have been an option if our primary purpose was to protect the landings.

The Central Group, under the command of Vice Admiral Kurita, was the major striking force. It consisted of 5 battleships, including the super battleships Musahi and Yamato, 10 cruisers and 17 destroyers. His orders were to steam for Leyte Gulf via San Bernardino Strait.

The Southern Force was split into two groups. The van was under the command of Vice Admiral Shoji Nishimura, which included 2 battleships, one heavy cruiser and 4 destroyers. Following 50 miles behind was Vice Admiral Kiyohide Shima with 2 heavy cruisers and 8 destroyers. These groups would approach from the south through Surigao Strait. If all went as planned, the Central and Southern forces would meet at Leyte Gulf in a pincers movement and destroy all of the shipping present. This would leave MacArthur without naval support, just as on Bataan in 1941-42. It required timing and luck. Through the dispatches flowing from the ships to the Commanders and CinCPacs to his Admirals, we had some knowledge of what was going on.

Halsey, in spite of MacArthur's belief that the gulf area was too restricted for a fleet action, kept a lookout, hoping an engagement might take place. On Monday 23 October at 0600, he ordered DesDiv 100 with the Washington and Alabama to join TG 38.4. At 0740 the Ingersoll was on station. The submarines Darter and Dace reported that Kurita was off Pawlawan passage. The Darter fired 6 fish, making 4 hits on Kurita's flag ship, the Atago, which sank her. Admiral Kurita was rescued and transferred to the Yamato. The Darter fired at the Takao making 2 hits. The Dace fired 4 torpedoes into the Maya, which exploded and sank. The submarines tracked the Japanese until the Darter went aground on Bonbay Shoal at 0105 the next morning. The crew was transferred to the Dace.

With these sightings, Halsey ordered planes to search for Kurita. He was spotted at 0812 heading for San Bernadino Strait, which was too far away for any surface engagement. We changed to a westerly course with a speed of 20 knots. Excitement began building with the prospect of seeing some action.

On 24 October, with the exception of TF 38.1, which was returning from Ulithi, the Third Fleet was deployed on a broad front off San Bernardino Strait. TG.38.3 was to the north. From dispatches we knew that 3 raids of 50 to 60 Japanese land-based planes were attacking them. Many were shot down, but a Judy hit the carrier Princeton. The bomb penetrated 3 decks and exploded in the bakery, killing many of the crew. The destroyers Irvin and Morrison with the cruiser Birmingham attempted to save her, but were unable. While the Birmingham was alongside, torpedoes stowed in the stern exploded, showering the crowded deck with deadly steel debris. 229 were killed and 400 wounded. Mitscher ordered the Princeton destroyed.

While this was happening, TG 38.4 launched strikes against Kurita's forces in the Sibuyan Sea, the first hit at 1026, the second at 1245 and the third at 1550. The super battleship Musashi was sunk after taking 19 torpedo and 17 bomb hits. Many ships were hit including the Yamato, Nagato and Haruna. The heavy cruiser Myoko, with both shafts damaged, headed for Borneo. At 1600 Kurita retired. Halsey was relieved, believing the exaggerated reports of his pilots that Kurita was no longer a threat. In actuality, he had 4 battleships, 6 heavy cruisers, 2 light cruisers and 10 destroyers, which was a formidable force.

In early afternoon our Task force rendezvoused with TG 38.2 and operated in the vicinity awaiting further orders. Halsey knew the Japanese were out in force and prepared to do battle, but he didn't know where. In preparation he sent out his "Battle Plan" at 1512 on 24 October to Mitscher and his Task Group Commanders. He named the battleships, cruisers and destroyers which "will be formed as Task Force 34 under Admiral Lee. It will engage decisively the enemy."

Admirals Nimitz, Kincaid and King were information addressees. For unknown reasons, both Nimitz and Kincaid took it to mean that TF 34 had been formed and was guarding San Bernardino Strait.

At 1700 Halsey received reports on the sighting of Admiral Ozawa and his carriers to the north of Luzon. Halsey believed this to be the major force of the Japanese Navy, just as Toyada had intended. At 1847 our speed was changed to 25 knots, course due north. At dinner Pardee asked, "What's the hurry?" Veasey replied, "Halsey believes his primary responsibility is to destroy the Japanese Fleet. Unfortunately no one seems to know where the main body is. If I were the Japanese, I'd try to destroy the landing forces at Leyte. The group our planes attacked today was quite sizable and there's probably more just behind them. The ships to the north maybe decoys."

I had the 20-24 watch when radar reported enemy planes, bearing 024 degrees, distance 34 miles. They were quickly driven off by our CAP. When Will relieved me, I said, "We're headed due north, speed 25 knots. There's been one helluva battle going on around Leyte. We seem to be winning, but there's a lot of ships unaccounted for. I'd like to stick around, but I'm going to hit the sack while I can."

Soon after I left the bridge, scout planes reported that Kurita's central force was heading for San Bernardino Strait and could sortie out at day break. Halsey said to his communication officer, "They're no serious threat to the 7th Fleet. They don't have enough ships to do any damage." He didn't even warn Admiral Kincaid. Pardee and Veasey heard the other Task Group Commanders over the TBS expressing their concern at the beaches being unprotected. Halsey's staff officers gave them the brush off and assured them Halsey knew what was going on.

None of us were aware that at 1600 the previous afternoon, Kurita had sent a dispatch to Admiral Toyoda, "I have been under repeated attacks by more than 250 planes. It is considered advisable to retire temporarily from the zone of enemy air attacks and to resume the advance when the battle results of friendly units permit." At 1714 he and the others received from Toyoda , "All forces will dash to attack trusting in divine guidance."

Kurita couldn't make the dawn rendezvous in Leyte Gulf. The Southern Forces of Vice Admirals Nishimura and Shima were sighted by scout planes at noon on 24 October. Halsey heard this, but believed the 7th fleet could take care of them. Admiral Kincaid estimated they would enter Leyte Gulf via Surigao Strait that night. He ordered Admiral Jesse B. Oldendorf, Commander of all fire support ships in the Seventh Fleet, to prepare to meet the enemy. Admiral Oldendorf placed his 6 battleships, 4 heavy cruisers and 4 light cruisers in a line covering the 15 mile entrance of Surigao Strait. 2 destroyer squadrons, one under Captain McManus and the other under Captain Jesse Coward, my former skipper, were ready to thrust down the Strait to deliver torpedo attacks on either side of the Japanese Force. A third was to stand by and follow up. 39 torpedo boats under Lt. Commander R.A. Leeson were sent south to patrol and act as "eyes of the fleet."

The night was dark. Vice Admiral Nishimura's van with 2 battleships was arriving in Leyte Gulf at the same time as Kurita's. He received a dispatch from Kurita at 1830 saying that he (Kurita) had been delayed, but Nishimura confidently continued on. Admiral Shima's strike group was 50 miles in the rear, but Nishimura saw no need to wait for them. Darkness was his best protection. At 2013 he sent a message to Toyoda and Kurita saying he expected to be off Dulag at 0400 on 25 October. At 2236 the PT Boats picked him up 2236 and began attacking in waves at 2254. Little damage was done.

At this time, while we were heading north at 25 knots, Nashimura advised Toyoda and Kurita that he would enter Leyte Gulf at 0130.

Our PT's ceased attacking as Captain Jesse Coward prepared to strike. Nishimura had his ships in a single column. At 0250 Coward hit with his 3 destroyers. Torpedoes were fired at 0301 from 8,200 to 9,300 yards. At 0308 Cmdr. Phillips attacked with his 2 from the other side. 47 torpedoes were launched. The battleship Fuso was hit repeatedly and exploded. The destroyer Yamagumo blew up and sank. The bow of the Asagumo was blown off, and the Michishio was lying dead in the water. The 5 American destroyers retired at 35 knots without damage. At 0323 Captain McManus's DesRon 24 attacked. The Michishio was sunk and a hit was made on the Yamashiro. Admiral Nishimura steamed straight ahead taking no evasive action, and at 0330 notified Toyoda of the attack and that he was breaking into Leyte Gulf.

Admiral Oldendorf was ready. His cruisers and battleships were in a line across the strait, forming the top of the T. The Japanese were in a column steaming straight into it. With this disposition, the guns of all of

Oldendorf's ships could be brought to bear on the Japanese. Only the leading Japanese ships could fire effectively without hitting the ones in front. At 0323 American radar screens picked up Nishimura's force, consisting of the battleship Yamashiro, the cruiser Mogami and the destroyer Shigure. Our battleships had the latest Mark-8 fire control radar and at 0351, opened fire at 26,000 yards. The concentration was terrific.

At 0407 the destroyer Albert Grant was hit by friendly fire and many were killed and wounded. As a result, firing was ceased at 0409. It was just as well. The Japanese ships had been hit repeatedly with shells of all sizes, as well as torpedoes. The Yamashiro sank at 0411, taking down Admiral Nishimuro and most of the crew. The Mogami was badly damaged, and by some miracle, the destroyer Shigure was uninjured. This ship lived a charmed life: it had been in the November 13,1942, night battle at Guadalcanal without receiving a scratch.

Admiral Shima, following, knew a battle was going on, but was unaware of the damage. With his 5 cruisers and 4 destroyers, he entered Surigao Strait just before 0400. The light cruiser Abukuma was hit by a torpedo from a PT and dropped out. He passed burning hulks of Nishimura's ships, but thought he was going to the support of the other ships. At 0420 his lookouts mistakenly identified an island as a battleship, attacked and fired 16 torpedoes. No damage was done to the island. Hearing nothing on his radio, he sent a dispatch, "This force has concluded its attack and is retiring from battle area to plan subsequent action."

Admiral Oldendorf went after the cripples. The Mogami and Asagumo were finished off by gunfire, torpedoes and bombs from planes. At 1018 Cmdr. Nishino, skipper of the Shigure, sent a dispatch, "All ships except Shigure sunk. Went down under gunfire and torpedo attack."

At 0408 when the Mississippi fired its 12" guns at the Yamashiso, an era in Naval warfare ended. It was the last naval battle in which air power played no part. We had 39 men killed and 114 injured. In no battle during the entire war had there been such a complete victory.

From dispatches, Halsey knew about the furious fighting to the south. However, he remained convinced the main Japanese Force was to the north. At 0235 Mitscher launched search planes which spotted Ozawa. The radio transmission was garbled and Admiral Mitscher thought Ozawa was 100 miles away, when in fact he was more than 200. Believing the heavy ships might become involved, Admiral Lee was ordered to form up Task Force 34. I had been in my bunk 25 minutes when GQ sounded at 0430. The exact location of Ozawa was unknown, but our first strike was in the air at 0540.

When I went to the wardroom for breakfast, the talk was about the fierce fighting to the south. Captain Veasey said, "I don't know the details, but from what I've heard, the Japanese took a helluva licking." Elliott came in waving his dispatch board and exclaimed, "Planes have sighted the main Japanese force. We're going on the attack."

To the south the action continued. Admiral Sprague had his carrier groups in a line with Taffy 1 to the south, off northern Mindanao, Taffy 2 in the center off the entrance to Leyte Gulf and Taffy 3 to the north off Samar. At dawn Taffy 1 launched a strike against Shima's force fleeing Surigao Strait. Taffy 3 launched 12 fighters to cover the ships in Leyte Gulf. No one saw Admiral Kurita with his 4 battleships, 6 heavy cruisers and numerous destroyers sortieing from San Bernardino Strait. Under the cover of darkness he had headed south and covered 130 miles.

At 0645 a lookout on the destroyer Johnston saw the pagoda-shaped superstructures on the horizon and sounded the alarm. Admiral Thomas Sprague was surprised and frightened. Taffy 3 had only 6 CVE's, 3 destroyers and 4 DE's. The largest gun was 5 inches. Turning east, he bent on maximum speed of 17 knots, launched planes and had his ships lay down a smoke screen. At 0701 he broadcast in plain language his contact report, gave his position and called for help. The nearest assistance was Taffy 1, 120 miles to the south.

Fortunately for Sprague, the lookout on the Yamato thought Taffy 3 was Task Force 38. Admiral Kurita was told there were at least 2 battleships, 5 large carriers and 10 heavy cruisers. He panicked. Rather than forming a battle line, attacking and destroying Taffy 3, he ordered "General Attack". This meant every ship for herself and created confusion.[64] At 0706 shells were falling all around Taffy 3 and the Japs were closing. Sprague said in his action report, "With the volume and accuracy of fire increasing, it did not appear that any of our ships could survive another 5 minutes." In desperation he ran into the cover of a rain squall and ordered his destroyers to make a torpedo attack at 0716.

Veasey came on the bridge as our first strike was heading north. I followed, as Taffy 3 was coming under attack by Kurita and yelling for help in plain English. I asked the Captain, "What gives? Where did those Jap ships come from and where are all of our battle wagons and cruisers?"

"Must be a few ships that got through from the melee last night. From reports, it looks like we gave the Japs a good working over. Oley should be somewhere close at hand. We've got our own problems with those Japanese carriers. I know one thing. Last night both Admirals Bogan and Mitscher urged Halsey to leave some ships to guard San Bernardino Strait. He didn't see the need for Lee with TG 34 to remain behind."

Reports flowed in about the fighting to the south. Taffy 2 launched air strikes which began bombing and strafing the Japanese. Hits were made by both sides. Although Kurita's ships were capable of twice the speed of Sprague's, they never closed the range due to the evasive action they had to take. For the next two hours the battle raged. At 0911 Kurita ordered his ships to break off the action and signaled: "Rendez-vous, my course north, speed 20 knots." With 3 cruisers sunk and other ships severely damaged, and his staff believing Taffy 3 could not be caught, he steamed around in circles for the next two hours avoiding air attacks. When Taffy 2 was sighted, he thought this was more of TF 38 and wondered why no reinforcements had arrived from Shima or Ozawa. Misinformation abounded. At 1236 he sent a dispatch to Admiral Toyoda, "1st striking force has abandoned penetration of Leyte Anchorage. Am proceeding north searching for enemy Task Force. Will engage decisively and then pass through San Bernardino Strait."

At 0740 Taffy 1 was preparing to send assistance when it came under attack by the first suicide planes of the war. The Japanese had developed a new weapon with its "Kamikaze Corps," the forerunner of the smart bomb. The name meant "Heavenly Wind." In 1570 the Gods sent a typhoon, Heavenly Wind, to scatter a huge invasion force from China. The Japanese prayed the Kamikazes would do the same for them now.

The pilots were a group of enthusiastic men with little training. It was a one-way trip, so obsolete planes were used. They were taught to use the planes as bombs and crash into the enemy ships. Thousands volunteered since they were assured that by dying an honorable death in defense of their country, they would have a first class ticket on a non-stop flight straight into heaven.

Wave after wave of Kamikazes came in throughout the morning. Many were shot down. Others hit their targets with deadly accuracy. The carriers Santee, Suwannee, Kikun Bay, St. Lo and White Plains incurred varying degrees of damage and many casualties. By 1130 the action was over. A steward's mate summed up the feelings when he said, "We don't mind them planes which drops things, but we don't like them what lights on you."

When the smoke cleared, the Gambier Bay and St. Lo had been sunk, as had destroyers Johnston, Hoel and Samuel B. Roberts. Several other ships were badly damaged. 23 planes were shot down, 1,130 men killed and 913 wounded. The Japanese lost 3 cruisers, had many ships damaged and the number of casualties was unknown. The Battle of Samar was an expensive victory.

Admiral King, in Washington, DC, Admiral Nimitz in Pearl Harbor and Admiral Kincaid were amazed. Each of them thought Admiral Lee with TF 34 was standing guard off San Bernardino Strait. Admiral Halsey, believing Kurita didn't have enough ships to do any damage, was surprised by Sprague's cries for help. Halsey had a problem. He knew the northern force consisted of 4 fleet carriers, 2 "hermaphrodites", 3 light cruisers, 9 destroyers and a tanker. Believing this was his one chance to destroy the main body of the Japanese Fleet, he charged ahead. At 0830 our first strike attacked. Hits were made on the Zuiho and Zuikake. The Chitose and destroyer Akitsuki were sunk. The second strike hit within the hour. This was at the same time Kurita was breaking off action to the south.

Halsey was elated with the results of the air attacks until he received a dispatch from Admiral Nimitz: "Action ComThirdFleet info CTF 77 X Where is RPT X Where is TF 34 X The whole world wonders." The yeoman encoding at Pearl Harbor had tacked on the last phrase as padding, to throw off enemy decrypters. However, the yeoman on the New Jersey thought it was part of the message. Halsey was furious. He yelled at his staff, "I've been insulted before the entire world." At 1100 he dispatched: "Order Lee to break up TF 34, keep the battleships with him and have the other ships return to their respective Task Forces." Lee headed south with the battle ships and Task Group 38.2. Halsey went along in the New Jersey.

Admiral Mitscher assumed command. From the pilots' reports he knew Ozawa had several crippled ships. At 1115 he directed Rear Admiral Dubose, with the cruisers Santa Fe, Mobile, Wichita and New Orleans, together with DesRon 50, the Bagley and Patterson, to form a new Task Group when so ordered. The purpose would be to catch and destroy the cripples.

I had the 12-16 watch when the 3rd air strike hit at 1310 with 200 planes. The carrier Zuikaki was torpedoed and sank. The Zuiho was bombed repeatedly. At 1415 Mitscher detached Admiral DuBose's group. The cruisers lined up in a column and the destroyers formed a circular screen. Our course was 070 degrees, speed 25 knots. The talk on the bridge was about the fighting to the south. From the dispatches and the radio chatter we knew savage battles had taken place around Leyte Gulf.

The 4th strike hit at 1445. There were loud cheers when the pilots reported the Ise was hit several times and the Zuiho sunk. The 5th strike did little damage.

It was difficult to find the crippled ships. One pilot reported two cruisers burning ahead. Another spotted two destroyers circling a carrier dead in the water. A little later we heard a battle ship and four destroyers were seen leaving a damaged carrier and two damaged cruisers.

When Stinky relieved me at 1545, he was on his soap box, "I just finished telling the fellows in the wardroom, if what we're hearing is only partly true, MacArthur's intelligence guys ought to be strung up by their balls. The Japs wouldn't fight! They couldn't come through the Straits of San Bernardino and Surigao. No water! No room to maneuver! Our guys must be hallucinating and fighting ghosts!"

"I can't argue with that. Right now we've got our hands full. Radar reports several crippled ships just ahead. We'll see some action very shortly."

GQ sounded as I was leaving the bridge, and at 1612 the Japanese cruiser Hatsuzuki, two destroyers and a carrier were sighted. George said, "DesRon 50 has been ordered to form disposition 1-4. DesDiv 100 will be in column on the port quarter of the cruisers and DesDiv 99, plus the Bagley and Patterson, on the starboard quarter." At 1625 he exclaimed, "The cruisers have opened fire on the carrier which is dead in the water. The other ships are hauling tail. Control reports there are fires the length of the carrier with smoke everywhere. They can see personnel jumping over the side. The Healy has been ordered to torpedo it. Nope! The Healy reports that it's sinking and no need to waste a torpedo." At 1658 he said, "The carrier has capsized and is headed for the bottom." He continued, "We're chasing the other ships," then added, "The Callahan has been ordered to investigate an unidentified object." In a few minutes he said, "The Callahan reports a life raft with Japanese survivors. She is leaving them and rejoining the formation."

During the chase the talk was about home and what we planned to do after the war. One man commented, "The worse thing about being at sea so long is nobody has any new jokes to tell. All of us have heard them ten times over. It's a lousy life."

Jokes were forgotten when George reported, "Radar has ships at 20,000 yards." At 1851 he said, "The cruisers have been ordered to commence firing. Fires have started on what looks like the Hatsuzukia, a cruiser. The destroyers have been ordered to form up in four groups, with three in each one. We are with the Caperton and Cogeswell."

He exclaimed, "She's firing at us. The Mobile reported hearing shells passing overhead and splashes nearby. That ship may be crippled, but it's still fighting and making 21 knots. Bridge says bend on 33 knots and prepare for a torpedo attack."

At 1930 the Division Commander ordered the Cogeswell, Ingersoll and Caperton to attack. George said, "We're closing target. She's maneuvering and making it difficult for the torpedo men to get a solution. Admiral Dubose has ordered us to give up if we can't get into a suitable firing position." There was silence and then, "We're not giving up yet.

Target is 8,000 yards away. Mr. Wheeler is having a tough time getting a solution with us changing course so often at a speed of 33 knots."

It was 2012. I heard and felt the shock wave as George excitedly said, "We've fired five torpedoes. Can't tell about hits. Captain has ordered control to commence firing. Admiral Dubose has ordered the Wichita to sink the ship. She has made several hits and there's been a violent explosion. Hurrah! The Hasuzuki has capsized and is heading for the bottom."

I went topside just in time to see the Healy turning in front of us. Momentarily it looked as though the only casualty from this action would be us. The Healy's stern came within spitting distance of our bow. Several of the crew believed one of our torpedoes hit. The Captain thought differently and the entry in the log stated: "Torpedo fire of attack is not believed to have caused any damage due to excessive firing range."

The cruisers were rejoined at 2045. Admiral Dubose realized the other ships couldn't be caught before daybreak. By then they would be under the protection of land-based planes, so we headed south at 25 knots.

Halsey was too late when he arrived at Leyte Gulf at 0100 26 October. Kurita had passed through the strait three hours earlier.

When Stinky came to the bridge at 0745, I said, "We will be rejoining Task Group 38.3 and the tankers during the morning."

The Captain was standing close by and asked Stinky, "How did you sleep last night?"

"I had a horrible nightmare. I dreamed I was driving the Ingersoll up Fifth Avenue in New York in heavy traffic."

The Battle off Cape Engano was over, with four carriers and one destroyer sunk. Several other ships were damaged. Ozawa later said, "The strikes after the 3rd were not too damaging. My chief concern was to lure these forces farther north. We expected complete destruction." His chief of staff added, "I saw all this bombing and thought the American pilot not so good."

The four naval battles making up the Battle of Leyte Gulf would later be considered the greatest naval battles ever fought. There were 244 ships involved. The Japanese lost 3 battleships, 4 carriers, 10 cruisers and 9 destroyers. Our losses were one fleet carrier, 2 jeep carriers and 3 destroyers.

The Japanese Navy would no longer be a major threat. After the war the Japanese Navy Minister, Admiral Yonai, said, "Our defeat at Leyte was tantamount to the loss of the Philippines. When you took the Philippines that was the last of our resources."

Many valuable lessons were learned and quickly forgotten:

(1) Naval victories cannot be won without air supremacy.
(2) Pilots tend to exaggerate. Take their reports with a grain of salt.
(3) Communicate your intentions with the other Commanders.
(4) Assume nothing! Ask for clarification when in doubt.
(5) Listen to your subordinates. Don't be arrogant.

In the wardroom after the battle, Superfine said, "I don't know whether fate was kind or not. We were up north running around in circles and our regular group, TF 38.3, was in the midst of the action. The Princeton was sunk and several ships received hits. We might have been one."

Will responded, "North, south, east or west, it would have made no difference to me. I learned that I am in the wrong department, or maybe the wrong service. I got little sleep, saw only the bulkheads in the after engine room and heard only the noise of our guns firing. I could just as well have been in Times Square on New Year's Eve. I kept hearing we were in a furious battle, but you couldn't prove it by me. I'm going to be a flier in the next war."

Little did he know he would soon be in a battle for his life, and it wouldn't be with the Japanese.

-

CHAPTER 12

The Lull Before the Storm

The Ingersoll rejoined TG 38.3 and the morning was spent fueling. Admiral Kincaid requested that combat air patrols be continued over Leyte Gulf, as his land-based P-38's had not arrived. Halsey ordered Mitscher to have TG 38.3 and TG 38.4 "prepared to make strikes or furnish fighter cover over Leyte if directed."

Neither Halsey nor his commanders could understand why the Army Air Corps was unable to provide coverage and on 26 October, he sent this dispatch to General MacArthur: "After 17 days of battle my fast carriers are unable to provide extended support for Leyte, but 2 groups are available 27 October. The pilots are exhausted and the carriers are low in provisions, bombs and torpedoes. When will land-based air take over at Leyte?"

My midwatch was quiet. Air strikes commenced at dawn with the pilots having a field day. They sank several troop transports and 2 destroyers. At 1810 during my watch, radar yelled, "I have a contact, bearing 030 degrees, 3,000 yards." I conned the ship into an attack position, but lost contact and we rejoined the formation.

The Japanese weren't idle. A Kamikaze hit the carrier Intrepid killing 10 men. Others crashed into the Franklin and Belleau Wood. There were numerous casualties and many planes were destroyed.

In the wardroom the talk was about other parts of the world. Superfine said, "There is more fighting between ourselves than with the enemy in Burma. Stilwell has been recalled. He and Chiang Kai-shek can't get along. He believes Chiang is spending more time containing Mao Tse-tung and his communists than halting the Japanese advance. Chiang won't accept Stilwell as commander of his armies, but will accept some one else."[65]

"In Greece Papandreau has set up his government in Athens, but there is still fighting among the various parties."

Stinky chimed in, "What those guys need is a good lawyer, and I'm willing to volunteer my service for free."

"And what you'd provide would be worth the same as your fee—nothing," Watson exclaimed. "All is not gloom and doom. The Russians have captured Belgrade and are advancing in Hungary. Our boys in Europe are moving forward slowly but steadily."

"That's true and if it weren't for winter settling in, Mark Clark and Alexander would be able to finish off the Germans in Italy. There is no love lost between MacArthur and the Navy, but at least we're working together with the same goal: destroy the Japs," Superfine concluded.

On Sunday, 28 October, the Fleet was off the Philippines. At 0627 the Ingersoll went alongside the Lexington. As a man in the breeches buoy was being pulled over, he was almost dunked into the ocean. Everyone was surprised when the Captain came on the PA and said, "Attention all hands! This is the Captain speaking. Stand at attention. Vice Admiral Mitscher is aboard."

All off duty personnel hurried topside to take a look. They were impressed. Following close behind was his Chief of Staff, Captain A.A. Burke.[66] They passed a few pleasantries with the men handling the lines before they went up to the bridge to visit with Veasey. For the next hour the Ingersoll was the flagship of Task Force 38.

At 0721 our distinguished visitors were transferred to the New Jersey. Their conference with Admiral Halsey concerned the forthcoming operation and how badly the men of TF 38 needed rest and the ships needed upkeep. At 0919 they were returned to the Lexington.

Tack remarked, "ComDesRon 50 must think highly of our skipper. It's an honor to be the taxi for the Commander of the Fast Carriers."

When I relieved Samony at 2345, I was delighted when he told me that we were enroute to Ulithi for rest and recreation. The talk on the bridge focused on the good time we'd all have swimming, drinking and shooting the bull with friends. GQ sounded at 1350 for gunnery exercises. At the conclusion, Veasey said to Mitchell, "I think Mitscher wanted to be certain your men still knew how to fire the guns."

On 30 October the Ingersoll was moored to the Cogeswell in the lagoon at Ulithi. Since I had urgent paperwork to do, I didn't go on liberty. At 2005 Ensign Paul Nushke, USN, reported on board and was assigned to the 1st Lieutenant's department. Everyone enjoyed the movie "Meet Me in St. Louis " with Judy Garland and Margaret O'Brien.

The next morning all ships received a copy of the dispatch General MacArthur sent to Admiral Halsey: "I send my deepest thanks and appreciation to your magnificent forces on the splendid support and assistance you have rendered in the Leyte operation. We have cooperated with you so long that we are accustomed to and expect your brilliant successes. You have more than sustained our fullest anticipation. Everyone here has a feeling of complete confidence and inspiration when you go into action in our support."

When I went on liberty, I discovered a change of command party occurring at Crowley's Bar. Vice Admiral John S. McCain was relieving

Marc Mitscher as Commander of Task Force 38. Mitscher was heading for the States. They celebrated at one end of the bar while I enjoyed visiting with friends at the other end. I was shown a little gem written by Lt. George Wright, the Yorktown's chaplain, entitled: "Beautiful Mog-Mog"

> Beautiful, beautiful Mog-Mog,
> Down where the sea breezes blow,
> We're proud of Crowley's Tavern
> Where the beer and whiskey flow.
> You may know of a cozier atoll,
> But you ain't seen no atoll at all
> Till you've seen beautiful Mog-Mog,
> Most beautiful atoll of all!

The next morning, Elliott announced, "Several attacks have been made on the Tirpitz, but she's still afloat. During October, Churchill and Stalin met in Moscow, and once again Stalin agreed to declare war on Japan as soon as Germany was defeated. They also discussed the Balkans and who would have jurisdiction over whom. We're on the move."

"I hate to report this, but Kamikazes are swarming all over TF 77 in Leyte Gulf. The Claxton has been hit and the Abner Read sunk. Casualties are heavy."

Prior to getting underway on 1 November, there was a meeting of the officers in the wardroom at which Veasey said, "Admiral McCain has reorganized the Task Force into 3 Task Groups. We are assigned to Task Group 38.3 under the command of Admiral Sherman, consisting of the Essex, Ticonderoga, Langley and San Jacinto; battleships North Carolina, Washington and South Dakota; heavy cruisers Mobil, Biloxi and Santa Fe, together with the light cruiser Oakland and 18 Destroyers. McCain and his staff have learned that one in 4 Kamikazes find a target and one in 3 sink a ship. Tokyo doesn't know how much damage is inflicted due to our tight security."

Stinky interjected, "They may not know precisely, but Tokyo Rose is certainly putting out some good guesses."

Veasy responded, "As long as it's a guess, it doesn't matter. McCain is putting into effect important tactical changes to lessen the damage being done. On strike days, picket destroyers equipped with the latest radar and aircraft homing devices will be stationed 60 miles from the Task Force on each side of the target bearing line. Their job will be to give advance warning of enemy aircraft approaching the carrier groups. Returning strike planes will be required to make a full turn around picket destroyers (known as Tom Cats) on their return flight to the carriers to be 'deloused'. This will weed out any Kamikazes who might follow the returning American pilots to the carriers. Combat air patrols known as 'sheep dogs' will be stationed above the destroyers to spot the enemy and swoop down on him. Our radar screens should be clear of friendly aircraft on the line of the enemy's most likely approach."

"Sounds mighty complicated to me," Mitchell said.

"Not really," Veasey replied. "Any planes deviating from the standard approach will be classified as enemy and we will shoot them down. McCain has also changed the mix of planes on the Essex class carriers to 73 fighters, 15 dive bombers and 15 torpedo bombers. The Hellcat and Corsair fighters are modified so they can carry up to 2,000 pounds of bombs unescorted, fly CAP or intercept enemy strikes. This should double the carrier's effectiveness. Any questions?"

There being none, I headed for the bridge. The signalman said, "You'll be interested in this dispatch." It was from Nimitz to MacArthur: "Release the Third Fleet as soon as possible." Veasey, standing nearby, said, "His airfields aren't completed and air coverage is needed over Leyte. Only TF 38 can do the job."

At 2345 the Task Group was off San Bernardino Strait. As I prepared to relieve Samony, I heard loud explosions and learned that a torpedo from a Japanese submarine had hit the cruiser Reno 4,000 yards on our starboard quarter. She was listing to port, and with the heavy seas looked as though she were sinking. She was kept afloat through skillful damage control. 2 men were killed and several were injured. The fleet tug Zuni took her in tow for Ulithi.

On 5 November the Fleet was off Luzon with strikes planned for the next 2 days. Each Task Group had a specific target area. Ours was between 14 and 15 degrees north, which included shipping in Manila Harbor. The fighter sweeps were airborne at 0615, catching the Japanese by surprise. At 1100 enemy aircraft were picked up on radar. CAP was vectored out and shot down a twin engine bomber.

During the afternoon Kamikazes began attacking while the Ingersoll was on picket station. We couldn't see the action, but heard some of it on TBS. One plane crashed into the Lexington, damaging the island structure, the signal bridge and anti-aircraft guns in the vicinity. There were many casualties. Admiral McCain transferred his flag to the Wasp, and the Lexington was sent to Ulithi for repairs.

When I relieved the watch at 2345, Stinky said, "We're in night picket station No. 1 with the formation bearing 085 degrees, distance 24,500 yards. The pilots had a field day yesterday and strikes will be resumed at dawn."

My watch was uneventful. At 0850 I saw a Jap plane explode above us and a parachute descending into the water. The body of the Jap pilot was picked up and searched and at 0933, he was buried at sea.

Later in the day Admiral Bogan's TG 38.2, together with Admiral McCain, left for Guam to pick up another air group. Rear Admiral Frederick C. Sherman, in the Essex, assumed tactical command. During the 2-day strike, in spite of intermittent rain, 439 planes were destroyed and many ships sunk, including Vice Admiral Shima's flagship, the Nachi. We lost 37 planes.

Veasey said, "General MacArthur wants to land on Mindoro on 5 December, which his Generals don't consider reasonable. The securing of Leyte is taking much longer than expected. He's going to have to change the landing date which will mean a delay of the Luzon landings until at least January."

"So who's going to benefit from that?" Mitchell asked.

"It's a trade-off. Our Generals are going to breath a sigh of relief because they'll have extra time to free up the necessary forces. On the other hand, the Japanese will be flying in additional planes and landing more troops."

Heavy weather curtailed flying on 7 November. Elliott announced, "There's a typhoon nearby. The meteorologist on the Essex is trying to locate the center so we can stay clear of it".

"With the wind howling and those waves 15 to 20 feet high, he'd better find out in a hurry. We're going to have a helluva time fueling," I said. At 1356, with much difficulty, the Ingersoll went alongside the South Dakota, receiving 66,000 gallons of fuel.

During my 16-20 watch, the TBS boomed, "This is the Healy. Man overboard! Man overboard! All ships in the vicinity keep a sharp lookout." The man turned out to be the Healy's executive officer, and his body was not recovered.

With the waves pounding the forecastle, the muzzle cover on the No. 1 gun came off, pouring water through the gun barrel into the handling room. Veasey yelled, "Tell those gunners mates that No. 1 handling room is flooding. Stop the water and get the mess cleaned up." The Ingersoll was corkscrewing into the waves. Richard Murphy, with a line around his waist and catching the giant waves on the ebb, was able to secure the gun muzzle.

In spite of the weather, there was some comic relief. With the crew's heads having boards as seats which ran fore and aft, instead of flushing, pumps maintained a continuous flow through the troughs. When the ship pitched, the water sloshed forward and everyone was soaked. When the bow came high out of the water, the water sloshed aft and everyone aft was soaked. No one stayed longer than necessary, and the smart fellows selected the center seats.

During my 00-04 watch on 10 November, MacArthur sent an urgent request: "Need help immediately. The Japanese are sending in a large number of reinforcements. Must be intercepted and stopped." Our course was changed to 220 degrees, speed 26 knots. By dawn the Task Force was 200 miles east of San Bernardino Strait and strikes began taking off. The pilots located the troop transports and sank most of them. Of the 10,000 Japanese on board, only a few survived. In addition, 4 destroyers were sunk. Later in the day 2 other destroyers went to the bottom. Our losses were 9 planes.

This catastrophe caused a stir in the Japanese high command. Losses in planes, ships and men were heavy during November. General Yamashita, responsible for the defense of the Philippines, was convinced Leyte could not be held and wanted to withdraw and write it off. Field Marshall Terauchi overruled him. He knew another landing was eminent, but didn't know the time or the place. His 260,000 troops on Luzon were short of equipment, and his 25,000 naval ground forces were divided between Manila, Clark Field and Legaspi. He was hoping the Kaitens might save him. He had 759 of these boats, which were similar to our PT's except they had a bomb on the bow. When they rammed the target, it exploded. It was a one-way trip for the operator. With only 450 planes available, Yamashita was ordered to do his best, but realistically he knew this would only be a "strategic delaying action."

At breakfast Veasey said, "Halsey has been after Nimitz to make strikes against the Japanese home islands. The OK hasn't been given because Admiral Nimitz believes air support is still necessary at Leyte. I'd say he is right."

On 12 November the Task Group spent the day fueling. At dinner Elliott exclaimed, "It's reported that the Tirpitz has been sunk by the RAF. It has been playing hell with our convoys and was the most feared battleship in the Atlantic."

"If that is true, it'll be easier for our ships to get through. Not only that, but they can sail closer to Norway and shorten the distance to Russia," Superfine responded.

The next morning the pilots were ordered to concentrate on shipping in Manila Harbor. Over the next 2 days, the results were sensational. The light cruiser Kiso, 5 destroyers and 7 transports were sunk. Also 84 Japanese planes were shot down. Our losses were 25 planes.

When I relieved Samony at 2345 on 14 November, he said, "TG 38.3 has been ordered to Ulithi for supplies and provisions. The other two groups are staying off Luzon and will continue to work over the shipping and planes." Radar contact was made with Ulithi during my midwatch on 17 November. In the morning the Ingersoll moored to the Dixie, a destroyer tender. In the wardroom Veasey said, "One of our Task Groups had bad luck. Our planes attacked Yap with a secret weapon, 'napalm bombs'. They didn't ignite and the pilots said, 'We might as well have been dropping empty beer bottles.' "

At 1300 a diver went over the side to investigate our sound dome. He told Veasey that the starboard side of the dome was off. Veasey exclaimed, "Other repairs can be delayed, but with our sound gear out, the Ingersoll is of little use to the carriers." The next morning the Ingersoll was in a floating dry-dock. At 1000, as senior member, I convened the Hull Board. Tack and I inspected the hull and underwater fittings and found conditions to be normal.

Repairs to the dome were completed on 19 November, and the Ingersoll moored to the Dixie.

At dawn the next morning, I felt a sudden jolt and heard a loud explosion. Coming topside, I saw a huge column of smoke in the vicinity of the tankers. I learned a torpedo had struck the Mississinewa, fully loaded with oil and gasoline. I watched with horror as she capsized and sank with the loss of 50 men.

SOPA, believing midget submarines were in the lagoon, ordered a search by all ships. Contacts were made with attacks following. One was rammed by the destroyer Case outside of the harbor. 2 others were destroyed inside the lagoon. Superfine said, "They are manned torpedoes. Scuttlebutt reports that the Japanese Navy agreed to try them if an escape hatch were available for the pilots to use. Ulithi is a prime target with the large number of ships at anchor."
None of us knew that 4 of those torpedoes had been strapped to each of 2 big submarines and fired. Fortunately, only one hit was made.

Once this menace was eliminated, liberty continued as usual. That night Ensign Nushke, our newest officer, was complaining, "The exec put me in charge of the liberty party. What an experience that was!"

"What happened?" Mitchell asked.

"I told the men to wait under a palm tree while I drew the beer. When I returned, I handed out the beer and left for a few minutes. When I came back, I found one case of beer missing. I told the men if it wasn't found I would take back all the beer. In about 15 minutes a fellow came running up with a case, claiming it had been swiped by a guy from another ship. I didn't buy that, but having made my point, I let the subject drop."

"Sounds like you made out all right," Elliott replied.

"For the moment. When we got ready to return to the ship, I counted heads and found 5 men missing. The launch went back to the ship and I began looking. I can't describe what I saw. There were a couple of hundred men lying around drunk, and they all looked identical. I finally found 4 of mine, which left one missing. I don't want that detail again." Everyone agreed he had done a good job keeping the missing to only one. On 22 November the Ingersoll was underway with TG 38.3. At breakfast Tack said, "At muster I had one quartermaster by the name of K.F. Walsh missing. One of the fellows said the last time he saw him he was lying under a Palm tree with a beer in his hand.

The monotony was broken in the afternoon when explosions sounded throughout the ship. Men were scurrying everywhere. One told me, "The last batch of raisin jack was placed in glass jars to ferment. No holes were punched in the cover, resulting in a buildup of gases and an explosion."

"Somebody is going to catch hell when the skipper finds out," I replied.

When the alcoholic aroma reached the bridge, the Captain, realizing the cause, shouted, "If every bottle of that damn liquor is not brought topside immediately and thrown overboard, the entire crew will be restricted to the ship at the next liberty port." The jars were found and the contents emptied into the sea.

During October the B-29's were moved from India and China to the Mariana's. Cheers were heard on 24 November when the PA boomed, "Attention all hands. Over 100 B-29's from the Mariana's bombed an aircraft engine factory in the suburbs of Tokyo this morning. This is only the first of many. We're on our way." The loss of bombers in subsequent raids was high. Daylight high altitude bombing traumatized the Japanese psychologically, but did little physical damage.

The next morning, 25 November, the fleet was 165 miles east of Manila. Planes began flying at dawn. The pilots sank the cruiser Kumano and several troop transports. At noon bogeys filled the radar screens and GQ was sounded. George exclaimed, "There are 5 Jap planes attacking. All ships have taken them under fire. Bombs and shrapnel are dropping all around us. 2 of the planes have been shot down." In a few minutes he continued, "3 have been destroyed by our fighters. My God, one Kamikaze has gotten through and crashed on the flight deck of the Essex."

The radar screens cleared at 1357 and GQ was secured. In the wardroom Elliott was saying, "You think we had it bad? 38.2 had the carriers Cabot and Intrepid hit by Kamikazes with many casualties."

Stinky exclaimed, "Somebody is hallucinating. The pilots keep reporting they are destroying an astronomical number of planes. Where do the Japs keep finding more? Intelligence has said they're running out. It doesn't make sense."

"Nothing about this war make sense," Superfine responded. "From the beginning, if any writer wanted a bestseller plot, all he'd have to do is use the propaganda we get filled with daily. Pay no attention to what you hear, just to what you see."

With 3 carriers damaged and destroyers needing fuel, Halsey decided to withdraw from the Philippine Sea. The air strikes had been successful, but a high price was being paid.

On 28 November at 1745, the Dortch came alongside to deliver mail. Rocky Rothschild was OOD and we had a pleasant visit. Going below to the wardroom, I found everyone off watch sharing the news. For some it was good; for others sad, especially for the ones with sickness and death in the family. For me there was nothing exciting. I said, "I have a letter from Lil Hair, a long-ago girl friend. Took her on a house party in 1940. She ditched me and went home. Never thought I'd hear from her again. She claims she's doing her part for the war effort by writing me."

"Maybe she's at loose ends and dragging the bottom of the barrel," Tack remarked.

"Could be. I doubt anything will come of it."

Veasey said, "Our support for the Leyte operation is over. The island probably won't be secured for a couple of weeks, but the Japanese in the Philippines are isolated. Few ships with supplies and reinforcements have gotten through. They're in big trouble."

Halsey, thinking the same, dispatched MacArthur and Nimitz: "Further strikes don't appear profitable; only strikes in great force for valuable stakes will justify exposure to the suicide attacks, at least until better defensive techniques are perfected." He also pointed out that we had been at sea almost continuously for 84 days and the strain on the ships and men was beginning to show. The following day the Ingersoll was moored to the Healy in the lagoon.

I was up early Sunday 3 December. At breakfast I announced, "You fellers are unaware that a most important person was born on this day 24 years ago, namely me! To celebrate the occasion, I'm throwing a birthday party at Crowley's Bar for all who can attend. The drinks are on me, but don't pass that word around, or I'll end up buying for all the officers in the Third Fleet. Uncle Sam isn't paying me that kind of money yet."

There was good and bad news on the radio. We had missed most of the football season and our Annapolis graduates weren't happy hearing that Army was the No. 1 team in the country. Will exclaimed, "Just because they've got Doc Blanchard at fullback (Mr. Inside) and Glen

Davis at halfback (Mr. Outside), both self-proclaimed All Americans, that doesn't make them No. 1."

"Well, if it makes you happy, neither will get the Heisman Trophy. Les Horvath, quarterback at Ohio State, is scheduled for that," Mitchell responded.

At Crowley's Bar in the afternoon, everyone enjoyed my party and I ended up with a sizable bill. The only things missing were girls.

Due to the prolonged fighting around Leyte, MacArthur announced the Mindoro landings would be delayed until 15 December.

One night when I was on the bridge day-dreaming, a voice on the TBS caught my attention. "Now hear this, all of you f-cked up SOB's out there. This whole navy is f-cked up! Halsey is f-cked up! I'm f-cked up!" There was momentary silence and a stern voice came on: "This is Commander Allgood. Obscenity is not permitted on this circuit. Identify yourself!" Another pause and then the familiar voice, "Sir, I may be f-cked up, but I ain't that f-cked up!" Everyone on the bridge had a good laugh.

On 10 December our honeymoon was over. The Ingersoll was underway with TG 38.3. It was a beautiful day in the South Pacific, puffy white clouds and a warm breeze out of the southwest. Ships were scattered as far as the eye could see. Most of the day was spent at GQ, conducting a variety of exercises. Intermittently I read the operation order. The Fleet was enroute to Mindoro to support the landings on 15 December. Mindoro was strategically placed, being 90 miles from Manila and defended by only 500 Japanese. By seizing it, we by-passed several enemy strong holds.

Admiral Kincaid's 7th Fleet was providing air coverage and transportation for the landings. General Kenney's land-based planes were covering Mindoro and the Visaya's. Our job was to prevent the enemy from launching air strikes against the landings from Manila Bay and northern Luzon.

At dawn on 14 December, the Third Fleet was 87 miles east of the northern coast of Luzon. Planes took off and landed throughout the day. A couple crashed and the crews were rescued by other destroyers. In keeping with Admiral McCain's doctrine, "The Big Blue Blanket" umbrella of fighter planes stayed over the airfields day and night. No enemy aircraft could take off. 208 planes were destroyed on the ground and 32 in the air. We lost 27 planes in combat and 38 operationally.

The landings on 15 December were virtually unopposed. Tokyo propagandists broadcast to the Japanese people a different story, saying: "The Americans are slipping away in a squeeze play on Leyte. They are forced to make the Mindoro landing due to terrific pressure exerted by our victorious troops on Leyte Island. We have the enemy in a position on Mindoro to deal him a stunning blow. General Douglas MacArthur, having escaped our traps many times, will not escape this time." When Elliott reported this at dinner, Stinky remarked to the Captain, "Guess this ends the war. Let's all pack up and go home."

The news from Europe was mixed. The Greeks were not satisfied with their government and engaged in sporadic civil war with many casualties. Patton, with clear skies, was advancing in the Saar toward Cologne. Belgium, southern Holland and all of France had been liberated. Alexander's 8th Army had advanced to the Senio River and Mark Clark was dug in for the winter.

In writing of the Mindoro operation and the new strategy used, McCain said, "Before the innovation of suicide attacks by the enemy, destruction of 80-90% of the attackers was considered an eminent success. Now 100 % destruction is essential. New developments have been designed to achieve 100% destruction." He noted: "2 cardinal principles have evolved: (1) defend the force with adequate patrols, and (2) blanket the threatening enemy opposition day and night with the most air power available. Regardless of the attractiveness of the targets, responsible commanders must not be lulled into diverting so much of their strength from the 'blanket' that the enemy's air is no longer held thoroughly helpless while it is being systematically destroyed."

That was excellent doctrine with which to beat the Japanese, but what about the awesome forces of nature soon to be unleashed? For many, it was the most terrifying battle of the war.

-

CHAPTER 13

Typhoon: Terror of the Sea

On Sunday 17 December, the Ingersoll was the linking ship midway between TG 38.3 and TG 38.2. To the south was TG 38.1. The Fleet was 500 miles east of Luzon. After fueling, air strikes were planned for the next 3 days in preparation for MacArthur's landing. Task Group 30.8, under the command of Captain Jasper Ascuff, consisting of 24 fleet oilers, 5 escort carriers, 3 fleet tugs, 10 destroyers and 5 destroyer escorts, was picked up at 1030. Admiral McCain signaled the fueling course. The wind was gusting to 30 knots and the seas were running 10-15 feet. I was in the wardroom getting bounced around and asked Superfine, "What makes McCain think this weather is going to improve? It's getting worse."

"He gets weather reports 4-8 times a day from Radio Kwajalein and Manus. Weather Central at Pearl sends out forecasts twice a day. The reports from the search planes are at least 12 hours late because they can't break radio silence."

"That's all fine and dandy, but none of that does us much good so far as the here and now."

"Each carrier has a meteorologist. Halsey's is Commander G.F. Kosco. He's a graduate of MIT and supposed to be quite good."

"I hope you're right."

At 1100 the sky was overcast and the wind gusting to 45 knots with the barometer reading 29.80. Stinky was OOD and said, "Our brothers haven't had much luck fueling. Hoses have parted and there have been collisions, with more oil going into the ocean than into tanks. The Spence is down to 15% of her capacity and has been alongside the New Jersey since the start. How are we?"

"We're OK for now. I'd hate to try and fuel in this sea."

The Collette, who was alongside the Wisconsin, had her hoses part. 4 other destroyers had to stop. The San Jacinto was able to get 172,000 gallons from the Monongahila before having to stop. The Hull, which was carrying mail for the entire Task Group, was able to transfer only 40 bags to the South Dakota. Mail for many of the ships would never be delivered. Carriers canceled air operations at noon, and planes were lashed down with steel cables. Halsey changed course 3 times trying to get a smoother ride, but was unsuccessful. Fueling ceased at 1330. The

Spence received only 6,000 gallons. A fueling rendezvous was set for 0600 in the morning.

Halsey changed course to 290 degrees and ordered the Spence, Hickox and Maddox to stay with the oilers and fuel at the first opportunity. The Ingersoll was ordered to return to the linking station between Task Groups 2 and 3. Before arriving, we were ordered to rejoin the screen.

Kosco knew there was a tropical disturbance in the area, but thought it was 450 miles to the east. The barometer now read 29.70, a drop of .13 inches in 3 hours. In the wardroom Will said, "The Captain believes there's a severe storm close at hand. When the barometer drop is .02-.06 inches per hour, the rule of thumb says the storm center is 150-250 miles distant. I hope Kosco knows what he is doing."

When I relieved Hollander at 1545, he said, "We're on course 270 degrees, speed 14 knots. No zigzagging. Halsey changed the fueling rendezvous to 14 degrees north, 127 degrees 30~ east. At 1500 the carriers were pitching and rolling too much for any kind of landing and the pilots of the 2 planes aloft were ordered to bail out. A destroyer picked them up. It doesn't look good with the barometer still dropping."

The ship was pitching and rolling so much I had to keep one hand fastened to a stanchion to keep from falling. Even though the bridge was 50 feet above the water, I was getting sprayed in the face. After the watch had settled in, I said to Ensign McCabe, my JOOD, "Do you realize we're only one week away from Christmas? My folks have the tree decorated and are probably wrapping presents. This is one year I'll be missing, but I can't complain. I've made most of them. What about you?"

Ed replied, "I was raised outside of New York City. Always at Christmas we'd go to Rockefeller Center to see the enormous tree and the ice skaters. The streets were filled with crowds of shoppers. Christmas decorations were everywhere and on every corner was a Santa Claus. There's nothing like New York to get you into the spirit of the holiday season."

"I wouldn't mind being there now. I'm a little concerned about this weather. With this 30-40 knot wind out of the NNE, fueling isn't going to be easy."

The seas continued to get higher. At 1745 the Captain got on the PA: "This is the Captain speaking. This weather looks like it is going to get worse before it gets better. I want everything movable lashed securely to the deck and bulkheads. Anything not secured will act like a missile and injure or kill. Do it on the double."

He turned to me and asked, "Chief, what is the fuel situation?"

"Could be worse. We're about 60% full."

"How long will it take to shift the oil and take on ballast?"

"Probably 3 to 4 hours".

"Let's get on with it."

Calling the oil king, I said, "Captain wants us to take on ballast. Shift the oil and fill the empty tanks with salt water. The barometer is continuing to drop. With full tanks we'll have more stability."

With nightfall, the sky and sea became black. The Kwajalein reported she was taking water over the flight deck. The barometer dropped to 29.76 and the wind was gusting to 40 knots from the northeast. The quartermaster, a veteran seaman, said, "I don't like those cross swells I'm seeing. The wind is out of the northeast and those swells are from east southeast. That's a sign of a typhoon."

Kosco and Halsey didn't seem concerned, but Halsey canceled the third fueling rendezvous and established a new one at Lat. 15 degrees 30' N, Long. 127 degrees 40' east. When Ascuff conferred a little later over TBS with the skippers of 2 escort carriers, they both thought this rendezvous would put them directly into the path of the storm.

Will, relieving me at 1945, said, "We're taking a fair amount of water over the sides and some of it is getting through the vents into the engine rooms. You ought to check on it."

Stopping by the wardroom to get dinner, I saw Doc MacGilpin, Elliott and Stinky holding fast with both hands to their chairs, which were secured to the bulkhead. Sideboards had been set up around the table to keep the dishes from sliding around. Stinky, waving, exclaimed, "Welcome to a gourmet meal. These sideboards are for looks only. The dishes move vertically as well as horizontally. They're called jumping plaques."

"I'm not hungry, but this weather is going to get worse before it gets better, and I need nourishment." The only way I could eat was with my hands, or with my head buried in the plate. A fork or knife became a lethal weapon. I gulped down a few bites and said, "I've got problems in the engineering spaces. Save me some food."

My major concern was to keep the engines running. Loss of forward motion, and the ship would broach. Once parallel in the deep canyon walls of water, it would capsize and death would be certain! With the tropical heat, the engineering spaces needed ventilating with fresh air. The architect hadn't visualized waves crashing over the ship and burying the vents under water.

As I climbed down into the forward engine room, I was greeted by the chief, who said, "We've rigged canvas ducts under all of the vents allowing the water to run into the bilges where it can be pumped out."

"Looks to me like you've done a good job."

"This rigging is satisfactory for most of the machinery, but the stupid architect perversely located vents over the main generators in both engine rooms. There is some leakage through the canvas. Any more water, we'll lose power and be in real trouble."

"You've done the best you can. Let's hope it does the job."

I went to my stateroom and took off my shoes, kept on my clothes and lay in my bunk. Sleep was impossible with the ship rolling, pitching and corkscrewing in and out of the waves. I wedged my body into the space between the bulkhead and the mattress, then braced my right leg against the guard rails on the side of the bunk. I could rest without getting thrown out. "Just like the North Atlantic," I thought.

By 2300 the barometer was reading 29.50, a fall of .07" in 2 hours, and no one knew where the center was located. Based on inaccurate information, Halsey ordered the Fleet to change course from west to due south at midnight and at 0200, northerly. Many ships were now heading into the center of the typhoon.

At 0400 on 18 December, Halsey, realizing the fleet was confronted with serious storm conditions, conferred by TBS with Admiral McCarney in the Essex and Bogan in the Lexington. Neither knew where the center was, or recognized its seriousness. At 0500 Halsey canceled the fueling rendezvous, changed course to due south and ordered the fleet to fuel when possible. He was concerned about the low fuel in some of the destroyers. The center was now 90 miles ESE from the New Jersey. The wind was gusting to 54 knots. There was a hard, driving rain and the seas were running 20 to 30 feet. The Ingersoll was heading straight into them. Repeatedly the bow would plunge into the wall of water, and with much shuddering, come up shaking it off.

A course change to a southeasterly heading was ordered at 0616. This moved the fleet closer to the typhoon. At 0710 McCain ordered TG 38.3 to commence fueling, and changed course to a northeasterly heading, which put us on a collision course with the center of the typhoon. The Captain, calling me on the phone, said, "Chief, get your men ready to fuel. It won't be easy, but give it a try."

"Captain, we're going to get more oil on the deck and into the ocean than we'll get in the tanks. We might lose men over the side. This is an impossible situation."

"Just stand by and we'll see."

Ascuff's group to the east was closer to the center, and the weather was much heavier. The Kwajalein, with engines full ahead, was making only a few knots. The Nehenta Bay and Rudyard Bay, with the Kwajalein, left the formation due to the pounding. Attempts to fuel, even from the lee side of the carriers, was unsuccessful. Nothing worked, and at 0803 Halsey discontinued all attempts to fuel and changed course to due south. At 0818 he sent a dispatch to General MacArthur: "Sorry. Will be unable to strike targets on Luzon on the 19th. Fleet caught in typhoon."

At 1000 the barometer began falling rapidly. Samony, OOD, notified the Captain, "This thing is taking a nose dive. It's down to 29.55. We've got real trouble."

The Captain said, "Pass the word for all hands to wear life jackets and make damn certain everything movable is secured."

Ships were being scattered all over the ocean. Station keeping was difficult to impossible. Some ships could only make a few knots with both engines full ahead. The wind was beginning to howl through the rigging at over 70 knots. The waves became mountainous, 50-60 feet high.

The Ingersoll was engulfed with the crashing waves. Visibility was almost zero. Elliott, who had just come from the bridge, said, "Even with radar I couldn't keep station. Ships weren't designed for these conditions. These monstrous waves are engulfing the bridge."

At 1100 I received an urgent call from the chief in the after engine room: "We've got an emergency and you're needed right away." He was a 20-year veteran who knew his business. I headed topside. There were 50 yards of open deck from wardroom country to the engine room. The safest way to get there was to catch the roll of the ship at the top when the lee rail was up and dry, then run and duck into the after engine room. This would work as long as there was some rhythm to the roll. Unfortunately, there wasn't. The ship would start to roll gently to the weather side, and without any warning, catch a rogue wave and lurch back to starboard like a truck hitting a brick wall. A steel cable was strung about 2 feet inside of the guard rail to act as a lifeline. I was scared, but had to go. The ship rolled to port and the deck cleared of water. I started running down the starboard side when suddenly the ship lurched violently. I was thrown off my feet and a huge wave crashed down on me. I blindly and desperately grabbed. My hands closed on the inboard steel lifeline. The force of the water began tearing me loose from the cable. This was it! What a helluva way to go! Suddenly, just as rapidly as I had gone under, I was free of the water. The deck was clear. I ran to the after engine room and scurried down the ladder.

The machinist mate on the throttle had a line tied around his waist secured to a stanchion. He was being kept busy. Every time the shafts came out of the water, he had to cut back on the steam to the turbines so the they wouldn't turn too fast. Men in the fire room had to decrease and increase the steam to coincide with the throttle actions. They were working as a team.

Ransom, chief electrician mate, was waiting for me. We stood on the steel catwalk circling the engine room, which had a one inch side rail designed to keep the men from slipping off. Now it was holding water which dripped on the machinery below. Ransom quickly explained, "The canvas above the generator is keeping it operational. I don't know for how long. The generator in the forward engine room and the main switchboard have shorted out. They're being dried off. All of our power is going though that." Pointing with his head to the main switchboard, he said, "Unless we can get the main power switch cleaned up, we're going to be in serious trouble."

"I don't understand."

"I have by-passed the switch, but the fuses are going to blow if gun circuits, or any other main circuits, are cut on. I need to pull the switch, dry it off and put it back. It can't be taken out from the front. Someone has to go behind the board and remove it. There are uninsulated 440 volt bus bars behind that board. With this wet catwalk and the ship plunging and rolling, that's dangerous work. Touch one of those bars and you're fried."

I asked, "Is there any alternative?" I was holding firmly to the guard rail to keep from being thrown on the machinery below.

"None that I'm aware of."

This was my responsibility. "Let's get on with the job. I want you to explain how to remove the breaker. I'll get it out."

He responded, "Oh, no! Let's get one of the electrician's mates. They do this all the time."

"Hell, no! This issue is not up for debate. Just tell me how to get the switch out."

He told me exactly what to do. I went behind the board and each lurch almost threw me into the bus bars. Sweating and with my hands shaking, I wondered why I had agreed to do such a stupid thing. One way or another, I was going to die, but I hadn't envisioned it being by my own hand. After what seemed like eternity, I got the switch out and gave it to Ransom.

He, too, was sweating as he said, "I didn't think you'd make it. The whole board could have blown up if you had failed. I think we can jury rig something so no one will have to go behind the board again." I thought, "That is one helluva note. I risk my neck and now he decides he can jury rig the goddam thing."

While I was in the engine room, the Captain had the oil king trail oil from barrels over the port side of the fantail. This quieted down the wave action and there was less of a crashing effect with the tons of water. It was a dangerous job for the men involved, but this was a battle, not with the Japanese, but with the age-old demon sea.

When I relieved Samony at 1145, I heard Halsey on the TBS: "Disregard formation-keeping and take best course and speed for security." Samony exclaimed, "Halsey has finally realized this is a monster storm. Everyone has already been following the age-old seaman's rule 'don't fight the sea'. Ships are scattered all over the ocean. Some have hove to waiting for this thing to pass, and there have been many near collisions."

"Why don't you just keep the watch? You're experienced and I'm a novice."

"Not on your life. I'm happy to let you take over," he replied as both of us held to the bulkhead with both hands.

"As you can see, visibility is zero. No pun intended. These waves are 60-70 feet high and we're operating more like a submarine than a ship. No one can stand on the wings of the bridge. Station-keeping is by guess and by God. The radar men can't distinguish ground clutter from ships. This place has been wild. The squawk box (TBS) hasn't stopped. 10 destroyers report fuel below 20% capacity. The Maddox, Hickox and Spence are down to 10% and can't make it another 24 hours. The CVE's Nehenta Bay, Cape Esperance and Rudyard Bay left the formation. The Independence reported a man over the side. Loose planes have started fires on the Monterey. The fleet tug Jicarilla has engine trouble," he paused.

"Don't you have any good news?" I asked.

"Only that we're still afloat. Ships have been reporting life boats, search lights, radar antennae, planes and depth charges washing over the side. Carriers and destroyers are catching hell, flooding, with inclinometer readings of 70 degrees and barometer readings down to an unbelievable 28.84.30. At 1100 the Spence reported rolls of 70 degrees and was unable to come about. The Monaghan is unable to come about even with full speed. The Hull doesn't sound like she is going to make it. We've had several course changes and presently are on 200 degrees, speed 11 knots. It's all yours and good luck."

"I've never experienced anything like this, even in the North Atlantic. The only plus is this water is warm and I won't freeze to death. I'll relieve you. Get some rest if you can."

I surveyed the scene. With rain pounding down in sheets, the wind gusting over 125 knots and 70-foot waves, the Ingersoll was rolling over 50 degrees. All destroyers were taking a brutal beating. The light carriers, with flight decks 57 feet off the water, had green water crashing over the bows. Planes were breaking loose from their moorings, becoming high speed missiles. The Monterey, Cowpens, Kwajalein and Cape Esperance were blazing and men were being killed putting out fires. There was a cacophony of sounds on the TBS; horror story after horror story was being reported.

Watching with fear, I saw the inclinometer move to 40, then 50 degrees. The Ingersoll was hanging on its side. Subconsciously I found myself and other crew members trying to push it upright. A few ships which were poorly ballasted had the off-watch crew stand on the weather side to keep the ship from capsizing.

At 1200 Halsey ordered a change of course. With the wind gusting over 100 knots, the Ingersoll answered the helm sluggishly, but finally came around. I was hanging on to the guard rail trying to keep station, while the Hull was experiencing its own hell. The skipper had served on destroyers during frightening North Atlantic storms and experienced the worst. His fuel tanks were 70% full and he hadn't taken on ballast. A gust of wind pinned the Hull on her side and her helm failed to respond to any combination of rudder and engines. She lay in irons rolling 50 to 70 degrees. She recovered from several, but a 140-knot gust pinned her down. Water flooded into her pilot house and engineering spaces. Power was lost and she capsized shortly after the noon hour. By a miracle, 7 officers and 55 men were picked up out of a complement of 264.

The Spence started ballasting too late. Water entered through the ventilation system and short-circuited the main distribution board. With the loss of power, the rudder jammed at hard right. At 1110 she broached and was swallowed up by the sea. Only one officer and 23 enlisted men were rescued out of a complement of 300.

The Monaghan was to the south near the center of the Typhoon. Her fuel tanks were only 15% full. At 0925 her skipper notified the Squadron Commander that he was unable to steer the base course and was leaving the formation on a heading of 330 degrees with the wind on the starboard bow. At about 1100 he tried ballasting the empty tanks. The ship foundered and water came crashing into the engine and steering room spaces. All power was lost. She stayed afloat for a short while, but capsized just after 1200. Only 6 enlisted men survived.

Luckier was the Dewey, whose Captain was Lt. Cmdr. C.R. Calhoun, a former shipmate of mine from the Sterett. In avoiding a collision with the carrier Monterey, the Dewey got in irons, broadside to the sea, rolling heavily to starboard, and was unable to answer the helm. Her tanks were 75% full and with the concurrence of the Squadron Commander, Calhoun jettisoned everything topside that was movable, including torpedoes and depth charges. He ordered the partially-emptied port tanks filled with sea water and ordered the off-watch crew to go below and stand on the port side. The ship rolled some 60 degrees to starboard, hung there and recovered. A speed of 3 knots was maintained with the starboard engine. At 1100 sea water began entering her ventilators and shorted out the switchboard in the steering engine room. This knocked out steering from the bridge. Lube oil suction was lost and the port engine had to be secured. Heavy seas crashed through the engine room hatches and short-circuited the main switchboard. There was a total loss of power and lights. Calhoun organized a bucket brigade to keep the steering engine room bailed out so the men on manual steering could keep her helm hard down. Submersible pumps were rigged and run off the diesel generator. At 1210 the Dewey rolled 65 degrees to starboard. The barometer was down to 26.60, and she was in the eye of the typhoon. No. 1 stack pulled out, and although more water went into the boiler room, it reduced the ship's sail area and stability was improved. By 1300 the center had passed, the pumps were working and conditions were improving. Through luck, competence and courage, her power was restored. At 1800 she was underway on a westerly course. Her survival was a miracle.

While these catastrophes were occurring, I was kept alert avoiding collisions with ships which kept appearing out of nowhere and were out of control. I was afraid to answer the phone when a call came from the engineering spaces. I knew I'd hear a horror story. Each time, I was relieved to learn the problem was minor.

At 1228 the Cape Esperance reported a fire on the flight deck. The crew extinguished it in a few minutes. The San Jacinto reported 4 planes loose. The Cowpens said, "We have put out all fires."

Stinky was plotting our position and muttering to himself. I asked him what his problem was.

"Do you know what that nut Mitchell is doing?"

"Can't say as I do. Probably trying to keep from getting thrown over the side."

"As senior officer, he has convened a summary court martial in the wardroom to try the case of a signalman. There certainly is no urgency. The guy isn't going anywhere. There's no sitting in any of the chairs, just holding on. With this bouncing around, the judge will probably end up in the lap of the accused. This must be unique in naval history. No trial has ever occurred under such terrifying conditions, especially when thousands of us seemingly are on trial by the Supreme Judge of all. Incredible!" I agreed.

The typhoon was at its peak at 1345. Halsey, recognizing the seriousness, changed course to 120 degrees, putting the wind on our port quarter, giving us a more comfortable ride. He notified Nimitz of his position and that the typhoon was intensifying. At 1358 Admiral McCain reported that the center of the typhoon was showing clearly on his radar bearing OOO degrees, distance 35 miles. Ships close to the center were reporting wind gusts of 200 knots and the Mascoma had a barometer reading of 27.07.

At 1500 the quartermaster said, "The barometer is rising and the wind is dying down a little."

"It does look like the worse might be over, but that's relative. The wind is still gusting to 80 knots and those waves are 40 to 50 feet high. The sky is a little brighter and that's encouraging.

At 1520 our course was changed to due south in search of better fueling weather. As Elliott was relieving me at 1545, Ascuff came on the TBS, "My flagship is dead in the water and my radios are out."

"What was that all about?" Elliott asked.

"You ain't heard nothing, my friend," I replied and gave him a rundown on all of the catastrophes that I knew. Finally I said, "Now for the good news. The New Jersey reports the wind gusts have dropped to 35 knots out of the west. The barometer has risen to 29.46. Your watch should be an improvement over mine."

Checking the engineering spaces, I was happy to find both generators back on the line and no other major breakdowns. We had survived! At 1630 I learned the summary court martial was adjourned until 0900 19 December.

Halsey, knowing men were washed overboard, at 1848 ordered a search for them. Conditions weren't ideal, with waves 10 to 15 feet high and pitch black dark. When I relieved Will at 0345, he said, "Halsey didn't find that out several ships had capsized until an hour ago. He still doesn't know which ones. The OTC and guide is in the Essex." And with a chuckle he added, "What a difference a day makes. The stars are out and I can see the other ships. These 10 to 15 foot waves don't make living too comfortable, but they're sure better than yesterday."

"I agree. Any special orders?"

"We're supposed to rendezvous with the tankers this morning. Many ships need fuel badly. I don't think there's any reason to wake up the oil king. We don't need to start getting rid of our ballast before 0700."

The rolling made eating breakfast uncomfortable, but it was much better than during the previous 2 days. The conversation centered on "Cobra", the granddaddy of all typhoons. Mitchell commented, "Halsey's meteorologists might be well-trained, but common sense they ain't got. Any midshipman knows to how to find the center. Face the wind, and the center is 10 points (112 degrees) to his right. Any jackass would have known that with the wind off due north (13 degrees), the center was SE by E (125 degrees)."

Superfine remarked, "Sure, right, hindsight is always 100%. Many lives were lost due to poor judgment. Someone deserves a general court martial."

At 0922 Halsey dispatched Nimitz: "Typhoon center passed 30 miles north of fleet guide midday 18th. Tracked by surface radar. Fleet took beating. Tabberer (DE 418) reports Hull (DD 350) capsized with little warning 1030. Only 10 survivors at time of report. Several other stragglers still unreported. Mataco towing disabled Jicarilla to Ulithi. Monterey, Cowpens, San Jacinto being sent to Ulithi for survey of damage and repairs. Estimate Monterey will be sent to Pearl. Dyson, Laws, Benham, Hickox, Alywin and Tabberer, with assorted derangements, will escort cripples. Fueling now proceeding in calm weather, Lat, 12 degrees 00' N; Long. 129 degrees E."

At 1207 the Ingersoll was alongside the Monongahela. Fueling was completed at 1320; we received 121,787 gallons. After delivering a quick release coupling to the San Jacinto, the Ingersoll was back on station at 1427 and Mitchell had reconvened the summary court martial.

At 2335 ships reported hearing cries for help. The Screen Commander ordered the Ingersoll, Knapp and Cogeswell to move to a stern position in the formation and search for survivors. We neither heard nor saw any. The Knapp rescued 3 and the Cogeswell one. The Tabberer picked up 41 from the Hull and 14 from the Spence.

The next morning at breakfast, the Captain observed, "Looking over the deck log for the past two days, you'd think we've been on a pleasure cruise. There is absolutely nothing in it to indicate the hell we've been through. Anybody got any ideas how to improve on it?" There was a heated discussion. The consensus was for the Bureau to assign a reporter to each ship and let him describe the happenings.

Elliott came in and said, "The Russians are advancing on all fronts, but a big battle is brewing in Europe. Our intelligence is convinced Hitler has insufficient troops to mount an offensive even though[67] his panzer divisions
have cut our forces in two and are on the move."

"I thought we had control of the air."

"We do, but nature is on the side of the Germans. The fog has been so heavy, no planes can fly. To brighten your day, you might be interested in learning that Major Richard Bong has just broken Eddie Rickenbacker's record by shooting down his 27th Jap. He is now the number one Ace."

"What's this about Glenn Miller?"

"Apparently he was flying from England to Europe to conduct his band at USO shows. His plane is long overdue and presumed lost."

When I relieved Stinky at 1145, he said, "We are on course 315 degrees, speed 20 knots. Unless plans change, strikes against Luzon will be made tomorrow. Everything is under control, so have a good one."

The Fleet overtook the tail of the typhoon and the weather became so bad the air strikes had to be canceled. The Third Fleet was ordered to Ulithi for rest, repairs and replenishment.

The news reported that Bastogne was surrounded and the Germans demanded that Brigadier General Anthony McAuliffe surrender. The commentator noted that his was a classic reply when he said, "Nuts."

The talk on the bridge was about home and Christmas. The quartermaster said, "One of us ought to dress up like Santa Claus and give the men a thrill. If we don't do that, we ought to recite 'The Night Before Christmas' over the PA." Someone else remarked, "Great idea, but wait until tomorrow night, please."

I spoke up, "One of my earliest memories of Christmas was Virginia's letter to the New York Times asking if there were a Santa Claus. The reply was a classic." Someone asked, "Can you recite any of it?"

"A little. It goes like this: 'Your little friends are wrong, Virginia. They've been affected by the skepticism of a skeptical age. Nothing can be which is not comprehensible by their little minds. There is a Santa Claus.....'"

There was momentary silence then applause. I had been concentrating so hard, I didn't notice the entire bridge watch had gathered around me. "Thanks fellows. That is my one and only performance."

After fueling, the Ingersoll moored starboard side to the Cotton in Ulithi Harbor. A motor launch came alongside with beer. The men drew 400 cases, not only the Ingersoll's allotment, but that for the rest of the division. It was placed in the forward hold and the hatch door secured. It was to be distributed the next day. Unfortunately, the hatch was not locked and most of the beer disappeared for a short while. Soon it appeared in berthing spaces, offices and even on the bridge. The men became rowdy and noisy and the smell became overpowering. By the time Veasey and Superfine realized what was happening, half of the crew were stoned. The Captain came on the PA, "Attention, all hands! This is the Captain speaking. I am ashamed of your behavior. I want all beer removed immediately from this ship. None will ever be permitted aboard again as long as I am Captain. If I could get replacements, I'd put all of you in the brig. Those men sober enough, put your buddies to bed and clean up the ship." Only the watch was awake when Santa Claus arrived.

On Christmas day, while we were on liberty at Crowley's Bar, Stinky got on his soap box, "Do you guys realize that 3 ships and some 790 men were killed with 80 missing? At least 146 planes were blown overboard or damaged beyond repair. 28 ships suffered a severe battering; 9 will be out of commission for several months. This includes the badly needed light carriers San Jacinto, Monterey, Cowpens, Cabot, Langley, Cape Esperance, Anzio and Altamaha. Only the battleships and large carriers had only minor damage."

Will asked, "How do you know that?"

"I have a friend on the Admiral's staff."

"What are you trying to prove?"

"It shouldn't have happened. It doesn't take an Einstein to realize that Halsey or someone on his staff is responsible for this disaster. They should be court martialed."

No one disagreed, but we preferred to listen to the tales of heroism and human tragedy. One survivor told how the wind and sea stripped life jackets off men while they were struggling to get off the capsizing ship. Another from the Monaghan reported how 40 men had gathered in the after gun shelter feeling safer than below decks. When the ship took its final roll, opening and getting out of the door was almost impossible due to the wind and waves. A gunners mate, Joe Guio, without any thought for his own safety, stood outside of the hatch pulling men out.

Lt.(jg) A.S. Krauchunas, the sole surviving officer from the Spence, related how he was sitting on the bunk in the Captain's cabin talking with the ship's doctor when there was a sudden lurch and he was thrown out. The ship rolled over and he was able to crawl topside on his hands and knees and fight his way clear of the ship. Only 50 to 60 men were able to make it with him; the rest were trapped below decks and died. He and others were picked up on the morning of the 20th.

I learned some had no life boats, only rafts, debris and float nets. Water and food was limited. Some had none. Many men became delirious; others died and had to be pushed into the ocean, where schools of ravenous sharks tore into the bodies. Hearing these horror stories and recognizing for the first time the magnitude of the disaster, I stayed sober. Stinky spoke for everyone: "I got no more idea than a preacher in hell why we're alive, fellows. We're damn lucky! I propose a toast of thanks to Almighty God for seeing us through."

On 26 December, a court of inquiry was convened at 1000 on board the destroyer tender Cascade. The purpose was to determine who, if anyone, was responsible for loss of ships and lives during the typhoon. It was presided over by Vice Admiral John H. Hoover, together with Vice Admiral George D. Murray, Rear Admiral Glenn B. Davis and Captain Herbert K. Gates. After deliberating for several days and examining 50 witnesses, they concluded Admiral Halsey was responsible for the storm damage and losses. No negligence was imputed to him. The court felt his were errors in judgment committed under stress of war operations and stemming from a commendable desire to meet military requirements. The court recommended: measures to reduce topside leakage on destroyers and other alterations to improve stability; upgrading the

Navy's meteorological service; a new weather central at Guam; properly staffed weather ships, and reconnaissance planes in areas of operations.

The logic of the court's decision not to punish Admiral Halsey was discussed. Stinky opined, "That logic is like freeing a bank robber because he was under the stress of being hungry and commending him for responding to the needs of his family. That is pure, unadulterated bull shit. Halsey demonstrated his incompetence only 2 months ago at Leyte. Look how many men were killed and ships lost needlessly. How many chances is the SOB entitled to? It makes no sense at all."

Nimitz sent a letter to the entire fleet emphasizing the rules of seamanship: "100 years ago a ship's survival depended solely on the competence of her master and on his constant alertness to every hint of change in the weather. His own barometer, the force and direction of the wind and the appearance of the sea and sky were all that he had for information. Seamen of today should be better at forecasting weather. The general laws are catalogued and readily available in various publications. Familiarity with Bowditch and other authorities is something no captain or navigator can do without. Any seaman is culpable who regards personal weather estimates as obsolete. The safety of the ship is always the responsibility of the commanding officer. This is also shared with his immediate superiors. The senior officer's responsibility is to think in terms of the smallest ship and most inexperienced officer. There is no little red light that is going to flash on and inform commanding officers or higher commanders that from then on there is extreme danger from the weather. The time for taking all measures for a ship's safety is while still able to do so. Nothing is more dangerous than for a seaman to be grudging in taking precautions lest they turn out to be unnecessary. Safety at sea for 1,000 years has depended on exactly the opposite philosophy."

At dinner Veasey remarked, "Our battle with typhoon Cobra is over but will never be forgotten. It affirms what seafaring men from the earliest days have known. The number one enemy for those who go down to the

CHAPTER 14

The Landings on Luzon;
Cruising in the South China Sea

Thursday 28 December was a beautiful day. At breakfast somebody asked Elliott what was happening in Europe and Italy. "I've got some good and bad news. The Battle of the Bulge is see-sawing back and forth. The weather is horrible, ice and snow, bitter cold. Things are so confused that prisoners on both sides are being liberated and recaptured. It's unreal. Thousands have been killed. Montgomery's Army from the north, Bradley's from the south and Patton's 4th Armored Division are relieving Bastogne. A pincers move was put on the Germans and forced them to withdraw. The Ardennes front is being reestablished to where it was a month ago. In Italy the advance is stopped due to the severe winter weather, but Clark and Montgomery have kept the Germans tied down for several months. The Russians are encircling Budapest and are successfully trapping the Hungarians and German divisions there."

"Maybe those guys will get to Berlin before we reach Tokyo," Superfine said.

Going out on deck, I watched a PB4Y make a perfect landing 1,000 yards away. Several boats, one with an Admiral's Flag, headed toward it. Admiral Nimitz was returning from Leyte where he had conferred with MacArthur. He was now stopping at Ulithi to meet with Halsey and his staff. I worked on the backlog of paperwork. Every breakdown during the typhoon was to be reported, with recommendations on how to keep it from happening again. Will was lying in his bunk and said, "Why don't you tell those guys to get a new crop of naval architects? That's the only way these breakdowns can be prevented."

"They might tell Veasey he needs another engineering officer. The one he's got is nuts," I replied.

At dinner on 30 December, Veasey said, "We're going to be busy for the next week. Our schedule calls for air strikes on Formosa on 3-4 January, fueling on the 5th, strikes on Luzon on the 6th and 7th, fueling on the 8th and Formosa again on 9 January, which is D-Day for MacArthur in Lingayan Gulf."

Stinky responded, "We'd get this war over twice as fast if we didn't have to keep fueling these damn destroyers."

"Yeah, and we'd spend less money if the Japs came to us instead of us wasting oil going to them," I replied.

The next morning the crew was exercised at General Quarters. When I relieved Stinky at 1145, I asked, "Why in the hell did we go to GQ?" He chuckled and replied, "Task Force Commander signaled 'exercise crew at GQ.' I guess that was to replace calisthenics."

When I relieved Pardee the next morning at 0345, he said, "We're enroute to Nansei Shoto and will pick up the tanker group during your watch." They were sighted at 0615. When I went to breakfast, Elliott was saying, "My boys picked up short-wave broadcasts from the States and heard some of the celebrations going on in Times Square and other places on New Year's Eve night. They also got the bowl scores. For your interest, it was Southern California 25, Tennessee 0 in the Rose Bowl; Tulsa 26, Georgia Tech 12 in the Orange; Oklahoma A&M 34, Texas Christian 0 in the Cotton Bowl and Duke 29, Alabama 26 in the Sugar Bowl."

The news reported that Churchill had been in Greece and assured all parties that Britain respected Greece's independence. He warned them that they needed to resolve their differences and establish the defeat of Germany as their first priority. In Burma the allies were advancing slowly.

When I relieved Samony at 1945, he said, "We're beginning a speed run to Formosa. The air strikes will be launched at dawn. Our pilots have been assigned central Formosa and Okinawa airfields."

A front moved in with clouds and rain. At dawn the fleet was 140 miles from the nearest Formosa airfields. The pilots said complete surprise was achieved, but the weather was so foul only a few of them could reach the targets. The Japanese planes didn't get off the ground. Visibility decreased and the rain got heavier. Flight operations were stopped after our guys destroyed 100 Jap planes. Our losses were 22.

At breakfast Veasey said, "With the weather so rotten, Halsey has called off all air strikes. The fleet is retiring to the southwest." Stinky said, "That's one of the few intelligent actions he's taken in the past several months."

Throughout the day unidentified planes were picked up and GQ was sounded. There was little work or rest for anyone. The only excitement occurred on 4 January at 1619 when the Ingersoll was ordered to destroy a mine off our starboard bow. The machine gunners hit it with 425 rounds of 20mm and 40mm shells together with 21 rounds of 5" shells. It didn't sink. Paul Horton exclaimed, "If we can't sink a lousy iron can, how in the hell can we do any damage to a Jap ship?"

The next morning Elliott said, "Admiral Oldendorf has been having a rough time. He left Leyte Gulf on 1 January enroute to Lingayen Bay with 164 ships. He passed through Surigao Strait without difficulty, but on the 4th, a Kamikaze slipped in and hit the carrier Ommaney Bay. 93 men were killed and 65 wounded. She couldn't be saved and was sunk by a torpedo. Today the cruisers Louisville and Australia were hit. I've had no report on the damage."

"Well it's obvious MacArthur is going to need our help for the landings on 9 January," Superfine said.

The tanker group was picked up and the morning was spent fueling. At 1220 the Knapp came alongside and delivered mail. Shortly thereafter the PA boomed the familiar words of mail call. After being relieved I went to the wardroom and opened my mail. I was ecstatic. "Have I got good news! My father tells me I have been accepted into the September class at the Medical College of SC." Stinky piped up, "You're nuts. You'll make more money, work less hours and be happier if you go to Columbia Law School."

Tack added, "You haven't got a snowball's chance in hell of making a September class. I suggest you tell your father to have them give that spot to somebody else."

Doc MacGilpin chimed in, "Don't let Stinky talk you out of medicine. I wouldn't go into law if they promised me a position on the Supreme Court."

Everyone voiced his opinion and then the discussion switched to "When is this damn war going to get over?"

When Will relieved me at 0345 on 6 January, I said, "We're supposed to strike airfields on Luzon at dawn, but with this lousy weather we may not." The planes took off, but due to the foul weather, few found airfields. Only 32 Jap planes were destroyed. With D-Day for the landings at Lingayen Gulf only 3 days away, Admiral Kincaid requested that coverage be continued.

The weather improved and McCain kept a blanket of planes over the air fields. Only a few Japanese planes took to the air and they were shot down. Air strikes resumed the next day. During my watch at midday, the Ingersoll went alongside the North Carolina to fuel. After the lines were in place, the Ingersoll was ordered to discontinue the exercise and proceed to our screening station without receiving any fuel. Later, in the wardroom, Will asked, "What was that all about? We could use some fuel. Why didn't we get it?"

"Don't ask me. I guess Admiral Sherman wants to be certain we haven't forgotten how to handle fuel hoses."

Elliott spoke up, "Be thankful that's your only problem. Yesterday was a nightmare for Oldendorf. His group was attacked by 32 Kamikaze planes. The New Mexico was hit twice. The Long, a destroyer-minesweep, and the cruisers Australia and Louisville, who were hit the previous day, got hit again. Other victims were the destroyers Walke and Allen M. Sumner, the battleship California, the cruiser Columbia and the destroyer-transport Brooks."

"What about casualties?"

"I don't have a complete rundown, but among those killed were the Skipper of the Walke, the Commander of Cruiser Division 4, the Skipper of the New Mexico and Churchill's personal liaison officer at MacArthur's headquarters. Many injuries resulted from men being sprayed with burning gasoline. They became human torches with burn areas covering 50-100% of their bodies. Few will survive."

Stinky exclaimed, "With all the damage the Kamikazes are causing, you'd think those brainy desk jockeys in Washington could come up with a solution."

The day passed uneventfully, and when Samony relieved me the next morning at 0345, I said, "We're supposed to rendezvous with the tankers this morning. If we don't, you might have to paddle 'cause we're in bad need of fuel."

Contact with Ascuff's tankers was made 160 miles east of Cape Engano and all ships fueled. The Captain held mast for a seaman and awarded him a deck court martial. In the afternoon the Cogeswell delivered mail. Fleet speed was increased to 25 knots. When I relieved Elliott at 0345, he said, "We're supposed to be at our launch site 100 miles from Formosa at dawn. With this rain, McCain may cancel." The weather became so bad the pilots were unable to find the airfields. Later in the day when the sun came out, 42 Jap planes were destroyed, 5 ships sunk and several others damaged. The greatest excitement was hearing that B-29's from the Mariana's had again bombed the Tokyo area.

Veasey said, "This week was not one of our best. We did accomplish our objective and prevented the Japanese from bombing the landings in the Lingayan Bay area. Hundreds of American lives were saved. Our major problem now is protecting the supply route from Mindaro to Lingayun Gulf."

"We control the air. What's the big deal?" asked Burt.

"The Japanese have a network of airfields from which they are operating Kamikazes and bombers. In addition, their combined fleet is scattered, but within attack distance. Formosa is only 345 miles from Manila, Hong Kong, 600 miles, and Camranh Bay in Indochina, 715 miles. Singapore is 1,400 miles and the center of oil production. These bases can only be reached with carrier planes. Nimitz has given Halsey the OK to swing through the South China Sea and destroy whatever he finds."

"From what the dispatches have been reporting, Admiral Toyoda still has a respectable fleet under his command. In the South China Sea are the battleships Ise and Hyuga, and up north in the Inland Sea of Japan are the battleships Yamato, Nagato and Haruna," said Elliott.

"Intelligence estimates he has approximately 950 planes. He's not ready to surrender yet," Veasey added.

Japan was getting desperate for certain critical supplies. Oil imports were down 65%, as were coal, iron and rice. They were still building aircraft and ships and manufacturing munitions. As a result of the shortages and our advances, the Japanese high command had designated Formosa, Iwo Jima, Okinawa, Shanghai and South Korea as the new outer defense perimeter. The "final decisive battle" was to be fought on Japan proper. Ground forces in the outer defense perimeter were not to be reinforced. Our submarines were sinking an average of 50 merchant vessels a month. With our 150 boats, the sea lanes between Japan and its Empire were being shut off. Halsey had been itching to attack the bases in the South China Sea. Now he could and the Fleet headed west.

At dinner 9 January, Elliott said, "The landings this morning went off without a hitch. There was no opposition on the beaches, but the Kamikazes played hell with some ships."

"No surprises?" Pardee asked.

"Not really. They brought out the Kaitrens, the same suicide boats they used at Leyte against the Jeep carriers. They sank 2 LCI's and damaged 4 LST's. Once the surprise element was lost, their effectiveness ceased. The 70 boats were so badly shot up, they disappeared."

"Those guys can think up more ways to kill themselves than we can to keep living. What's happening with the Russians?"

"The Germans have been on the attack and moving toward Budapest, but it's expected they'll run out of steam and the Russians will counter attack."

"Does that mean the European war is coming to an end?"

"Nope," Elliott replied, "but the commentators say Hitler has gambled too much on this operation. 150,000 men have been killed or captured and they had to leave behind hundreds of tanks and artillery pieces. There's a helluva lot of fighting ahead, but daylight can be seen at the end of tunnel."

The implications of these developments were discussed until I relieved the watch at 1945. The Fleet was passing through Luzon Strait into the South China Sea, and unidentified planes were picked up throughout the night. The night was spent at GQ.

When the Task Force began its run into Camranh Bay, Halsey sent a dispatch to all ships: "You know what to do—give them hell—God bless you all." The strike was launched at dawn when the Fleet was 50 miles from the bay. Bombing and strafing continued throughout the day. At dinner Veasey said, "From dispatches I've seen, Halsey was disappointed none of the ships of the Japanese Combined Fleet were present. The pilots sank 41 ships, including 9 fully loaded tankers as well as 125 planes. We lost 23 planes."

When I relieved Samony at sundown, he said, "We are retiring on course 073 degrees, speed 20 knots. Tomorrow we rendezvous with the tankers." The clouds rolled in, the wind picked up and the waves became higher. When Hollander appeared at midnight, I gave him the pertinent information and added, "If this weather gets any worse, we're going to have one helluva time fueling." Sleeping was difficult to impossible. The ship pitched and rolled. I wedged myself in and catnapped. The weather improved slightly and the next afternoon the Ingersoll went alongside the Neches and managed to take on board 30,700 gallons. The weather deteriorated and fueling had to be discontinued before many other ships received any oil. All ships were successfully fueled and the Fleet headed for Formosa.

At dinner Elliott said, "The Lingayan Bay area was secured yesterday. MacArthur and Kruger went ashore to boost the morale of the troops."

"What about the Kamikazes?"

"They returned on 12 January and crashed into the D.E. Belknap and 4 Liberty ships. The next day one hit the escort carrier Salamana and the casualties were heavy."[68]

With the rolling and plunging of the Ingersoll, sleeping was fitful that night. At dawn on 15 January, the Fleet was at launch site 250 miles ESE of Hong Kong and 170 miles south of Formosa. The wind died down, but the skies remained overcast. Unidentified aircraft were reported and most of the day was spent at GQ. In spite of the weather, our pilots sank one transport, one destroyer and one tanker. 16 planes were shot down and 18 were destroyed on the ground. Our losses were 12 planes.

The Fleet headed west for Hong Kong, and at dawn on 16 January, strikes were launched. The overcast skies and high seas handicapped the pilots and caused problems for the destroyers. During my 12-16 watch, the Cogeswell rescued a man who had been washed overboard from the San Jacinto. When Elliott relieved me, I said, "This weather is causing problems for the pilots, but flight operations are continuing and we're steering various courses at various speeds. This should be over by sundown. Hopefully, we'll steady down on a course that will give us a smoother ride."

In the wardroom Superfine was saying, "The pilots encountered very effective anti-aircraft fire today. To add to the problem, the depth settings on the torpedoes were set too deep and they nose-dived straight into the mud. However, they did sink 4 freighters and 3 tankers. We lost 49 planes."

Elliott said, "My men picked up a broadcast from Tokyo Rose. She said the Third Fleet was bottled up in the South China Sea and concluded, 'We don't know how you got in, but more importantly, how the hell are you going to get out?' "

"Halsey wants to hit Okinawa, but unless this weather improves, it isn't going to happen," Superfine said. "All destroyers are in need of fuel and we're going to try again in the morning."

The rest of the day and night was spent just hanging on. Fueling operations began at daybreak on 18 January. It was slow and difficult. All ships were pitching and rolling with the gigantic waves. When Elliott relieved me at 1545, I went to the wardroom and tried to drink some coffee. Everyone was bitching about the weather and the war. My reveries were broken by the phone ringing. "You're wanted in the after engine room, Chief," Stinky said. "Water has come in through the ventilators and is shorting out part of the main switchboard."

I hurried topside and while I waited for the right time to run down the deck, I saw Verne Braman, storekeeper 2/c, climb out of No. 4 gun turret. From conversations I had had with him, I knew he had a wife and was a competent, well-liked shipmate. He was expecting to go to college when he got out and get a degree in Business Administration. While he was climbing down the ladder of the after deck house, the ship rolled to the windward side. His feet had reached the deck when a gigantic rogue wave hit. The ship gave a violent and unexpected lunge to starboard. The mountainous wave crashed down on him. He lost his grip and I never saw him again. I yelled up to the bridge, "Man overboard." The Caperton, the ship astern of us, searched in vain for him.

As I was sliding down the ladder into the after engine room, the chief said, "Everything is under control. It was a helluva lot worse last month. As you can see, canvas has been spread over the generator. Little water is falling on it. Power was lost briefly to steering. We switched to the forward engine room generator and that's no longer a problem."

When I relieved Samony at midnight, he said, "The crew is really shaken up over Braman. It's a real tragedy. He was a good kid."

"I feel sick about it. He was on my watch from time to time. Always talking about his family and what he was going to do after the war."

Samony responded, "Thankfully, the sea has calmed down a little, so that shouldn't happen again. We're suppose to fuel in the morning."

With the improved weather, everyone had a good night's sleep. On 20 January, the Fleet was 100 miles west of Luzon. Enemy planes were picked up off and on by radar, but none were seen. Our fighters shot down 15 Japanese transport planes attempting to evacuate personnel from Luzon to Formosa.

The Balingtang Channel north of Luzon was transited at 2200 during my watch. There were sighs of relief and the quartermaster exclaimed, "Thank God we're out of that boxed-in China Sea. What's Tokyo Rose going to say now?"

During the 11 days from January 10-20, the Third Fleet had logged 3,800 miles with no major mishap. Nimitz said, "The sortie into the China Sea was well-conceived and brilliantly executed." Stinky commented, "You can't prove that by me, but the horrible weather is prima fascia evidence that God hasn't been on our side."

The news reported that the Allies were advancing on a broad front toward the Rhine and the progress in the Philippines was slow, but steady.

Veasey said, "Our next landings are scheduled for Iwo Jima on 19 February and on Okinawa, 1 April. Nimitz is going to need every ship he can get his hands on." Stinky spoke up, "I thought he lent a number of battleships, cruisers, destroyers and escort carriers to Admiral Kincaid for MacArthur's landings on Leyte and Lingayan Gulf."

"He did. There's been some haggling, but MacArthur has assured Nimitz he would release them."

Intelligence reported to Kincaid that there were 2 Japanese battleships at Singapore. Being so close at hand, he didn't believe he had sufficient forces to protect the beachhead. After much wrangling, Nimitz agreed to give Kincaid 4 battleships, 4 light cruisers, 17 destroyers and 6 baby flat tops.

There was a need for a strong naval force during the critical period between the withdrawal of the Third Fleet and the installation of MacArthur's air forces on Luzon. Admiral Spruance later wrote: "The planning for the Iwo Jima operation was affected to a considerable degree by the operations in the Philippines. It reduced the number of ships allocated to the Iwo Jima operation and necessitated last minute changes."

The Philippine campaign had been a thorn in the side of Nimitz since its beginning. He wanted to get on with the Pacific war. The bickering as to how to best use the naval forces was ongoing.

Admiral Halsey was carrying out his plans regardless of the discussions between Nimitz and MacArthur. After completing the passage through Balingtang Channel, the Fleet headed north. At dawn on 21 January, 120 miles east of Formosa, air strikes were launched. They continued throughout the day in the best flying weather of the month, for us and for the Japanese.

Radar picked up unidentified aircraft all around us at 1212. GQ was sounded. Upon my arrival in the forward engine room, George said, "Kamikazes are attacking. The Langley has been hit by 2 bombs and many fires have been started." He paused and then excitedly continued, "A Kamikaze just dove into the flight deck of the Ticonderoga. Bridge believes it exploded between the hanger and flight decks. Holy cow! Another just crashed into the Ticonderoga's superstructure and fires have started on the planes preparing to take off on the next strike. Men looking like blow torches are jumping over the side. We've been ordered to rescue them."

While searching for the survivors, the second raid arrived. George said, "They're attacking from all directions. The flake is heavy. One's down. Another just missed the Essex. One has gotten through and crashed into the destroyer Maddox. That's all for the moment." Many fires were started on the Maddox; 7 men were killed and 33 injured.

During the attack, the Ingersoll was busy rescuing survivors. By 1337, 10 had been picked up with several seriously injured. The Ticonderoga's crew had all fires extinguished within the hour, but a 9-degree list had developed. She had 143 men killed, 202 wounded and 36 planes lost.

The attacks stopped, but the other Task Groups were not so fortunate. Admiral McCain's flagship, the Hancock in TG 38.2, was hit by a 500 pound bomb which exploded between the flight and hangar decks. Fires were started. They were quickly controlled, but 52 men were killed and 103 wounded.

When I relieved Stinky at sundown, he said, "All is quiet. We're on course 070 degrees, speed 24 knots. The damaged ships are supposed to leave the formation during your watch and return to Ulithi. I hope things stay settled down so I can sleep."

At 2105 the Ticonderoga, Biloxi, Flint and Cogeswell formed up and left the formation. When Elliott relieved me, I said, "We're headed for Okinawa. Weather and Japs permitting, we're supposed to fuel during the morning." The destroyers fueled from the battleships and 4 seriously wounded crew members of the Ticonderoga were transferred to the North Carolina. Unidentified planes were reported throughout the day. GQ was sounded, but no Jap planes were seen.

When I relieved Samony at 2345, he said, "We should be off Okinawa at dawn. Our primary objective is to obtain photographic coverage in preparation for the landings in February. Our pilots will destroy any ships or planes found."

The strikes were launched at dawn. The pilots flew 682 sorties, of which 47 were photographic. There was no air opposition and 28 planes were destroyed on the ground. The operation was successful and the Fleet headed south to Ulithi.

The next day was beautiful: 5-knot wind on our port quarter with little roll; clear blue skies with a few white cumulus clouds. Pardee remarked, "It's hard to believe there is a war going on. I'm coming back when it is all over."

I had the watch in the afternoon when the Ingersoll went alongside the Dortch to receive mail. I enjoyed talking with my former shipmates. The joyous sound came over the PA: "Mail call for the crew in the mess hall; for the officers, in the wardroom."

Gunnery exercises were conducted the following day. When Will relieved me at 1945, I said, "We're getting to Ulithi tomorrow. I'm ready for a drink and some relaxation. How about keeping things quiet so I can get a good night's sleep."

The news reported that Warsaw had been liberated on 17 January and the Russians were advancing on a broad front. In one area, they were crossing the Rhine. Some 53 German divisions had been cut off and Germany was being flooded by refugees.

On 26 January during my watch, Ulithi was picked up on radar at 0502. After fueling and replenishing our ammunition supply, the Ingersoll moored to the Knapp in Berth #327. Immediately Lt. Cmdr. Albert W. Draves reported aboard to relieve Lt. Cmdr. Superfine as executive officer.

Admiral Spruance and his staff had arrived at Ulithi on the New Jersey on 25 January and conferred with Halsey. Halsey was throwing a big farewell party at Crowley's Bar with all of the trimmings. Neither I nor my shipmates were invited. We didn't get off the ship. At midnight Spruance assumed tactical command and the Third Fleet became the Fifth Fleet.

From dispatches, we knew MacArthur had captured Clark Field on the outskirts of Manila, and during the Luzon campaign, 300,000 tons of Japanese shipping was sunk and 615 aircraft destroyed. Our losses were 201 aircraft and 165 pilots and crewmen. In addition, 205 sailors were killed by the Kamikazes. However, our ships and men had proven their ability to operate continuously in bad weather.

"The outer defenses of the Japanese Empire no longer include Burma and the Netherlands East Indies. These are now isolated outposts," wrote Halsey.

In his parting message he said: "I am so proud of you that no words can express my feelings. This has been a hard operation. At times you have been driven beyond endurance, but only because the stakes were high. The enemy was as weary as you were. We have driven them off the sea and back to their inner defenses. Superbly well done."

"Nobody is going to argue with him about that," exclaimed Stinky. "Since we left Enewetok 5 months ago, we've been surrounded by Jap bases. They've thrown all the ships and planes at us that they had. The seas have gone berserk and we haven't had time to breathe. I'm tired just thinking about it."

"So how do we top that?" Will asked. We were surprised when we found out.

-

CHAPTER 15

Home is the sailor home from the sea;
And the hunter home from the hills

At breakfast the next morning the talk was of home. Scuttlebutt proclaimed that the Ingersoll was heading Stateside. I said, "The engines need repairs only a Navy Yard can do. One of these days while we're operating in Japanese waters, everything is going to break down at once. We'll just watch the Fifth Fleet slowly disappear over the horizon."

Elliott said, "I'm looking forward to seeing my wife. I'll have her fly out when I find out our port of embarkation." The other married officers had similar ideas. Stinky spoke up, "I'm glad I don't have a wife. I've got good contacts everywhere on the West Coast. If we're close to L.A., I'll be in hog heaven. I know Donna Reed, Virginia Mayo and several other starlets. I'll get you a date, Chief. How'd you like that?"

"Sounds great to me. I don't have a true love. Months ago she indicated it wasn't true and no longer love. Recently I've heard from a girl I call 'Little Miss Magnolia Blossom'. It's just a friendly relationship."

"Doesn't sound very exciting to me," responded Stinky. "How'd she get that name?"

"The girls at American Airlines gave it to her. A couple of years ago when I was changing planes in Washington, DC, I asked about Lil Hair. I was told she'd gone back to Columbia. With her thick southern accent, they'd called her 'Miss Magnolia Blossom'. Her last letter indicated she's at loose ends. I am available for any of your starlets. What about one of those long-legged chorus girls you've always been talking about?"

"Have no fear," Stinky replied. "I'll fix you up with the hottest number you've ever had."

I was summoned to the Captain's cabin and was pleased to find him smiling. He said, "Admiral McCain believes many deserving men and officers have not been properly recognized for their performance of duty. He ordered all Commanding Officers to submit names to him of deserving personnel. I have recommended you for a Bronze Star."

I gulped and replied, "Thank you, sir, but I don't deserve it. There are many others who warrant it more than I do."

Veasey snapped back, "Cut out the crap, Chief. Almost every ship in our Task Group has had a major breakdown and several have had to return to port for repairs. You've had your problems, but never once have you failed to answer the bell. I know you didn't personally put the feed pump back together or do any of the other repairs, but you are the responsible party. If things had gone to the bad, I'd have chewed your ass out. You're a damn fine officer and I am pleased to have you aboard. Now get on with your work."

In the afternoon at Crowley's Bar, a staff officer said the Ingersoll was going to the States for an overhaul. As soon as the word got around, my shipmates and I became the most popular officers at the bar. "Call my wife, my mother, girl friend." They had a variety of gifts they wanted us to carry home.

At breakfast, Captain Veasey announced, "We're heading for the west coast. I don't know the navy yard yet. Fusfield, see if you can get us some good movies to show on our way back."

The world news was good. The German garrison at Warsaw was threatened with encirclement and withdrew. Although slow, the Allies were advancing down the Burma Road. The 20th Bomber Group was attacking Iwo Jima with B-24's and B-25's. The Japanese High Command issued directives for the defense of Japan (Sho-Go) and sent reinforcements to Iwo Jima and Okinawa.

On 28 January the Ingersoll was underway with the Ticonderoga, California, New Mexico and Caperton. There was excitement in the air as Ulithi disappeared over the horizon. We were going home! Except for

Admiral presenting the author with Bronze Star.

gunnery exercises, all department heads were kept busy preparing work orders for the navy yard. There were movies in the wardroom and the crew's mess hall at night.

On 1 February Eniwetok Atoll was sighted and the Caperton delivered passengers to the Atoll. The weather was ideal: balmy tradewinds and gentle waves, which were perfect for sleep. It was another world. Elliott reminded us there was a war on. At breakfast he said, "Our boys are moving ahead in the Philippines. The X1 Corps has landed north of Bataan, the 11th Airborne Division has landed at the entrance to Manila Bay and the X1V Corps has reached the outskirts of Manila."

Superfine added, "The Russians have crossed the German frontier in force, and our boys are advancing toward the Roer Dams."

"It's rumored the Germans are going to open the floodgates and wash everyone away," Horton said.

"They'll try, but won't succeed. Our Chiefs of Staff are meeting with the British to decide on the next move. Eisenhower wants a broad advance to the Rhine. Montgomery and the British favor a single thrust so we can beat the Russians to Berlin," Superfine said.

On 5 February Elliott announced, "5,000 allied prisoners of war have been freed at Manila. It won't be long now."

During my 16-20 watch, Veasey remarked, "Chief, I suspect I'll need to designate one officer to fly back to the States with the work orders. This will let the Yard make plans and speed our repairs. I'm appointing you. Familiarize yourself with the work requests of the other departments and coordinate the leaves with the exec. All hands will get 20 days, one-third at a time."

All of the off-duty watch was on deck at 0645 7 February to see Diamond Head and Waikiki. Rather than following the heavy ships into the harbor, the PA boomed, "Now hear this! This is the Captain speaking. The Ingersoll and the Caperton are proceeding to a firing range for gunnery exercises. It won't be for long." The bitching started, "What jackass gave that order? Why? It's not fair. We haven't had a decent liberty in 8 months." The exercises lasted 2 hours.

At noon the Ingersoll was moored at Pearl City with the Caperton on the portside. Commander Francis Blouin reported on board to relieve Commander Veasey. Two hours later Superfine departed to report to ComDesPac. I was summoned to the Captain's cabin. When I entered, he said, "Just as I thought. ComDesPac wants one officer to fly back to the States carrying all of the work requests. You'll probably leave tomorrow."

"Aye, aye, sir. I'm going to like this assignment."

There was bedlam in the wardroom. Every one had someone for me to call and a message to give. I finally had to shout, "Hold up, fellows.

I'm so confused I don't know which direction I'm going or what I'm suppose to do when I get there. Please! Each of you write your name on the top of one page of this notebook. Under that, put who I'm to call, the telephone number and what I'm to say."

I slept soundly when I finally got into my bunk. At breakfast Elliott said, "You're going to be carrying dispatches from ComDesPac Fleet to Com 12th Naval District and will be designated a special courier, which makes you immune from the usual search. This will be an ideal time to take your contraband to the States."

"Sure would be if I had any. If you know of someone with priceless jewels, send them to me and I'll sneak them in for a price."

On 8 February at 0910, a car took me to the transportation office. At the same time, the Ingersoll and Caperton got underway for the States. The duty officer declared, "Everything is in order, Lieutenant. I'm sending you out to the Naval Air Station. A plane is leaving at 1800." The PB4Y lifted off on schedule. It was with great excitement that I watched Diamond Head and Waikiki pass by. I reflected, "What a world! How lucky can one guy be? I've seen action in both the Atlantic and Pacific, been present at the most furious naval battles of all time and haven't received a scratch. Many far more deserving than I are at the bottom of the ocean. Is life just a roll of the dice?" I didn't have an answer and fell asleep.

Arriving in San Francisco the next day, I reported to the duty officer and asked about the Ingersoll. He replied, "I don't know what yard is assigned to do the work. Check with me tomorrow. There are no quarters available in the BOQ. Just get yourself a room downtown." He paused and continued, "Enjoy yourself. You guys have been having a rough time of it. Sure wish I could get on a ship." He nervously shuffled the papers on his desk and added apologetically, "I'm just so damn busy." How many times would I hear that in my life?

I checked into the Fairmont Hotel and called my mother. She said, "We're all doing fine. Herbert is somewhere in the Pacific. Maybe you'll run into him."

"I might, but right now I'm coming home. I've got 20 days leave and should be home in a week or so."

After showering, I went across the street to the bar at the Top Of the Mark Hopkins. It was jammed with naval officers, some heading out and others just coming in. I found a couple of friends, drank and shared experiences. Girls appeared, which added to the gaiety. How I got to my room I'll never know. The next morning, with my head bursting open, I swore off all alcohol.

The duty officer said, "I'm not certain, but I think the Ingersoll is going to San Diego. I'll give you a priority chit to fly down by NATS."

It was a beautiful flight down the coast to San Diego. When I reported to the duty officer, he said, "I haven't heard anything about the Ingersoll coming here. Check into a hotel downtown and come back tomorrow." In the morning a smiling duty officer said, "I've got the scoop. The Ingersoll will arrive in San Pedro, Long Beach, California, on 15 February." I caught a bus for San Pedro.

With only 5 days, there was one helluva lot of work to do. Drinking and partying were out. I went over the work orders with the yard personnel and met with the transportation officer. One third of the crew and officers were going on leave as soon as the Ingersoll docked. I had to arrange for airplane, train and bus tickets to be ready when they arrived.

I followed the war through the radio and newspapers. My problem was discerning fact from propaganda. Churchill and Roosevelt were meeting at Yalta and agreed: (1) Nazism would be eradicated, but the country would not be destroyed. (2) Germany would pay reparations for war damage. (3) The Big Three with France and China would sponsor a United Nations meeting in San Francisco on 25 April. (4) Pledged to assist liberated countries in establishing democratic governments. (5) Discussed Poland and Yugoslavia, borders and governments. Commentators noted that Roosevelt appeared to be a very sick man. Ernie Pyle was still writing from the front lines. He was quoted, "You begin to feel that you can't go on forever without being hurt. I feel that I have used up all of my chances. And I hate it. I don't want to be killed."[69]

Each night I listened to various shows on the radio: "Bob Hope", "Bing Crosby" and "Information Please", a quiz show. Sometimes it would be the music of Tommy Dorsey, Benny Goodman or one of the other Big Bands playing "Irresistible You", "Long Ago and Far Away" or "Dream" with the Pied Pipers singing. There was no war.

Later I was told that at midday on 14 February, the change of command ceremonies took place on the fantail of the Ingersoll. Commander Veasey said to the crew, "I am honored to have been the first Commanding Officer of the Ingersoll, to have taken her into battle and brought her safely home. I commend you, the officers and men of this ship, for a job well done. I will always cherish these experiences." Commander Francis J. Blouin stepped forward and read his orders. He then turned to Veasey and said, "I relieve you, sir." Commander Veasey responded, "I stand relieved."

One of Blouin's first orders of business was to hold mast at 1735 for 6 men who had been caught gambling. He let them off easy; each got a warning.

On 15 February the Ingersoll anchored in Los Angeles Harbor. The transportation officer and I arrived on board at 0855. He immediately began handing out air, train and bus tickets to a happy group of officers and men. They wasted no time in heading home. Captain Blouin said, "If you didn't accomplish anything else on your early trip Stateside, getting the transportation set up made you a winner. Those guys would probably elect you the mayor of Long Beach."

On Wednesday 21 February, I was summoned to the Captain's cabin and he said, "I have received the awards Veasey recommended to Admiral McCain for you and the others. We are going to have the ceremony this morning." At 1000 the ship's company was assembled on the fantail. Rear Admiral F.G. Fahrion, ComCruDiv 4, (SOPA) made the presentations to me and 14 others.

I was a little embarrassed as he read: "For distinguishing himself by meritorious achievement in connection with operations against the enemy during the period 20 July, 1944, to 2 December, 1944, while serving as engineering officer of a destroyer attached to a fast carrier Task Force. His efficient maintenance and skillful operation of the engineering plant under fire and at high speeds for prolonged periods contributed materially to the success of the ship in operating against enemy aircraft, surface craft and shore establishment. His personal leadership and conduct were a fine example to his men, and at all times in keeping with the highest traditions of the United States Naval Service." I didn't feel like a hero. I had performed my duties competently. My men deserved the accolades. I felt like a fraud. I was a survivor! Others receiving awards were Hollander, Davis, Schwartz, Lang, MacGilpin, Young, Ray, Thurmond, Bueti, Mangun, Steadham, Bartlett, Schaffer and Cantalini.

The news from abroad was good. The Soviets were running over the Baltic Republics, had captured Budapest, and 1,000 plane attacks were being made on Berlin, Magdebug and Dresden. Germany was ringed on all sides. In India, Mandalay was being threatened from the north and west.

The talk in the wardroom and the bars was the landing on 15 February by the 38th Division on the southern tip of Bataan and securing it on the 21st. With the landing of the US Airborne on Corregidor on 16 February, the end of the Philippine Campaign was near.

On 19 February cheers rang out when we heard the 4th and 5th Marine Divisions had landed on Iwo Jima. Resistance was slight and 30,000 troops were landed the first day. On the 21st, Kamikazes attacked, sinking the carrier Bismarck Sea and badly damaging the Saratoga.

In Europe the Allies were advancing into Saarland and into the Roer Valley. There was scuttlebutt that the Germans in Italy were willing to make a unilateral truce. Heinrich Himmler, realizing Germany's defeat was inevitable, had suggested that the Germans join forces with the western allies to prevent Russia from over running Europe. This was unacceptable.

As I left on leave on 24 February, the front page of all newspapers carried a picture of Marines raising Old Glory on Mt. Suribachi at Iwo Jima. I flew via Kansas City, Chicago, Washington, DC, Charlotte and finally into Columbia, SC.

As we circled the city I was filled with excitement. When I entered the waiting room, I saw Lil Hair at the Delta counter smiling and waving. Hugging my parents and passing a few pleasantries with them, I excused myself. Embracing Lil, I exclaimed, "I had no idea you'd be here. What a wonderful surprise. How about showing me the town?"

"I'd love to, but I'm tied up tonight. How about tomorrow?"

"It's a date." Hugging her, I left.

My father proudly showed me the car he had bought. Getting in, I said, "Boy, this is going to be great. For the first time in my life, I'm not going to have to find a ride and double date."

The next night Lil and I went to the Carrollton Club, where we danced, talked and visited with friends. The days went by rapidly blending into one another. I kept discovering things about Lil I had never known: her family, her likes and dislikes, the traits she most admired in others, her deep religious convictions and her goals and aspirations. Somewhere along the way, I began realizing we had much in common. Sitting in the car one night on the corner of Laurens and Senate Streets with my arms around her, I knew I had found the person I had been looking for and wanted to spend the rest of my life with. I didn't propose, knowing the future was too uncertain to make any commitments.

The war was on another planet, but I kept up through newspaper and radio. Corrigedor was secured on 2 March, followed by Manila the next day. The city was devastated and in ruins. The Japs had contested our advance house to house. There were 6,500 American casualties, and over 100,000 Filipinos had died.

In Europe the advance was steady. By mid March, US Armies had reached the Rhine, then the outskirts of Cologne and by the 21st, the Rhine to the south. Through a Swiss contact, I learned that talks were continuing in Geneva between high ranking German officers and Allen Dulles, head of the OSS. Nothing was settled.

Lil and I enjoyed listening to records, dancing and singing "I Fall in Love Too Easily", "The More I See You", "June is Busting Out All Over", "Put Your Dreams Away" and many others. We joined Frank Sinatra, Perry Como and Doris Day in singing all of the hit songs. Occasionally we went to the movies. Time got away.

The day arrived when Lil had to leave with her mother to visit relatives in Orlando, Fla., and I was going to Charleston to visit mine. Kissing her good-bye, I felt a warmth and glow I had never experienced before and said, "I love you. Take care of yourself. God willing, we will have a future together, and always remember, 'I'll be seeing you again whenever spring comes through again.'"

With the war news so good and believing the end might be near, I again put in an application for medical school.

I wrote Lil on 9 March, "You sound like you had a very interesting and entertaining trip. I'm extremely jealous of your traveling companions. With 3 children along, you probably weren't too wicked. It's been terribly lonesome here without you. I called your house as soon as I got back from Charleston just to be sure you had gone. The realization hasn't sunk in yet that it's going to be months, or maybe years before I see you again. You haven't seen the last of me, and the next time, you're not going to run out as you did this time.

"Had a pleasant visit to Charleston. You don't have to have eyes to bring back memories, just a good nose: that inimitable pluff mud, smelter and paper mill.

"Reed Boyd and I had dinner uptown today, and it was on him. Ordered the most expensive steak on the menu. Your ears should have been burning. We talked about you, and now I'll tell you a secret. Last night I missed you more than I thought I could ever miss anyone.

"Took my mother to a Sigmund Romberg concert last night. The music and singing were beautiful. You would have loved it.

"Reed and I have a couple of nags lined up for this afternoon. We're going to ride if the horses agree. I don't know how long we'll last. Something interesting might happen. Go on and laugh.

"How about giving me your phone number and the name of the people you're staying with. Last night I had my first and last date since you left. We went to the Elk's Club and saw several friends. Almost made me feel like home, but not quite. It's not the same with you not around. Enjoy your stay in sunny Florida. Don't run into too many millionaires.

"Just remember that out there somewhere there's a guy who's just living for the time that he'll see you again; that guy is me."

From letters he had written, I knew brother Herbert was somewhere in the Pacific and I told my mother, "I'll find him. It's a big ocean, but somehow we seem to run into friends and relatives. It's mysterious how it happens."

"Maybe each of you has a guardian angel that leads and protects you," she replied.

"From some of my experiences, I think you might be right."

My plane left on 10 March. After saying my good-byes, I added, "The war won't last much longer and I'll be home to stay."

My Delta flight arrived in Washington, DC, and there was the usual snafu. All direct flights to Los Angeles were filled and I was stranded until the next day. The banks were closed and with my ticket costing an extra $152, I had a problem. Phoning Johnny Carroll, who had been stationed in Washington ever since our graduation from the Prairie State in 1941, he said, "Good to hear from you, old buddy. I expect you to spend the night with me."

"Thanks, but I've got another problem. My airline ticket is costing an additional $152. I told those people to bill me. I was going back to fight their war and wasn't that worth a lousy $152? No soap, they said."

"Don't worry. I can take care of that. I'm going out with Carl McElveen and Betty Jane Gawler tonight and I expect you to join us." When I arrived at Johnny's apartment, we embraced and shared experiences. Our talk turned to the news of the day. General Curtis LeMay had taken over the 20th Bomber group, loaded 339 B-29's with incendiaries, and bombed Tokyo. The results were devastating. 16 square miles made up largely of wooden houses were destroyed.

Johnny said, "If they keep that up, you might be getting home quicker than you thought."

"I'm not going to bet the family jewels on it. LeMay used incendiaries and low-level bombing on Chinese cities with great success until he ran out of bombs. I just hope that doesn't happen this time. At any rate, I'm looking forward to this night."

Author on left, Johnny carroll, Betty Jane Gawler, and Carl McElveen.

Betts was one of Lil's oldest and dearest friends from junior high school days. I had known her for many years. Carl McElveen grew up in my neighborhood and his older brother had been in my class. He was a corporal in the Army and heading for Europe. This was to be his first combat experience and he had concerns. We tried to cheer him up. I assured him, "Old buddy, as a limey told me at the beginning of this war, your number can come up just as easily walking across the street as it can fighting the Germans. Let's just enjoy our time together." We did.

Johnny got the money and on Sunday I was on my way. The highlight of the milk run was the 5-hour lay over in Salt Lake City. I toured the city and visited the Mormon Tabernacle. Another plus was the cute stewardess on the flight into L.A. I dated her the night of our arrival in Los Angeles and we went to the Coconut Grove in the Biltmore Hotel. The food was excellent. There were many celebrities to be seen and Freddy Martin provided the music. We talked and danced the night away. It was a fitting end to my leave.

I reported on board the Ingersoll at 0800 the next morning and was immediately summoned to the Captain's cabin. Blouin had a big smile on his face. "Have I got a surprise for you! Just look at this," and handed me a dispatch. I read with astonishment that following our navy yard work and full speed runs, I would report to the USS Conner DD 582 as executive officer. "I'm surprised! Pardee is qualified to take over the engineering department here. I thought he would get transferred to new construction and I'd finish up the war on the Ingersoll."

Blouin replied, "I'll miss you, but this is a great opportunity. This is your first step toward getting your own command. How many V-7 engineering-only officers have gotten into the command structure so quickly? You're well thought of." I had never reflected too much on my fitness reports. I knew I was better qualified than some, but not as competent as others.

While we were dry-docked, the officers were billeted in the BOQ and the men in the receiving station. Liberty was every other day. The paperwork was horrendous. All repairs and maintenance performed had to be documented. If the ship were sunk, the records would be up to date.

I wrote Lil on 18 March at 2215, "I finished my flight in a memorable manner. A message was waiting for me asking me to check my overcoat. I discovered it was much too big. Mine was in San Francisco.

"I placed a phone call to you, but fell asleep and didn't wake up until a few minutes ago. It's one o'clock on the east coast and I didn't want to get your family down on me.

"Guess your mother thought I was out of my head asking you to fly up to Washington. Well, I was—crazy to see you again. I am listening to

J.C. Thomas singing the 'Lord's Prayer. It's beautiful and moving. Wish you were here.

"Betts gave me your Florida address. What does the 'P' stand for in your name? Is it Patricia, Petunia or what?

"Why don't you become a lady welder? They are needed and you could get a job out here. You probably couldn't do my welding 'cause I'd disturb you all the time. Hope you and your mother are enjoying Florida. I'm still missing you, loving you and wanting you.

"PS What's the idea of your telling me not to love you too much?"

On 19 March I wrote Lil, "It was good hearing your voice last night, even to the tune of $15. You're going to make a pauper of me yet! The telephone operator pushed the wrong button 'cause my money came right out of the slot. I put it right back in. That's how I was able to talk so long.

"I got talked into triple dating with a couple of shipmates last night. When I finished talking with you, I went back to the table and told my date I had been talking with my wife, that I had been married 5 years, had twin girls, 4 years old, and triplets, 2 boys and a girl, 2 years old. I spent the rest of the night discussing my family.

"My date had a car and when the place closed up, we rode around town just chatting, no hanky-panky. Didn't get in until 0330 this morning.

"Tonight I'm staying at home catching up on my sleep and plan to do a little dreaming. Maybe I'll see you. I sorta think that I will. If I don't, I'm going to be awful mad at the feller that makes dreams."

From that night on, I let my dates know I had a girl back home!

On 21 March the Ingersoll left the dry-dock and moored to the Cogeswell. The shore patrol kept bringing back crew members for disorderly conduct, fighting, drunkenness, AWOL and other things. The Captain was busy holding mast. The coming on board of new crew members and the leaving of old ones kept the yeomen busy.

The news reported that LeMay had bombed Nagoya, Osaka and Kobe with incendiaries. The results were devastating. Iwo Jima was secured and the British Fleet under Sir Bruce Frazer joined the Fifth Fleet.

Hitler issued a "Scorched Earth" order. Everything was to be destroyed: factories, houses, food, communication lines, anything the Allies might be able to use. It was just as well, because during the week of 22-31 March, Patton, Montgomery and the French crossed the Rhine.

I wrote Lil on 27 March, "Saw the movie tonight that impressed you, 'The Life of Chopin'. The music was superb and deeply moving. I saw something else in the movie I hadn't considered, the tragedy of George Sand's life. She was a genius. Her early life was a struggle and so

perverted her that she could never fully recover from it. She failed to develop those ideals and feelings which average people cherish. If she had
had a normal family life, her terrific will-power and intellectual abilities
would have been a force for the good of all mankind rather than for personal gain. It's sad that a person of Chopin's talents came under her influence. I saw portrayed 2 of my basic beliefs: in the majority of cases,
the woman is the force which shapes a man's life. She guides him to the
heights or drags him to the depths. He is always trying to please her no
matter what other people think. If she is pleased, then so is he. What this
world needs is more intelligent, compassionate, deeply religious women.

"In addition, I believe no individual can do his greatest work or
achieve his greatest fame without dedicating himself to a task that en-
compasses all of humanity. Most men are not talented enough to touch
all of us, but the ones that do are the greatest. In music we find a medium whereby everyone can be reached.

"There's a beautiful full moon out tonight and I'm going for a
walk. It should be peaceful and good for thinking. I am certain my
thoughts will be straying in your direction."

On 30 March the engines were tested. At muster each morning,
more of the crew were reported AWOL. This meant the Ingersoll would
be leaving the States soon.

I wrote Lil at midnight, "It was good talking to you, but to econo-
mize, I'm now writing.

"You are always reluctant to express yourself positively in matters of
the heart for fear of hurting the other person. Nothing in relations with
other human beings would ever hurt me except for a loss of ideals or
faith by the person involved. I think you like me. Let's make it a game
and play it for all it's worth. May not last long, but let's enjoy it while it
does.

"I went into town tonight with two fellows, had a couple of drinks
and chatted with a couple of girls. I excused myself and came on home.

"I started thinking of you so much that I had to call. Hope I didn't
wake too many people. Have lots of wonderful dreams."

Churchill and Montgomery got upset when Eisenhower told Stalin
the Allies' advance would not have Berlin as the objective. They wanted
to meet the Russians as far to the East as possible. They believed Berlin
was "the most decisive point" in Germany.

On 1 April, I wrote Lil at 2202, "Happy Easter! I missed going to
church this morning. At Christmas and Easter the music and whole service is so beautiful and impressive. Would like to have gone to the sunrise service at the Hollywood Bowl, but there was too much work to do.

"How about your Easter bonnet? I suppose it was one of those crazy jobs that women seem to go for. I've only been ashore a couple of times recently. I'm getting so many gray hairs, I'm going to be an old man before my time. I would be if I were the worrying kind.

"The last letter I wrote probably didn't make much sense. I had much too much to drink.

"I've decided this new job I am going to is not going to be much fun. I don't like it and think I'm getting a lousy deal. It's all in the game and maybe it'll turn out for the best. Maybe! Ain't hope or plain ignorance wonderful.

"Sure wish you and I could have been in the Easter Parade. We'd have knocked them cold. You, because you'd have looked so beautiful, and I'd have been such a contrast, sorta an oddity. It would have been wonderful to have had you at my side. You might have even let me hold your hand in church. Tell me, was I drunk when I named our 5 adorable children or just nuts? Sounded like I was naming a flower garden rather than a family. Maybe we should call them No. 1, 2, etc.

"I wish you'd quit complaining about my handwriting. It's not going to do you much good saving my letters. I can't read them either. That's why I've got to have a wife who can write legibly. I can recline on the sofa and just dictate.

"Just think of me half as much as I think of you."

At breakfast the talk was about General Simon Buckner's 10th Army landing on Okinawa. The beaches were not defended and 50,000 troops landed the first day. Admiral Kuribayoshi, Jap Commander of Iwo Jima, committed suicide.

The Russians captured Danzig and were heading for Vienna. In Italy Himmler, believing the Generals were double-crossing him, ordered all peace talks stopped.

Stinky proclaimed, "The word from the Philippines is that the Japanese are well-entrenched in the mountains to the north and in the south. They've got little food and ammunition. We're probably going to let them stay there until the war is over. There's no sense losing any American lives digging them out."

On 3 April the Ingersoll was standing out in San Pedro Harbor and at 0850, we began our full speed trial runs. We didn't have the responsibility for mishaps, as yard personnel supervised our activities. I wasn't pleased when the chief in the after engine room reported, "I'm having to shut down the engine. We're losing lubrication pressure on the main engine." This ended our trial run and at 1245, the Ingersoll was again moored at Pier #1. After the engine was repaired on 5 April at 1235, the Ingersoll successfully completed its run, making 34.5 knots. Everyone in the "black gang" cheered. We'd passed the test.

I wrote Lil at 2220 on 6 April, "I'm feeling very, very chipper today. Why? 'Cause I've practically finished my work. The tests have been satisfactory and I'm almost ready to leave. This time 2 days ago, I was utterly exhausted and deep in the throes of despair and despondency. Everything had gone wrong. It's OK now and I'm happy about the ship.

"I won't be getting any leave. I've been sticking close to the ship. Your letters have been the bright spot in my life. Fate was kind when it allowed me to see as much of you as I did. Knowing you has been, is and will always be the most wonderful thing that has ever happened to me.

"Switching to the heavy side, how about giving me the 'blow by blow' description of your dilemma. You say you don't wish to encourage me any further because it isn't fair. Remember what Shakespeare said, 'To thine own self be true, and it must follow as the day the night, Thou cannot then be false to any man.' You make me feel sorta bad about my being so forward. It makes me feel that I'm not playing fair; that I've been taking unfair advantage of another's absence for my gain.

"Remember what the cat said to Alice, 'We're all mad here. I'm mad. You're mad.' That's me, too, except I'm nuts. Whoops! The lights started flickering and I automatically head for the engine room when they do. They did go out and I had to stop writing for an hour. It's sorta late and I'm heading for the sack. Keep up your good work with the letters."

The talk at breakfast was about the massive Kamikaze attacks on the Fifth Fleet. Blouin said, "From reports I've seen, the results have been devastating, 28 ships hit and 3 sunk." Stinky responded, "They're going to run out of planes before long. I just hope it's before we get back out there."

"I'm leaving you guys today. We've had a ball together and my only regret is I never had that date with Donna Reed. Stinky, you owe me one. I'll provide you with a Geisha girl in Tokyo."

At 1400 Lt. William Pardee relieved me of my engineering duties. I picked up my orders, which instructed me to proceed to Seattle, Washington, and report to Com 13th Naval District for transportation to the Conner DD 582 as executive officer. At 1500 I was officially detached. I saluted Stinky, the OOD, as I asked, "Request permission to leave the ship."

"Permission granted," he replied and added, "Good luck and good hunting. See you in Tokyo."

CHAPTER 16

The USS Conner DD 582:
Return to the Philippines

There were no flights available and I was assigned a berth on a troop sleeper train. I had no option and quickly discovered it was no "sleeper". It was packed with men who had just come from overseas and men heading out.

As I told Lil in my letter of 10 April, "This place is a mad house. Loud cussing, gambling, outrageous lies of heroism and horseplay. The aisles are full of men, and moving around is difficult to impossible. We had a layover of 12 hours in San Francisco, just long enough for everyone to get tanked up. A West Pointer got on, pulled rank to bring peace, and succeeded in catching hell. From one end of the car to the other voices would yell out, ' Who does that little bastard shave tail think he is? Let's send him home to mother. The little mother f-cker. No wonder we're still at war.' The Lieutenant would shout out repeatedly, 'Who said that? You're going to be court martialed. I want your name and rating.' He never got any names and could never identify the source of the cussing. The riding continued and he left the train before it reached Seattle. I felt sorry for him, but he brought it on himself.

"I have been thinking about your year in college and the subjects you'd have to take, like Chemistry, English. It's going to be tough, but you can do it. I'll be rooting for you."

When I arrived in Seattle, Washington on Friday 13 April, the headlines read, "Roosevelt is dead. Harry Truman is President." At 1pm on 12 April while he was sitting for a portrait, he rubbed his neck and said, "I have a terrific headache." These were the last words he would speak. He was pronounced dead of a cerebral hemorrhage at 3:55pm. Like millions of Americans I felt like I had lost a father. He was the only President I had ever known. Life magazine said, "At the moment of his death, he was the most important man in the world. He was one American who knew, or seemed to know, where the world was going. The plans were in his head. It was easier to let him worry for the whole country." His body was placed in a casket on the Presidential train. The cortege left Warm Springs, Ga., at night. People lined the tracks with tears in their eyes. At Charlotte, NC, there were 10,000 blacks and whites standing separately, but singing together "Onward Christian

Soldiers". It was a day of mourning for the entire nation. In Berlin, Hitler celebrated, believing his fortunes were about to change for the better.[70]

Roosevelt had been a great leader, but my immediate concern was: where is the Conner? The duty officer relieving me said, "Lieutenant, the Conner is just completing her repair and overhaul. She's at berth 24 in the Bremerton Navy Yard. I'll get some one to drive you over."

When I arrived, I got out of the car with mixed emotions. Was I qualified? Could I handle the job? What a challenge! Second in command! A great opportunity. Walking up the gangway at 1607, I saluted the OOD and said, "Request permission to come aboard. Lt. Jervey reporting for duty."

He replied, "We've been expecting you. I'll get some one to take your luggage to your stateroom and I'll show you to the Captain's cabin."

Walking forward I thought: "What is the Captain like?" A lot depended on him. I had seen some who were first-class bastards. My fears were allayed when he said, "Glad to have you on board, Mr. Exec. Your reputation has preceded you. I'm Bill Sissons." He looked like a Bill: blond, disheveled hair which he nervously kept running his hand through, steel-rimmed glasses which gave him a square face, and an impish, contagious smile! I liked what I saw.

"I'm Academy class of '38. Took over the Conner on 18 February. We've got a good bunch of officers and men. Some haven't had much sea duty so you'll have to whip them into shape."

"I'll do my best."

We chatted for an hour and I learned he was single and his mother lived in Ontario, Canada. I then went to the wardroom and met with some of the officers. Lt. Robert Austin, 1st Lieutenant, blond, slender, from Vermont; communications officer Lt.(jg) Felton Wyatt, black hair, short, slender, from California; the doctor, Lt.(jg) Ellsworth Wareham, balding, grayish hair, 6' tall, from Oregon. Next to him was the engineering officer, Lt.(jg) Marcus Creager, black hair, slender, of medium height. I told Creager, "Every time the lights flicker, I'm going to head for the engine room. It's an acquired reflex. Just yell if I get in your way."

The ship was named for Commodore Conner who joined the Navy as a midshipman in 1809 and served on the USS Hornet during the War of 1812. In 1841 he became Navy Commissioner, and during the War with Mexico served as Commander of the home squadron.

The Captain held a general inspection on 14 April, which gave me an excellent opportunity to get a feel for the men.

At 1900 I wrote Lil, "Just arrived. The skipper is Academy class of '38, and we have several friends in common. It's going to be a good ship. Just remember I still love you even if you don't want to encourage me.

"I had dinner with the former executive officer and his wife last night. Had a real southern meal with fried chicken, rice and gravy. The Captain was present, along with two other officers and their wives. I wished for a date. Wanted to call you and have you fly out and marry me. I never thought the day would come when I would want one person as much as I want you. Remember the poem, 'If I were king, the stars would be your pearls upon a string. The earth, a ruby for your finger ring, and you would have the sun and moon to wear, if I were king.'

"PS What does the 'P' in your name stand for and when did you first come into this world?"

The next afternoon the Conner with the Charrette was underway for San Diego. I remarked to Sissons, "I'm going to be uncomfortable not standing deck watch."

"You'll have plenty to do. Once we get squared away, I'll let you take the conn coming into port, fueling and other maneuvers. For the moment, I've got to get the feel for it myself," Sissons said.

General MacArthur and Admiral Nimitz were drawing up plans for the invasion of Japan: Kyushu (Olympic) about 1 December followed by Honshu (Coronet) on or about 1 March 1946.

The Russians captured Vienna and were advancing into Czechoslovakia. Bridgeheads were established over the Elbe, and Eisenhower ordered the troops to halt and advance no further. Omar Bradley was moving south to link up with the Russians, and Montgomery was securing Hamburg and the German North Sea naval bases. In Italy the British, Americans and Poles were advancing, as were the British, Indians and Chinese in Burma.

San Diego harbor was entered on 19 April. There was excitement at breakfast upon hearing that Germany was being squeezed into a vise. Sissons said, "Hitler is about finished. The Ruhr pocket has been cleaned with over 300,000 prisoners taken. The Russians are attacking Berlin from all sides."

Bob Austin remarked, "I don't understand why Eisenhower ordered our men to halt. They could have secured Berlin before the Russians got there. Doesn't make sense."

"It makes political sense. He wants to keep peace in the family. Stalin believes the Russians have suffered the most and should have the privilege of accepting the Germans surrender in Berlin," Sissons replied.

"It's prolonging the war and costing lives. It's going to create more postwar problems than it solves," Bob responded.

After mooring in a nest with the Charrette, I watched as the fuel barge came alongside and said to Bill, "I'm going to enjoy watching this operation. For too many years, I've been in charge."

"You're not going to do much watching. There's an inspection team coming aboard to see if we're ready for combat duty. Pass the word to the department heads and make certain everything is shipshape." At 1402 Commander Johnson came aboard with an inspection team. Upon completion, Commander Johnson said, "You look ready for sea. Good luck and good hunting." The next morning 20 April the Conner was underway for Pearl Harbor with the USS Lamson.

At 2320 I wrote Lil. "I have been assigned the Captain's stateroom which is much more spacious than anything I have ever had. He's living in the cabin on the bridge. All I brought with me from the Ingersoll was one suitcase, and I'm keeping the laundry busy washing my two uniforms.

"I get tired hearing how dumb you are. You've got an excellent mind. Use it! Your pictures are in my box which may never catch up with me. Our doctor is Ellsworth Wareham, who worked a couple of years in Alaska and has been telling me about its beauty. Let's take a vacation there sometime."

The next morning the British reached the Elbe. Leipzig had fallen to General Hodges and Nuremberg to General Patch. Hitler was celebrating his 56th birthday and turned the defense of Berlin over to the army group Vistula. Of more importance, the Russians were now shelling Berlin. It was good news, but we still had the Japanese to contend with.

My battle station was Combat Information Center (CIC), the heart of the ship. All information from radar, lookouts, gun control and the bridge came through CIC. It was my responsibility to give the Captain pertinent information so he could fight the ship intelligently. I was familiar with the operation and the petty officers were experienced veterans, so I didn't think there would be any problems. That's what I thought!

At breakfast on 25 April, Felton Wyatt came in waving his dispatch board and exclaiming, "Berlin is completely surrounded. Hitler has declared he will commit suicide rather than fall into Russian hands. In addition, the Russians and the western allies have joined up on the Elbe at Torgau. Germany is now split in two and the Battle for Berlin is in its last stages."

"Sounds like Hitler is about done for and it won't be long before we can all go home. What's happening in Italy?" Bob Austin asked.

"Our boys are on the move. Bologna has been captured and they are just outside of Genoa. Mussolini won't be around for long," Wyatt replied.

On 26 April Oahu was picked up. I was on the bridge at dawn looking at Diamond Head and Waikiki. I told Bill, "I've always been in the engine room. This is my first time to see the beach and Pearl Harbor."

He asked, "Would you like to take the conn and tie her up?"

"Sure."

I was a good ship handler, but maneuvering 2,100 tons and tying up to a another ship was going to require as yet untested talents. However at 0845, the Conner was moored to the Lamson. With this victory behind me, I was ready to celebrate. Shortly after 1600 I was in the officer's club with former shipmates and friends. The talk focused on the meeting of the United Nations being held in San Francisco. Bob said, "They've got delegates from all over the world and I hear they started off wrangling over the Charter and how the organization is to function."

"Their goal is to establish peace on earth for all time, by negotiation or force. Whatever is necessary," Wyatt added. "They've got as much of a chance as a snowball in hell, little to none. They can't even get started. How are they going to stop anything?"

For the next 3 days, the Conner, with the Charrette and Wadleigh, conducted gunnery, radar tracking, anti-submarine and anti-aircraft exercises. The goats on Kahoolawee Island were shelled and Sissons kidded Ken Miller, "You gunnery guys have been shelling those goats for the past 3 years. From reports I've read, the population has grown beyond the island's ability to feed them. I hope it's because they know where to hide and not your poor marksmanship."

The Russians were closing in on the Reichstag and Chancellery. Hitler denounced Himmler for negotiating with Allen Dulles and ordered Goering placed under house arrest. With his world falling apart, he married Eva Braun and appointed Admiral Karl Doenitz his successor. In Italy the Germans signed unconditional surrender papers effective 2 May. Two days earlier, Mussolini's convoy was ambushed by partisans and he was killed.

At 2158 I wrote Lil, "There's one thing about this job I don't like. Navy protocol requires senior officers to fraternize with their peers. I'm supposed to be partying with the Captain and his peers. Commanders and Captains who are older, they ain't my peers! I do have one advantage. My freedom of speech is not curtailed, whereas everyone else is on their P's and Q's.

"Just discovered today we have a steward's mate who has been in the Navy for 3 years and didn't know it. His draft board told him he would be put in the Army. When he got aboard a ship he said, 'I done figured dat dis was jus da ship-board Army.' This came to light when friends contacted Army headquarters in Washington looking for him. I got a letter asking if he was on board. It's incredible, but a true story.

"The moon is showing its head tonight in all its radiant beauty. Would be great to be under the stars with soft music, quiet talk and peaceful thinking. Guess who I'd be talking to? Not myself, I can assure you. How's about a little stroll?... Sorta makes me feel closer to you when you tell of visiting my family...I must warn you. My mother believes my business is hers and anything I want I should get...

"Some of the things you write make me think you want to change the Navy system like DO for DD...So let's go to the top of the heap together and change the whole set-up...Which reminds me of a verse from the Rubiyat:

'Oh love, could you and I with him conspire,
To grasp this sorry scheme of things entire,
Would not we shatter it to bits,
And remold it nearer to our heart's desire.'

"Right now my heart's desire is to get a little sleep. I was up all of last night, and it wasn't on the beach...I had a wonderful dream about you. I'm going to try and contact you again in the spirit world...and remember, 'I'll be seeing you in all the old familiar places that this heart of mine embraces...'"

The Conner shifted berths on 30 April. I went on liberty. When I returned, I wrote Lil at 0030, "I saw Manny Reid today. Only had time for brief chat...We both agreed you were a d— nice girl and ended the subject there...

"Had party at a friend's who lives on the beach. The skipper stole a 'girlie' calendar and it ain't going to make my friend happy...

"I've decided you should just forget me for awhile... count me out. The old bucket's gone to the bottom of the well too many times to suit me...I'll be around...You're a wonderful girl and I wouldn't take anything for the time I've spent with you. Fate is laughing like hell at me and I deserve it...I'll be looking at the same moon and stars as you and wishing we were together. I'm happy I found what I wanted even if it was at the wrong time.

"PS Probably had one too many drinks tonight so anything objectionable, just forget."

On 1 May the Conner was underway as a Task Unit of one, on a westerly course at a speed of 21 knots. At breakfast on 3 May Wyatt exclaimed, "You won't believe it! Hitler and Eva Braun have committed suicide. That was followed by Goebbels, his wife and 6 children. It's wild. Berlin has surrendered and the Russians have taken 480,000 prisoners."

"They're mad. Just goes to show you what twisted minds will do. Killing your own children! Thank God the world is rid of them," Bumalough responded.

"Don't you have some decent news?"

"Admiral Doenitz broadcast to the German people that the only reason to continue the fighting is to save Germany from destruction by the Bolshevik enemy. They are deathly afraid of what the Russians will do. In Italy, the war is officially over and the Allies have entered Rangoon in Burma," Wyatt said.

At 2040 on 4 May, I wrote Lil, "I had a long chat with the doctor today. He wants me to study medicine…What's your idea on my being a doctor? Think I'll be a good one? Could I doctor you? I've always had it in mind…

"Had to pause for a minute. The mess attendant just brought me a cold glass of orange juice and a ham sandwich. I know what you're thinking. What an easy life!…That last letter showed you had a flair for writing. And when are you going to put your brain to work? You've got ability and you're not my idea of a girl that just flitters around doing nothing. Horseback riding is fine, but put your brain to some use.

"Tonight the movie in the wardroom was 'Two Senoritas from Chicago.' As the reel ended and the climax approached, the movie operator announced in a weak and pleading voice, 'I'm sorry, but I didn't get the last reel of the movie.' Just imagine! I'll never know how it ended.

"The skipper and I are getting along fine. We see eye to eye on most everything. The weather is good and my spirits are high. I've been having to crack down on the men and officers. I'm not going to be liked for long…If you assure me that you still love me, I can stand anything…

"My box from the Ingersoll finally caught up with me and was soaked in fuel oil. My clothes were ruined and I threw them over the side. More importantly, books I had bought all over the world had to be 'deep sixed'…Fortunately your pictures were in good shape except for a fuel oil smudge on your nose. Makes you look even more attractive and natural…

"So you didn't think I'd remember our song? There are any number of them. No matter how old I get, whenever I hear the popular songs of the day, especially 'Every Time We Say Good-bye', it will bring the memories of you flooding back…I've been humming all day 'Did I remember to tell you I adore you?' I didn't, but I'll tell you tonight in my dreams…"

On 6 May the Ingersoll fueled at Arno Atoll, Marshall Islands. The next afternoon the Captain welcomed Davy Jones aboard, who told the polliwogs to be prepared to greet His Royal Majesty Neptunis Rex the next day.

While the polliwogs were trembling with fear, the Germans signed an unconditional surrender document at 0240 at Reims in SHAEF Headquarters. This was leaked to the press and our radio operator picked it up. At dawn on 8 May the PA boomed, "All hands, and I do mean all hands. Now hear this! This is the Captain speaking. The war in Europe is over! I repeat! The war in Europe is over. The surrender papers have been signed. All hostilities are to cease at 2301 on 8 May." There was momentary silence, then loud cheering throughout the ship. Miller summed it up pretty well when he said, "I'm happy for the guys in Europe. I hope they are sent home. We don't need them, or any more ships, out here! I can't keep track of the ones we've got. And I know one thing. There's a shell out here with my name on it, so lets get this damn thing over."

The Conner crossed the equator at Longitude 153 degrees 27' east and the polliwogs were properly initiated into King Neptune's Domain and became trusty shellbacks.

The war didn't stop because of our ceremony. Russia told Japan it was renouncing their 1941 non-aggression pact. The Japanese government of General Kuiaki resigned in protest at being left out of the decision making Admiral Kantaro Prime Minister.

At 2205 on 8 May I wrote Lil, "It's a beautiful night; peaceful and calm. I can faintly hear the sounds of the movie in the wardroom, feel the vibrating of the ship and the quiet rustle of life. I can easily escape from the noise by walking out on deck. It's like another world, a mighty vastness, an empty void covered by a canopy of stars and a few clouds drifting by...I don't believe any man can think evil thoughts of anyone when he is alone at night with only the stars for company. I'm looking at the 'Big Dipper'. I pretend you are, too, and it makes me feel ever so close to you...

"How about reminiscing? Some things stand out so clearly and others are lost in the mist of memory...I remember meeting you at the ration board on my first leave in 1942. We had a coke and long talk at Eckerd's. I remember hearing about 'Little Miss Magnolia Blossom' when I was passing through Washington. And meeting you again at the airport when you worked for Delta. I'm not superstitious, but I am beginning to get the feeling that the man upstairs has plans for us. He has done his part and from now, on I'm going to take over and keep you with me always...

"Listening to Brahms 1st symphony this afternoon brought on this nostalgia. It's a beautiful piece of music...Have you ever read Byron's,

'She walks in beauty, like the night
Of cloudless climes and starry skies,

And all that's best of dark and bright,
Meets in her aspect and her eyes,
Thus mellowed to that tender light
Which Heaven to gaudy day denies.'

Can't remember anything more but the last two lines:

A mind at peace with all below,
A heart whose love is innocent.'

"I'll dedicate it to you...Right now I'm going to bed, but before I go to sleep, I'm going to read some of your back letters..."

On 9 May the Conner anchored in Berth #330, Admiralty Islands. I went on liberty and at 2230 wrote Lil, "Had an unpleasant task today. Several men broke into the beer locker. I had to lecture them and dole out punishments. We're going to have the best ship in the Navy! I'm confident of it...

"I had a few drinks on the beach this afternoon and played ping pong (I won); also played some cards in between. Feeling slightly 'tight' right now...Had to leave and give my little talk. I'm back now...I'm doing my damnedest to get my ideas across. I'm not doing badly, but I'll reserve further opinion until a later date.

"We got the news of Germany's surrender. There is no noticeable difference in our outlook or morale. We've got a long, hard pull out here. It's just another working day...

"I'm glad to hear you're going back to school. You'll never regret it... Everything will work itself out for the best whether to my advantage or not. Fate deals the cards right and if you deserve the breaks, you'll get them. I don't deserve them, but I have a feeling you're going to have to put up with me for a long, long time..."

The next morning the Conner was underway with the USS Pressly and Fremont and several screening destroyers for Leyte Gulf. There was a lively discussion of the surrender ceremony held by the Russians in Berlin. They had expected the announcement to be made jointly with Churchill and Truman and were unhappy they had been up-staged. As a result, VE Day was celebrated on 7 May by the US and Britain and by the Russians on 8 May.

Wyatt said, "We can't get along with the Russians when we're Allies. How is it going to be when the war is over?"

"Worse. We'll probably be at war with them within the next 10 years," Miller responded.

I wrote Lil at 2113 on 13 May, "...I've been playing pinochle with the Captain and several of the other officers. I only learned it 3 days ago and been winning ever since. Beginner's luck I guess...I'm sending pictures made with Betts in Washington. Frankly they stink. Somehow a camera just doesn't do me justice. Can't figure out why...Don't you try!

"Yesterday afternoon I organized a recreation party on the forecastle. We sun bathed and tossed a medicine ball around. I tried to take off all the excess poundage on my midriff in one afternoon. Am I feeling it today!...

"I haven't used a typewriter in a long time. Probably will have sore fingers tomorrow...Hope you haven't gotten bored. Just hang in there...I'm still missing you, wanting you and loving you..."

At breakfast on 15 May, Wyatt announced, "25,000 of an estimated 2,000,000 soldiers have received their honorable discharges and are returning to civilian life."

"How were they chosen?"

"The Army established a point system based on length of service, overseas duty, campaign awards, age and dependents. To add to your pleasure the Secretary of the Navy announced there would be no demobilization of the Navy until Japan surrenders. How do you like them apples?" There was some discussion, but everyone thought the policy was fair.

In the early afternoon we attacked and dropped depth charges on a sonar contact. Results unknown. This was followed by the sinking of an oil drum after firing 139 rounds of 40mm ammunition. At dinner Miller said, "That was one expensive oil can. Why do we have to keep wasting ammunition on these things?"

"That's to keep you guys sharp," Austin replied.

The next day the Conner anchored in Leyte Gulf, Philippines and I wrote Lil, "...Got no letters today and I was disappointed...Guess you and Arnie Childs are the best of friends and you're getting set for school...It won't be much fun for awhile...Just hang in there. I know doggone well you'll do okay...

"You know how music can shorten the years and make the yesterdays seem alive today? The fellows in the wardroom are playing records from 'Oklahoma'. It was a big hit in summer of 1943 when I was in New York putting the Dortch into commission. Everywhere you went you heard the tunes. I was living at 166 East 66th St. with 3 other fellows. There were dances and parties almost every night...It was a gay city that year and I had a wonderful time.

"No sooner had I finished this reverie than I heard 'Indian Summer', and I was transported to the fall of 1938. That was my junior year in college and I had found my true love. I was very much in love. Everything was bright for me that fall: had a girl, was making almost straight 'A's' with little effort, had a little cash in my pocket. I was having a big time. It was a great year in so many ways, but I wouldn't go back. You know why? 'Cause the next song was from 'Showboat'. It was 'You could make believe you love me. I could make believe that I love you'. It brought you back into my arms and the time you and I played at making love. Eons have passed since then and we're still making believe. It's been fun, darling. I wouldn't have wanted to pretend with anyone else. Just don't get tired of pretending and if you do, make it become a reality...

"...You told me about your bridge game. I used to be a fan, but I've switched over to pinochle. Nothing lower than a 9, mostly face cards. Much prettier hands and fewer cards to keep track of...

"And before I stop. How do you manage to keep the skin I love to touch, what with all of your chairwoman's work...One of these days I want to hold hands with you...You'd better take good care of them and of the rest of my girl too...

"I'm going to do what all good men should do this time of the night...Spare one dream, will ya?..."

On 18 May the Conner went into a floating dry-dock for 24 hours to repair the sonar sound dome. I wrote Lil, "I saw my first USO show of WWII last night. It was 'Oklahoma'...It was a wonderful performance, held in a big outdoor theater under the stars with a small crescent moon peeking out from under the clouds. Broadway never had anything to offer like this. They had a cast of 12 girls (Um-and what looks) and 13 men...Everything went off in the best Great White Way manner. All of us enjoyed it immensely. Wish you might have been here...

"We had a short visit with the cast after the show at the officer's club...It was one helluva long boat ride to where the show was being performed. Didn't get back to the ship until 0300. It was worth it...

"Got word today that I will be giving up my cabin and bunking with the doctor. The squadron commander, a 4-striper, is moving on board. Sure hate to give up this comfortable stateroom...You just wait! In the next half of this ball game, I'm going to be either sitting on the top or else the bottom. This gent is not going to be playing a middle position...

"By the time you get this you'll be reembarked on your college career. Keep me posted on your problems and progress...

"It's 2300 and I didn't get much sleep last night. There's lots of pretty music on the radio tonight and it's beautiful outside. I'm an awful sentimental fool. The Star Spangle Banner is being played right now and it is sending chills up and down my spine; always has and I guess it always will…"

On Sunday 20 May Captain H.J. Martin, Commander of Destroyer Squadron 51, shifted his pennant to the Conner. He was a short, wiry, sharp- nosed fellow of indeterminate age. I knew nothing about him which, to my misfortune, would change rapidly. In the afternoon the Conner was enroute for Manila. The weather was perfect and various exercises were conducted. The Commodore started showing his colors immediately. Nothing Bill Sissons could do was right. "Your men are out of uniform. Instruct your mess attendants how to make coffee." I told Waresham, "My only experience with a Squadron Commander was Captain Warlick soon after the war began. He gave the skipper hell, but he was like a father to me. Always asking me to play acey-ducey with him. I'd like to wrap a chair around this bastard's neck."

In the early hours of 22 May, Cape Calavite and Corregidor lights were passed. At 0844 the Conner anchored in Berth #50, Manila Bay, Philippine Islands. When I went on liberty, I was shocked at the devastation. I knew Manila was one of the 2 most bombed out cities of the war. It was horrifying to see. The Japanese had fought house to house and few residences didn't show damage. The Filipinos believed all Americans were friends and wanted to share their bananas, papayas and other fruits, which I declined. My first priority was to locate my brother Herbert, who was somewhere in the Philippines with the 249th Port Company. I found a friend at headquarters who promised to check for me.

At breakfast the next morning Wyatt said, "Admiral Doenitz and his governmental officials have been arrested by the British. That should put an end to all fighting in Germany."

"Where do the Russians stand?" Austin asked.

"That's going to be the real battle. There has been no agreement amongst the Allies on how much reparations Germany will pay, to whom and with what. They haven't settled on what territories Russia, Britain, France or the US will control. Truman has stopped all lend-lease to Britain and Russia, which hasn't made anyone happy."

On 23 May Sissons met with members of Admiral Kincaid's staff. When he returned, he said, "Harold, you are now going to discover how the other half lives. We are going to be with Kincaid and the 7th Fleet. They have been busy to the south operating with General MacArthur and the Eighth Army.

"I've heard reports that MacArthur has been liberating other islands."

"That's correct. He was given no direct authority to liberate the southern Philippines, but having strong feelings of loyalty, he believed the people should be freed as quickly as possible. From 28 February until 1 May, his forces liberated Palawan, Zamboanga, Cebu, Mindanao and other islands. He was able to quickly establish civil governments. The Filipinos consider him to be God."

"So what's his next goal?"

"The securing of Borneo, which is a major source of oil for the Japanese. Churchill and his high command have wanted the British Navy involved. Admirals King and Nimitz didn't, believing they'd get in the way. A truce was declared and the British will participate. MacArthur is in overall command and the operation has begun. We're going to have an exciting time. I've got some reading material for you," and he handed me a packet of papers.

I learned that the Borneo Campaign was primarily an Australian show and we were assisting them. Borneo was a mountainous isle twice as large as the entire Philippine Archipelago and was civilized only in coastal regions. Headhunters still existed in the interior. Brunei, Sarawak and Labuan on the north shore were British protectorates. The Dutch controlled Tarakan, Balikpapan and the south shore. Lt. General Sir Leslie Morshead, Commander of the 1st Australian Corps, was in charge of the landings. The 7th Fleet under Rear Admiral Royal was handling the naval operations. Tarakan on the eastern shore was to be liberated early on.

The first landings were on 1 May. It involved 18,000 men, most of whom were Australians. The area was secured by 8 May. Captured Australians were freed, but of the over 2,000 taken prisoner in 1942, only 6 had survived.

Mail caught up with us! My father said the Dean at the Medical College told him I had a place in the freshman class whenever I arrived. Bob Austin exclaimed, "You must be nuts! School is starting September 4th. It's now the 23rd of May. It'll take a miracle for you to get there. Even if you do, you're 4 years away from chemistry and other college subjects. It's going to be tough. I don't see how you're going to make it."

"Whether I get there or not is in the hands of a higher authority! I'm not worrying about passing. Our brains have not been in neutral. Those 100-page operation orders and memorizing them in a couple of days? Hell, medical school will be a snap. For the moment, I'm going to have lunch with Charlotte. She has invited me to her field hospital which is on the outskirts of Manila."

With no taxis, my only chance of getting there was hitching a ride with someone going that direction. I went to the motor pool and asked the officer in charge for suggestions. He responded, "You're in luck! There's a fellow going out to the field hospital right now," and he pointed to a jeep about 50 feet away. My teeth were almost shaken out, the road was so bumpy, but it was worth it. Charlotte showed me around and introduced me to her friends. Lunch was excellent and the company even better. I was the only naval officer present and surrounded by a bevy of good looking females.

Hoping to share this bonanza with my shipmates I asked, "Couldn't we arrange a get-together with you girls? My men are lonely, good-looking and good company. In addition, they are gentlemen. It says so in their commission." They laughed and Major Susan Jones spoke up, "Sounds like a great idea! A wealthy Filipino has given us a house on the water for recreation, and transportation can be arranged with the motor pool. Let's make this a big shindig. We know some officers on the other tin cans. Let's invite them all. We'll find music and can bring the food. You provide the beer and drinks. Will you guarantee only to bring gentlemen?" I was dumfounded and quickly replied, "You betcha. I don't know how long we'll be in port, so the sooner the better. What about tomorrow?" The girls looked at each other in a knowing way. Susan responded, "I think that can be arranged. When you get back to the ship, give Charlotte a ring and tell her how many gentlemen you can provide. By that time I will have checked on the house, food and transportation."

Charlotte got me a ride back to the ship and I immediately sought out Sissons. I told him about the girls and the planned party. "It'll be a real wing ding. What do you say?"

"Proceed. The sooner the better."

Calling Ensign Royal Randall to my cabin, I said, "You have just acquired a new title, Randall. You are now recreation officer. Find out how many officers on the nearby destroyers can come to our party tomorrow night. It's going to one they'll never forget." I told him about the nurses and what information I needed within the next hour. He went about his job with enthusiasm. By the time I hit the sack, everything was in place.

It was a party to end all parties. The house was on the water. There was something for everyone: swimming, sunning, talking, necking and dancing to the 4-piece combo the girls had found. There were tubs of ice cold beer and assorted drinks. Everybody had a partner. It seemed like months since any of us had enjoyed ourselves with real live American girls. Plans were made for follow-up dates.

My letter to Lil at 2300 May 25th said, "...We had a party with about 40 officers from several tin cans anchored close by and with Army nurses from a field hospital. We even had a 4-piece band from some Army unit. Everyone enjoyed themselves. I contributed two bottles of scotch that I had been hoarding. I managed to salvage one drink.

Course, I ain't going to mention what various and sundry other stuff I consumed. We broke up about 2300 and it took forever to get the girls home. I didn't get back to the ship until 0300.

"I spent most of the night sitting alone or just wandering from group to group and dancing a little. Sure is a rough life. This ole Navy is changing fast. It would have been a perfect night if you had been present. I managed to stay unattached until just about time to go home and then my luck failed. Somehow or the other, I got latched on to by a young lady from 'Bahston' and had to take her home.

"Some of the guys invited the girls over to eat supper on board the next night. So the ship was livened up by the presence of several girls at the supper table and movies...

"I've arranged for church services on Sunday. How about going along? The seat will be sorta hard, but it should be cool as it'll be held on the forecastle...

"...Your brother's right. Love is a dangerous game, but it is thrilling and one of the things that makes life worth living. I like it and I like your brother. You can tell him for me that I love his sister and he'd better tell his sister to quit talking so much, or people will say we're in love, and that would be simply wonderful..."

We didn't have the church services. On Saturday morning 26 May, the Conner was underway for Subic Bay. Enroute gunnery exercises were conducted and by mid-afternoon, the Conner was moored to the Nicholas in Berth 173.

I quickly found the bar at the Subic Bay Officers Club. It reminded me of Mog-Mog, except it was half as long as a football field. Finding former shipmates, I told them about my Stateside visit and asked, "How did you guys get along without our help?" I was rapidly brought up to date. "You missed a dilly," Hartwreck, a gunnery officer, said. "Before you left, plans had been made to land on Iwo Jima, which is only 4.5 miles long and 2.5 miles wide. The High Command thought the B-29's flying from the Mariana's to Tokyo needed an emergency landing field. Also, it was a desirable base for the fighters which accompanied the bombers. Far too many were being shot down. We heard that on the nights of 9-10 March, incendiaries were dropped on Tokyo and the city was devastated. Over 250,000 homes destroyed and 80,000 Japanese burned to death with one million homeless.[71] Anyway, you would have thought: Iwo Jima, that little island? Nothing to it! We bombed and shelled that spit of sand for days. Didn't phase the Japs. They had dug in with miles of underground tunnels. 30,000 of our guys landed on D-Day 19 February. We had 2,400 casualties. The Marines could only advance yard by yard. The Kamikazes were active and caused incredible destruction to our ships. Several were sunk and a helluva lot were badly damaged. They brought out the Kaitens again with the smart torpedoes."

"I thought they'd learned their lesson at Ulithi," I said.

"The Kaitens were ineffective. Just another way to commit suicide." He paused took a drink and continued, "There was a flag-raising on Mt. Suribachi on 23 February. You saw that in the paper. You would have thought the battle was over. The Island was not secured until 26 March. 3 Marine divisions were chewed up. There were 6,821 Americans killed and 20,000 wounded. Unofficially, the Japanese lost 21,000. They still think it's a sin to be captured alive. There were only 216 POW's."

"Wow!" I exclaimed. "Sounds like Iwo should have been by-passed. If every B-29 crew in the world were to make an emergency landing, it still wouldn't justify the losses."

"You're damn right. For the first time, we had more casualties than the Japs. It was one costly mistake and will forever be a monument to official bungling."

I asked a few questions and said, "Remind me to tell you of my battle with one Commodore. He is the most irascible SOB I have ever been around. But tell me about Okinawa. That must have been hellacious."

"It was unbelievable," Hampton, a communication officer, exclaimed. "D-Day was 1 April, Easter Sunday. How ironic! We got mauled by the Kamikazes. They came in swarms. Over 100 planes at a time. Prior to the landings, the carriers Wasp, Yorktown, Saratoga and Franklin were badly damaged. By the time Okinawa was secured, it's estimated there were over 3,000 Kamikaze attacks. There were 34 ships sunk and over 300 damaged. The Navy had 5,000 deaths and 4,800 wounded. The 10th Army had 7,600 killed and 31,000 wounded.
"Where in the hell do they keep getting these Kamikaze pilots? Must be a lot of stupid Japs," I said.

"They played hell with our ships. I hope we've seen the last of them. Interestingly, the British carriers didn't have to withdraw when hit. They've got heavy armor on their flight decks. When a Kamikaze hits, it just dents the deck. We did get word of Roosevelt's death on 13 April. There was no cease-fire. Business as usual."

Hartwick added, "In ships and Marines, this may have been the costliest Naval campaign of the war. There were 11,900 killed and over 32,000 wounded. 29 ships were disabled.[72] Winston Churchill sent a message to President Truman saying, "This battle is among the most intense and famous in military history.....We salute your troops and the Commanders engaged."

"I'll second that motion," I said.

We continued reminiscing and drinking. I never saw these friends again.

CHAPTER 17

The next morning Major J.W. Calder, an Australian, reported on board with 4 enlisted men. The questions started. Why did we need them? Where were we going?

While I was wondering about the Aussies, Stalin was telling Harry Hopkins, President Truman's special envoy, that Russia would go to war with Japan in mid-August and insisted they share in its occupation.

I wrote Lil on May 30th, "...Things have really improved. The fellows are cooperating with me and we're working well together. I just started a newspaper to send home. It gives me and the men something to do, and it'll give the folks back home an idea of what's going on....Brother Herbert is out here somewhere. Hope I can find him. Miss you."

The next afternoon at the officer's club, a familiar voice said, "G'day, mate. Mind if I join yah?"

"Glad to have you, Major Calder."

"No need for formality. Just call me Johnno."

"And I'm Harold. What are you drinking?"

"I'll 'ave a tinne, T'anks. Beer to you."

"What do you call the dialect you have and where are you from?"

"It's called 'Strine'. It was developed by the early settlers and the aborigines. My folks have a ranch out from 'Marvelous' Melbourne. The first Calder got t'rown out of Pommeyland (England) and I don't know how 'e got into ranching."

"Having you on board is deja vu for me. My first exposure to war was with the British Home Fleet at Scapa Flow in the winter of '41-'42."

Johnno said, " 'Arold t'ere has not been a year since the Empire was established that we 'aven't been at war somew'ere in the world. You learn quickly to make the most of the good times, 'cause the bad are right around the corner. And bye the bye, you don't talk like most of the Yanks I've met."

"You're right. I'm a rebel! I live in the south and the Yanks live in the north. We've got our Confederate flag, national anthem 'Dixie' and our own language. I come from the South Carolina low country where it all started. This 'Geechie' dialect was developed by the early settlers and the slaves from Africa."

He laughed and broke in, "You sound daffy to me. In Australia the outback has nothing to do with the blokes in the city. We've got different customs, but we ain't gone to war yet. T'ere was a movement to secede from Pommeyland after World War I, but the depression came and we needed each other so we stayed together." Pausing for a moment, he asked, "If you've got 2 countries, why don't you let them damn yanks fight this war?" I didn't have an answer.

The next morning the talk was about A.B. "Happy" Chandler, former Kentucky senator, succeeding Kenesaw Landis as baseball commissioner with a 7 year contract at $50,000 a year. Wyatt exclaimed, "I'd go AWOL from the Navy for that kind of change." We talked about how successful our submarines were in mining Japans major waterways and the ships sunk. Everyone agreed the crews were the unsung heroes of the war.

At dinner on 3 June the Commodore came in with his usual scowl and without even waiting for the blessing, shouted at the Captain, "What in the hell is wrong with your mess boys? Look at this silver." He slammed a fork on the table. "Your good for nothing mess boys haven't shined this stuff since I've been aboard." He got up abruptly, threw a knife on the table and as he strode out, exclaimed, "Take the necessary action and report to me." Johnno, sitting next to me, whispered, "You've got a nutty one there, matey."

Later I went to Bill's cabin to cheer him up. "Harold, that's the system. I don't like it, but it must be a requirement to get 4 stripes. It's the rare one that doesn't act like a horse's ass occasionally."

"I couldn't take it. I can't wait to get out of this man's Navy."

"You better learn. Just take a deep breath and count to ten."

On 5 June the Conner was enroute to Brunei Bay on the North shore of Borneo, where the next landing was scheduled for 10 June. Borneo was 5 times the size of England and once been connected by land to Southeast Asia. Some believed a more advanced civilization than the one in the middle east once lived there. Before the Pyramids were even built, their temples were falling apart. The Chinese arrived first looking for gold and other metals. After intermarriages, 90% of all shops were owned by them. The Javanese brought the Hindu religion, followed by the Malays, who brought the Islamic religion. As with many islands in the South Pacific, head-hunting persisted in the interior. The more heads a man had, the better off he was. They were suspended in conspicuous places throughout the house. Women often times lured their lovers into the jungle to be killed by relatives. Then she'd decorate her hat with fingers or other parts.

At dinner Austin was exclaiming, "The Russians can't get along with friends or enemies. Before the Allied Declaration of Defeat was signed in Berlin yesterday by the Allies, the British and Americans had to agree to withdraw troops from the zone that Russia is to control."

"That's easy to explain. They want to be in charge of Europe. They've suffered the most and are entitled to the greatest reward," Wareham replied.

"Well, from my point of view, it's going to start another war before we get through with this one."

At the same time, the Japanese Supreme Council was passing a resolution to fight until the end. The Japanese "national essence" must be upheld. With the 2.35 million troops backed up by 4 million Army and Navy civil employees, together with a newly created civilian militia 28 million strong, they intended to destroy our troops as they attempted to land on the beaches.

Major Calder briefed us on our duties and pulled out a chart of Brunei Bay. He showed us where the spotters would be located and some of the potential targets. He assured us he'd worked with these men before and our only problem would be understanding what they were saying. That's why he was along.

I asked, "Where will you and your men be stationed?"

"I'll be in CIC with you. One of my men will be with the gunnery officer, one on the bridge and one on the deck. He'll keep an eye on the beach and the landing craft to be certain we're not firing at any of them."

After the briefing Johnno said, "About the only book my mum read was the Bible and she was determined that I go to college. I stayed with relatives and friends in Melbourne and worked the ranch in the summer and holidays."

"Where were you when this war began?"

"I was in my senior year of college and offered a commission. I joined up. My buddies were either in or just signing up. I'm not much into religion. Sorta like you guys. When your number comes up on the board, that's all there is, mate. I'll never forget what my mum said as I was leaving. 'Johnno,' she said, "I'll be praying every day that the Lord will surround you with his angels, to guide you and protect you.' And you know 'Arold, I'm believing 'er prayers were answered. I've been in some tight spots. Men all around me 'ave been killed. So far, I 'aven't been scratched. Sure wasn't just coincidence. 'Er last words were 'there may not be any bands playing when you come home, but the angels will be singing.'"

"I'm not going to argue with your mum. I sorta believe that way myself. Did you know any of the coastwatchers in the Solomon Islands? They did one helluva job."

"I knew a couple of those bloody blokes. They were mostly loners. Not many men would go into the bush with a couple of natives and set up housekeeping, especially with Japs running all around the place."

"What do you know about Borneo?"

"Some of our blokes were stationed t'ere before the war. We've been pretty well briefed. In many areas the females dominate the males, may even beat them. And one of the screwiest customs I've run into is 'ow the 'usband is treated before he goes on a long 'unting trip. A piece of sharp bamboo is used to pierce 'oles in the foreskin of his penis. A bone is inserted through the holes and stays t'ere while the wound heals. Some chastity belt, eh 'Arold?" He paused and laughed, "Sure would make you lose interest in sex in a 'urry. They believe in free love but with a little different twist. An unmarried male and female may take a liking to each other. T'ey build a small 'ut and live together until one or the other calls it quits. This may 'appen several times before they settle down and get married. Now get this: the natives believe all females are virgins w'en they marry. T'eir reasoning: since there are no virgins, all girls are considered to be equally chaste; if all are chaste then they must be virgins." He laughed, "How do you like that reasoning?" I could only scratch my head in bewilderment.

Before we got to Borneo Johnno had learned "Dixie," "Give My Regards To Broadway" and other songs. I learned many popular Australian songs, including the unofficial national anthem, "Waltzing Matilda." It didn't mean dancing with a girl, but walking through the bush with your "swag" on your back, swag meaning your personal possessions.

On Thursday 7 June North Borneo was sighted and the Conner conducted drills. The next morning we were on station in Brunei Bay and Calder made contact with our spotter, Henry. He moved us around and seemed pleased as he said, "Looks like you've made a direct hit on an ammunition dump. The whole area seems to have blown up. Nice shooting."

In the afternoon the Conner with several other ships went to sea and spent the night steaming around in circles. In the morning the Conner was back in the harbor covering the mine sweeping unit. In the afternoon Henry was again directing our pre-landing bombardment of Labuan Island.

The Commodore persisted in harassing me by looking over my shoulder and asking me to explain everything I did. It was difficult getting messages to the bridge. In private, Calder remarked, "That bloke's crazy, mate." I agreed.

When firing was completed at 1557, I whispered to Calder, "Thank God we're through. Hopefully I can get a few hours relief from the Commodore."

The night was spent at sea and on 10 June, the Conner was on station firing at the pill boxes and gun emplacements near to the beach. Underwater demolition teams reconnoitered the beaches and cleared away mines. The Australians landed on Papuan Island at 0915 and advanced rapidly inland, securing the airfield. No additional calls for support fire came.

On the morning of 12 June the Metcalf relieved us of our fire support duty and picked up Major Calder and his men. As he was leaving he said, "It was great serving with you, 'Arold. I'm beginning to feel like a rebel. You're first class blokes. I'll look forward to seeing you again."

Various drills were conducted and at 2300 GQ was sounded when enemy planes were reported. The Commodore stalked into CIC in his skivvies and barked, "What's going on? Bring me up to date. How am I going to fight this ship if you don't give me the poop?" He kept yelling. I had no chance to reply. I thought: "Thank God you ain't fighting this ship." Without waiting for an answer, he ran out on deck and yelled at the Captain. Not satisfied, he climbed up the ladder to the bridge. With his drooping drawers, he was a pathetic, comical sight. It would have been funny if it weren't so serious.

When GQ was secured, I told Doc Wareham, "I'm getting damn tired of the Commodore and his behavior. I'm going to do something even if it's wrong. He's either got combat fatigue or he's a crazy SOB. He's driving everybody nuts. Sissons has had it. We've got to get him a medical." Wareham looked at me like I was crazy and asked, "What do you want me to do? To support such a diagnosis, you need someone with more clout than I've got."

"You're to keep your mouth shut. The next time we're anchored close to a hospital ship, you and I are going to pay a visit to the staff medical officer, explain the problem and ask for his help. It may not work, but it's worth a try."

Wareham shook his head and exclaimed, "I'm not certain who is crazier, but I'm on your side. Let's sleep on it."

On 15 June the Conner relieved the Charrette as the fire support ship off Pappan Island, and a contingent of Australians under the command of Captain Peter F. Cleland reported aboard. Our spotter had no need of us, so the next afternoon I was on the bridge when a lookout shouted, "Tell the Captain there's an LCT flying a 5-star General's flag approaching our port quarter." I recognized General Douglas MacArthur with his hat and pipe. He was accompanied by his staff who were heading ashore to evaluate the situation. Bill and I stood at attention and saluted as he passed.

"I've been with him on several operations, but have never seen him before," I said.

"Neither have I. He looks just like his pictures," Bill replied.

After completing his inspection, MacArthur sent a congratulatory dispatch to Admiral Royal: "The execution of the Brunei Bay operation has been flawless. Please accept for yourself and convey to your officers and men the pride and gratification I feel in such a splendid performance."

As Admiral Royal was leaving on 17 June, General Morshead sent a dispatch: "On the eve of your departure, I wish to express admiration and appreciation of the thorough, efficient, gallant and successful manner in which the naval force under your command carried out its vital role in the Borneo operations."

With Brunei secure, Task Group 74.3 was underway on Sunday 17 June. The next morning Bill called me to the bridge. "I've got sad news, Harold. Admiral Royal has fought his last battle. He died of a massive heart attack this morning while enroute to Leyte. What a shame. We'll miss him."

"How ironic. Dying of a heart attack rather than a Jap shell. He's been through many naval battles. It just proves, when your number comes up on that board, it makes no difference where you are."

Going below, I found Peter Cleland and told him what I had learned from Calder. He had told me that the natives lived in large houses divided into apartments, with the most important family living in the center, then children, followed by uncles and aunts and at the ends, the cousins. Pigs and chickens live underneath. "They know something we don't," I remarked. " We can't get along with just our parents in the same house." Calder told me they used blow guns and poisoned darts for hunting. For large animals, they dig pits 7 ft. square and 8 ft. deep which are covered with leaves and brush. The animals fall in and are trapped. He said rice is their staple food. They plant gardens whenever and wherever the spirit moves them, maybe in the middle of the street or on the sidewalk. It's claimed they'll eat anything that moves, grubs in rotten trees to poisonous snakes. The jungle is filled with tropical fruits of all kinds.

On 19 June the Conner was anchored in Twai Tawi Bay, which the Aussies had secured early on. During the next 2 days, it was normal shipboard routine. Everyone enjoyed the movies "They Were Expendable" with John Wayne and Robert Montgomery, as well as "The Picture of Dorian Gray" with George Sanders and Hurd Hatfield. The Commodore continued with his irritating ways.
Peter Cleland and his men left the ship at 1300 on 21 June.

I wrote Lil on Friday 22 June, "...Doc and I didn't go to the movie tonight. We're geniuses! We have acquired Russian language records. The book says we can learn to speak it in a couple of months. We've also been learning Spanish. I'll be able to make love in many languages. Isn't that exciting? Can't figure out why we haven't tried Japanese. That's what we need in this part of the world...

"Am enclosing pictures of 'Crossing the Line Ceremony'. Also some of the party we had out side of Manila. As you will note, there are no females in the pictures. This was in deference to the married guys...

"We acquired a mongrel puppy a couple of weeks ago. Her name is Schultz. She's growing rapidly and beginning to look like a dog. She's a great source of pleasure for the crew.

"I have written BuPers and requested permission to attend medical school. Fat chance! Nothing ventured, nothing gained!...Your letters are getting shorter and shorter since you left Orlando. You ought to go back..."

Emperor Hirohito was telling the Supreme Council that steps toward peace must be taken. Earlier he had accepted the decision to fight to the end, but with his people suffering from shortages of food, clothing, oil and other resources necessary to wage war, continued loss of life was senseless. A lively debate ensued with no firm decision.

In the morning I told Wareham, "We're anchored as close to SOPA in the Nashville as we're going to get. Let's pay a visit to the staff medical officer and see if he can help us with the Commodore." Going aboard, I found the doctor and told him about the problems the Commodore was causing. "It's impossible. He's driving everyone crazy, especially the Captain. He needs to get some rest. If he isn't suffering from combat fatigue, he's just plain crazy and unsuited to command."

The Commander looked at me as though I were a lunatic. Scratching his head, he said, "Lieutenant I've heard some lulus, but this beats them all. I couldn't present this to the Admiral unless you first put it in writing. Even if the Admiral agreed, there'd be a court of inquiry, a panel of medical experts to verify the facts. That would take forever, and in the meantime, you'd be in big trouble. I suggest you just learn to live with the bastard. He won't be on board for long. Just hang in there." Recognizing he spoke the truth, I said to Waresham, "Well, I tried. He's right. I might as well learn to live with the SOB."

At noon 24 June the Conner was underway with the Nashville, Phoenix and DesDiv 102. The next morning the Conner and Burns were detached and on 26 June, we were anchored in Morotai Harbor. On liberty, Bill and I found the bar and were told there was an Australian field hospital with pretty, friendly and accessible nurses close by. An added attraction was an USO troop with Carol Landis as the leading performer. They put on a great show and afterwards dropped by the officers club. The war was forgotten for a few hours.

I wrote Lil the next day, "...You are the most inconsistent, illogical, but adorable individual I have ever known. You start off by saying you love me and then give me 15 reasons why you really don't, why you shouldn't...

"...Lately all I've been doing is sitting around day-dreaming, doing a little work (very little), a few visits to the beach, an occasional movie. No mail—but oh! A great time is being had by all. Last night I fiddled with my Spanish. Seems like a simple subject, but I don't concentrate unless the pressure is on. Terrible habit.

"...I was reading aloud some passages today from a series of lectures given by Dr. Osler, probably the greatest man in medicine this country has produced. They weren't technical. Just a way of life. You would have enjoyed them, and I would have given anything to have you here to read them to me...Right now on the medical advice given by my roommate, I'm going to take a good, warm shower and hit the sack. I'll probably read a little (do you mind people reading in bed?). After that, well, I just might dream of you as I've done before. Who knows, maybe I'll see you tonight. Think of me once in awhile."

OBOE 11 landings were scheduled for 1 July at Balikpapan, the oil center, which was on the east coast across Makassar Strait from the Celebes. The entire area was heavily fortified with coast guard defense guns, revetments, tunnels, pillboxes and tank traps.

The minesweeps had taken a helluva beating from mines and enemy gunfire during the two weeks of operation prior to F-Day. The UDT teams did a super job of reconnoitering and clearing the obstacles. It was said that this was one of the best and bravest jobs done by the frogmen during the entire war.

At dawn on 28 June the Conner was underway with TG 74.3. The next morning Task Group 78.4 was sighted. Rear Admiral William Sample had the CVE's Suwanee, Chenango and Gilbert Islands with escorts. The Phoenix had Vice Admiral Barbey, Commander of the Balikpapan Attack Force, aboard and Rear Admiral Berkey was in the Nashville. At 0830 the Conner was ordered to join Task Group 78.4.

Watching the ships from the bridge, Sissons said, "Take a good look. This maybe the last amphibious landing of the war. The scuttlebutt floating around is that we have developed a superbomb which might end the war."

"I hope it's true. There are too many people, including Eisenhower, who believe blockading and bombing will starve the Japanese people into surrendering."

"They're dreaming. These bastards don't think like Europeans. Death is better than losing face, and they have no intention of giving up. They've got thousands of Kamikazes just waiting for us to land."

"I hope politics don't play a part in the decision to drop this bomb. It'll save thousands or even millions of lives, both Japs and ours. I might even get to medical school."

At 1408 the Burns came alongside and delivered mail. There were shouts of joy when the PA boomed: "Now hear this! Mail call for the crew in the mess hall; for the officers, in the wardroom." I had letters from my parents and friends; none from Lil.

Task Force 78.2 bombarded the shore on F-Day, 1 July. Major General E.J. Milford, 7th Division, 1 Australian Corps, had 35,000 troops and encountered little resistance. The area had been under air and naval bombardment for 16 days prior to the landings, the longest of the war. The Conner was offshore with the carriers searching for Japanese planes.

That evening I wrote Lil, "...Had a great night. Saw movie 'I Love a Soldier' ...Everyone enjoyed it...Doc talked me into taking a little Benzedrine this afternoon and I am exuberant and just bubbling over...Just wanted to see the effects...

"I'm still eagerly awaiting the end of this month. I'll know then what the future holds...It takes some people a long time to find themselves. I'm one of those, both in regards to medicine and you. Both of them were in front of me all of the time and I never knew. I now know and it's a great feeling..."

The next morning the Conner anchored in Makassar Straits, Balikpapan, Dutch East Indies. Several officers and men reported on board to serve on Captain Martin's staff. At noon Captain Richard Nix, an Australian, came on board with 3 enlisted men. At sundown the Conner was on fire support station and Nix established contact with our spotter, Russell. The Aussies wanted the beach illuminated so the Japanese could not sneak up on them under the cover of darkness. At 2030 firing was commenced with star shells, one every 30 minutes until dawn the next morning.

At 2200 I wrote Lil, "...I am the one that's probably stupid...just plain thick...just remember I'm deeply in love with you...I got your picture and it's truly terrific...so radiantly fresh and lovely. The Doc and I both agreed you looked good enough to eat...

"...I'm not complaining about my lack of sleep...still I could use a little more...Doggone it, Lil, your letters aren't telling me much. They used to be long and newsy, and I sorta knew what you were doing and thinking. Now you seem always in a mad rush to get through...Wish I could be with you for 5 minutes so we could have a complete understanding...

"We're getting rather crowded on this vessel. The junior officers are really having a tough time finding a place to live. This thing of having a staff on board is not very convenient from any angle...

"...Tell you a secret! I haven't taken a shower in a week. In deference to my associates, I'm determined to go through that ordeal tonight...

"PS This is another night. It's been a long day. Got a letter from my folks saying you'd dropped by with those pictures I sent...Got a letter from Herbert written on a transport heading this way...I'm sorry to see him come because my mother will be worrying twice as much...Many think I have a chance to get home to med school...Keep your fingers crossed..."

Wednesday the 4th of July, all of the American ships gave a 21-gun salute. The Conner proceeded to our fire support station. At 1041 firing was commenced and continuing until stopped by a familiar sounding voice coming over the TBS: "Whole yah fire! Whole yah fire! Ya'll is shooting at us."

"Tell the bridge to hold fire," I told the telephone operator. "I want to check the gun bearings."

Captain Nix asked, "W'at is that bloke talking about? I can't understand a word 'e's saying."

Going out on deck to see where our guns were aiming I explained, "That was a southern boy who's with a landing party and shells are coming from this direction." To my chagrin, our guns were aimed in the direction of the assault boats. We were the guilty party. Ken Miller was looking out of the fire control hatch, glanced at me and shook his head. Fortunately, no damage had been done. Firing ceased at 1225. The Commodore found shore bombardment boring and didn't show up in CIC.

Firing commenced again after lunch. Our spotter moved us around and seemed pleased with the results. At dinner the Captain commented, "This is the way to fight a war. After a leisurely meal, we bombard an enemy we can't see, kill a few, get a good night's sleep and start again in the morning. All that's lacking is a couple of drinks."

The next morning I found Dick Nix in the wardroom and I asked him where he was from.

"I'm from Brisbane. I've worked with both Calder and Cleland. Bloody good bastards."

"When did you get into the service?"

"I got a commission in 1941. I don't know why I didn't join the Navy. I've been in more jungles than I thought existed on this planet. There's no sleep to be had and they are stinking! When the Nips took Singapore, we were ordered home to defend Australia. It looked like the Nips would be right behind. Then you blokes showed up and Guadalcanal turned the war around."

"What do you know about orangutans? This might be my only chance to see one. Borneo has plenty."

"You don't want to meet one in the jungle. They are ferocious and enormously strong, weighing up to 350 pounds. The word means 'wildman of the forest', and the natives believe they can talk, but don't for fear of being put to work. Their heads are thought to be as powerful spiritually as human heads. However, if killed by a rifle, all magical strength is lost."

"That's fascinating. I'm going to get ashore and see if I can observe one from a distance—a great distance!"

On Friday 6 July the Conner relieved the Burns of fire support duty. After firing for most of the day, we went alongside the LST 67 and unloaded our ammunition. I said to Sissons, "This might be my only chance to see an orangutan. Do you object to my going ashore? We could use some fresh fruit and there's plenty to be had for the picking."

"Just don't do anything stupid," he replied, "and don't stay too long."

An Australian officer was at the dock and offered to show me around. As we were walking down a road leading into the jungle, he explained where the battle line was and the problem they were having with snipers behind the lines. "They're not concerned about their lives. Just want to harass us."

About a half hour later while I was admiring the bright foliage and the chirping of various birds, I heard the sound of firecrackers. My friend shouted "down" and pushed me to the ground. The men on either side fired into the trees ahead. I saw a body falling and realized a sniper tied in the top of a tree had been shooting at us. That ended my sight-seeing and I returned to the ship.

In the afternoon Captain Nix and his men were ordered to the Phillips. As he was leaving, I said, "I hate to see you leave. It's been a real pleasure serving with you blokes. If everyone fought wars like you and the limeys, they might never end."

"'Arold, it's been my pleasure. Look me up if you're ever in Brisbane. Thanks for 'aving us. Just hope we don't meet on another ocean with another war."

Although the island would not be secured until 22 July, there was no further need for the Conner. The Commanders praised the minesweeps and UDT's for their excellent performance and the outstanding fire support given by the US and Australian Navies. On Saturday 7 July, the Conner was underway with the Phoenix and Bell on a northeasterly course.

On 9 July I wrote Lil, "...Am I being presumptuous in calling you Sweetheart?...Hope is one of the saving graces of mankind. Wonderful thing! Tonight I feel splendid. Don't know why. Guess its because I've caught up with all of my paperwork. If we spent half the money on munitions as we do on paper, and half as much time shooting as we do pushing a pencil, this war would have been over a long time ago.

"Great life!...Our former puppy Schultz is growing up to be a dog and getting plenty of attention. The other morning I noticed a large group of men on the forecastle...The poor ole pooch was being given a bath by about ten men...

"Saw a movie tonight, 'Journey to Margaret'...enjoyable and impressive. Made me realize what a wonderful country we have. Think of it! Until a few months ago, it was the only place of consequence on earth where people could find the cities lit at night, find some semblance of a normal life, a sanctuary from the strife and suffering so prevalent elsewhere...the hope and the inspiration of people, mighty and weak, sick and poor, throughout the world. I hope the folks at home realize their position and are thankful...I'll stop on that subject...

"I haven't had any dope on med school...Think you could fall for a struggling young doctor? (probably won't be very young, tho)...

"Can't get anything out of you...for the next few hours, I'm going to recline into the arms of morpheus. Jealous?"

Sissons gave me the conn the next afternoon, and after fueling and replenishing our ammunition supply, the Conner anchored in Berth 173 in Subic Bay.

In Switzerland, Japanese employees of the Bank for International Settlements approached a member of Allen Dulles' OSS. They were interested in discussing peace and wanted to be assured the position of the Emperor would be safeguarded. The Japanese continued seeking Russian approval for an envoy to visit Moscow. They wanted to seek a separate peace, but Ambassador Naotake Sato attached a stipulation to the visit: if the USA and Britain insisted on unconditional surrender, Japan would fight until the end. Knowing this, the Russians refused to agree to the visit.

On 15 July I wrote Lil, "Hello, Wonderful...you are, you know... glad to hear you're once again a school girl...and by George, you'd better make good grades...

"I can now tell you I was at the invasion of Brunei Bay on the north shore of Borneo...Had a ringside seat and saw the friend of the people, General Douglas MacArthur, make his entrance with all the cameramen cranking away...He wanted to see how effective our firing had been. It was a pretty torn up hunk of land...

"It won't be long before my entire bulkhead will be plastered with your likeness...You've been watching me like a hawk...My mother seems to be working on you over time. Guess she knows a good thing when she sees it...Haven't been able to sit still the last couple of days. The die is cast by now, and either I'll be there in school with you in the fall of the year or else it'll be some other year...the suspense is terrible...

"...You've got to learn to 'Samba'. Tonight's movie had a lot of 'Samba-ing' in it...I need some tutelage—by you.

"That dog (hound would be more correct) has started dining in the wardroom. Remember what I told you about Manny Reid's female pooch?...she got into trouble and had 9 puppies. How she managed it on the high seas I don't know. They had more dogs on that ship than they knew what to do with...Hope ours doesn't have similar difficulties...

"Tonight I'm sitting in the wardroom...Across from me is Henderson, the staff communication officer. He's thumbing through dispatches with a worried look on his face...Next to him is Wilson, a good ole Georgia boy with a big chart in front of him making corrections. At the end of the table, Florence is pounding out a letter to his wife on a broken down typewriter (and he hasn't got a shirt on—really embarrassing). The radio is turned to a program called 'Words and Music', very low, melodious and beautiful. Does that description bring you just a little closer?...

"The Captain has been letting me handle the ship quite a bit recently. Going alongside a tanker, I had everybody concerned. I ended up bending a couple of stanchions. My next landing was perfect...

"I have heard nothing from the all powerful Bureau...not expecting favorable action...

"Got a payday tomorrow and I have a grand total of $2.00 on the books...it's a rugged life...They don't even pay me!...

"Did I tell you of the most thrilling memory I have of you? It was on our first date when I was home. We'd stopped in front of your house and were listening to the radio...and as a boy and a girl do, I put my arm about you and kissed you. Your remark will always remain with me: 'I've waited 3 years for you to do that!' (How did you figure 3?) Anyhow, what I should have said is: 'I've waited 24 years.' It won't be that long again...I'm around to stay. Will you let me ?..."

On 21 July Captain Martin, ComDesRon 51, shifted his flag to the Haradan. As he and his staff went down the gang plank, I remarked to the Sissons, "The only thing that could bring greater joy to me is for Japan to surrender. I feel sorry for that bunch on the Haradan. He gets my vote for being the most contemptible SOB I have ever known."

I wrote Lil, "...Just a note to tell you how wonderful your pictures are...You look beautiful...Your letters mean so much...

"Did I tell you how proud of you I am? You're probably a future star... What is the name of this production?...How many times do you have to rehearse the love scenes?...I'm jealous!... So what have I been up to?...Down to Balikpapan (on Borneo). Not too much excitement. Routine work. Nothing more...

"Our Squadron Commander has betaken himself elsewhere and I'm back in my old stateroom. Life isn't too bad. Of course, I'm considered a so and so, but that is part of the game. I can handle it as long as you don't develop that attitude, too...

"Nothing but Jimmy Durante on the radio and he doesn't inspire me...Do me a favor. On our first date, wear that Easter dress. You look sweet 16, just waiting to be kissed..."

The next morning 23 July, the Conner was underway with the New Orleans, Shields, Killen and Lampey. President Truman was in Potsdam, Germany, conferring with other Allied leaders. A Council of Foreign Ministers was established with Britain, China, France, Russia and the US. Their job was to draw up peace treaties with Italy, Hungary, Romania, Bulgaria and Finland, but there was wrangling between Russia and Britain which the US tried to arbitrate. Churchill alleged that Stalin was sabotaging efforts to establish democratic governments in the liberated countries. Stalin claimed Churchill agreed to leave the Balkan countries to Russia and now he was meddling in the their affairs. More important was the disagreement on Poland's eastern border.

The Conner conducted a number of simulated submarine attacks and the dropping of depth charges. All went well until a souvenir Japanese shell exploded in the hand of a gunners mate in No. 4 gun mount. There were no eye witnesses, hence the status of misconduct could not be determined. All the fingers of his left hand were blown off and those of the right hand badly lacerated. The left eye was swollen and he had lacerations of the nose, chest and left thigh. Upon our return to Subic Bay, he was transferred to the HMS Oxfordshire for treatment.

The Potsdam Conference was adjourned so Churchill and Clement Attlee could fly back to England for the general election which was being held.

I convened a deck court to hear the cases of 3 of the crew, but had to adjourn it at 0915 when all hands were needed for drills: gunnery, battle and simulated torpedo attacks. Late in the day Sissons showed me a dispatch he had received from Admiral Kincaid, Com 7th Fleet: "USS Charrette and USS Conner report to me for special assignment."

"What do you think that means?" I asked.

"I have no idea, but we'll soon find out."

What a surprise!

NAVPERS – 136 (REV. 1–44) DECK LOG—LIST OF OFFICERS CONFIDENTIAL

LIST OF OFFICERS
ATTACHED TO AND ON BOARD THE U.S.S. CONNER (DD582) , COMMANDED

BY William A. SISSONS, Lieutenant Commander U.S.N. , DURING THE PERIOD COVERED BY THIS LOG BOOK, WITH DATE OF

REPORTING FOR DUTY, DETACHMENT, OR DEATH, FROM 1 May , 19 45 , TO 31 May , 19 45

NAME AND FILE NUMBER (Show file No. below name)	RANK	DATE OF REPORTING ON BOARD / DATE OF DETACHMENT (Show detachment date below reporting date)	PRIMARY DUTIES	NAME, RELATIONSHIP, AND ADDRESS OF NEXT OF KIN (Show address at which BuPers may most readily communicate with next of kin in an emergency)
William A. Sissons (81129)	Lieut. Comdr.	2-5-45	Commanding	Mrs. Marie Ball (Mother) Route #1, Fletcher, Ontario, Canada
Harold E. Jervey, Jr. (102461)	Lieut.	4-14-45	Exec. Officer	Mr. H. E. Jervey (Father) 2906 Duncan St. Columbia, S. C.
Robert O. Austin (166441)	Lieut.	6-8-43	First Lieut.	Mr. A. O. Austin (Father) 6 High St. Orleans, Vermont
Kenneth M. Miller (165527)	Lieut.	9-28-44	Gunnery Off.	Mrs. K. M. Miller (Wife) 1479 Gardner Blvd. San Leandro, Calif.
Val W. Ringer (184919)	Lt.(jg)	6-8-43	Asst.Gunn.Off.	Mrs. V. W. Ringer (Wife) Waldoboro, Maine
John de P. Hansen (187335)	Lt.(jg)	6-8-43	Sound Officer	Mrs. D. J. Hansen (Mother) 7235 Merrill Ave. Chicago, Illinois
Robert T. Bumbalough (224451)	Lt.(jg)	6-8-43	C.I.C. Officer	Mrs. R. T. Bumbalough (Wife) 805 Mile End Nashville, Tenn.
Elroy Florence (225938)	Lt.(jg)	11-29-44	Asst. First Lieut.	Mrs. E. Florence (Wife) 342 Water Street Stevens Point, Wisconsin
Marcus O. Creager (227723)	Lt.(jg)	6-8-43	Eng. Officer	Mr. C. C. Creager (Father) R. R. #5 Eaton, Ohio
Felton M. Wyatt (267838)	Lt.(jg)	5-5-44	Communications Officer	Mr. F. G. Wyatt (Father) 12 Downey Plade Oakland, Calif.
Richard K. Leininger (258954)	Lt.(jg)	4-7-44	Torp. Officer	Mrs. R. K. Leininger (Wife) 511 W. Sandusky Street Findlay, Ohio
Edward K. Waters (343508)	Lt.(jg)	2-26-45	Asst. Comm. Officer	Mrs. E. K. Waters (Wife) 206 W. Mulberry St. Normal, Illinois
Ellsworth E. Wareham (373735)	Lt.(jg)	3-26-45	Medical Off.	Mr. Dayton Wareham (Father) 722 S.E. 61st Ave. Portland, 16, Oregon
Alvin T. Stubel (288404)	Lt.(jg)	4-20-45	Asst.Gunn.Off.	H. C. Stubal (Father) 33 Hamilton Ave. Fairview, New Jersey
Royal W. Randall, Jr. (340397)	Ensign	4-8-44	Navigator	Mrs. L. W. Randall (Mother) 1566 Blair Avenue Mobile, 19, Alabama
Albert G. Siewe (376840)	Ensign	12-28-44	Supply & Disbursing Off.	Mrs. A. G. Siewe (Wife) 737 Gondert Avenue Dayton, Ohio
George C. Willetts (338788)	Ensign	12-23-44	Asst.Eng.Off.	Mr. W. P. Willetts (Father) 175 Warner Ave. Roslyn Hts., L.I., N.Y.
Conrad T. E. Beardsley (358303)	Ensign	2-18-45	Asst.Eng.Off.	Mr. T. E. R. Beardsley (Father) 381 Park Place Brooklyn, N. Y.
Stephen R. Steinhauser (401506)	Ensign	4-30-45	Temp. Duty in CIC Operation	Mrs. Lois H. Steinhauser (Wife) French Hospital San Francisco, Calif.

EXAMINED AND FOUND TO BE CORRECT:

CHAPTER 18

The Capture of the Taschibana Maru;
Blown to Oblivion by the Atomic Bomb

Following night battle maneuvers, Captain W.H. Martin, ComDesDiv 102, was ordered to report to Admiral Kincaid in Manila. Upon anchoring on 26 July, Clement Atlee's landslide victory over Winston Churchill was the headline story.

I exclaimed, "I don't understand the British. Throwing Churchill out like a dirty towel after he led them to victory. Don't those limeys have any sense of decency and fair play?"

Sissons replied, "That's not the point. Churchill represents the many hardships the British have endured: rationing, poor housing, limited fuel, bombings and death. Atlee promises improved times. He's an unknown quantity and anything is better than what they've got."

To the north, the Indianapolis was departing Tinian after unloading parts for 2 atomic bombs.

Sissons and Joyce met on the Charrette to learn from Captain Martin what Admiral Kincaid planned for our next operation. Upon returning Bill gestured for me to follow him to his cabin and exclaimed, "You don't want to miss this trip! Get the ship and crew ready for one helluva operation." At midday Lt.(jg) Henderson reported on board, followed by Sergeant George Lawrence Gillick, Jr., USMC, with 7 combat-outfitted Marines. There was excitement in the air as the Conner and Charrette weighed anchor at 1707 for Morotai.

In Europe, Atlee, returning to Potsdam, joined his Allies in demanding that Japan[73] (1) surrender unconditionally or face prompt and utter destruction; (2) end militarism; (3) punish all war criminals; (4) accept military occupation of Japan; and (5) evacuate all territories except the home islands. In return, the Allies would (1) establish a democratic political order; (2) assist in rebuilding Japan's industry; and (3) end military occupation when a responsible government was established. These demands were unacceptable to the Japanese.

At my first opportunity I asked Henderson, "What are your orders?"

"To report aboard. I'm fluent in Japanese. I know nothing else." Sergeant Gillick wasn't of any help either.

In the morning Premier Suzuki told the Japanese people that unless the Emperor's survival was assured, they were to ignore the Potsdam Agreement.

Entering Morotai Harbor on 29 July, imaginations were working overtime, up to and including a raiding party on the Japanese homeland. Liberty parties left at 1600, but I stayed aboard doing paperwork, listening to the radio and reading "The Egg and I" by Betty MacDonald. During the morning, both destroyers received hand grenades, walkie-talkies and barbed wire. "What the hell are we going to do with these?" I was asked repeatedly. I had no answer.

At 0002, 600 miles west of Guam, Lt. Cmdr. Hasimota, Captain of the I-58, fired a spread of torpedoes at the Indianapolis. It plunged to the bottom of the ocean with its crew of over 900.

After departing Morotai on 31 July, the Captain called a meeting of all off duty officers. "Gentlemen, we are embarked on one of the most exciting missions of the war. We have been ordered to intercept, board and search for contraband, and if any is found, seize as a prize vessel of war, the Japanese ship the Tachibana Maru. Each destroyer will furnish a boarding party of 40 men including the Marines." There was absolute silence. He continued, "Intelligence has learned that the Japanese are using hospital ships to evacuate healthy troops from the by-passed islands. A ship was boarded and searched a year ago and allowed to proceed. It isn't to happen again. This ship is enroute from Tocal, Kai Islands, to Soerabaja, Java. If the reports are accurate, we should intercept her north of Timor in the Banda Sea."

"My God," Wyatt shouted, "That's the dream of every sailor. Grappling hooks, cutlasses and hand-to-hand combat. Just like Blackbeard." Everyone began talking at once. The Captain waved his hand for silence, "Don't get so carried away. We're not a bunch of pirates. This operation will go down in naval history. We'll be operating in enemy waters and if unexpected trouble develops, there will be no help by air, land or sea."

After the meeting he told me, "Lt. Cmdr. Ernest Peterson, executive officer of the Charrette, has been designated prizemaster. You will be assistant prizemaster, if you're willing. This is a voluntary assignment."

"Of course I accept. I wouldn't miss it for all the tea in China!"

Sissons suggested officers who might be included in the boarding party and added, "Get with the chiefs and officers involved. Have them recommend the men they want. Just remember! This is a voluntary assignment." The word spread rapidly. Everyone was eager to go. It was a tough decision, but within 2 hours, the list of 32 men and officers was complete.

Proficiency in small arms fire was a talent few of us possessed. The fantail began to look like a shooting gallery at the state fair. Cans were hung on stanchions and thrown over the side for targets. With the roll of the ship and our poor marksmanship, few were hit. What we lacked in ability was made up for in enthusiasm. Sgt. Gillick, a decorated Guadalcanal veteran, was our instructor. Only his constant vigilance kept us from blowing up each other and the ship. In the morning small arms practice continued on the fantail. Excitement began building in the afternoon when the Charrette signaled,

"Have received contact report. Hospital ship sighted at Latitude 05 degrees 18' south; Longitude 131 degrees 37' east, speed 5 knots."

The frightening aspects of our operation began casting their spell. Human and mechanical failures took on sinister meanings. Sonar made false contacts. Lookouts made mistaken sightings. The wind began gusting to 20-30 knots and the Conner began plunging and rolling. At 1440 Mangoli Island was passed 25 miles on the starboard beam. Farewell letters were written to love ones. There was the taunting: "You guys are wasting your time. Who's going to deliver this mail if none of us get back? Gabriel?" The boisterous bravado diminished. Quips were exchanged. "Who wants to live forever? It ain't time for my number to come up on the board yet!"

At 0220 Thursday 2 August, the Conner entered the Banda Sea. The frantic gunnery practice continued and the whale boats were loaded with supplies and ammunition. With the wind from the south and white, puffy clouds, it was a typical south sea island cruise except for persistent sounds of gunfire.

The air was electrified with excitement when, at noon, the Charrette signaled, "Have received report from plane: unidentified hospital ship spotted at Latitude 05 degrees 40'; Longitude 129 degrees 45' east. On course 245 degrees, speed 10 knots." Men began gathering in small groups, waving their arms wildly. I was on the bridge at 1532 when the Charrette signaled,

"Continue course and speed until 2200, at which time change course to 245 degrees, speed 13 knots. Charrette will continue course and speed to be at earliest meeting point, assuming enemy speed 10 knots. If contact is made by either vessel, adjust course and speed to maintain contact. Upon gaining contact, communicate by VHF. If not possible, by Task Force Common 2748 KCS or CSP 1270. Reverse course at 0630 if contact not made."

Sissons exclaimed, "It won't be long. Tell the boarding party."

I briefed Gillick on the reports and said, "Shut down the shooting gallery. Tell the men to hit their sacks early. This might be their last good night's sleep for several days."

Night fell suddenly. I stayed on the bridge and talked with Sissons and the watch officers. At 2150 the Charrette radioed, "Have made contact with Tachibana Maru. Can see lights. Course 255 degrees, speed 10 knots. Am maneuvering to take station 15 miles astern. Join up."

At 2319 the radar man reported, "Have unidentified object bearing 359 degrees, distance 36,400 yards."

Bill slapped me on the back and yelled, "That's it! That's the Tachibana Maru!"

At 2335 the Conner took station 7.5 miles on the port beam of the Charrette, 16 miles astern of the Tachibana Maru. There was little sleep for anyone. GQ was sounded at 0505. The boarding party ate breakfast first. Speed was increased to 23 knots. I first saw the Tachibana Maru at 0552 on Friday 3 August, with lights blazing. The wind began gusting to 22 knots and the Conner was rolling and pitching.

At 0600 I ordered, "Visit and search parties, stand by the whale boats."

At 0637 the Commodore signaled the Tachibana Maru to lie to and one shot was fired across her bow. At 0650 she was dead in the water. The Conner was 1,000 yards off her port beam and the Charrette on the starboard side. I saw large red crosses on her sides and top. She was 249 feet long, 40 feet wide and weighed 1,772 tons.

At O658 the Charrette's visit and search party, with 5 officers and 25 enlisted men, was dispatched in 2 boats. The seas were rough and they rolled and pitched. Each man had a 45 Colt automatic as a side arm and several submachine guns hidden under blankets in the bottom of the boats. At 0705 the men began climbing up the gangway. The officer meeting Peterson was waving his arms and speaking. Lt.(jg) Henderson, interpreting, said, "He wants the officers to meet with Captain Yasuda in the wardroom." Peterson reached the wardroom and after much bowing, he said to the Captain, "We are here to search the ship for contraband." Henderson replied, "He will be happy to assist and will provide officers to accompany your men."

Peterson kept contact with the search parties through a long lead cable and the voice tube connections in the engineering compartment. Henderson interrogated Captain Kishire Yasuda and told Peterson, "The crew consists of 13 officers and 63 men. They are two days out of Teel, Kai Islands, with a large cargo of medical supplies and 1,562 patients enroute to Soerabaja, Java."

Later Dr. Catrall said, "The patients are quartered in 3 wards: one on the main deck forward and 2 below deck, one midship and one aft. A crude platform has been built in the holds halfway between the deck and overhead. Conditions are so crowded they are stretched over each other. The lighting is so poor I can't see the opposite end without a flashlight. With no forced draft ventilation, the heat is stifling. I found only 2 large heads on the port side of the ship aft, one on the main deck and the other on the first platform deck. All patients are ambulatory and none are sick enough to require bedside care. This ship resembles a hospital ship only because she is marked like one."

The search party in the forward compartment opened boxes marked with red crosses and found 77mm shells. The Japanese officer knew nothing about them. When this was reported to Peterson, I heard a voice yelling over the walkie-talkie at 0745, "Mickey Finn! Mickey Finn! 77mm ammunition found."

At 0750, "Everything going smoothly." At 0757, "Send both boats immediately."

At 0759 our gig was lowered into the water and Captain Sisson's voice rang out, "Boarding party away! Boarding party away!"

When we had cleared the Conner, the men on deck kept up a barrage of encouraging banter: "Put my name on one of those Jap nurses." "Don't drink up all of the sake." "What a break for you guys; wine and women on a floating south sea island." The voices began fading out and our quarry started looking ever more sinister. The 500 yards was becoming a strip of eternity. The waves were 5-7 feet high. The silence was broken by Quartermaster Lyles when he n sighted the lowered gangway on the starboard side: "What the hell! All my work on those grappling irons for nothing. I ain't going aboard unless I can climb." This evoked a ripple of nervous laughter.

As we went up the gangway, the stench from human, monkey and rat feces and urine was overpowering. The men joined the Charrette's men in stringing barb wire in the passageways and over the portholes. While our second boat was unloading, I ran to the bridge. Peterson said, "Yasudu seemed more surprised than anyone when contraband was discovered. I told him we were seizing the ship as a prize vessel of war and taking it into port for further searching. He didn't seem disturbed and volunteered to have his men run the engines. There was no evidence of violence."

"That is astounding," I exclaimed. "Nothing like this has happened in 4 years of war. There's got to be a catch! They must have been caught with their pants down. Just wait until tonight!" Peterson, rubbing his chin, replied, "Could be. Those 5" guns on our ships are mighty good persuaders. Maybe they don't feel as secure about their souls at sea, especially if they can't swim." He chuckled as he continued, "The most logical explanation is sea sickness. With these 6 to 8 foot seas and them being confined to those hot, stinking quarters below decks, they probably don't give a damn who's running this ship or where it's going. Separate the officers from the men and send as many as possible to the destroyers. Put the rest put under guard in the wardroom. Without leadership, there'll be less chance of an uprising."

I encountered Dr. Cartall who said, "This ship normally carries 700 patients. It's jammed with 1,562, all lying with their eyes closed. I removed some of the bandages but found no wounds."

"What about facilities for taking care of the sick?"

"There are no operating rooms, treatment rooms or x-ray facilities. There is no laboratory or diet kitchen. These are combat troops."

"Sounds like we're in for more trouble than we thought."

Continuing my inspection, I saw barbed wire being strung across all of the portholes which opened onto the maindeck and the passageways. I thought, "This is going to require a road map to go from one place to another."

I saw the small staterooms on the second deck in the forward part of the ship where the officers slept, one in the bunk and 2 or more on the deck with pillows and blankets. I was called to the quarter-deck at 0900 where Young reported, "The officers are separated from the enlisted men. They range in rank from lieutenants to the colonel in charge."

"This is incredible! Where are the dedicated sons of the Emperor who preferred death to a life of dishonor? The greatest shame of all is being captured alive," I replied. Turning to Gillick, I ordered, "Split the senior officers up into two groups. Some will be sent to the Conner and others to the to the Charrette." At 0920 the Captain of the Tachibana Maru and 27 officers embarked for the Charrette and 22 others departed to the Conner.

Sissons later said, "Before they came aboard, I ordered the prisoners to take off their white hospital gowns. I wanted to be certain they had no concealed weapons. Two at a time showered on the fantail. They were put in the vegetable locker under armed guard. The gowns were sent to the laundry. Wrist watches were taken into custody."

"How did they look?"

"Good except for 3. The doctor got the name, rank, age and complaints of each one. After a physical examination, he made a diagnosis and ordered the necessary treatment. The laundered gowns were returned and we fed them from the crew's mess. A couple were seasick, but the others ate like they were starved."

The Charrette placed the prisoners in the forward crew's compartment. With the exception of those too seasick, all were bathed and their clothing laundered. No trouble was experienced. The remaining officers were placed in the wardroom under the bridge. With the large windows, the guards could easily watch them. The Captain of the Tachibana Maru sent his thanks for the excellent care they received.

At 0935 the formation was underway on course 355 degrees, speed 10 knots. With the wind gusting to 30 knots and waves 6-8 feet, the ship was rolling and pitching. The Conner took station 1,500 yards ahead of the Tachibana Maru with the Charrette on the starboard quarter.

Fear and revulsion overwhelmed me when I looked into a compartment the first time. Little could be seen without a flashlight, and without ventilation, it was stifling. The 500 sweaty bodies glistened ominously. I said to the Marine guard, "This looks like the hole of an eighteenth century slaver. I'd like to know what's under those straw pallets the Japs are lying on, but that'll just have to wait." There were no evaporators and no water for bathing or personal hygiene. Fresh water was carried in storage tanks and doled out in small amounts for drinking purposes. Dr. Cartall thought it was contaminated with E.Coli and our men were ordered to avoid all of the ship's water.

The galley, located on the main deck near the fantail, contained large black iron kettles heated by steam from the engine room. Rice was stored in open bins with rats, cats, monkeys and cockroaches swarming everywhere. I told Hawkins to find out from the cooks what they eat and when. After some unintelligible gibberish, he replied, "They eat boiled rice and dried fish chips. They are fed at 0830 and 1600. They are given one canteen of water at dark to keep them from moving around at night." Later I saw the rice being dumped into large wooden kegs and the fish into buckets. These were passed from patient to patient. Each grabbed a double handful of rice and fish. They fashioned it into a ball and ate with their fingers.

At 1145 the Charrette came alongside and lines were rigged from below the bridge of the Charrette to the starboard quarter of the Tachibana Maru. Boxes of canned goods and bottles of water were sent over and stacked on the deck. After the transfer was completed, I asked, "You guys ready to eat? They've probably sent us the best goodies in the storeroom." As the boxes were opened, I was astonished to discover we had more turkey a la king than I thought existed in the entire South Pacific. To vary the menu, there was pork and beans and apple sauce. It wasn't appealing, but everyone ate enthusiastically. Food and drink was taken to the Captain and the bridge watch.

After eating, I continued my inspection. In the head there was an endless line. With limited flushing capacity, urine and feces sloshed over the deck. It was repulsive and I felt the urge to vomit.

Going to the bridge, I said, "Pete, everything is secure below decks. We've set up a watch of 4 hours on and 4 hours off. All hands will be needed when the prisoners are fed. Guards have been stationed at all entrances and exits to the compartments. It was a good decision to keep the medical corpsman, the doctors and engineering personnel on board. It'll make life a little easier for our men."

The afternoon passed uneventfully. Fear was always present! The first time I walked through a compartment alone was most frightening. Pfc. James Miller, the Marine guard, noting my hesitancy, said, as he directed a stream of tobacco at a rat, "Don't go in there, sir. Just ask if they've got any complaints and tell them to throw all weapons on the deck. Tell 'em any bastard that disobeys will be court martialed."

"You're real funny, Private! I'm going to walk through this compartment. My 45 will be on ready, which will do little good if they decide to grab me. If that happens, shoot and shoot to kill. If you hit me, so be it. They are not to use me as a hostage to take over the ship. Do you understand?"

"Yes, sir."

Starting down the narrow aisle, I kept brushing against out stretched arms and legs. I didn't try to look under the pallets. The men gave me an occasional grunt and a look of intense hatred. I breathed a sigh of relief when I reached the end. The other two compartments were the same.

When I came topside, the clean ocean breezes were a welcome relief. Gillick was close by holding his nose and exclaiming, "This is turning out to be the stinkingest campaign I have ever been on." For the first time, I really saw him: a rangy, tow-headed youth with creases around his gray eyes. The grim set of his jaw and the leathery, sun-tanned skin added years. His experience had not made him callous, but a realist, a craftsman in the science of death and the art of living. It was comforting to know he was on my side. It had been a long day. Standing on the wing of the bridge, I thought, "Only 12 hours? Fresh bodies tolerate acute strain well, but the sustained and unrelenting pressure we were experiencing would drain the strength from Superman."

With the fall of night, childish fears began increasing and sounds were magnified. The wind was dying down, but the rolling of the ship in the shallow troughs took on a new significance. The creaking of the timbers sounded like hundreds of stealthy footsteps. Visions of the fanatical Banzai charges appeared. Shaking off this feeling, I threaded my way over the sleeping Japanese seamen in the pilot house. Peterson was in his cabin looking over a pile of assorted watches and jewelry. He smiled wanly as he said, "These are a few of the souvenirs I have recouped in accordance with the Commodore's latest directive. He's going to make an honest disposition of them when we get to port."

I responded angrily, "That bastard! He'll give them to his buddies just to impress them. The only way we'll keep our men from taking souvenirs is to put guards on the guards. I refuse to do that. They're entitled to something for their effort. I've got to check below. Send a search party if you don't hear from me in an hour or so." Leaving by the ladder on the starboard side, I entered the athwartship passageway on the main deck leading to the radio shack and the officer's quarters. Paper and debris were scattered everywhere along with clothing. Pictures were partially ripped off the bulkheads. Nothing had been overlooked in the search for weapons and souvenirs. It looked like a typhoon had struck. Walking forward, I glanced through the window into the wardroom. The officers of his Supreme Highness were scattered around, with some sitting on the deck, others squatting on their haunches and a few sleeping on the tattered over-stuffed chairs and transoms.

Pfc. James Miller, the Marine guard said, "There's been nothing unusual. I've been watching them closely. Don't act like any Japs I have ever seen."

Going aft, I passed several groups of our men talking quietly. Not the usual laughing and joking. Entering a compartment with the prisoners, I threaded my way down the passageway, brushing bodies on either side. They seemed to be sleeping.

In the corridor behind the prisoners' quarters, I stopped to talk with the guard who was supervising an unending line of Japs. "Are these the same men that have been here since morning?" I laughingly asked. "I don't know if they're the same, but we've had standing room only. This is the most popular place on the ship. They have been going to the head ever since we boarded, an unbroken stream you might say." The miracle of 1,600 men with only 3 urinals and 2 commodes all reaching their goal without mishap was a topic of heated discussion.

Passing the engine room hatch, I glanced in. The throbbing, swishing sound of the reciprocating engines sounded like accentuated heart murmurs. The Japs, with white bandannas on their heads, and our men were working side by side. A sign language had been established between them. A few of the watch were asleep on the grill work. The only unusual part of the scene was the guards standing around leaning on their rifles.

Going up the ladder to the bridge, I could hear Hammond, chief engineer, declaring in an angry voice, "I don't care what the exec says. I'm not going to even close my eyes in the engine room and neither are my men. We aren't going to get murdered while we sleep." He lashed out as I entered, "And I hope you heard what I said." I was more amused than angry. "Go on, Hammond. You're just blowing off steam. Everyone is being treated fairly. The safety of the ship comes first. You've got it a lot easier than you'll ever know."

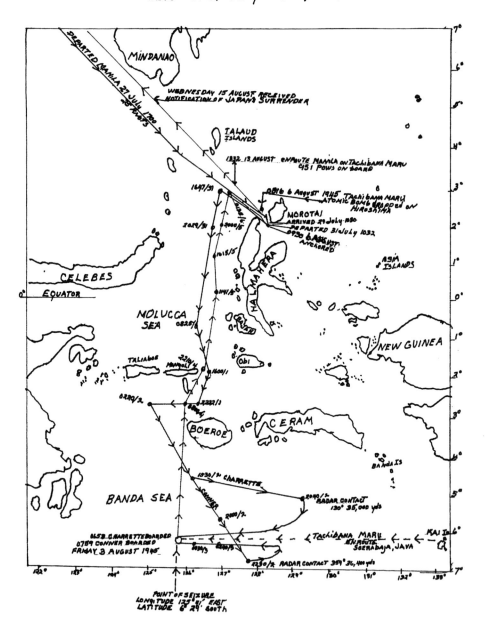

TRACK CHART OF USS CHARRETTE DD581 AND USS CONNER DD582
INTERCEPTION AND SEIZURE OF JAPANESE SHIP
TACHIBANA MARU 27 JULY TO 15 AUGUST 1945

MINDANAO

DEPARTED MANILA 27 JULY 1700
w/ TROOPS

WEDNESDAY 15 AUGUST RECEIVED
NOTIFICATION OF JAPAN'S SURRENDER

TALAUD
ISLANDS

1332 13 AUGUST ENROUTE MANILA ON TACHIBANA MARU
451 POWS ON BOARD

1647/31

0816 6 AUGUST 1945 TACHIBANA MARU
ATOMIC BOMB DROPPED ON
HIROSHIMA

MOROTAI
ARRIVED 29 JULY 1830
DEPARTED 31 JULY 1032
0930 6 AUGUST ANCHORED

2029/31   2000/5

ASIA
ISLANDS

1618/5

CELEBES
0°   EQUATOR   HALMAHERA

0940/6

MOLUCCA
SEA   0825/1

GEBE

NEW GUINEA

TALIABOE   2300/1
MANGOLI 4
1600/1   Obi

0220/2   0222/1

BOEROE   CERAM

BANDA IS

1530/2 CHARRETTE

CONNER   2040/2
RADAR CONTACT
130° 35,000 yds

BANDA SEA   2000/2

0453 CHARRETTE BOARDED
0759 CONNER BOARDED
FRIDAY 3 AUGUST 1945

TACHIBANA MARU
ENROUTE
SOERABAJA, JAVA

KAI IS

0300/3   0400/3

0230/2 RADAR CONTACT 359° 36,400 yds

POINT OF SEIZURE
LONGITUDE 125° 41' EAST
LATITUDE 6° 24' SOUTH

TWO UNIQUE EVENTS OF WWII
OCCURRED AT THE SAME TIME

1-DROPPING OF FIRST ATOMIC BOMB ON HIROSHIMA

2-SEIZURE OF THE TACHIBANA MARU, A JAPANESE SHIP CARRYING 1,653 HEALTHY
COMBAT TROOPS

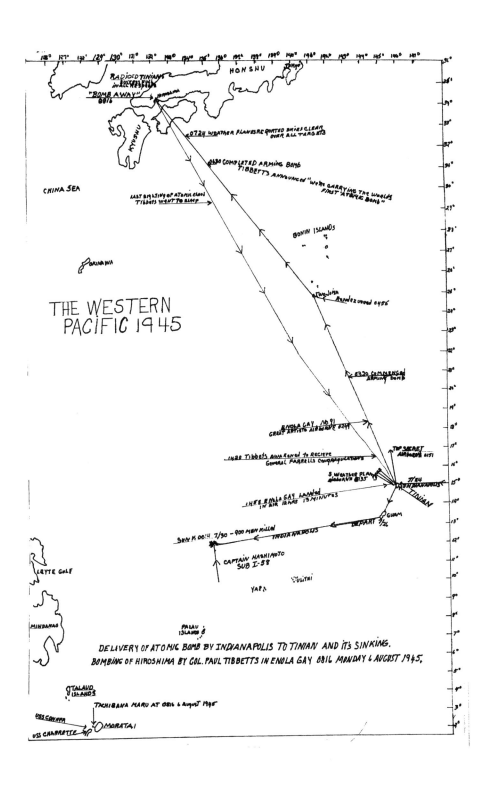

THE WESTERN
PACIFIC 1945

HONSHU

RADIOED TINIAN
in code 9:15 AM
"BOMB AWAY" 0816
0724 WEATHER PLANES REPORTED SKIES CLEAR
OVER ALL TARGETS
0630 COMPLETED ARMING BOMB
TIBBETTS ANNOUNCED "WE'RE CARRYING THE WORLD'S
FIRST ATOMIC BOMB"
LAST SIGHTING OF ATOMIC CLOUD
TIBBETS WENT TO SLEEP

HIROSHIMA
KYUSHU

CHINA SEA

OKINAWA

BONIN ISLANDS

TWO JIMA
Rendezvoued 0456

0320 COMMENCED
ARMING BOMB

ENOLA GAY No 91
GREAT ARTISTE AIRBORNE 0247

1420 Tibbetts AWAKENED TO RECIEVE
General FARRELLS CONGRADULATIONS

TOP SECRET
AIRBORNE 0151

3 WEATHER PLANES
AIRBORNE 0135

7/24
INDIANAPOLIS

TINIAN

1458 ENOLA GAY Landed
IN AIR 12HRS 13 MINUTES

SUN K 00:14 7/30 - 900 MEN Killed
INDIANAPOLIS

GUAM
DEPART 7/26

LEYTE GULF

CAPTAIN HASHIMOTO
SUB I-58

ULITHI

YAP

MINDANAO

PALAU
ISLANDS

DELIVERY OF ATOMIC BOMB BY INDIANAPOLIS TO TINIAN AND IT'S SINKING.
BOMBING OF HIROSHIMA BY COL. PAUL TIBBETTS IN ENOLA GAY 0816 MONDAY 6 AUGUST 1945.

TALAUD
ISLANDS

TACHIBANA MARU AT 0816 6 AUGUST 1945

USS CONNER
USS CHARRETTE

MORATAI

Marines attached to USS Charette.

Our discussion was halted with the sound of a rifle shot. We waited for the cries and fusillade to follow. Instead, absolute silence! Running out to investigate and scampering down the ladder, I pushed my way through a group of men gathered around the engine room hatch. A red-faced, stammering seaman was attempting to explain how his rifle had gone off, all by itself!

There was no respite from fear. The questions haunting us were still unanswered. How long could our 80-man boarding party successfully control the 1,562 POW's? Why had they offered no resistance when we boarded the ship? Why had they remained so docile? More importantly, what was concealed under the pallets?

From my vantage point on the bridge, I could see the comforting silhouettes of the two accompanying destroyers. Pete came over and said, "Well, Mr. Exec, maybe we can relax."

"Everything is relative, Captain. There will be little sleep for anyone. We'll be watching the Japs and they'll be watching us."

The dawn of Saturday, 4 August, was greeted with brightening spirits. The creaking timbers sighed with relief. The formation changed course to 045 degrees. I heard the voice of Chief Boatswain's Mate Lewis Kelly, alias Scharpie, saying, "What's this mess you call chow? Ain't you got any imagination? If you're interested in our health, you'll let me sell you this Hawaiian doodle bug, which is guaranteed to catch fish." Harvey, the chief cook, laughingly replied, "You wouldn't know the difference between fish and seaweed. You're getting scrambled turkey eggs for breakfast and you just ain't used to eating high class food." Breakfast wasn't the Waldorf's delight, but the men were gulping it down with little comment.

I asked Gillick, "How are things going below decks?" Swallowing, he replied, "For the moment, too good. The men are getting over their initial fear and I sense a let down. They can't believe these pathetic, bedraggled specimens of humanity are the same ones we've been fighting for 4 years. Wish I could tell them about the human bombs, torches and Banzai charges at Guadalcanal. Death before dishonor and capture. I've got to keep them alert. Any guy who slacks off has got to be disciplined. Our lives are at stake."

"What's your plan for today?"

"I'm going to take working parties into the holes and open up the rest of the boxes. That'll keep them busy and the findings may impress them."

I took a turn around the ship. One group of men was scrubbing down the decks, others working on the lines, and the ever-vigilant guards were at their stations. I sat for a moment on the rusty old anchor on the bow. With the sun beaming brightly, a 4 to 6 knot breeze out of the east, and a gentle roll to the ship, it was hard to realize how tenuous life was. I had feared, hated and despised the Japanese. With a shipload full of them, it seemed different. I shook off the feeling of pity and complacency. If I couldn't maintain vigilance, how could I expect the men to?

The tensions were relieved by the dispatches from the Commodore. Even Peterson, Annapolis Class of 1940, appreciated the humor. At 1230 he smiled as he read the dispatch, "Rig line aft. Have working party stand by to receive provisions." Grimacing he commented, "All we've got on this tub is an 80-man working party. The Commodore must think we're on a yachting cruise. I'm just waiting for him to order us to shift into the uniform of the day."

I went to the wardroom and told Pfc. James McNamara to have the young medical officer come out. He spoke fair English and I asked, "How long have you been on this ship?"

"I came aboard on 17 December, 1944, in Manila. Previously I served 3 years on Army troop ships. The Tachibana Maru has made trips between Saigon, Takeo, Java, Singapore, Celebes, Sumatra and other Japanese-occupied islands in the southeast."

"How many doctors are on board?"

"Two others and 33 medical corpsmen. The senior doctor had one year of internship with no other training. The youngest has recently been inducted into the Army and is still in an apprentice status."

Lt. Cmdr. Ernest R. Peterson USN—Prize Master, Executive officer of Charrette

"And what is your training?"

With obvious pride, he said, "I am an EENT specialist and have had one year of postgraduate training. I have the roster of all of the patients, if you are interested." Handing me several sheets of paper, I read the name and diagnosis for each patient. There were 40 different diagnoses, including 550 cases of Beriberi, 400 of malaria, 60 with pulmonary tuberculosis and a variety of others, such as 4 with kidney stones, 6 with sciatica, 4 with hemorrhoids, 8 with chronic appendicitis, 7 with prolapse of the rectum and 11 with neurasthenia. Thanking him, I went to the bridge to report my findings to Peterson. Reading the roster, Ed exclaimed, "Somebody had one hell of an imagination putting that list together."

After chatting briefly with Peterson, I went aft to check on Cook Harvey. He smilingly said, "See that pile of cans? Each one contains the same thing. We're going to have turkey a la king in ways never tried before and probably won't be again. Before we disembark, those fish heads and rice are going to look appetizing."

1,000 miles to the north on Tinian, Colonel Paul Tibbets, pilot of the B-29 Enola Gay was briefing the crews of the other B-29's on their bombing mission to Japan. There were three potential targets, with Hiroshima being primary. Intelligence reported fewer American POW's in that area and more military industrial targets. If Hiroshima were socked in, he would bomb either Kokura or Nagasaki. If he failed to complete the mission, Captain Charles McKnight in Top Secret on Iwo Jima would pick up the other bomb and carry out the plan. The crews were shown pictures of a similar bomb explosion and were told there would probably be a mushroom cloud rising anywhere from 30,000 to 60,000 feet.

My reverie ended when Sgt. Gillick reported, "One of the Japanese doctors is trying to stir up trouble. He is insisting on death before dishonor and is trying to get the others to riot. He is waving his arms, clenching his fists and has the attention of everyone in the wardroom."

"Tell the guards to get him out of there and put him into one of the small cabins. We'll transfer him to a destroyer as soon as possible."

With the sinking of the sun, fear returned. The seas picked up, the creaking timbers became louder and the rats bolder. Speculation about what was under the pallets continued.

On Sunday 5 August, the wind freshened. The swells grew increasingly higher and the ship rolled and pitched in the deep troughs. The chasing of the bold rats, the cats and the monkeys kept us fully occupied. In between inspections, Peterson and I speculated on the future. "This time next month, I'm supposed to be a freshman medical student. I put in an application when the war ended in Europe. Never thought I had a chance, but I was accepted. Classes start in 3 weeks. Maybe I ought to stay in the Navy. You don't suppose those Japs are waiting until we get close to shore before they attack? They might stand a chance of getting away alive."

"I'm not worried. Those guys are just too damn seasick to think about escaping. My future is fixed. Another ship on another ocean, but hopefully no more wars."

At 1100 came the familiar signal, "Have working party ready to receive supplies on the starboard quarter." During the transfer, a line on the breeches buoy snapped and cracked like a 20mm cannon. The loose end hit Dr. Cartall in the chest and knocked him on his back. Momentarily, he didn't breath. I opened his shirt. There were no signs of any injury. "You're okay," I said. "You've had the wind knocked out of you." He got up slowly, explored the area on his chest and smiled with relief.

When the transfer of supplies was completed, Dr. Cartall and the Japanese officer trying to foment trouble were sent to the Charrette.

The wind died down at dusk and the sea became placid. The men seemed more reflective and tense. There were no small groups engaged in conversation. The ship had the air of a hearse. The closeness of the shore brought the much-welcomed heavy fragrance of the tropics. It was a South Pacific night with the Southern Cross hanging low on the horizon and a faint sliver of a moon trying to stay aloft. Nature was outdoing herself in radiant magnificence. There could never be another night like this and might not be.

My tours of the ship revealed nothing unusual. The engines continued to complain. Men with a common purpose fought the valves. The end of the line at the head was still not in sight. A few unfamiliar monkeys and rats put in an appearance. None of our men were asleep. Only the Japs seemed relaxed.

At midnight on Tinian, the crews were fed. Colonel Tibbets had told them that weather-wise, it would be a good day for the mission. They'd be flying at 30,000 feet and should be over their target by 0800. Paul Tibbets, before climbing into his cockpit, touched the small metal box in his pocket containing 12 capsules. Each had a lethal dose of cyanide. At the first sign of trouble, he was to distribute them. No one was to be captured alive. At 0242, Tibbets became airborne. His flight was uneventful. At 0630 the bombardier reported, "The bomb is armed. No problem so far." Tibbetts then announced over the intercom that they were carrying an atomic bomb, a first. It's destructive power was greater than 20,000 tons of TNT. President Truman believed it would force Japan to surrender. Tibbits said, "Keep a smile on your face. The photographers on board are going to record your reactions for posterity."

On Monday 6 August 1945 the sun cast its first rays on a group of dirty, unshaven, foul-smelling sailors looking like beach bums. The day which we thought would never come had arrived. Morotai was sighted at 0805 just as the navigator on the Enola Gay announced, "Ten minutes to drop point."

At 0815:17, as the Tachibana Maru approached the harbor entrance, the bombardier on the Enola Gay announced, "Bomb away." At 0816 there was a blinding flash which spread from one horizon to the other. There was no noise at ground center, where the temperature was estimated to be 6,000 degrees centigrade. A mushroom cloud ascended and the plane rocked. There were tornado-type winds. It was Dante's inferno. Out of a population of 240,000, 78,150 were killed, 37,425 wounded and 13,983 missing. Out of the 90,000 buildings, 62,000 were destroyed. Few identifiable landmarks were left, and planet earth would never be the same.

At 0830 the Charrette signaled, "Super bomb of immense power dropped on Hiroshima. May result in peace talks. Don't tell the prisoners." There was little reaction to the announcement. All of us were too exhausted to care. War over? War was a way of life. The grown-up world we had entered consisted of the peace of living with war. The bomb only added to the hazards. We had adjusted to the uncertainty of life. Now we were haunted with the specter of death. What if the Japs rioted as we entered Morotai Harbor with them not even knowing of The Bomb?

At 0925 the Tachibana Maru was anchored in Berth C-21.

At Hiroshima Captain Mitsuo Fuchida, leader of the attack on Pearl Harbor, was returning in a Navy bomber. He saw a large cloud, huge fires and debris. After he landed, all he remembered was coming face to face with "A procession of people who seemed to have come out of Hell."

At 1358, when the Enola Gay touched down on Tinian, thousands lined the field. There was loud cheering as Tibetts led his crew through the hatch.

Taschibana Maru entering Morotai Harbor at 8:16 August 6, 1945. The precise momment when the atomic bomb is exploding over Hiroshima Japan.

The Tachibana Maru moved to the Navy Pier at 1545. Several thousand troops lined up on either side of the dock with rifles at ready waiting to relieve us of the POW's. It looked like the entire 93rd Division of the US Army under Major General Johnson was on hand and the 13th Airforce commanded by Colonel Troop Miller.

Taunts were flung at the armed men: "Where's MacArthur? Looks like you've got everyone else here." "Just like always. We do the work and you get the glory."

"How ironic," I thought. "80 had lived with the 1,562 prisoners. With the Army taking over, several thousand men were required." As much as I sympathized with my men, I didn't want to have an inter-service war. I yelled, "The next feller that opens his mouth is going to get a court martial."

The Japanese made a pathetic picture as they shuffled down the gangway with their shoes tied around their necks and hands over their heads. Their faces were expressionless and their heads bowed.

After the last POW disembarked at 1900, I heard Gillick's loud cursing. Peterson and I ran to the compartment. The sergeant was standing in the passageway with a mounting pile of pistols, bayonets and grenades being passed from under the pallets where the POW's had been sleeping. Gillick was pointing and muttering, "They could have blown us all to hell and back. I don't get it. 4 years of fighting these SOB's. They never did nothing like this before. Why?" And he looked around as if to find the answer. We were dumbfounded and silent. Peterson said, "Just stack the weapons up on the fantail. We'll inventory them tomorrow. Tonight all of us are going to get a shower, have a hot meal and get a good night's sleep in our own bunks."

When the final inventory was completed, we found 30 tons of assorted ammunition, including 8cm field howitzer shells, knee mortar projectiles, hand grenades and rifle and machine gun ammunition. Also, 400 hundred rifles,15 light machine guns, 45 knee mortars and four 8cm field howitzers.

A messenger came up, "The Commodore wants you to know the island is swarming with reporters. He told them they can take all the pictures they want, but there will be no interviews until tomorrow. You are to cooperate with them to the best of your ability. Answer all questions except those involving confidential or secret information."

On Tuesday morning, 7 August, the boarding party looked as though they had been on leave. Food, rest, fresh uniforms and a shave made a remarkable difference. Photographers and reporters from national wire services and major magazines such as Life and Time were everywhere. This was an unprecedented story! The capture of a Japanese ship with the largest number of able-bodied Japanese troops ever taken prisoner during the war, with no casualties! The American public and the world needed to know at once! It didn't happen. The headlines and lead stories screamed, "World's First Atomic Bomb Dropped on Hiroshima". The capture of the Tachibana Maru was relegated to a supporting role.

Then the roof caved in. "The Commodore wants to see you on the dock," a messenger said.

"You wanted to see me?" I asked, noting he was surrounded by a group of high ranking Army and Navy officers. Taking me to one side he said, "Lieutenant, I want you to have your men clean Tachibana Maru from stem to stern. I want it to be in good shape when we turn it

August 7, 1945 on bridge of Taschibana Maru—Photo taken by *Life Magazine* photographer.

over to Com 7th Fleet." I was momentarily stunned! He's crazy I thought.

After I recovered, I said, "You don't mean that, sir! These men have been living on this stinking ship for 4 days and they need rest and a little time off. There are plenty of men around here sitting on their butts doing nothing. Why can't they do it?" His face reddened and his jaws clenched as he snarled, "Lieutenant, I didn't ask your opinion and don't need it. Do you intend to carry out my orders or not?"

"Sir, I have a responsibility to my men. If an order is unreasonable, I have a duty to point it out." He interrupted, "You are insolent! I should have you court martialed. Carry out my order and don't let me hear any more of your lip. In addition, have all swords and other souvenirs placed in the wardroom where I can inspect them. I'll hold you personally responsible."

"Yes, sir," I replied and turned away. Without much enthusiasm, I mustered the men on the fantail and passed on the Commodore's orders. The bitching started. "Remember, fellows," I said, "This is the Navy. 'Ours not to question why, ours but to do or die.' Think positive! You may discover hidden treasure. I won't tell, if you don't."

When I returned to the Conner, I reported my confrontation with the Commodore to Sissons. "Just forget it, Harold. Everybody is a little tense."

On 8 August the news reported that the Japanese government was willing to surrender with conditions. This was unacceptable to the Allies. The war continued and the ship-cleaning proceeded. Spirits improved when working parties showed up from both the Charrette and Conner. My fight with the Commodore came to a head when I heard he was giving Samurai swords and other mementos to several high ranking officers. I searched him out. "Commodore! May I ask, sir, what your plans are for the swords and other mementos? I understand you have given them as presents to several officers."

He glared and snapped, "And what business is that of yours? I have had about all I can take of your arrogance."

"I am sorry," I replied. "I have no desire to anger you, sir. My men boarded that ship and brought it into port with 1,562 Jap prisoners. They are due some consideration." His face flushed, his fists clinched and he shouted with his face stuck into mine, "You are finished! You have absolutely no respect for senior officers. I'm going to speak with your Captain and have you disciplined! You should be court martialed." He stalked away.

When I returned to the Conner, Sissons called me to his cabin, "Sorry, Harold, I know how you feel, but the Commodore means business and insists you be disciplined."

"I agree. You are a career officer and I'm getting out as soon as I can. My only fights with the Navy brass have been when I tried to protect my men. You've got to stay on the good side of that SOB. He writes up your fitness reports. I suggest you confine me to the ship."

"I hate to do it. I have no choice. As of now, you are restricted to the ship for liberty purposes. Continue with your regular work activities. I don't want the men to hear of this. It will not be placed in the log, but I will notify the Commodore."

The next morning, Thursday 9 August, the cleaning continued. I spent lunch on the Conner. Finishing my paperwork, I heard cries and cheering, "The war is over! The war is over!" The radio man had received a message in plain English: "An atomic bomb was dropped on the city of Nagasaki this morning. Peace talks are under way!" Bedlam reigned on the deck for over an hour. The primary target was Kokura, but Major Charles Sweeney could not identify the aiming point through the clouds and flew on to the secondary target, Nagasaki. 35,000 were killed, 5,000 missing and 6,000 severely wounded.

Adding to our elation was news reporting that Russian troops had invaded Manchuria. There was nothing official, but everyone believed the war was over. Even though it was a little premature, two thirds of the officers and the crew were given liberty to celebrate.

The Japanese Supreme Council deliberated all day. The civilian members and the Navy Minister, Admiral Misumasa Yonai, argued that the Potsdam Proclamation should be accepted, but the military wanted to fight to the bitter end. No decision could be reached. Premier Zuzuki called in Emperor Hirohito to break the impasse. Foreign Minister Togo said he believed the terms of the Potsdam Proclamation should be accepted provided the Allied demands did not "prejudice the prerogatives of His Majesty as a Sovereign Ruler." At 2am on 10 August, Hirohito stated, "I am in complete accord with Minister Togo," and left the room.

Standing alone on the bridge while the Japanese were debating, I reflected on my Navy experiences. My first exposure to combat was with the British Home Fleet at Scapa Flow in February 1942, my last with the Australian Navy at Borneo. This was a sad climax: being the assistant prizemaster of the Tachibana Maru in "hack" and disgrace. Turning to the bridge radio, which I didn't know was live or on tape, I heard the announcers describing the hilarious celebrations in Times Square, the Chicago Loop and San Francisco's Market Street. On the beach I could see and hear the loud merry making, the constant barrage of flares, fireworks and gunfire. The sounds of the radio and beach merged into one. The whole world was engaged in revelry. I had never felt so lonely and deserted in my entire life as I pleaded, "My God! My God! Why hast thou forsaken me?" Little did I know....

Japanese troops sqeezed into compartment.

Unloading Japanese prisoners on deck at Morotai August 6, 1945.

Unloading prisoners on deck August 6, 1945.

Contraband found in boxes on Tachibana Maru.

-

CHAPTER 19

"It's the orders you disobey that make you famous."
General Douglas MacArthur

When we returned to the Tachibana Maru the next morning, I supervised the cleaning. The Commodore and I established an uneasy truce. He sent his orders by a staff member and I carried them out.

Truman accepted the Japanese terms and drafted a reply stating that from the moment of surrender, the Emperor and his government would be under the authority of the Supreme Allied Commander. When approval for Truman's reply was requested from the Allies, only the Russians were skeptical. Molotov stated they would continue fighting in Manchuria, which was not satisfactory to Truman. After more haggling, the Russians agreed to the terms and the dispatch was sent.

When I returned to the Conner at 1600 I said to Sissons, "One day of grace. I had no confrontation with the Commodore and I'm thankful. I don't want my problems rubbing off on you."

"I'm not concerned. It's part of life. I understand why you were upset with the order to clean up the ship, followed by the Commodore's giving the swords to senior officers. I don't blame you for blowing your stack. You were protecting your men. But! This is the Navy and you carry out orders, like them or not."

"True, but every time he sees me, he's going to get mad all over again. When he writes your fitness report, he'll take it out on you. This war is about over. I've been accepted into medical school. School starts next month and the Navy doesn't need me."

"Let's just forget it for now and play it by ear. I put on your last fitness report that you are qualified for a destroyer command. I'm not backing down, Commodore or no Commodore. I'm beginning to believe you've got a higher authority on your side and you will make medical school. What about marriage and the future?"

"I've finally found the girl, if she'll have me. I want to find out if medicine is what I want to do before I settle down. That'll take at least one year."

"How did you decide on this girl?"

"Fate played a big part. I had dated her before the war and she keep showing up every time I went on leave, even though we only spoke and never dated until just this year."

"There was more to it than just that."

"Yes, there was. I desired that each of us begin life on a level playing field."

"Now what in the hell is that suppose to mean?" Sissons exclaimed.

"Genetically speaking, that is. My family has been successful as far back as I have been able to trace. Lil Hair's has also. Her father was a dentist and President of the SC Dental Association. On her mother's side, her grandfather founded Pearce-Young-Angel, one of the largest wholesale food distributors in the southeast. All Lil and I have to do is provide the right environment for our children to be productive, happy leaders. Don't you agree?"

"You're way ahead of me. My best wishes to you and all those children."

The men searched the trash for intelligence material, and the most useful information was sent by air to Com7thFlt. Less important stuff was kept on board. At the completion, 200 truckloads of trash was unloaded and burned.

When I finished my work, I went to the officer's club and refought the war with present and past shipmates. The enigma of why 1,562 armed combat veterans remained docile was discussed ad infinitum. Wyatt suggested, "To ride through the pearly gates and hear the heavenly choir singing, you have to be mentally alert. These guys were so seasick, they wouldn't have known if they were in Heaven or Hell, whether God was welcoming them or the Devil."

On 11 August the Conner was underway for Manila with the transport Yochow, with 700 of the POW's on board. During my patrols, it appeared that the POW's were contented. Since we knew they didn't have any weapons, everyone was more relaxed. 951 POW's were loaded onto the Tachibana Maru and at midday, the ship was underway with the Charette headed for Manila.

Truman's dispatch was not received in Tokyo until 0100 of 13 August. A group of hard-line Japanese Army officers were planning to mount a coup and intended to seize Hirohito, whom they believed had been misled by evil advisors. The demand that the ultimate form of government should be decided by free elections did not guarantee the position of the Emperor and widened the gulf between the military and civilian factions.

In Japan, with no movement toward peace being made, Hirohito called the first Imperial Conference since the war began. Ordering acceptance of the Allied terms made the meeting highly emotional with much weeping. Late that night, the Emperor prepared a recording to be broadcast to the Japanese people so they would acknowledge the surrender. The rebellious junior officers, realizing their only chance of success was to destroy the disk before the message was broadcast, stormed the palace, killing the Commandant of the Imperial Guards and sealing off the Palace. They searched the Household Ministry, but found nothing. Other conspirators seized local radio stations and searched for Prime Minister Suzuki and Marquis Koiichi Kido, believing they had advised the Emperor to surrender. General Shizuichi Tanaka, Commander of the Eastern Military District, learning of the revolt, went to the Palace and ordered the troops back to their barracks. He reminded them it was their duty to commit suicide rather than surrender. Many did.

Hirohito was asleep during the chaos. The unprecedented recording was broadcast at 1110 local time. The Japanese people were in tears when they heard the Emperor's voice for the first time. There were scattered acts of defiance, but the vast majority laid down their weapons.

At 0805 Wednesday 15 August 1945 the Charrette signaled: "President Truman has announced that the war is over. Peace has been declared. Don't tell the prisoners."

The few cheers were barely audible. The talk was of home, their goals and fears. On the bridge I encountered another heated debated. Should the bomb have been dropped, killing so many innocent women and children? Was it a humane act? Was it morally right? The war was won without it. Peterson was adamant, "Without the bombs, the loss of lives would have been in the millions. They're still hiding out on some of the islands. The suffering is indescribable. With the larger population on the home islands, it would have been horrible. The agony and deaths is beyond imagining."

The formation arrived in Manila Harbor on Friday 17 August, and barges relieved us of the POW's. Com7thFlt ordered us to remain on board.

In Japan, a new government under Prince Toshihiko Higahikuni was being formed.

Mail arrived! My father's letter was the big news. I let out a yell. "Just listen to this, fellers! My place in the freshman class at medical school is being held. The Dean has told my father it's mine whenever I arrive. Ain't that something?"

Later when Bill and I were alone, he said. "I'm going to be asked for recommendations for awards for the boarding party. What are your thoughts?"

"Only a couple. Peterson is entitled to the Navy Cross and the men some sort of blanket recognition. No event of this magnitude occurred in 4 years of war. The only Japanese ship captured. The largest number of armed combat troops taken by the Navy, and without a casualty! And all of this in Japanese- held territory. My getting into medical school is all the reward I want or need."

When I arrived at the Conner the next day, I was greeted by an excited OOD. "We received an AlPAC dispatch this morning, and the Captain wants to see you immediately."

"What's up?" I asked Bill.

"Take a look at this," and handed me a dispatch I read with astonishment and joy. Commanding officers of all ships were authorized to discharge up to 10% of their deserving personnel for reassignment. This was to alleviate the logistical problems when all reservists were released from active duty. With my heart pounding, I asked, "What's your reaction?" Laughingly he said, "It may be a way out for you and for me. Orders for executive officers come directly from the Bureau, but it doesn't say I can't."

"I agree. If the Bureau didn't want you to have the authority, they would have said so. Wow! Just think, the Commodore won't have me to look at anymore. More importantly, you'll get a fair shake and I won't be an anchor around your neck." Bill scratched his head, twirled his glasses in his hand and after what seemed like eternity, said, "I'm going to do it. Not because of you and the Commodore! I don't give a damn about him. You've seen this war through from the beginning to the end, and few have experienced what you have. If you aren't deserving, there ain't a cow in Texas. Get your things ready. I'm not going to ask anybody. I am the Captain."

I could only say, "Thanks."

Although I hadn't been officially relieved of my duties on the Tachibana Maru, I began briefing Bob Austin, who would be my relief. Getting a box, I made off to pack my belongings.

On Sunday, 19 August, US and Japanese delegations were meeting in Manila to arrange the Allied occupation of Japan. I wrote Lil, "...I haven't been able to do much writing recently. You possibly saw in the paper where a Jap hospital ship was boarded, taken over and brought back into port about two weeks ago. I was in the party and have been playing nursemaid to about 1,600 Japanese troops...I'm still on the ship, but the Japs aren't...They were packed in like sardines. Supposedly they were sick and wounded, but out of the 1,600 men, only about 15 could be classified as patients...After we got them off the ship, we discovered they were lying on hand grenades, rifles, ammunition and other weapons of war...All of this happened before the peace negotiations began...It was an exciting experience. I'll tell you all about it when I see you...

"Last night the Captain and I talked until 2am...He's going to recommend me for a discharge and transfer me...I'll have to go to Pearl Harbor first....Under the present point system, I might have 2 more years to serve...If I'd gotten married, I'd be on my way. Why didn't I?

"Probably best for you not to write for a while until I know where I'll be...I heard from my father who said, 'Lil did an exceptionally good job in the play...she was head and shoulders above everyone else.' Now don't get swell- headed on me. I am very proud of you. Keep it up.

"Haven't seen Herbert as yet. I've had little liberty time since 1 August... When are you going to take up piano again? If you're going to create the beautiful atmosphere with soft lights and song, you're going to have to furnish the music...You're going to get courted in style, so prepare for it..."

Admiral Kincaid notified Peterson that his staff would inspect the Tachibana Maru on the morning of 20 August. After their inspection and the ceremonial procedures, the ship was officially turned over to Com7th Fleet. As we were mingling around the quarter-deck saying our good-byes, Peterson said, "Men, many of us will never see each other again. I am going to ask Simmons to say a farewell prayer." After we removed our hats and bowed our heads, with several of us holding hands, Simmons began, "Lord, we thank you for guiding and keeping us safe through the greatest conflict of our lives and of the 20th century. We ask you to glorify those who made the supreme sacrifice to keep our nation free. Let them never be forgotten. Let us ever be mindful that you have been our Captain as we sailed through violent storms and battles, in the end leading us to victory at sea. As we go our separate ways, let us continue to accept you as our leader so this world will be a better place for our having passed through, and victory will always be ours through you."

When we were alone, Peterson said, "What a climax to 4 years of war. Hemingway couldn't have dreamed up this ending. I wonder what awards will be given out?"

"For me, it's an honorable discharge. You ought to get the Navy Cross and every one of the prize crew should get some recognition."[74]

I resumed my regular duties on board the Conner at 1915 Tuesday 21 August 1945. After I completed my packing and after lengthy bull sessions with the men, I wrote Lil at 2300, "I've been detached and will be on my way to Pearl tomorrow...Don't know what the future holds, but I'll keep you posted...Don't write until I can give you a mailing address...Got a lot of work to do tonight..."

In the morning the yeoman handed me my orders:

ORDERS 22 August 1945 USS Conner DD 582
    Ref (a) ALPAC 140-45

-1- In accordance with Ref(a), you are detached from duty as executive officer on board this vessel and from such other duties you may have been assigned. You will proceed via first available transportation and report to Command Service Force Pacific Fleet for further orders.

With mixed emotions, I went to the bridge and said, "Bill, it's till we meet again for now. I'll never forget you. I wish you well in your Navy career, and I hope the day will come when I can repay you for your many kindnesses to me."

Putting his arm around my shoulder he replied, "You owe me only one thing, Harold: be a good doctor. You have the ability. Your only weakness has been caring too much for your men. You've picked the right profession. You'll be an outstanding doctor. I look forward to seeing you again. God bless."

I went to the quarter-deck, saluted the flag and OOD John Hanson and said, "Request permission to leave the ship, sir."

"Permission granted."

At 0500 Wednesday 22 August, 1945, as the whale boat pulled away, I waved to the officers and crew who lined the rail. My eyes misted. A new life lay ahead. At 0647 the Conner was underway for Subic Bay.

I had a pleasant surprise when I reported to the transportation office and saw my former yeoman from the Dortch. "Harry Dunbar!" I exclaimed. "It's good to see you again. How is the world treating you?"

"Couldn't be better. I like this shore duty." We swapped stories and I showed him my orders. He shook his head, saying, "Sir, we may have a problem. All surface transportation east is filled with the wounded and prisoners of war. There's no way I can get you out of here for weeks."

After I explained to him that medical school was starting, he scratched his head and replied, "There's one thing I can do. Do you object to flying?"

"Hell, no!"

"Nobody's going to say anything if I fix you up with a Class 3 priority on NATS. Your baggage will be limited to 55 pounds. The rest of your stuff will get there whenever. How does that sound?"

"That's great! But I don't want you getting into any trouble because of me."

"Have no fear. I can take care of myself."

After he wrote up my orders and arranged transportation to the Naval Air Station, I was soon in my assigned BOQ quarters. I called Don and asked if he had any more information on Herbert. "I've found him, and he's stationed close to you." I went to his company's quarters and we had a wonderful time sharing stories. Before I left, I said, "My flight doesn't leave for two days. Let's do some sight-seeing and night-clubbing." We did.

As I was parting on the night of 24 August, Herbert said, "I'm happy for you. I'll be following shortly. Give the folks my love."

The next morning I was at the dock with my heart pounding as I climbed aboard the PB4Y. After an eternity, everyone was seated and

Lt. Herbert V. Jervey (my brother).

the plane roared down Manila Bay for our take-off. To my dismay, the Captain cut the engines and over the PA announced, "We've got a problem with one engine. I can make it on 3, but it wouldn't be the smart thing to do. I'm going back to the dock. Shouldn't take long for a mechanic to get us ready to roll." I learned there was a policy: no take-offs after dark. It was going to be close. With the repairs completed, the plane again roared down the harbor just as the sun was sinking in the west. There were loud hurrahs and clapping of hands as the PB4Y slowly left the water and lifted into the air. The huge round orange ball in the west and the city of Manila below were beautiful sights.

After we reached our cruising altitude, snacks were served. My seat was uncomfortable and I began looking for somewhere to stretch out and relax. Finding a place in the tail with the luggage, I fell asleep. Immediately I was awakened by an apologetic crewman. "Sorry to disturb you, sir. The pilot says the tail is too heavy and we need to shift some weight forward."

"What a bummer," I thought. "For the first time in my life I am accused of weighing down a plane." I went forward and settled in my seat.

When we landed on Kwajalein to fuel, everyone got out to stretch their legs. Upon arrival at Pearl Harbor Saturday at 1900 26 August, I was assigned quarters in the BOQ. The duty officer noted my orders and said, "No action has been taken yet on officers with orders like yours. They're reporting in each day. I suggest you do the same."

The Houvners were glad to hear I was heading home to medical school. Audry was enjoying Stephens College and they assured me the door would be open and a bed available anytime I wanted to spend the night.

I wrote Lil on 28 August, "Things are looking pretty good, wouldn't you say?...Just swim, sun and take life easy...I am doing what is known as 'sweating it out'...When and if they give credit for overseas duty, I'll be on my way. Shouldn't be more than a couple of months.

Lil Hair.

"You must be just finishing up the summer session...With gas rationing off, we could take trips to the beach and have a great time...

"Saw Herbert and spent a couple of days with him...He's putting in 13-14 hour days and looks tired. We took in some of the night spots and did some sight seeing...Sorry to leave him. It was a let down for him...

"I've been catching up on 'Life' magazine...The bathing suits being worn this year are really something. Wow! Are you girls wearing those things at home? I've sure been missing something..."

On 31 August I wrote, "...This is the life...beach in the morning, bowling, playing pool or ping pong in the afternoon, usually movies at night...no entangling alliances with the fairer sex...

"I've run into many fellows I've known over the years. Right now I'm staying with a friendly group of guys who have nothing to do, just like me. We've been having a good time together. Sure hate to let these beautiful Hawaiian nights go to waste. You ought to be here, darling! We could do a powerful lot of courting under these skies...

"I have a hunch I'll be home for Christmas this year...we ought to spend this Christmas and New Year's together. Can't think of any better way to begin the year than with you in my arms.

"Tell me all about what you're doing. I am getting starved for news of you..."

On Saturday, 2 September, the talk in the lounge of the BOQ was of home and the surrender ceremonies which were to be broadcast. Officers were saying: "I've been waiting 4 years for this." "Seems like it's been forever." "I never thought I'd make it." At midday our ears were glued to the radio as the music was interrupted by the announcer saying, "I am broadcasting live from the deck of the USS Missouri in Tokyo Harbor. General Douglas MacArthur has just come aboard from the destroyer Buchanan." Chills ran up and down my spine! Containing my excitement was difficult as the announcer continued, "With MacArthur are Admirals Nimitz and Halsey. He also has at his side Lt. General Jonathan Wainwright and Lt. General Sir Archer E. Percival, both of whom have been prisoners since 1942. Both of these latter officers are emaciated and gaunt. I can just imagine the thoughts going through their minds. The Japanese delegation consists of Foreign Minister Memaru Sigimitsu and General Yoshiziro. The others I don't know by name but there are 3 representatives from the foreign office, Navy and Army."

As he described the signing ceremony, I wondered if any of my destroyers were present. My attention returned to the radio at the sound of MacArthur's voice. "It is my earnest hope—indeed the hope of all mankind—that from this solemn occasion, a better world shall emerge out of the blood and carnage of the past; a world founded upon faith and understanding. A world dedicated to the dignity of man and the fulfillment of his most cherished wish for freedom, tolerance and justice."

The announcer described the signing of the surrender papers and MacArthur concluded, "Let us pray that peace is now restored to the world; that God will preserve it always. These proceedings are now concluded."

"And that's how a war ends?" I thought! Not quite! The announcer said, "And now General MacArthur has some words for the American people." Again the deep resonant voice, "Today the guns are silent. A great tragedy has ended. A great victory has been won...A new era is upon us..."

Varying thoughts flooded my mind. I had goose bumps.

"Men since the beginning of time have sought peace. Various methods through the ages have been attempted. The utter destructiveness of war now blots out this alternative. The problem basically is theological and involves a spiritual recrudescence and improvement of the human character. Today freedom is on the offensive. Democracy is on the march. And so, my fellow countrymen, today I report to you that your sons and daughters have served you well and faithfully."

There was absolute silence. This was a unique and precious moment that could never be repeated or shared. Finally someone spoke up, "This is incredible. Here we are at Pearl, where it began. The irony of it all! On the one hand, these islands will be remembered for the war and the dead. And yet each of us will remember their beauty, the genuine friendliness and love these Hawaiians radiate, the aloha spirit. I feel covered by a blanket of peace. It's what MacArthur was talking about and what the whole world is praying for. These islands cast a magic spell over anyone who has ever been exposed to them. Would that I could bottle it and give it to all the nations of the world. Only then would we have peace for all men, for all time."

There was nothing to add. That night at the officer's club we philosophized on MacArthur's speech. "Do you really believe this was the war to end all wars?"

"I can give you two opinions," I replied. "One was given to me by a limey sailor at Scapa Flow just after the war began. He declared, 'There will always be wars. It's God's way of keeping this earth from becoming over-populated and using up all of its resources.' The other I heard at Borneo during the last amphibious landing of the war. An Aussie officer stated, 'As long as a minority of men are motivated by avarice and money, lust for power and a callous disregard for the feelings of others, so long as they exist, wars will continue.' The consensus from both sides of planet earth is that this will not be the last war and I agree."

My dreams were shattered when, as I reported in to the duty officer on Monday, 4 September, he said, "Your orders have arrived." With astonishment and anger I read:

Orders 4 September 1945
    From: ComServPacFlt
    To: Lt. Harold E. Jervey, Jr., DE USNR
    Subject: Change of Duty

-1- Report Com 14 for first available transportation to port where USS President Hayes APA may be. Upon arrival report to CO for duty as replacement for Lt. Cmdr. Clyde M. Braden, USNR.
-2- Travel via NATS Class 3 priority certified.

I was stunned and asked, "Who in the hell is responsible for these orders?"

"Commander Wilson is the staff officer responsible for making assignments."

I searched him out and exclaimed, "Commander, I only lack a couple of points of being eligible for a discharge. Scuttlebutt has been floating around for weeks that points for sea duty will be awarded at any time. I'll have far more than necessary when that happens. The war is over. The Navy doesn't need me."

He listened and quietly said, "Lieutenant, your skills are needed. The war is over, but the need for you isn't. Just simmer down. This will only be a short tour and you'll be home."

I knew medical college was out for now and perhaps forever. I drowned my sorrows at the bar ranting and raving about the callous, stupid asses running the navy. A friend slapped me on the back and exclaimed, "Don't give up the ship, ole buddy. Transportation is tight. It'll be at least a week before anything is available. Time enough for a miracle. Maybe the President Hayes will be blown up."

The next day I wrote Lil, "Seems I'm the Navy's most indispensable officer. It's wonderful to feel needed so much. I'm flying out of here for

Tokyo in a couple of days. A Lt. Cmdr. is sick and needs hospitalization, and, you guessed it, I'm his relief. My new address will be the USS President Hayes, one of the luxury liners of the pre-war days, now a troop transport. I'm supposed to be a chief engineer, but I'm going to be a sack time Charlie and a wardroom Joe...

"I did some fancy cussing, because only a few days ago I turned down an XO's job on a tin can going to the States. Nobody asked me about this one.

"When the Commander said, 'You'll be doing this other fellow a good turn because he needs medical care,' that calmed me down and resigned me to my fate. Some good is going to come of it for somebody. However, my sweet, I'll be home for Christmas even if I have to drive that ship overland.

"Got quite a lot of mail today, mostly from you. Spent yesterday at the beach. I'm getting so dark I'm beginning to look like a Hawaiian. Went to see 'Random Harvest' last night. It was wonderful and I'd like to talk with you about it when you ain't busy...

"Do you know what it is like to be so much in love that all you can do is think of your loved one? You just lose interest in everything and everybody, just as though a part of you is missing. Well, that's me! You beautiful thief, when you get through with my heart, please send it back. I need it!"

It was pool and cards the next day. That night, I wrote Lil, "The realization of how the years have passed just struck me as I was writing the date on this letter. It's unbelievable—1945! I've got a lot to make up for, and darling, you're going to be the one to help me. I haven't celebrated any of the momentous events of this past year. Will ya help me?

"Okay! First, we'll visit the moon for a short while. Then we'll go to the stars, every one of them (we couldn't slight any because they've been such good friends). By the time we finish our tour of the heavens, we'll be pretty old people. It'll take a lifetime to see everything. I'm going to pin you down to a yes or no answer.

"I'm going to phone you tomorrow. Don't know what we'll talk about. Probably won't get around to anything but 'How yah feeling and what yah doing' and other such dribble. Will be worthwhile just hearing your voice again.

"Saw 'The Clock' tonight. Somebody appropriated the pool balls so that's out for now. Today I ain't had nothing to do.

"The radio is playing a program of organ music, soft and beautiful. So many people are coming and going, it's very distracting. I can't listen too attentively...I keep forgetting you are sitting by me, and I must devote some time to you. I wish you'd snuggle up a little closer; that's better. And now put your head on my shoulder. It's wonderful just like this. Okay! I can dream, can't I?

"After glancing back over this letter, something I never do, I've come to the conclusion we both must be nuts! People are really amazing...ain't it great though? I feel just like a kid and hope that 50 years from now I feel the same way,[75] silly or no.

"Stand by! I hope to hear your voice tomorrow. We'll have 3 minutes to cover 6 months. I am very excited about it..."

I spent 3 hours the next day trying to get my call through to Lil. The stupid operator told me the number was not listed. I immediately wrote, "...It was partly my fault. I told the operator I only knew it had two '6's and two '8's', but I couldn't remember the order. Unfortunately your letter with that info is somewhere between here and Manila. Maybe it's best. I saved a few dollars. I'd be insulted if a person couldn't remember my phone number.

"Other than waiting by the phone, I checked on the mail, which didn't exist, and on my transportation out of this place. Couldn't play pool as the balls are still missing. I haven't been able to scrape up much competition at ping pong so I have given that up.

"How is your mother doing? How does she feel about this great romance between her daughter and myself? I've got to get on the good side of her...

"The scuttlebutt continues about extra points for sea duty...It'll happen when I'm about as far west as I can get...

"After my strenuous day, I'm going to turn it in and hope I hear from you tomorrow..."

The next night at the officer's club, I met Horace Marko, former gunnery officer on the Charrette. "What's with you?" I asked.

"Just got in from Manila. I'm here for reassignment. I've got some bad news for you. About a week after you left, 29 August to be exact, Sissons was returning from liberty, fell getting out of the whale boat and ruptured his spleen. He was taken immediately to the hospital, but he died before anything could be done. The Conner had to leave without him, and Bob Austin was put in command temporarily."

I was stunned. "My God, what a horrible tragedy! I can't believe it. He was one fine, decent guy and looked forward to making the Navy a career. I wouldn't be here tonight except for his caring about me. There's not a damn thing fair about this world. What happened to that all-loving God? Bill Sissons went through the entire war, didn't get a scratch. The war ends, he dies. There's something wrong with the system. Somebody, anybody, tell me why!" I buried my face in my hands.

Marko put his arm around my shoulder and said, "I wish I had an answer." I went to my room sobbing and finally fell asleep.

When I wrote Lil on 8 September, I said, "...Bad news comes in 3's. Just heard Bill Sissons died of a ruptured spleen about one week after I left the ship. One of the finest men I ever knew. There is no one I can even call to express my sympathy. His mother lives in Canada and I'm not certain where. What a horrible tragedy. I'm waiting for the second shoe to drop. Maybe it's my turn next.

"Spent all of yesterday at Kailua lying on the beach. They've got an excellent officer's club. There's plenty to drink (and I did), not much to eat (didn't want to anyway) and lots of sun. I'm turning a lovely shade of black."

"Ran into Hazel LaBorde. He lived around the corner from me in Columbia. We had a brief, but nice visit.

"...I haven't heard from you in ages. Have you dropped me from your list of correspondents? No, honey, I expect it's just the mail service...Sorry I told you to write to the President Hayes..."

In the morning the duty officer said, "You'll be flying out on NATS on the 11th. The President Hayes is still in Tokyo Harbor."

Good-bye, medical school and all of my dreams. Why me? My only option was to go AWOL, and with the closest land 2,500 miles away, that wasn't much of an alternative. Realization hit! Bill Sissons and thousands, millions of others were never going home. I was. So what was a couple of months?

My flight didn't leave until Tuesday and on Sunday morning, I was sunning by the pool, reading the paper and day-dreaming. Music was playing over the PA system. I went into the bath house to dress. I was going to Waikiki for one last visit. Suddenly the announcer broke in, "I have an important bulletin just issued by the Navy. As of today, credits toward discharge will be given for sea duty. One fourth point for each month of sea duty. I repeat..."

I let out a loud, "Yippee! I'm out! I'm out!" Others standing around in various stages of dress looked to see what the yelling was all about. "I'm supposed to be flying out to Tokyo on Tuesday. With points for sea duty, I've more than enough to get my discharge. I'm going to call ComServPac's duty officer right now and see about getting my orders changed."

The duty officer was sympathetic, but said, "I don't have the authority to change your orders. Commander Kirven is the senior officer today. Let me put you in touch with him." I explained to Kirven that if my orders weren't changed, I would have to give up the goal of medicine as a career. "I am on your team, Lieutenant. Get down here the first thing in the morning and I'll take care of your orders." I just uttered, "Thanks."

I wrote Lil, "Tonight you're talking to a civilian, or practically one. I feel happier than I have in years. This afternoon while I was in the bath house dressing..." I told her about the broadcast and wrote, "I'm going to be sent to Charleston, SC, for a discharge. Ain't that wonderful? I'm coming home for good!

"Probably can't make med school, but I'll take a couple of courses at the University. I'll be there for the football games, dances and those beautiful autumn nights. Will you spend a few of them with me? How about a date on October 1st...

"Don't try to write. It'll probably take me a week or so to get out of here. I'll call you from Frisco if I can get your phone number.

"I'm too excited to write anymore. There must be a good God who looks after fools like me.

"PS This place is a mad house. Everyone's figuring and recalculating their points. How many you got? I'm out! Quite a sight."

I reported in to ComSerPac's and received my orders:

<u>2nd Endorsement</u> 10 September 1945
   Subject: Change of duty.

1- Report to ComServPac this date for instructions. Your basic orders are canceled. Resume your duties in the Officers Pool.

The next day I wrote Lil, "...I'm still in a whirl...Got a letter from my father saying they were definitely expecting me for this class at med school. Just think! Two days ago I had given that up...today everything is going according to plan. It's not such a bad world, is it?

"My only black spot is none of your mail has gotten through. Everything is being sent to that ship. I'm burned up! It's a miracle the letter about med school slipped through...Fate again...

"Can't help but laugh. Some joker is conducting a music appreciation class at the other end of this room. Just came out with the statement that we'd appreciate music more if we knew something about the composer's life, such as Beethoven's father beat his mother; very interesting and enlightening.

"Tomorrow I'm going out to a Navy rest camp for a couple of days and take life easy. Got to get ready for that terrible grind. Think I can make the grade? I'll give it a good try.

"I'm spoiling you with all of these letters...You'll soon be getting the idea that I love you...and I do...

"PS My writing isn't improving, is it?"

I put in a call to my father and the operator said there would be a 6 hour delay. When I did get through, I said, "Dad, I'm coming home. I don't know how quickly. I'll be in that class. Tell them to hold my place."

I enjoyed the next couple of days until my new orders were issued.

ORDERS 13 September 1945
   From: ComServPacFlt
   To: Lt. Harold E. Jervey, Jr., DE USNR
  Subject: Change of Duty

-1- Proceed to Com14th Naval District by first available transportation to port on west coast of US. Report for temporary duty pending further assignment Chief of Naval Personnel.

My hopes for a quick return vanished when I discovered that there were hundreds of men with reasons just as urgent as mine who were trying to get to the States. I didn't know when, or if, I would ever return to these islands. I enjoyed my visits to Waikiki, Kialua and the Houvners and the farewell parties! I wore myself out.

On Tuesday morning, 25 September, I was on the bow of the Monssen DD 798 as Waikiki and Diamond Head glided by. I had mixed emotions. My eyes moistened as I thought back to my only experience as a passenger on a destroyer (the Stack) in Hamilton Harbor, Bermuda while I awaited the return of the Sterett. The Stack would never return. The wheel had come full circle. The voice of Lieutenant Steve Black interrupted my reverie. "What are you thinking? You seem lost to the world."

"The past, the present and the future." I wiped the tears off my face.

"Among other things, about the legend of the islands that if you throw your lei overboard as you past Diamond Head and it drifts ashore, you will some day return. I can't test the validity of that because I don't have a lei."

"Would you like to come back?"

"I will return, but like the thousands we're leaving behind buried in the sea and on those soon to be forgotten islands scattered all over the Pacific, part of me will always remain. This is 'Aloha' for me." I paused and continued, "I became a man out here, learned the value of life and the certainty of death. More importantly, I regained a part of my childhood's lost beliefs: there is a loving God who looks after each one of us. He is the Captain of our ship. All we need is faith no larger than a mustard seed."

"I agree," Steve responded. "And the irony is you will never be able to completely share this with the ones you love the most, only with the ones you have been with and may never see again."

As I took one last look and headed below deck, I added, "How long do you think it will take for me to forget everything I just said?"

"Never."

The conversation in the wardroom turned to the cost of the war. Steve exclaimed, "I've heard there were 50 million people killed and over 100 million wounded, many crippled for life." Another guy added, "Yeah, and in excess of 21 million tons of merchant shipping sunk and 2 million tons of major warships such as aircraft carriers, battleships and cruisers, to say nothing of destroyers and smaller ships." They talked about the devastation of cities and countries, how tens of millions had been left homeless and how the Germans attempted to eradicate the entire Jewish race by killing over six million of them. No area of the planet had escaped the horror.

The consensus was that the United States had emerged as the most powerful country in the world. Only 300,000 had been killed. No damage had been done to the cities or factories, and the economy was flourishing. More importantly we had "the bomb". My acey-ducey partner added, "Now that we got it, what are we going to do with it? I predict that until the second coming of Christ, Earth will never be free of wars. With the ability to destroy all of mankind, there'll probably be smaller and more restricted geographical conflicts. Every country with the cash will have atomic weapons. The killings and mass destruction will be forgotten. You and I, when we reminisce 50 years from now, will feel this all happened to someone else in another life. Fights will continue over property, national interests and religion."

I was on the bridge when land was sighted at 0700 1 October. The Golden Gate Bridge represented all of the reasons why I had been in the Navy for four years: home, loved ones and the land of the free.

When we docked at Mare Island, my orders were endorsed and I got a room in the Fairmont Hotel. My first call was to Lil. "Guess where I am?"

"Honolulu."

"I'm in San Francisco. How about coming out and marrying me? Right now. I can't wait."

"Is this a proposal? Pretty informal. I'll have to ask Mother and you will, too." Then laughingly she asked, "You're not serious?" We had a good visit and agreed to wait.

I was pleasantly surprised when the duty officer handed me my orders after only a 2-day stay.

ORDERS October 3,1945
      From: Commandant Twelfth Naval District
      To: Lt. Harold E. Jervey, Jr., DE USNR
     Subject: Release from active duty

-1- Detached. Proceed to separation center US Naval Station, Charleston, SC.

With no air priority, it was catch as catch can. The airport was jammed.
    "Will you fly stand-by, sir?"
    "You betcha. I'll fly stand-by, stand-up, stand-down or lying-down."
    I was on my way at 1830, flying all over the country and arriving in Charleston, SC, on 5 October, 1945, at 0200. My parents and Lil met me. I was tired, but happy.
    The next 2 days were spent resting and getting together civilian clothes. My orders were quickly written at the Charleston Navy Yard:

Separation Center 8 October 1945
By Direction of Commanding Officer

Detached 9 October 1945. Proceed to your home. You are granted 1 month and 27 days leave, upon expiration of which at midnight, 6 December 1945, you will regard yourself released from all active duty.

I was pleased to learn I had been promoted to Lt. Cmdr. With my uniform on, I went downtown and reported in to my new station: Medical College of SC. At the registrar's office I filled in forms. "Do you want to start right now?"
    "You bet," I replied.
    I was apprehensive when I was introduced to Dr. Cy O'Driscol, Professor of Anatomy. He did nothing to allay my fears. "Where have you been? This class has been going for 5 weeks. We've finished one dissection and we're almost through the second." I knew I had made a big mistake. The feeling changed when he put his arm about my shoulder and with a smile said, "Let's meet your classmates."
    When I entered the door I was overpowered with the stench of formaldehyde and grotesque looking cadavers. Why had I thought I wanted to study medicine? This was the war all over again, and a stinking one at that.

O'Driscol said, with his arm still around, me, "This is Lt. Cmdr. Harold Jervey, your long-awaited classmate. Give him a big welcome." I stared at the ghoulish creatures nonchalantly chewing gum and fingering cadaverous flesh. They looked at me and my ribbons as though I were an alien from outer space. Would this be another war on another ocean with another ship? Or would Tennyson's prediction come true:

"Till the war-drum throbbed no longer, and
the battle flags were furled
In the Parliament of man, the Federation of
the world.
There the common sense of most shall hold
a fretful realm in awe,
And the kindly earth shall slumber, lapt
in universal law."

THE END

EPILOGUE

Today I'm reminiscing following the elegant party hosted last night by our 7 children celebrating our Golden Wedding Anniversary. During the last six months of World War II, in my letters to Lil, I shared my hopes and dreams as to what our marriage and life would be like 50 years in the future. Did we succeed or fail? We didn't visit the moon and stars, but we traveled all over planet Earth. I learned early on and, yet quickly forgot, to be prompt in expressing admiration and love for my fellow voyagers. Too often there was no tomorrow and feelings were never expressed. To my sorrow, I continue to repeat this mistake. More importantly, is this world a better place for us having passed through? Only the readers and God can pass judgment on this.

What is most vivid in my memory? Seeing the Stature of Liberty in New York Harbor with the skyscrapers in the background when I returned from the North Atlantic brought a tingle to my spine and tears to my eyes. The same was true of the Golden Gate Bridge when entering San Francisco Harbor after returning from the Western Pacific. They represented what the war was all about: family, loved ones and home. My first sighting of the Aurora Borealis in the northern climes, and the Southern Cross low on the horizon in the southern hemisphere will remain indelibly printed in my memory.

I recall distinctly the debates on whether this war was the one that would end all wars. The consensus was: World War ll would not be the war to end all wars. Since the final surrender on August 14, 1945, there have always been confrontations somewhere on this earth. Today as I write, the headlines announce there are 5 major wars and 13 lesser conflicts simmering and boiling across Europe.

Although this ship Earth has sailed millions of miles since I signed on board, my 4-year tour of duty in the Tin Can Navy was a microcosm of my entire voyage. The events described in the past pages have reaffirmed in a dramatic way what I experienced at the time of happening. Beings like myself, as well as nations, learn little from their mistakes. Intelligence has little to do with it: smart or dumb, young or old, rich or poor, we're all subject to the same failings. The young and the poor have a better chance of avoiding these pitfalls than the wise and the rich.

The conclusion I reached following the Tachibana Maru caper has been validated on numerous occasions. The time and place is more significant than the happening itself. There was little publicity given to the seizure and capture of a ship with 1,562 healthy, armed, veteran Japanese troops—the only Japanese ship captured in 4 years of war. This unique event was preempted by the explosion of the first atomic bomb. Many times during my life, I have seen awards presented and individuals memorialized due to circumstances rather than merit. This is especially true when a person dies while holding an office in an organization. I have learned to share the happiness, or sadness, with the family and friends even if not recognizing the appropriateness of the honor. My reason: God is kind and loving; he is a fair judge.

Whereas neither I nor others from the Conner received any medals, we acquired a far more precious gift: life and life more abundantly. This has proven to be true throughout my voyage.

For me, the long trek is almost over. It has been an exciting and challenging passage. I learned in the Tin Can Navy that it's not the destination, but who your shipmates are. I was privileged to share the cruise with competent and jolly crew members. Only one, my first mate with the flawed name of Little Miss Magnolia Blossom, stayed for the entire passage. Others completed their tours of duty, disembarked at various ports, signed onto other vessels, or became Captains of their own ships.

Words can not adequately express my praise and admiration for my first mate. In fair weather and foul, she has performed her duties superbly. She has been loyal and cheerful and the crew has been devoted to her. Without her advice and counsel, the ship would have floundered on several occasions. We sailed the world, and no matter where the port, we always found compatible sailors with which to share our experiences. Early on she convinced me, and everyone who came in contact with her, that God's son Jesus Christ was the Captain of the our ship. It wasn't just luck and good fortune that saw us through the storms. Thanks be to God.

I have always believed that when I finished my allotted time of three score and ten years, I would feel like John Masefield:

"I must down to the seas again to the vagrant Gypsy life,
To the gull's way and the whale's way,
Where the wind's like a whetted knife;
And all I ask is a merry yarn from a laughing fellow rover,
And a quiet sleep and a sweet dream when the long trick's over."

With the infirmities of age and spirit, I can only dream of such a life and now empathize more with Tennyson's Ulysses who said:

> "......Much have I seen and known, cities of men
> And manners, climates, councils, governments....
> I am a part of all that I have met....
> How dull it is to pause, to make an end;
> To rust unburnished, not to shine in use!
> ......Old age hath yet his honor and his toil;
> Death closes all: but something ere the end...
> 'Tis not to late to seek a newer world.....
> To sail beyond the sunset, and the baths
> Of all the western stars, until I die.
> ...It may be we shall touch the Happy Isles,
> And see the great Achilles, whom we knew.
> Though much is taken, much abides; and though
> We are not now that strength which in the old days
> Moved heaven and earth; that which we are, we are;
> One equal temper of heroic hearts,
> Made weak by time and fate, but strong in will;
> To strive, to seek, to find, and not to yield."

BIBLIOGRAPHY

1-Deck Logs, action reports, war diaries and official ship histories of USS Sterett DD 407, USS Dortch DD 670, USS Ingersoll DD 652 and USS Conner DD 582.

2-*History of United States Naval Operations in World War II*. Samuel Eliot Morison Little Brown & Co Boston 1990

3-*The Chronological Atlas of World War Two*. Charles Messenger MacMillan New York 1989

4-*American Chronicles—Seven Decades in American Life*. Lois Gordon and Alan Gordon Crown New York 1990

5-*A Democracy at War, America's Fight At Home and Abroad in World War II*. William O'Neill The Free Press New York 1993

6-*Don't You Know There's a War On?* Richard R. Lingeman G.P. Putnam New York 1976

7-*War in the Pacific*. Clark G. Reynolds Military Press New York 1990

8-*Lonely Vigil*. Walter Lord Viking Press 1977

9-*Tin Can Sailor*. C. Raymond Calhoun Naval Institute Press/Annapolis Maryland

10-*Battle of Leyte Gulf*. Edwin P. Hoyt Pinnacle Books Inc. 1973

11-*The USS Ingersoll DD652 in World War Two*. Richard J. Murphy Published Privately Knoxville Tenn 1992

12-*New York Times*.

13-*The State Newspaper*, Columbia, SC.

14-*Battle Report*. Commander Walter Karig and Lieutenant Welbourn Kelly

15-Personal letters and communications from former shipmates

16-*Enola Gay*. Thomas Gordon Pocket Books New York 1976

17-*The Two Ocean War*. Samuel Eliot Morison Little Brown & Co Boston 1963

18-*National Geographic* Society December 1991 Page 50A

ENDNOTES

1 [1]4 became Generals, 2 became Adjutant Generals of the SC National Guard.

2 [2]He went into PT boats. Together with Lt. Comdr. John Buckley, he assisted in the evacuation of General MacArthur, his family and other high ranking officers from the Philippines. Kelly received the Navy Cross and Buckley the Congressional Medal of Honor.

3 [3]One became a distinguished Congressman, one a long-time Attorney General of SC, and several others, prominent civic leaders in Columbia, SC Each one who survived contributed toward bettering the lives of those with whom they came in contact.

4 [4]After graduation, I didn't see him again until 1993, at which time he was District Attorney for the island of Manhattan. We enjoyed sharing the happenings of our lives.

5 [5]I never forgot that advice. On more than one occasion, my wife and children wished I had.

6 [6]Kabot distinguished himself on another destroyer which was sunk. His arm was bitten off by a shark and he was discharged from the Navy.

7 [7]Captain Moon received many honors and was promoted to Admiral. He was in charge of Naval Forces on D-Day at Normandy Beach. He was commended, but obviously depressed. Several days later, he was found dead with a 45 revolver in his hands.

[8]Many years later a friend brought me some Danish pastries from Iceland. They didn't taste the same. It reinforced what I knew: there is no carry-over in tastes or spatial memories from youth to old age.

[9]Her fame followed her to the distant reaches of the Pacific. When men reminisced about the States, Tassel Gertie's name would surface.

[10]In later years, he became Chief Justice of the US Supreme Court.

[11]We never got to Washington, and I never dated Dina.

[12]He was my division officer on the USS Quincy when I took my apprentice seaman cruise in November, 1940.

13 [6]Bill Farrow, a classmate of mine at USC, was one of those executed.

14 [7]I told this story to my wife-to-be. On our wedding night, as I waited in the anteroom of the church, I heard the strains of this familiar melody. My betrothed had asked the organist to play it as a surprise. It was, one that almost backfired. The memories came flooding back and the tears started dripping down my cheeks. I looked like the reluctant groom as I entered the sanctuary, handkerchief in hand.

15 [8]Hitler and Mussolini decided to invade Malta on 10 July.

16 [9]Over the next several months, the RAF slowly regained control over the air with the planes supplied by the Wasp, Eagle and other carriers.

17 [1]In 1978 my wife and I visited Tonga and stayed in the Dateline Hotel.

18 [2]In 1970, when his older brother became King, I wrote a letter congratulating him, wishing him a long and prosperous reign and reminding him of my visit. I received a cordial reply with an invitation to visit.

19 [3]So named because it became the graveyard for more sailors and ships than any body of water on the earth.

20 [4]Ultra, the name for the British code breakers, had early-on broken the Nazis secret code and given the RAF warning of the convoys departure and destination.

21 [5]This was only one of many such snafus that occurred during the war.

22 [1]Mitchner, in his "Tales of the South Pacific", mentioned this. The planter played a major role in Rogers and Hammerstein's musical "South Pacific."

23 [2]I never saw him again until after the war.

24 [3]The chief engineer was Herbert Kabot, my former roommate on the Stack. He distinguished himself and was rescued, but not before a shark had chewed off his arm.

25   [4]Learned to be from Japanese submarine I-176

26   [5]She was out of the war for 9 months getting repaired.

27   [1]50 men, including the executive officer, Commander Mark Crouter, were injured. The wounded were transferred to the President Jackson. Crouter insisted on staying. This decision cost him his life that night.

28   [2]Everyone on the bridge was killed, including Admiral Callahan and his staff.

29   [3]3 of them were rescued and returned to the ship.

30   [4]There was no submarine. These were damaged depth charges fired from No. 4 gun.

31   [5]He had been in his 2nd year of surgical residency training when called up. Few, if any, destroyers had a doctor with his background. He was the right man in the right place.

32   [6]For his timidity, Admiral Yamamoto relieved him of his command and assigned him to shore duty for the remainder of his career.

33   [1]The total killed was never accurately established.

34   [2]Following this tragedy, Navy policy was changed, and brothers were not permitted to serve on the same ship.

35   [3]From later reports, I learned that there were 100 survivors who were able to cling to flotsam. Of that number, only 10 were rescued.

36   [4]Captain Hoover was relieved of his command for not leaving boats and life rafts.

37   [5]As the plank was tilted, the flag was raised. The next body was then placed on the plank.

38   [6]Fifty years later, I can clearly see those men standing at attention just as though it were yesterday.

39   [7]This was a prestigious club for unmarried females. Lil was an officer.

40   [8]I've long since forgiven the chairman. I see him often, but somehow I can't forget, even after 50 years.

41   [9]In April, 1946, in Charleston, SC, I recognized Frankie Jenkins shuffling toward me, wrinkled, jaundiced, with head bowed. He was the most outstanding boxer USC ever produced, going to the NCAA finals on two occasions. Before I could greet him, he said, "I've changed, Harold. I was with the 1st Marine Division on Guadalcanal." My eyes moistened and I put my arms about him. He lived only a few more years.

42   [10]It was estimated that 118 fliers were rescued during the war.

43   [11]I did not communicate with him again until 1992.

44   [1]I did not learn of Myrtie's death until many months after the fact.

45   [2]I didn't see "Oklahoma" until 1945 when a touring company visited the Philippines.

46   [3]He had an illustrious career, becoming an executive officer of the Los Angeles Times Corporation, one of the world's most influential newspapers. He was also listed in Who's Who in America.

47   [4]A renowned female-only hotel.

48   [5]All of my life, whenever I hear songs from "Babes in Toyland", the goose bumps return.

49   [6]Three of his former students were sitting Justices on the US Supreme Court and consulted him on occasion. A room in the Law School is named in memory of him.

50   [7]I talked to him on the phone several times, but never saw him again.

51   [8]His grandfather founded the St. Paul Insurance Company, one of the largest firms in the country. In due time, Carl became President and Chairman of the Board. My brother Herbert, a lawyer, went to work with them after the war.

52   [9]My former division officer on the USS Quincy.

53   [10]Since spring, the Japs had been combing the island for coastwatchers and Australian scouts. In March, a US sub evacuated 8 women, 27 children and 3 nuns.

54   [11]This was the last naval engagement in the Solomon's.

55   [12]This was the only black mark I received during my Navy career.

56   [1]Lt. Cmdr. Frank Luongo, formerly engineering officer and executive officer of the Sterett, was chief engineer.

57   [2]Several mishaps occurred during her repairs and she was nicknamed "The Evil 1".

58   [1]Nineteen year old Ensign George Bush was the pilot of the "Barbara", a torpedo bomber.

59   [2]Later, in the war in the Philippines, MacArthur's bombers were off target. I was OOD and watched with horror as the planes strafed and bombed the UDT. All efforts to contact the flight leader failed, because he was not guarding the emergency frequency.

60   [3]The Ingersoll had 5 killed and several injured. Other ships suffered casualties from the crossfire.

61   [1]They were. Rommel was implicated and committed suicide on 14 October.

62   [2]It became an important recreational base, entertaining as many as 20,000 officers on one day.

63   [1]He had been skipper of the Hornet, which had sunk off Guadalcanal.

64   [2]This equaled the worst mistake any of the US Commanders ever made.

65   [1]Roosevelt sent over Generals Albert Wedermeyer, Daniel Sultan, and Raymond Wheeler. This was acceptable to Chiang.

66   [2]I had met him when he was CO of a destroyer at Guadalcanal.

67   [1]He had massed his panzer divisions and infantry with over 1,000,000 men and burst through the Ardennes Forest in Belgium.

68   [1]This proved to be the last casualty by a Kamikaze during the Philippine Campaign.

69   [1]Only a few weeks later, he was killed on Okinawa.

70   [1]Roosevelt was buried at Hyde Park on 14 April. It was noted that this was the same date on which Lincoln had been assassinated.

71   [2]Most destructive raid of the war, including the atomic bombs.

72   [3]1,465 Kamikazes were lost and 150,000 Okinawans were killed.

73   [1]Known as the Potsdam Declaration

74   [1]Due to the chaos resulting with the end of the war, only Peterson received the Bronze Star, and that was in 1949.

75   [2]Amazingly enough, I do.